A Home-Concealed Woman

A
Home-Concealed
Woman

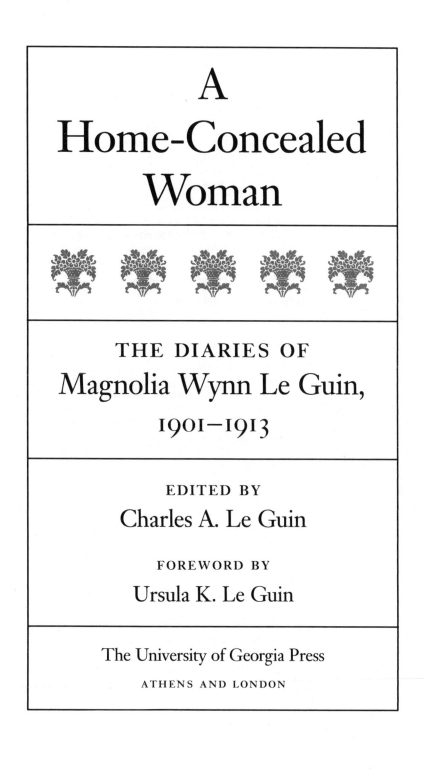

THE DIARIES OF
Magnolia Wynn Le Guin,
1901–1913

EDITED BY
Charles A. Le Guin

FOREWORD BY
Ursula K. Le Guin

The University of Georgia Press
ATHENS AND LONDON

Published by the University of Georgia Press
Athens, Georgia 30602

Designed by Kathi L. Dailey
Set in Janson Text by Tseng Information Systems, Inc.
Printed and bound by Maple-Vail Book Manufacturing Group
The paper in this book meets the guidelines for permanence
and durability of the Committee on Production Guidelines
for Book Longevity of the Council on Library Resources.

Printed in the United States of America

94 93 92 91 90   5 4 3 2 1

Library of Congress Cataloging in Publication Data

Le Guin, Magnolia Wynn, b. 1869
 A home-concealed woman : the diaries of Magnolia Wynn
Le Guin, 1901–1913 / edited by Charles A. Le Guin ; foreword
by Ursula K. Le Guin.
   p. cm.
 Includes bibliographical references.
 I S B N 0-8203-1236-3 (alk. paper)
   1. Farm life — Georgia — Henry County — History. 2.
Henry County (Ga.) — Social life and customs. 3. Women
— Georgia — Henry County — History. 4. Le Guin, Magno-
lia Wynn, b. 1869 — diaries. 5. Women — Georgia — Henry
County — Diaries. I. Le Guin, Charles A. II. Title
F292. H73 L4 1990
975.8'435 — dc20   90-34163
                                                                      C I P

British Library Cataloging in Publication Data available

Frontispiece: Magnolia Wynn, 1888

The photographs in this book have been provided by
Frances Le Guin Snoderly, Trella Le Guin Brewster,
Dorothy Le Guin Phillips, La Trelle Brewster, and the editor.

For Magnolia's daughters
Frances Le Guin Snoderly
and
Trella Le Guin Brewster

CONTENTS

FOREWORD

BY HER LONESELF

THOUGH WOMEN HAVE BEEN WRITING BOTH PRIVATELY AND
professionally for as long as they have had access to education, men
have generally controlled not only education but criticism and pub-
lishing; and so, with few exceptions, the canon of what constitutes
literature and what is excluded from it has been a male one. Recently, scholars and critics influenced by feminist ideas have begun
to question that canon and to enlarge its limits, re-including works
and genres previously rated as not worthy of serious attention, and
thereby bringing much refreshment to readers and writers alike.

Only such extraordinary diaries as those of Samuel Pepys or Vir-
ginia Woolf have been published and appreciated as literature; most
journals and diaries have been valued mostly for their usefulness as
documents, as source material for historians and other researchers.
This usefulness of course remains; but following the feminist prin-
ciples of looking "outside," looking "down," we may now read a diary
kept by an ordinary woman doing nothing unusual in an unremark-
able place during an uneventful time — a diary such as this one — and
find it altogether worthy of being read, like a novel, for pleasure: a
work that is "artless" and yet which may interest and satisfy as does
a conscious work of art.

Even for the famous diaries there is little theory or vocabulary of
critical appreciation. As more critics take an interest in the aesthetics
of the form they will sharpen our appreciation of its possibilities and
peculiar faculties. For instance, I have thought that the inevitable
repetition of events and wordings that characterize the unselfcon-
scious diary are more appropriate than any device used by the conventional novel to describe the actual gait of most people's lives — in

which dramatic episodes punctuate and change, but do not climax or culminate, a long, returning rhythm, or complex cycles of rhythms, or a riverlike ongoing the essence of which is its incessance. In this appropriateness is an aesthetic power—like that of the refrain or burden of a ballad or song?—which our conventional narrative forms almost entirely lack.

Magnolia Wynn Le Guin's diary is naturally valuable as a social document: a picture, as clear and intense as it is narrow, of life on an American farm at the turn of the century. What is a little unusual or unexpected about the picture is that it is all indoors. Magnolia's farm, Magnolia's world, is the house: the bedrooms where the children were born and where the grandparents lay ill and died, the stove room where every day's three meals were cooked and cleared, the sitting room where the endless visitors were entertained. "I always welcome washdays," she says in October of 1909, "because I can get out doors one half of each day each week." Sweeping the side yard can be a holiday, a festival—"I was truly glad when I felt the sprinkling of the rain. I was so glad I couldn't content myself indoors washing dishes, sweeping floors, making beds, etc etc, so I just postponed those things and churning too awhile and betook myself out in the misty rain with a new brushbroom and swept a lot of this large yard and inhaled the sweet air scented with rain-settling dust."

The husband is in the fields or at the mill or gone to town, the boys as they get nine or ten go out to pick cotton, the children go off to school, but Magnolia lives indoors—in her phrase, "a home-concealed woman."

This is a woman shaped by local cultural definitions of woman's role, accepting them and the teaching of the local form of Christianity as a sufficient code of expectation and behavior. By so limiting her womanhood to the duties of daughter, sister, wife, and mother, Magnolia may disappoint a reader longing for evidence of questioning, rebellion, the declaration of the independent self. All the same, it is as a feminist that I personally find the diary most fascinating and impressive. What she accepted, what she endured, how she worked!—nine hard pregnancies, the last at age forty-one; eight children to bring up with no regular or reliable hired help in a house without electricity, running water, or a water heater; fifteen teeth pulled and wait two years till she can get back to town for a set of false teeth; a bad back and a chronic, probably uterine, disorder;

the hordes of visitors and house guests to cook and clean for; the moments when it was all too much—

> My feelings over came me today and just cried and could not help it. When Coz. Jno. came in and ask me why I was not going to camp meeting I could not controll my feelings again and cried and told him "there were nine of us—six babies—I had no chance to go." (1906)

> Oh what a busy day—full of drudgery—I do not complain particularly of that, but how embarrassed I feel when real intelligent people come in and find me completely worn out and children and house more untidy than when no one are here but homefolks. (When no one are here except homefolks I have more time to sweep, resweep, wash and rewash, wash faces) but when the house is so full of company I have to cook so long and so much and talk with company some and much is compelled to go undone when only one overtaxed tired woman is to do it all. Oh, how weary and fagged I do feel! (1906)

Much as I might like to I cannot say that Magnolia was one of Adrienne Rich's "stoic raging grandmothers"—the phrase is splendid, but neither adjective quite fits this particular grandmother. "Stoic" would not allow her to complain of her weariness, grumble about ungrateful relatives and graceless hired help, and pray fervently to be spared a visit from Marvin Wynn. And "raging" would deny her her constant tenderness toward her equally overworked husband, and the sometimes bright, sometimes brooding joy she takes in her babies and children. There is indeed stoicism in her willed endurance of all those miserable pregnancies (which she calls "sickness") and hard deliveries; there is indeed rage in her prayers for patience, in her refusal to give her fifth child a name for weeks and months. But there is much going on beyond anger and coping. Magnolia's is a strong and complex personality; again and again she rises above mere response, asserting her own unshaken, uncontingent being, betaking herself out into the misty rain.

She was the victim of a bigoted, male-supremacist oligarchy—only less a victim of it than her black neighbors, to whom she believed herself as a white inherently superior. One must regret this, resenting or grieving that her field of being was so mean and so hard. But to define her, however well-meaningly, as a victim only, is to condescend to her, just as did the authors of the patriarchal-patronizing eulogies in the local paper at her death—beloved wife and mother, etc. They meant well, too. But she deserves better. Similarly, one must condemn the racist epithets and phrases taught and sanctioned by her society, but may not simply dismiss her as a bigot, for that hateful language disguises, perhaps disguised from her, the extent and the quality of her actual, personal relationships with her black neighbors. In this respect more than any other her language was completely inadequate to express her reality.

In her diaries, Magnolia is not only a woman being but a woman writing. For whom was she writing? The question is probably not useful. Except for conscious public performances such as the diaries of Anaïs Nin, or journal-keeping in an eventful time, I think diaries are mostly written not for anybody but for their own sake—not as a record but as an act. For some people both reading and writing are imperative needs.

> I sometimes hunger to read—sometimes to write in my diary. (1903)

> I haven't time to write—am leaving sewing undone to scribble now—needed sewing too. I *love* to write. (1904)

> I have been sick ever since April and could not on these pages record many things that I so much wished to. I am so *hungry*, so impatient to write. I have written only one letter since April. I would lie down when not compelled to be doing absolutely necessary things in house for the family when not engaged trying to entertain company. This is 3d time I've moved since I began to write from Mary. I've just had to get up and slap Askew for worrying Fred and Fred may have needed the slap worse. . . . [The next day:] I am sorry I slapped Askew. A child should not be slapped strong about the head. He told me this morning he had a swimming of the head. I am sorry I did not use a hickory to punish him with for nagging or worrying Fred. I was so anxious to write—too anxious—and my impatience overcame me. (1905)

That passage is a good sample of Magnolia's style, which is effective, vivid, and agile. The syntax of the fourth sentence, with the two clauses introduced by *when*, perfectly expresses its meaning, and the disjointedness of the next sentence—"This is 3d time I've moved since I began to write from Mary"—while a bit extreme, certainly fits the situation of a mother trying to evade a relentless three year old. Usually her language flows easily, clear and colloquial, seldom impeded by the ornate elocutionary mannerisms of the time except in outbursts of prayer. What she copies from published authors is often florid and boring; what she writes herself is easy and lively. Sometimes she evidently reworks a description until she gets it said to her own satisfaction—her comparison of baby Ralph to a rose on page 54 works itself out this way. At other times the words pour out passionately:

> One of the strangest things I ever saw happened while Mama was sick. When she first became low, she had been, apparently, expiring all night—pulse growing weaker and most irregular all night and Papa said he didn't think she would last till day. So we thought she was dying and ceased pouring drops down her short while before day. At day light, or some short while after, she seemed to be gone—seemed to be out of flesh—pulse stopped, could detect no breathing. Miss Babe says her heart has not entirely ceased and lets rub her pulse, with whiskey. We (Miss Babe and I) began to rub her pulse, lips with whiskey and we found her pulse after so long were beating again. After awhile we saw a sign of returning breath and I knew her head was too low, so we were excited and asked some of them standing by to lift her up higher on a pillow. Misses Matt and Babe and Lil thought they couldn't and called on Cape. He had rheumatism and said he couldn't so I with a strength (not natural) I hopped up on bed, picked her body up and laid her higher on a pillow and then she breathed more freely and soon afterwards slowly opened her eyes like one just awakened. She seemed like one whose spirit has left body for another world and came back to this. She smiled as soon as her eyes were opened—and in few moments laughed out loud enough to be heard over house—face seemed radiated—a sweet heavenly expression seemed to flood her face. 'Twas something wonderful! wonderful! (1903)

The next line, written the next day, says, "Yesterday company came and interrupted me while I was writing in my diary." She did not get much time to be, in her eloquent phrase, by her loneself.

Some of the charm of the language is dialectical—such words as *didoes, wrathy, bonton* used as an adjective, or *pastime* meaning not a game but pleasure itself. She spells it variously *pastime, past time, pass time,* evidence that it was not a book-word. So she spells the southernism *lack, lacking* (wanting, missing, short of) as *like, liking,* the vowel in her dialect being the same or nearly so; and *right* as an ad-

verb (very) she spells *rite*. Aside from words she never saw written—
hollow for holler, *gotton* for gotten, labeled incorrect usage by gram-
marians of the time—and a few firm idiosyncrasies—*severel, controll,
swolen, appearantly, burried*—her spelling is conventional; so much so
that you cannot help but notice when she goes on spelling her son's
name three different ways for four years: Travis, Travys, Traviss.
This also may become a charm, a puzzle, the hint of a mystery.

She was at home with words; she was a writing woman. The peculiar fascination of her diary, hard to explain, for after all nothing
"happens"—her back hurts, a baby is born, another gets a tooth,
eight-year-old Askew chops cotton, a nurse-girl is insolent, Papa has
a fever, Ghu offends morality by drinking beer and eating pickles and
crackers with his friends, it is hot in August, it is cold in December,
she is "sick" again and prays God for strength, another sweet, merry
baby is born . . . on it goes, and in this endlessness of daily work
and feeling is the essence of a life—but the fascination, the delight
of reading about it, the pastime she gives us, must come direct from
her own delight in writing it, the relief, release, and freedom she had
in doing what she loved best to do.

Ursula K. Le Guin

ACKNOWLEDGMENTS

ALL BOOKS THAT GET PUBLISHED ARE IN ONE DEGREE OR another collaborations, this one to a remarkable degree. Magnolia Wynn Le Guin wrote her diaries; all the rest is collaboration. As editor of what my grandmother wrote, I have many to thank for their part in seeing her words appear in print. First, in point of time, are my aunts Frances and Trella, who willingly gave me free use of the diaries, and my cousin, Dorothy Le Guin Phillips, who, as keeper of the manuscripts, encouraged me to prepare a typescript of them. She was also an invaluable resource for matters of detail about people and places mentioned in the text. Then there are those friends and relations, many of whom knew little of the world portrayed by Magnolia, who urged me to seek a publisher because they were sure that her words were of more than family interest.

For help in preparing the text of the diaries for publication, I am particularly indebted to Diane Lynch, who computerized my typescript. Magnolia's diaries could not have found a more apposite or congenial publisher than the University of Georgia Press. I owe special thanks to two women at the Press, Debbie Winter, my editor, and Kathi Dailey, who designed the book. Their enthusiasm and courtesy made the task of converting my grandmother's fragile manuscripts into a solid, tangible book a pleasure.

Charles A. Le Guin

May 1990

INTRODUCTION

MAGNOLIA WYNN LE GUIN WAS BORN ON FEBRUARY 18, 1869, at High Falls in Monroe (now Lamar) County, Georgia. When she was three, her family moved to Wynn's Mill, Henry County, where she lived the rest of her life. Three months short of her seventy-ninth birthday, she died in Atlanta. Magnolia's whole life was spent in an area the radius of which was not thirty miles; indeed the majority of her life, including the years recorded in her diaries, was spent in an area approximately ten miles in circumference. Even so, she often found it difficult to get as far as Jackson, about seven miles away from her home, where she needed to go to have her teeth fixed. It was a small geographic space she inhabited, though there is little to indicate that Magnolia felt it so.

Magnolia's world was also an isolated one. In her extant writings, she occasionally mentions the death of well-known national religious figures, but only two events of general significance to the larger world are noted: the assassination of President McKinley in 1901, and World War I — that only in the context of the induction of her eldest son in 1916.

Her world was overwhelmingly rural. The three contiguous Georgia counties with which she was most familiar — Henry, where she lived; Monroe, where she was born; and Butts, adjacent to both — lie on the Piedmont Plateau, a band of rolling land across the center of the state. During the years of Magnolia's diaries, these counties contained no places defined as urban by the United States census, that is, no town had over 2,500 population. Even the county seats, McDonough, Barnesville, and Jackson, did not qualify as urban, though they contained more people than most of the other rural communities in their counties and provided services not available in the places where Magnolia lived.

The land of the area most familiar to Magnolia, "the red old hills of Georgia," consists of mica-filled schist and granite, sparsely covered by red soil. It is not a fertile region, topsoil having been steadily carried down to the sea by the many red-brown streams cutting through the Piedmont. Save where cleared for cultivation and dwellings, the land is covered by mixed forests, mostly pine and oak. Buckeye, small and bushy, grows prolifically, and the woods are scattered with mountain laurel and azaleas. Creepers of the entangling variety—honeysuckle, trumpet vine, muscadine, scuppernong, blackberry—complicate and thicken the fabric of the forests and make convenient refuge for small wildlife, including snakes, in which the woods abound. Seasonal wildflowers—violets, blue-barrel gentian—carpet the woods. It is a lonely, even melancholy, landscape, one to which Magnolia passionately responded. It was, she thought, "the sweetest spot on earth . . . and the saddest" (1907).

This rural region was home to some 53,000 people in the period of Magnolia's diaries, averaging about 54 persons per square mile. There were slightly more black than white inhabitants in the three counties: the average for the area in 1900 was 43 percent white and 57 percent black. The vast majority of both races was engaged in agriculture. Farms were generally of modest size, tenant farming and sharecropping being common. Ghu Le Guin, Magnolia's husband, found it necessary to supplement his arable land by leasing land from others, one such lease being taken from a black farmer. While Ghu hired hands to help him and his sons on his land, he and his sons also worked for other farmers in the community. The arable acreage of the Le Guin farm, representative of the pattern followed in the area where it was located, was planted in cotton (the cash crop), corn, and grain; remaining acreage was in pasture and timber. Livestock was limited to milk cows, pigs, chickens, mules for plowing, and a horse for the buggy. Like Ghu, most farmers of this part of Georgia were able to eke out a living, but it was often a subsistence living, as becomes evident in the pages of Magnolia's diaries.

Life in the rural, agrarian world Magnolia inhabited was not easy; climate contributed no more than soil to make it so. The weather of this area of upper central Georgia can be extreme. Summers were hot and long and often dry; Magnolia dreaded them and suffered through them. Winters, though brief, were often unpredictable and sometimes severe, quite cold and usually dank. Weather changes were precipitous and at times violent. Rain could be torrential; flooding was not uncommon. Winds could be destructive, and ice and snow might coat the red hills. Magnolia was intensely alert to climate, suffering from the heat, shivering in the cold, but delighted in the glories of beautiful autumnal days. For her October was the ideal month: "What a G-L-O-R-I-O-U-S month October is to me. How it thrills me and fills me with joy and life, as perhaps no other month in the year! . . . I feel as different as if I were another person when warm weather passes and October comes in" (1904).

MAGNOLIA WYNN LE GUIN began her life at High Falls and lived it out at Wynn's Mill, which became Le Guin's Mill after her father's death: both were rural communities, typical of her time and place. High Falls was a prosperous settlement, and Magnolia's father (along with T. S. M. Bloodworth) had major interests there: "Dr. J. A. C. Wynn owned the entire place. Everything was on the go then. They [Wynn and Bloodworth] operated two large general stores, grist mill, gin, blacksmith shop, shoe shop where handmade shoes were made, chair factory, bedstead factory, wool factory, and saw mills. They bought old rags which were sold to be made into paper, they bought cotton and sold mules. They also had large farming interests."*

By the time Magnolia was three, High Falls had begun a decline that was completed in the 1880s when the community was bypassed by the railroad. In 1872 Dr. Wynn moved his family from the banks of the Towaliga River in Monroe County to the banks of Tussahaw Creek in Henry County. Here he took possession of land, a house, and a mill that had belonged to the Childs family. Henceforth, the community became known as Wynn's Mill and, like the community at High Falls, was a thriving center of small businesses. Like High Falls, Wynn's Mill became a ghost town in the twentieth century. Before its decline and disappearance, "corn mills [lined] . . . Tussahaw Creek—Nail's Mill, Mayo and Farrar's Mill, Boatner's Mill and Wynn's Mill . . . in days when old time corn mills dotted the hills and

*Monroe Advertiser, August 4, 1966.

dales of Henry County."* At the height of its prosperity, Wynn's Mill also had a sawmill, a cotton gin, a thread mill, a carding mill, a tannery, a store supplying the needs of local people, Dr. Wynn's medical offices, residences, and nearby New Hope Church and school.

Overlooking the business center of the community on Tussahaw Creek was the house where Magnolia grew up and spent her life. The Wynn–Le Guin house, built before the middle of the nineteenth century, was on a wooded hill. Magnolia's love for it, as for her community, is frequently expressed in her diary entries. She especially loved "the oak trees around the house and the grove on [the] hill below the house" (1904). Indeed, Magnolia's "place" was central to her life. As a child she attended school at New Hope, and it was here that she was received into the Methodist Episcopal Church South: New Hope was at the heart of her spiritual and intellectual life. Among her family and many friends in the community she made her social life, found her husband, brought up her family, grew old, and is buried.

A GLIMPSE OF MAGNOLIA as a young woman is suggested in a few letters that have been saved. Most of these are to and from her brother Splint, a year her junior, with whom she had a deeply affectionate relationship. The letters, and an autograph book dating from the same period, indicate that the eligible young Magnolia was popular with both sexes and led a fairly active social life, going to parties and making visits to a variety of houses in and around the community. These early friendships continued into her adult life; against growing odds, she strove to maintain them.

When Magnolia was between eighteen and twenty-three years old, she met Ghu Gilbert Le Guin. Born February 20, 1870, in Butts County, Ghu was second of the seven children of James M. and Cinderilla Vashti Bridges Le Guin. Since early in the nineteenth century, Le Guins had been small farmers around Peeksville, a community several miles from Wynn's Mill on the Butts–Henry County line.

Exactly how Magnolia and Ghu met is not known, but several entries in Magnolia's autograph book were made in Peeksville, suggesting that they may have met at one or another of the various visits

*Vessie T. Rainer, *Henry County Georgia: The Mother of Counties* (Published by the author, ca. 1971), p. 71.

Magnolia made there. However or wherever they met, Magnolia appears to have formed a firm affection for Ghu, who reciprocated. That their affection needed to be firm is indicated in Magnolia's earliest recorded mention of Ghu, two brief diary fragments and an allusion in a letter to her from Splint, written about the same time. It is clear from this evidence that Ghu was not favorably regarded as a possible son-in-law. On April 9, 1892, Magnolia confides that her brother "wrote in regard to my marrying Ghu that I could do as I pleased and made apologies for his last letter where he advised me not to marry him because of his station. I love Splint so much and I am truly thankful that he will not oppose so seriously my love for Ghu. . . . I thanked God . . . because my favorite brother no longer bitterly opposes my love for Ghu."

Two days later she wrote, "I have been trying all day not to give way to my depressed feelings. I think wrong to give way to them. I do trust the Lord to help me be brave and cheerful. . . . He has given me the love of Ghu and a noble boy or man he is and that helps me a great deal to be cheerful." In a letter from Jackson at this time, Splint acknowledges Magnolia's "hint in your letter of the trouble." In an angry allusion to his father, Splint continued: "It nearly kills me to think how little pleasure you and Mama have at home," and concluded that his father ought "to try to do more to make home pleasant."

Just how tense the situation at home was is clear from Magnolia's diary entry of April 12:

> Ghu came yesterday and carried Minta and I to Mt. Bethel. He was here when our family ate supper and it was so sad to me that I didn't feel free to insist on him eating supper. I asked him of course but could not insist as Papa would have made he and I both feel so disagreeable at table—by treating him with contempt. Oh! Ghu! I was sorry but I could not help myself. I have some rite thorny places to go thro and Ghu's love is such a treasured gift and puts a silver lining to good many dark clouds.

Despite her father's resistance, Magnolia and Ghu were married by the Reverend D. C. Brown on a Sunday morning, November 27, 1892.

The couple set up housekeeping in the vicinity of Ghu's family in Peeksville. After the death of their first child, and before Ghu's family pulled up stakes and moved west to Louisiana, Magnolia and Ghu moved to Wynn's Mill, into the home of her parents. Here they were to live the remainder of their lives. That they had got through some "rite thorny places" becomes clear as Magnolia's diaries unfold. Her record of the first decade or so of their life at the Wynn homeplace indicate that Dr. Wynn abandoned his hostility to Ghu and came more and more to trust and rely on him. As his father-in-law became old and infirm, Ghu simply took over the management of his farming and business interests, and by the time Dr. Wynn died he had developed enough confidence and affection for Ghu to make him coexecutor of his will. Dr. and Mrs. Wynn and the growing family of Magnolia and Ghu lived together as companionably and happily as two families under a single roof could. It seems only natural that the Wynn home, mill, and a portion of the farmland should have passed on to Magnolia and Ghu and that in time the place should have become known as Le Guin's Mill.

Magnolia's life was focused on her families, the one she grew up in and the one she and her husband created. She had been born the tenth of eleven children, the fifth and youngest daughter, of J. A. C. and Mary Ann Wynn. She and Ghu had nine children, all but the first one of whom lived past infancy. These large families were close-knit, and both hinged on Magnolia's parents. There were tensions, naturally, but on the whole family relationships seem to have been affectionate and peaceful. Among her own siblings, Magnolia was especially close to Splint and to her sister Lillie, born four years before her. Her relationship with one sister, Anna, was strained by her aversion to Anna's husband, Dr. Jarrell. Magnolia's diaries, so much of which are devoted to her care of her parents and to the birth and bringing up of her children, make plain her commitment to the maintaining of a loving and harmonious family life.

It may appear from the evidence of Magnolia's writings that the crucial factor of her life, the fulcrum on which her world revolved, was her parents. The problems of her courtship with Ghu and her continuing concern with her father indicate that J. A. C. Wynn, farmer, businessman, graduate of the Medical College of Georgia (1847), was a forceful personality, a figure to be reckoned with in the home as well as in the community. Magnolia's mother, a housewife with a penchant for gardening and drawing, emerges as a gentler, less distinct personality. But despite her concern with her parents,

Magnolia's diaries show that in fact she herself was the linchpin of her families, the person on whom her aging parents, her siblings, her husband, and her children relied. It was she who filled "rural woman's God-given role . . . that of dutiful daughter, wife, mother, and homemaker. . . . She nurtured, sustained, and consoled. She maintained order and tranquility and was the fixed point of reference in a chaotic and uncertain world. . . . She was the armature of well-being—dispensing hospitality; nursing the sick and hurt; serving up food, cheer, and love; providing moral and cultural guidance."*

In the decade covered by her diaries, Magnolia Wynn Le Guin did all these things and more: she bore five children and cared for her parents during their final illnesses. And she did it all pretty much on her own. Her parents were too feeble to be of real help; her husband, who did what he could during emergencies, was too busy in the fields or at his mill to provide constant aid; hired help, both white and black, equally difficult to come by, was costly and temporary. Magnolia's concern with servants, particularly during pregnancies, is constant throughout the pages of her diaries. She preferred white "help" and occasionally had it (usually from outside the family). Black servants, though she hired them willingly, rarely satisfied her; she was critical of the temporary and uncertain character of black "help." In a community that was more than 50 percent black, she seemed never to have found acceptable or long-term servants. Jacqueline Jones notes that blacks had a tendency to move whenever they had the opportunity, up to a third of black families moving annually.† Moreover, Jones points out, field work was probably more profitable and desirable for black women, who preferred not to repeat their own household chores in a white home. Magnolia's experience would seem to confirm this observation. The uncertainty, or unreliability, as she saw it, of black servants neither solved her need nor softened her attitudes toward blacks. Her view of them was typical of her time and place, combining as it did a sense of social and racial hierarchy that held blacks to be inferior with personal concern and compassion and help for individual blacks in need.

Despite the lack of major distinctions between blacks and whites

*Norton Juster, *So Sweet to Labor* (New York: Viking Press, 1979), p. 13.
†*Labor of Love, Labor of Sorrow: Black Women, Work, and Family from Slavery to the Present* (New York: Basic Books, 1985), pp. 83–90.

Chart of
Magnolia Wynn
Le Guin's Family

James Abercrombie Wynn*
1821–1907
m. 1842 ————————————
Mary Ann Settle
1828–1904

John Paul Eve
b. 1848
d. 1864

Thomas Jefferson
b. 1849
m.
Mollie O'Rear
d. 1905

Martha Madora
b. 1852
m.
A. J. Wellmaker
d. 1939

James Owen
b. 1854
m. 1. Susie Le Guin
    2. Lucy Goodwin
    3. Sara Shaw
d. 1943

William Capers
b. 1857
m.
Josephine Bostwick
d. 1937

Mary Frances
b. 1860
m.
J. M. Wynn
d. 1934

Charles Oscar
b. 1862
m. Willie Read
d. 1908

Anna Jones
b. 1863
m.
A. J. Jarrell
d. 1936

Lillie Gordon
b. 1865
m.
W. B. Lewis
d. 1906

MAGNOLIA
1869–1947
m. 1892 ————————————
Ghu Gilbert Le Guin
1870–1950

Esca Splint
b. 1870
d. 1893

*M. D., Medical College of Georgia, 1847.

Daughter
1894

Alfred Askew
1895–1961
m. ———————————
Ella Peavy Du Pree
b. 1900

Fred Gilbert
1898–1974
m. ———————————
Grace Fields
1897–1980

Travis Lowery
1900–1941
m. ———————————
Marie Daniel
b. 1901

Charles Ralph
1902–1918

Mary Vashti
1904–1957

Maggie Wynn
1906–1955

Frances James
b. 1907
m.
Haden Snoderly
1907–1972

Florence Trella
b. 1910
m. ———————————
Joseph B. Brewster
1909–1969

Mary Bruce
b. 1922

Charles Alfred
b. 1927

Thomas Gilbert
b. 1935

Katherine Wesley
b. 1936

Martha Frances
b. 1938

Dorothy
b. 1923

Betty Ann
b. 1934

Joseph B.
1935–1985

La Trelle
b. 1941

in terms of earthly and creature comforts in rural, agrarian society, the white code of neighborliness and mutual cooperation in communities such as Wynn's Mill excluded blacks. It was, however, honored and powerful among whites. Magnolia's diaries are full of the neighborly practice of visiting. Though her own opportunities to visit others were limited by her household responsibilities and her babies, the Wynn–Le Guin home seems to have maintained a sort of perpetual open house, which, of course, only increased the burdens Magnolia bore. Community crises — sickness, death — were dealt with by mutual assistance. Ghu often responded to calls outside the home, since Magnolia could not; neighbors came to help during her confinement and especially during the long final illnesses of her parents. There are references to Masonic meetings and to socials, which Ghu attended; he seems to have got about quite a bit, while Magnolia remained at home.

The real center of their social and cultural life was New Hope Methodist Church; for Magnolia, religion was second only to her family in importance. New Hope Church, about a mile across Tussahaw Creek to the east of Wynn's Mill, was one of four churches grouped as the Locust Grove charge. The charge was served by a circuit rider, a preacher who came to conduct services for each congregation in rotation. Only on these assigned Sundays, or on special occasions such as quarterly meetings or protracted (revival) meetings, were there full-scale religious services. Other Sundays, when preachers were not present, were devoted to Sunday school, organized and run by the members of the congregation under the guidance of their chosen Sunday school superintendent, Ghu Le Guin, who held the office continuously until 1941.

New Hope Church was older than its Sunday school. A major event in its history was the building of a new, second, frame church building in 1902. As she proudly notes, Magnolia's father and husband made generous contributions to the new building. She was able to go to services in the new church far less often than she would have liked, but she saw to it that her children and her husband went. Ghu, who was a deacon as well as Sunday school superintendent, was active in all activities at New Hope, faithful in attending services and quarterly and protracted meetings, whether they were held at New Hope or at other churches on the charge. Ghu also went to the camp meetings in Butts County at Indian Springs, sometimes taking his older children with him. During the years of her diaries, Magnolia, who longed to go, generally had to stay home to prepare meals for the clergy and laity. She had to be content to satisfy her deep religious feelings with infrequent trips to New Hope, with prayers from visiting clergy, and with establishing nightly family prayer and Bible-reading sessions, which were to continue as long as she lived.

New Hope Church provided for the religious needs of the Wynn's Mill community; New Hope School across the road from the church provided for its educational needs. Magnolia, "when a little girl," had attended "the old New Hope School house" — the church building, used as a school during the week. Exactly when she began her schooling is not known, nor how long she attended New Hope School; she also went to nearby Philippi Church School and to the academy at Barnesville, where her older sister Dora lived. By the time her own children began attending New Hope School, there was a new schoolhouse. When the new church was built in 1902, the old church building was moved across the road to become a full-time schoolhouse. After several years, a second room and a porch across the front were added. The land and much of the labor for erecting the new schoolhouse were provided by Magnolia's father and husband, and the family's interest in the school was as strong as its interest in the church. Magnolia and Ghu were deeply involved in selecting teachers, some of whom they boarded and all of whom Magnolia respected and admired. New Hope School apparently ran on a somewhat irregular schedule, one no doubt related to the exigencies of an agricultural community as well as the availability of teachers. In time, as they progressed, Magnolia's children had to go beyond the offerings of New Hope School (as she had done) in order to complete their education. For example, her eldest son went from New Hope School to Philippi School to Locust Grove Academy and finally to Young Harris College at Blairsville in north Georgia.

Magnolia's diaries and letters make clear a devotion to books and learning, one that she wanted to pass on to her children. She received a thorough enough education to enable her to write, all her life, in a firm, clear, basically Spencerian hand and with a consistent and personal style. Her spelling is generally correct, exceptions arising from certain words that she heard with a "southern" ear, dialectical spelling, as it were. Certainly she developed early in life, and probably at school, a deep reverence and love for reading and writing. A survey of Magnolia's copybooks, in which she recorded "such things as I find a sweet pleasure to me [and that] I wish to retain," reveal a large number of quotations from religious authors (such as Bishop Warren A. Candler and Billy Sunday) and periodicals (such as the *Wesleyan Christian Advocate*). But she also quotes passages from the prose of Lew Wallace, Thomas Jefferson, Robert E. Lee, Harriet Ward Beecher, Charles Dickens, Ralph Waldo Emerson, and Oliver Wendell Holmes, among others, and the poems of Henry Wadsworth Longfellow, Elizabeth Barrett Browning, James Whitcomb Riley, Frank L. Stanton, George Herbert, and many others. The persistence, against heavy odds, with which she kept her diaries is proof enough of her love of writing. In them she frequently speaks of the pleasure that reading and writing gave her, a pleasure she had too often to forego. On evidence and by preference she valued learning and was an educated and cultured woman.

She was above all a woman of the time and place into which she was born, lived, and died. She and countless similar women were sustainers of a rural, agrarian world. As her diaries indicate, this was not an easy role. Magnolia's responsibilities were heavy and she took them seriously; her lot was wearisome, repetitive toil, work that seemed endless, never finished. None of this really fazed her: she liked to work and complained about it only when her health was delicate or help was inadequate. Through it all she was supported by the love she felt for and received from those whom she served; by her religion, which was both justification and haven for her; by sheer delight in the world around her, a joy she felt even when her duties kept her inside; and by the comfort of writing in her diary, an activity so important that she pursued it in the face of all interference. Magnolia Wynn Le Guin may have been defined by her world, but she was also confirmed by it and contributed immeasurably to it.

EDITORIAL NOTE

THIS BOOK CONTAINS THE DIARIES KEPT BY MAGNOLIA
Wynn Le Guin during the middle dozen years of her life. She wrote
them in what she had at hand, an odd assortment of long and narrow
ledgers, account and memorandum books. Some of these are par-
tially filled with farm records and she had to write over and around
these. There are six such books extant; the entries in them cover
the years from 1901 to 1913. There are also two others that Magnolia used as copybooks in which she put all "that I may see and
wish to retain for future enjoyment and reference." Some of the
material in the copybooks is highly practical—recipes, lists, remedies, and the like; much of it consists of poetry, adages, Bible verses,
religious lessons, and discussions, both secular and religious. Her
jottings are interspersed with her comments and ruminations and
with occasional verse of her own. Selections from these copybooks
are appended to the text of her diaries in this volume.

In addition to the diaries and copybooks, there are several random
diary pages, suggesting early attempts at journal keeping. Three such
pages and a small memorandum book give a revealing glimpse of
Magnolia on the eve of her marriage. Several loose pages from 1892,
1899, and 1901 serve as a prologue to the main body of the diaries.
There is also a small collection of letters that she preserved, dating
from 1887 to 1918, though on the whole these add little to the story
told in her diaries.

This is the material on which this book is based. It covers perhaps
the most trying years of Magnolia Le Guin's life, years of childbearing and child rearing under trying circumstances. The entries
are family centered and intimate, "a parade of the ordinary and the

infinitesimal, the daily job of coping and providing, or strategies, rationales, and costs of being female and being human."* By the time the entries end, Magnolia Le Guin was reaching the halfway point in her life. Though she remained an indefatigable letter writer all her life, there are no journals after 1913. Perhaps her diaries had simply served her purpose.

In preparing Magnolia's diaries little has been done to change her text. Her words, her style, are very much her own, and to change the way she wrote would have been to alter her character. Accordingly I have let stand her sometimes idiosyncratic spelling, her personal syntax, and the somewhat rambling structure of her entries. Occasional footnotes are used to clarify what seems unclear.

Magnolia dated her diary entries in a variety of ways—from "February 13th, 1903," to "Nov., 11th, 1905. Saturday Night." For the convenience of the reader, I have standardized the dates to month and day and treated them as headings; any additional information, such as "Fourth Sunday," is retained as part of the entry.

Diaries are often repetitive and parochial, and, as Margo Culley points out, this is particularly true of diaries kept by women, whose lives have traditionally been circumscribed by routine responsibilities.[†] Culley's observation is sustained in the essentially repetitive rhythm of Magnolia Le Guin's life as she recorded it. I have done nothing to alter that reality. Such excisions as have been made are of two types: (1) lists of guests who came to the Wynn–Le Guin house over the days and months of the years covered by the diaries; (2) the frequent use of parenthetical identification of family members of Magnolia's household, for example, her identification of her father parenthetically as her children's grandfather. I have retained an example of each sort of deletion I have made, after which I indicate excision by ellipses.

An editorial task of another order derived from the fact that Magnolia kept two more or less parallel diaries during the years from 1903 to 1906. The dual entries contain some common information, but the parallels are by no means exact. Not all entries are duplicated; those that are, differ somewhat in character. One entry is apt

---

*Juster, *So Sweet to Labor*, p. 1.

†*A Day at a Time: The Diary Literature of American Women* (New York: Feminist Press, 1985).

to be more factual, quotidian, than the other, which tends to be more candid, self-analytical, confessional. I have no certain idea why Magnolia kept two journals for these years, nor does she indicate any reason for doing so. Given the tenor of her life at the time, keeping one diary as regularly as she did must have been difficult; keeping two indicates clearly how deeply important writing in her journal was to her.

There was no question of deleting one or another of the two diaries; combining them into a single diary was attempted but seems undesirable. To do so would damage the repetitive character of the parallel entries and weaken the distinctions between them. To preserve the integrity of the separate journals and at the same time ensure some sort of narrative continuity, it was decided to collate the entries in chronological order, marking the distinction between the two diaries typographically. In the years 1903–5, then, there are sometimes two entries for one day—one from one diary and one from the other.

Another editorial task was to identify the people who inhabit Magnolia's pages. In this task I have been greatly aided by my cousin, Dorothy Le Guin Phillips, whose help is clearly reflected in the index, where the people mentioned in the diaries are listed. At times Magnolia refers to a person cryptically, as Dr. J or Bro. D. I have left it so, save for initial appearances, when the full name is given in brackets. Places mentioned, when they are not generally known or self-explanatory, are identified in footnotes.

The final editorial task resulted in two appendixes in which are to be found some of Magnolia's favorite recipes, especially those she mentions in her diaries (Appendix 1), and nostrums and remedies, some of which she tried on those of her large household who were ill (Appendix 2). These appendixes, I think, say as much of my grandmother's time as of her personality. They add detail to the portrait that emerges from her journals.

Biographers are conscious of the problems of dealing with persons very close to them in time and human relationship. I have been keenly aware of this concern in preparing these journals of a kinswoman whom I knew in the first decades of my life and the last of hers. Magnolia made my task easier than it might have been. I found in her diaries much that I remembered as basic and integral to the grandmother I knew: her gentleness and kindliness, her faith and dignity, her love of people and place. That she took time in a full and busy life to keep such extensive journals is consonant with my memory of her as a marvelously voluble and inexhaustible raconteuse, the delight of any grandchild. These grandmotherly verities, it seems to me, are evident in Magnolia's pages, written long before I was born. I did not have to place them there and I do not need to underline them.

But her diaries also present a woman I never knew. Rather than the soft, gray, bosomy grandmother smelling of lavender and soap, I found in her journals a somewhat harassed mother in her prime, a woman who explored with candor and vigor the busy, difficult, and demanding life that she led. This woman is a historical figure for me, removed in time and in personal acquaintance. I believe that in the process of editing her journals, I was able to view the historical Magnolia with a perspective that eludes me when I recall the personal grandmother. I found much to admire in the woman revealed in the diaries and, in having discovered her, I take even fuller pride in being her grandson.

Prologue
to the Diaries

April 9, 1892
Saturday night

I have enjoyed this week very much; spent from Sunday night till yesterday at Fan's, she brought me home and Minta came too. Minta will go back tomorrow I guess. Ghu called on me one night this week at Jim Buck's. I expect him tomorrow to carry me to Mt. Bethel. I received a letter today from Mr. Seaborn. I *never* did get a letter that I prized more in my life. Oh! what a good interesting letter it was—a long one too. He is my favorite preacher. I received a sweet and valued letter from Splint also today. He wrote a good deal about the protracted meeting he is attending. I believe he will be a christian. He wrote in regard to my marrying Ghu that I could do as I pleased and made apologies for his last letter where he advised me not to marry him because of his station. I love Splint so much and I am truly thankful that he will not oppose so seriously my love for Ghu. I never did get a letter from Splint that did me so much good. I went upstairs and praised and thanked God for Splint being interested in his soul's welfare and because my favorite brother no longer so bitterly opposes my love for Ghu. I see in both of these things an answer to prayer. The Lord is wonderfully good to me. I do thank Him for the two letters I received today. I've felt so happy, lighthearted and contented all day—and more than usual all week nearly. Minta and I went violet and honeysuckle hunting this eve and have the parlor decorated beautifully with them. This has been a real cold day for April. I fell in branch with one leg this P.M. and my leg and foot was so cold before I got to the fire.

April 11, 1892

Monday night

Wynn's Mill—Ga.

Diary:

I will pen a few lines to you tonight. I have toothache and neuralgia rite bad tonight. It hurts! it hurts! Mrs. Shaw and Little Sis spent today here. Little Sis was very quiet—something seemed to lay heavy on her mind. Mama has been looking sad all day, and for several days past. Poor Mama! poor Mama! I do wish you felt happy and well. I have been trying all day not to give way to my depressed feelings. I think wrong to give way to them. I do trust the Lord to help me be brave and cheerful, to keep my spirits up; to strengthen me spiritually for the duties I have to perform. He has given me the love of Ghu and a noble boy or man he is & that helps me a great deal to be cheerful. Blanch is over here this week staying with Sweetie and Alf. The children are troublesome but I am learning by the Lord's help to be more patient with them. They are sweet children tho' lots of trouble at times. Don't know whether Blanch will stay all week or not. Ghu came yesterday and carried Minta and I to Mt. Bethel. He was here when our family ate supper and it was so sad to me that I didn't feel free to insist on him eating supper. I ask him of course, but could not insist as Papa would have made he & I both feel so disagreeable at table—by treating him with contempt. Oh! Ghu! I was sorry but I could not help myself. I have some rite thorny places to go through & Ghu's love is such a treasured gift & puts a silver lining to a good many dark clouds. Lord help me to be made more like Thee thro' all my sorrows.

April 12, 1892

Tuesday night

This has not been a happy day with me at all. This A.M. I suffered some neuralgia. The children have troubled me good deal, but it was wrong in me to be so easily worried, I guess. Mama has been so still, so sad, so quiet. She looks like she might be sick, but she isn't unusually so, I don't guess. Just trouble and old age—more trouble that is making her look bad than anything else. I have not enjoyed anything scarcely this day, I had not as much life in my prayers as usual either. I feel so worried about the children being here and Mama not able to take care of them and me with hands full.

April 15, 1892
Friday Night

I am shut up in front room all alone by a splendid fire. I feel, when thus situated, like reading or writing. We have had some furious weather past two days, especially yesterday. Yesterday was the windiest weather I believe I ever saw unless 'twas during a storm and the weather was fair; tonight the wind has ceased and is now calm. The stars are peeping out thickly. I cooked early supper tonight; we ate before "candle light."

Mama and I have been quilting largest portion of today. Marvin came home with Alf yesterday and Marvin, Alf, Sweetie, and Blanch are all here tonight. Marvin and Alf remained home from school today because twas Friday and they didn't want to say a speech. The children have been all worry and no pleasure, or scarcely any to me this week, but the fault was with me, for I ought not to let myself be so impatient. I know they are lots of trouble and cause me to take many steps and keep me busy fixing up where the[y] tear down etc etc but 'twas Providence that placed them in my path way and I must be braver and do my part by them and *bear with them* tho' they are sometimes rude, unkind and say saucy things. I prayed lots last night over my impatience with them and today I've been more patient and long suffering. The Lord will help.

I would have gone to Mr. Bostwick's this P.M. or A.M. had not the windy weather prevented.

I received a note from Splint yesterday P.M. He has joined the M.E. church in Jackson. I am glad, glad! glad! He is certainly a noble boy. May the Lord guide and be with him all thro' life and at last receive him into the Pearly Gates.

Papa received a Telegram yesterday announcing that Uncle John Wynn was very sick and wanted to see him. Papa stays so closely here that he doesn't feel right to leave and I guess he will not go.

I may go to a fish-fry tomorrow at Jim Buck's bridge.

April 19, 1892
Tuesday Night

Well, before retiring I will scribble some. Have been busy today, quilting and ironing. Got my "bear's paw" out today. I have 14 quilts now.

Well we had a rite good S.S. last Sunday—first time we have had a sabbath school in severel months. Evie Mason and Lula Bostwick recited and we were pleased and little surprised too. The prayer meeting Sunday night was very good. Wayman Whitaker conducted it real well.

Ghu came after me Sat about 10.30 and carried me to the so called fish fry at Jim Buck's bridge. We had no fish but I had a very pleasant time. We came back just before Sundown. Ghu came back Sunday P.M. and carried me to S.S. and after that we went up to Mr. Barnett's and carried Sarah S. with us. I played on the organ most of the time but had a real nice time. I did enjoy Sunday P.M. *so very* much. We took supper at Buddie's and Wayman Whitaker did too. Received a note from Mr. Bill Harriss the other day saying he wanted to call next Sunday; that he was soon going to St. Andrew's Bay and wanted to see me before he went. I have not answered—one reason because it was written from Molena and letter was missent and he might not have gotten an answer early enough and another main reason I didn't think his visit would be any benefit to me and I wanted to be with Ghu. Ghu insisted last Sunday night on an answer about our wedding day; he insists that it be next Dec. I never gave him any decided answer but told him I didn't know when we would marry.

April 26, 1892
Tuesday Night

Well, this day has not passed off so very sweetly to me some how. Jeff McKibben came by here this A.M. and stopped two or three hours. He seemed to enjoy his call very much and I think Jeff a good hearted fellow and as he is an old schoolmate and a neighbor (when he is at his parents') I always welcome him to our house. He always calls on me when he comes home, and acts like I was a sister.

We are to have preaching at New H. next Sunday which is first of May on account of Bro. B. [Brown] being at Quarterly meeting at the Shoals last 4th Sunday. I went with Ghu on Saturday and never enjoyed a day better hardly.

I went to Jackson yesterday to buy Spring and Summer dresses etc etc. Was so glad to see Splint. He is such a darling sweet noble brother. I do pray the Lord to rule and reign in Splint's heart.

Sweetie came back this P.M. from Buddie's. I played a good while tonight. I love music and do wish I could take music lessons. My! My! I sometimes think I have very few advantages for a girl in my present position but surely it is all for the best. Oh, Lord, help me to *trust* in Thee all the way thro life. My! My! I have some trials to contend with and unless the Lord sustains me I can not be happy at home. Alf is some trouble to me. Mama never seems to see a happy day. A cloud seems to stay in our home. I long, oh I long for a different atmosphere and yet I say Lord help me to be a brave cheerful christian—help me to stay contented for thy name's sake.

Oh! Oh! I am not well tonight. I have a cough and my throat is little sore. Lord be my everlasting portion—be my guide. Oh, how my heart longs to know whether I ought to marry Ghu and by so doing displease my parents and some to the rest of family or stay single and break Ghu's heart. Lord! settle this question. I can't. Oh me! How bothered I am.

. . . . . .

February 18, 1899

In this book I purpose to write down such things as I find sweet pleasure to me I wish to retain in here.

Success seems to me in human life to be not what we have, but what we do with what we have, i.e., on the opportunity to use it. We see the truth of this when we look back on life.

Magnolia Wynn was born at High Falls Ga., Monroe Co. *Feb. 18th 1869.* I (Magnolia) am 30 years old today.

Magnolia Wynn and Ghu Gilbert Le Guin were married on Nov. 27th (Sunday morning) 1892. We began housekeeping two weeks before Christmas near Peeksville. We lived there some over a year when my health failed and we came to live with my father and mother (at Wynn's Mill).

A daughter was born to Magnolia and Ghu Le Guin on 11th day of May (near two o'clock P.M.) 1894, and died in three days after, in

P.M. at 3 or 4 o'clock. Dr. J. A. Jarrell (he lived in Peeksv[ille] then) was the physician we had when our first baby was born.

In thirteen months after first baby was born, Askew Abercrumbie Le Guin was born (just after midnight) August 18th, 1895. (Mrs) Dr. Tommie Aken of Jenkinsburgh was here when Askew was born. Askew weighed 10 lbs when he was born. Askew was one of the "best" babies—slept lots. Was very quiet. Amused himself. Often left him with Lil or Jane Miller when he was young as 3 months old. I left him at that age with Lil Miller and I went to Jackson. Askew walked at 14 months old. Was weaned at two years old; Askew did not eat early. Askew's eyes were dark blue until he was (I think) 2 years old. Then they turned light brown or hazel. Askew was baptized July 12th 1896. Dr. J. W. Heidt baptized him here (at Papa's) in the parlor. Our pastor, Rev. B. Sanders and Dr. Heidt took dinner here that day. That was Dr. Heidt's birthday. He was 55 years old.

On Feb. 11th 1898 (just about two o'clock after dinner time) Fred Gilbert Le Guin was born. Dr. Langston was here when Fred came to light. When Fred was born he weighed 7½ or 8 lbs. Fred never nursed a draw till he was 3 days old. My first baby [i.e., Magnolia's first-born daughter] never did nurse a draught. At one month old Fred weighed 10 lbs. At 2 months, 12 lbs.—at 3 months 15 or 16 lbs. 7 months old, one tooth—can't sit alone, 21 lbs. Fred was one year old on the 11th Inst. Fred (at one year) can stand by chairs, etc., but can't stand alone. He has 8 teeth and can say "Please," "Mama," "Papa," "kitty," "cat," and "Jim."

.   .   .   .   .   .

December 6, 1900

On Feb 11th 1900 Travis Lowery was born. Travis was born just after supper time, if I mistake not. Dr. Josh Thurman was here when Travys was born.* Travys weighed 8 lbs when he was born.

Travys likes a few days of being ten months old. He has one tooth and weighs 20 lbs. He can't sit alone without falling over. Can't crawl but can say "Mama," "Kitty," "Je" (for Jim).

---

*Magnolia uses various spellings for her third son's name: Travis, Travys, Traviss.

1901

February 18

I was 32 years old. Ghu's birthday was Feb. 20th.
Fred's was Feb 11th (3 years old).
Travis' was Feb 11th (1 year old).
Askew's Aug. 18th, 1900 (5 years old).
Papa's (Dr. J. A. C. Wynn) was August 8th, and he was 79 years old. Mama's (M. A. Wynn's) was Aug., 17th and she was 72 years old.

March 27

Went to Jackson and had 8 teeth pulled. Have suffered 7 years with neuralgia but most of the 7 years my health was not sufficient to go to town and have the teeth extracted.

March 28

Travys is 13 months old—small to his age compared to what Askew and Fred was at this age. Travys says several words now—such as "Bow-wow" "mine" "hoomtink!"

Travys learned to eat real well and was hearty (for that age) at 9 months. Walks around chairs. Fred never learned to eat till 16 months. Fred walked at 15 months and was weaned at 15 months old. Never could leave Fred or Travis. Both very cross—always restless till old enough to walk. Fred and Travys both were born with a hard swolen place on the right side of their necks—both same side. Fred's stayed there till about 2 years old. Travys has the swolen gland yet.

Strange it is, when a child is born into the world, to think what its destiny is to be, and what is to be the place it is to hold among men. You never can tell. Every new child is a hidden casket of possibilities, and only time can supply the key which will unlock the secret. Of course the great majority must be commonplace. They will simply go through the ordinary experiences; they will never be heard of 20 miles from home, their memory will perish from the earth fifty years after they are put in the grave; but what mother bending over the cradle of her infant, does not indulge in the hope and the dream that it may not be so with *her* child, that he may turn out to make a name in the world, and leave a good influence after he has gone?

March 29

Askew is 5 years old. He has a decided talent for writing, and some for drawing. I've never learned him, or tried to learn him his letters yet, tho I set copies for him because he loves to write. I haven't learned him, first because I have 3 small children, lots to do, and not stout at all, and 2nd because I don't much approve of children being put to books too early; especially if they are not healthy. Askew is not a robust child. He had a spell of tonsillitis (sorethroat) last fall and since then his health has not been what I expected. One remarkable thing Askew writes is these words (in capitals) "TERMS CASH." He drew it one day off of the old storehouse that his grandpa use to sell goods in. The words—"TERMS CASH"—are all over the old store-house door and have been ever since my earliest recollection. Now Askew is constantly writing the word and writes it plain and splendid, tho' he can not spell it at all. Askew and Fred have within the past month or two begun to say their prayers. I had for two or three years wanted Askew to say the little prayer "Now I lay me down to sleep" but somehow he wouldn't willingly do so, or by coaxing, only just a very few times. Now, after he began, he never fails and at night kneels by his bed and says it by heart.

'Twas an easy matter to get Fred because he, as is natural, is always doing just what he sees the older brother do. Fred doesn't know it by heart, so he repeats it after me.

April 1
All Fools Day

I'm suffering some with neuralgia and baby is cross—teething— but if I can, I want to make some cotton biscuit and some kind of a pie (an april fool pie) have outside covered with wheat-dough, and cook them, to fool Askew, Fred and some [of the] rest of [the] family.

Last night when Askew was saying his prayers, Fred says "I am going to say my prayers. I am going to say J. K. L. M." He evidently thinks saying prayers is something like getting a speach, or learning the alphabet, tho he will kneel down and sweetly repeat "Now I lay me down to sleep etc" after me.

Mr. Fowler, our P.C. [Pastor in Charge], took dinner here yesterday (5 Sunday). He gave them (our church) an extra Sunday, because so many 4th Sundays this year have been rainy days.

I went to Jackson last Friday and had 8 or 9 teeth pulled by Dr. Cantrell, so since then I am not well. One broken caused me lots of suffering and some of the time since I'm suffering good deal with neuralgia.

April 9

Ghu gave me these violets a few moments ago. Every year he brings me about the first violets I see. He knows I love the modest little blossom and that 'tis a special pleasure to gather or receive the little favorite, fragrant blossom. I am always pleased at the interest Ghu pays me by bringing me the first violets I see every spring.

Last Sunday was Easter. Saturday eve I colored 18 eggs for Askew, Fred, and Travys—cooked some colored ones for dinner Sunday. Anna J and Grace were here. Mama and Ghu went to High Falls last week. Mama stopped in Jackson two days with Dr. J's family. Askew went with them to H. Falls.

Parry Lee, a man whom I have lots of respect for as a Christian and gentleman, has sold the "Argus." We subscribed for it because he was editor—now a Mr. Shaver is editor.

April 17

Wednesday night

Last week was a busy week with me. We had some scouring done and I was busy fixing up for quarterly meeting at New Hope. Dr. Robbins, P.E. [Presiding Elder], and Mr. Fowler took dinner

here Saturday and Dr. Robbins spent the night. He is a great man—
a *very* wise man and I think one of the most original characters I
ever met. I heard him preach Sunday. Ghu, children and myself went
down to Joe Wynn's for dinner Sunday. Dr. Robbins had two books
with him. I will always wish I could read them I think. One was
"Eleanor" by Mrs. Humphrey Ward, and the other was "The Map
of Life." I forget the author of that.

Travys is 14 months old and is growing cuter. He can walk a little.
Jim (a negro boy about 14 years old, and one who has been here
ever since Askew was 3 months old) works now and so I get along
badly, at times almost miserably, with my baby and my work—baby
cries—climbs—calls etc etc. Travys tries to say lots of things after
being repeated by us. Nods his head and says "good morning." He
eats hearty. Has five teeth and I think six near through.

April 20

We are having unusual, *very unusual*, weather for this time of year.
The wind blows stormy all day and we keep good fires. I think 'tis
the windiest weather I ever knew. This strange weather (so much
wind) makes me very nervous. Children can't play out doors and the
noise they make is quite trying at times. Lewis Shaw says the fruit
crop will be killed tonight. Papa says he is afraid the wheat crop will
be killed too.

Travys is quite different from what either Askew or Fred were at
his age. Travys eats [a] good deal and with much relish. Milk and
corn bread is a favorite food. He began to eat a quantity of popped
corn and parch (big grain) corn long before he was a year old. Would
just cry for it if we refused to chew it and give him. Fred was 15 or
near 16 months old before he could be induced to eat, except tasting
a little. Weaned him on boiled cow's milk at 15 months. Travys says
lots of single words after we tell him what to say and a good many
without us telling him tho' he doesn't connect any. He will ask often
if what we give him is hot. "Hot? Hot? Hot?" he will say or ask over
and over, and sometimes he will say or ask if it will burn. "Burn?
Burn?"

April 27
Saturday Night

The ending of a busy week. All my weeks are *busy* ones. Three children—a heavy weight and no corresponding strength. When my first baby was born, Dr. J. (not knowing any better) injured me for life.

This has been a beautiful day—the warmest since Christmas. I cooked and swept and did many other things all forenoon. In P.M. I amused fretful Travis, milked, and went up to Mrs. Childs (rolled baby in baby carriage) a little while. 'Tis now past my bed time. Ghu is off with some folks fishing. I am waiting for him. I have read in my favorite magazine "Ladies Home Journal" for some time. It is such a delightful entertainer! How I do prize that magazine. How much pleasure a year's subscription is for me I can never express.

Travis can walk nicely for past two or three days. I gave Bro. Fowler a cake of butter and jug of milk this P.M. I wanted to go hear him preach today but our horse was busy—planting cotton—and I could not go.

Bro. Jim has a new girl baby. Mama and Papa have 46 living grand-children and 6 great-grand-children up to date. This beautiful weather and our interesting magazines and papers arouse a longing that is *deep* within me for some flowers—a flower yard. Mama has so many chickens that I can't have many flowers without pailings. How I do long for a little pailed-in yard full of flowers. I *love* them. I want to cause the love of flowers to be deeply implanted in Askew's heart by having him help me make a flower yard and I don't feel able to buy pailings to put on a yard of my own. Yet if we are going to live here I want to do it for *life* is passing and I have not the coveted treasure—a flower yard. Ghu has come at last.

June 4

Travys is nearly 16 months old. He calls lots of different words plainly. He is bright in many respects. He is teething and hasn't been well in over a week. He has for a few days been calling me "Mag." He hears Jim say "Miss Mag" and hears Mama call me "Mag." Travys likes onions and can ask for them tolerably plain.

Last Saturday eve Fred astonished us by spelling his name severel times and at any time since when we ask him he will say, slow and distinctly: "F-R-E-D" Fred. He pronounces it when he gets thro' spelling and sometimes he says "F-r-e-d Fred Gilbert" (pronounces his double name after spelling Fred).

He was talking to Ghu last Saturday eve and Ghu says "how do you know so much when you can't read?" and Fred says I can *spell*. Then he says "F-r-e-d FRED" and we are astonished. We have never yet tried to learn even Askew his alphabet, but Askew is certainly bright in writing and spelling a few things of his own get-up by asking me now and then the name of letters. He spells his name rite along "A-s-k-e-w-L-e-g-u-i-n," and he writes it thus (all in capitals) ASKEW LEGUIN. Fred spelled "D-o-g dog" too last Sat. after he spelled his name, without being asked to. He had heard Askew and Jim spelling his name after me, and I think that is why he learned it.

Recently Askew cut and made of small pieces of pine, several letters and brought me two—M.L. for my initials and A.A.L. for his initials. I was greatly surprised at Fred's spelling and have always been (since he learned how) at Askew's talent for writing names and spelling few words. Askew learned to write "Terms Cash" and his name sometime before he knew the name of any of the letters. After he had written those words about two or three months he learned by asking me a *few* times, the name of the letters that compose those words, how to spell "terms cash" and "Askew Leguin" and without any one's assistance he recently wrote "JARRELL" and astonished Papa and Ghu by writing it and showing to them and spelling it and did the same for me. He is remarkably bright in several respects for a child of his age and with as little pains as he has had taken with him. I compare him with other of Papa's and Mama's grandchildren, of his age, who come in here and I find that in conversation and in some other respects he seems their senior. He talked remarkably early, and always unusually plain. He was *never* like a baby. Fred talked early too and plainer than other babies of his age. Fred is greatly pleased when called a big boy. He wont eat in his table chair: says "Travys can have it—I am a big boy now." Fred tries to be a "big boy" in his talk and walk and certainly does act funny and always trying to "talk big" and "walk Big" and blare open his eyes to try appear "big." Fred is such a humorous 3 year old fellow and makes me so many funny faces that for a year or two I will at times call him a "clown." Askew asked me yesterday, when I called Fred "Clown" what was a clown? I told him 'twas a funny man in a circus and Fred says I'm a "snake eater." He went with Ghu and Askew to Jackson to the carnival last winter and there was a "snake-eater" on exhibition.

Mattie Lou Smith has been with me a few days helping me with my sewing. Mollie came few evenings ago for first time since she married Mr. Crumbly. Pearl Brown marries tomorrow and I expect Mamie Owens from Atlanta in a week. She will attend Pearl's wedding and come down here so she wrote. Met Mrs. Fowler last Fourth Sunday P.M.; she, her little boy (John Fletcher is his name) and Mr. Fowler came by here. Faith Jarrell spent a few days here recently. Askew, Fred, Travys and myself carried her home. We had a pleasant ride coming back. Let old Joe (Papa's old family horse) poke lazily along and we talked of things we saw along the way—the train, trees, birds, flowers, and God's loving kindness towards us, and His protection over us, all way to Jackson and back home. When we reached home 'twas about dark, and our playful dog "Rex" met us and was overjoyed to see all of us and the horse too; he just jumped up repeatedly to the horse's head as we were driving thro' the yard. On our way to town one of our buggy wheels began to creak and we stopped at an honest darky's, by name of Sandy Gordon, to get him to grease it for us, which he very kindly did and I felt very grateful for his kindness. He was unusually obliging for a darky. I appreciate kind words and acts even from darkies.

June 28

Traviss has had a bad time teething. We are very uneasy about him. Papa and Mama got up and stayed up the night he was worse off, until he ceased crying and dozed. He almost screamed a good while. We gave him medicine from Dr. Thurman. He is thin now and weak, the bowels trouble under good controll just now. I expect him to be sick all this summer as he is at the age to suffer from teething. We were afraid he would have cholera infantum.

Today I put on a clean dress and he noticed it and kept pulling at his and saying "dess" "dess." Trying to tell me to pull off the one he had on and put him on another, which I did. We carried him to church last Sunday and Askew and Fred were down on their knees while Mr. Fowler was leading in prayer and Traviss walked over to them and knelt down on his knees by them and asked what they were doing in these words "doing?" "doing?" Fred has been puny a month or two. I've been weak and sick with a cold—well now as usual. Askew's throat gave him some trouble while back. Mama is seriously ill now—she has a real bad cough. Was in bed a few days—up little while at a time. Askew was very kind and thoughtful of his grandma while she was in bed.

Mr. Fowler is here today—came just before dinner. He and Ghu are fixing to go to High Falls this P.M. on their way to District meeting which comes off in Forsyth tomorrow. 'Tis pouring rain now and Askew, Fred, Traviss and Jim are out in buggy shelter: Raining too hard to come in.

Traviss talks well for his age (16 mo's old). When he wants to go up stairs he goes to Ghu, holds up his arms and says "upstairs" "upstairs." Askew is very much interested in planting and cultivating flowers, in getting up eggs and in the chickens. My pen is sorry but my time for writing is so limited that I just use what I first get my hands on. *So much* work a mother of three babies has to do and so much ahead that I rarely even catch up, tho' doing all my health and strength will permit. I suffer so from loss of strength—more especially in summer.

July 15
Monday

Today Fred saw a top-buggy coming down the road and he says "that is a t-o-p (top) buggy." I heard Askew spelling it that way when he saw a top buggy several days ago and Fred's excellent memory retained it, from hearing Askew several days ago. Travys remembers well—unusually well too. He is learning new words and tricks and they cleave to his memory; he is quick to learn and retains so well what he does learn. Last week Jim's (Wynn's) little boy Acy was here and Travys called him Hines. He has never seen Hines or Acy very many times and I was surprised that he knew one of their names. He learned 'twas Acy tho' and ever so many times since he shows off to us how *smart* he is by saying "Acy!" "Hines!" etc etc. Sometimes he wants to show off and he begins to hollow out "I ain't!" "I ain't!" and other new words he has latest learned.

He has now for nearly a month taken possession of Fred's little table chair. (A chair I bought for Askew and he willingly gave to Fred when Fred could sit up in it.) Askew thought 'twould make him appear larger to give F. the little chair, for him to eat in an ordinary chair, and likewise Fred thinks he is a "big boy" and too large to eat in a little table chair, and so he gladly gave it entirely up to Travys and felt that he had grown a whole heap at once to eat in an ordinary chair. Fred and Askew like to do things that they think make them like "big boys." I hope not one of them will make premature boys — or men. I want them to be children; I'm going to teach them to be in no hurry to get to manhood. I despise premature young men and young ladies. I played with my dolls till sixteen and enjoyed them thoroughly. I went with a boy a few times too that year, but I was a *natural child*. I enjoyed my childhood. I did not hurry into womanhood. I was not anxious to be in the "social swim" of "beaux and belles" — in other words I was not seeking beaux. When I went in society I enjoyed myself but did not think I was a full fledged young lady. I felt like I was something of a child.

Papa was in bed seriously sick one week ago yesterday. He had Dr. Jarrell telephoned for. He had something like cholera morbus but was better by evening.

August 3
Saturday P.M.

Protracted meeting closed at New Hope after a continuance of 7 days. Rev. F. R. Seaborn assisted Bro. Fowler. We had Fred and Travys baptized last night. Fred being nearly two and a half years old I've felt like he was too large. I didn't think about it tho' until Mr. Seaborn asked me why I hadn't had them baptized earlier. I had never seen but two such baptizings before as old as I am (32 years) and had never given much thought to their being baptized after infancy. Fred and Travys were both asleep when baptized. I believe in infant baptism tho'.

August 21
Wednesday Evening

I've been suffering with neuralgia of the head, and other chronic troubles and after pain left, I was so weak that for one day, especially, I was very uneasy about myself. I have some very weak spells and suffer with my head so much. I think it must be nervous prostration that causes me to be so weak in summer.

Fred, Travys, and myself went to Joe Wynn's yesterday and spent the day. A thunder-clap drove us in Mr. Ingram's for a while.

My nerves are so weak, and have been for years, that I can't hardly live in time of a thundercloud unless I'm in house and lying down.

Askew spent the A.M. of his birthday (he was 6 the 18th, Inst.) at High Falls (having gone there the day before with Ghu and Alf W) and the P.M. was spent in coming home. I was real weak and sick the day he came and the day before so I didn't have his birthday cake. However, Mama had Jane to bake her one and I cut a generous slice and saved till Askew came and when he came in from Falls I kissed him 6 times and handed him his slice of cake.

Travys says many surprising things for his age. He often in the night gets frightened and he will say repeatedly "Keered" "Keered." This morning he put a morning glory to Ghu's nose and said in a course voice "Smell." He sometimes talks course. He is 18 months old now.

September 3

For a month I've been suffering severely with neuralgia of the head. Now my head is better for which I am truly glad, but Travys has been sick three days and very sick last night and today. Cutting teeth and a *severe* cold. Such a *hot* head he has when cutting a tooth and such high fevers.

Neither of the others had such awful high fevers. I think he is better some. I do need a good night's sleep. Has been so long since I slept well. What I suffer is not dreamed of only by Ghu.

Travys is nearly 19 months old and has only 8 teeth. I think it Providential that he didn't cut any more when weather was warmer as his fevers are dangerous. He is smart. This eve he livened up and

connected three words: said slowly, "Jimmie—catch—Joe." He saw
the horse and just begged Jim and I to catch him. He wanted to ride
in buggy. I've never heard him connect three words before.

This P.M. he was in front yard with me and Fred, was several feet
from the "Four O'Clock" bush, but Fred said something about the
"Four O'Clock" and Travys walked over to it and put his hand on
it and says "tock." Tried to tell us which plant was the "4 O'Clock"   ·
and I was certainly surprised that the precious baby knew it from any
other plant, but tho' it is in a thicket of others he certainly knows the
"tock" from all else and I think better than any other. I doubt if he
knows the name of any other tho' I saw him put his hand on a zenior
[zinnia] and call it "senie" but it was just a few moments after Fred
had said something about "Zeniors." Fred calls them "Ber-seniors."
Fred and Askew love flowers and Askew's love is remarkably strong
for them and all ways has been.

Travys nearly every day goes around them and pulls some and
always looks at Mama and laughs because she so often has told him
not to and he knows she cares. He is when well full of mischief.
When sick he calls "Mama Mama" and "Maggie" pitifully all day
and night.

September 4
Wed.

Fall is here again. My physical nature (or mental, or my whole
being) rejoices more over fall than any other season. My health in
some respects is always better. My heart rejoices because fall has
come and hot weather that so much of the time prostrates me is over
for a six months. Oh, how sweet nature is to me in fall! The breezes
that blow seem to be whispering sweet and helpful things to me
every day now since September has come in. All hail September I say
o'er and o'er, in my soul, as I busy myself about my household tasks.
When September comes in new life comes to me and strong desires
to visit my friends seizes me, more than any other month except
glorious October. I think I have experienced this thrill of pleasure at
this season of the year nearly all my life. If I was not compelled to
cook all A.M.'s and sew the P.M.'s (in order to get Ghu, children and
myself winter clothes) I certainly would visit several families this and

next mo., while my health will permit. If neuralgia of the head stays easy enough I think I will make a few visits anyway. I have my heart set on a couple of visits to Locust Grove.

September 13
Friday (A.M.)

I went to Jackson Tuesday A.M. and had 7 teeth extracted and roots of two and part of a third, besides, at one sitting and now I haven't a single upper tooth and I am truly glad they are out. I suffered 8 years, intensely, at times with those teeth. Dr. Cantrell said 'twas the hardest set he ever pulled. Said he often pulled some hard teeth, but he never saw anyone dread to have teeth pulled, who was so anxious for them to be extracted, as I did. Oh, it was just awful suffering, but I am *so glad* they are out.

Askew pulled his first tooth this morning. He was six years old last month. He has another loose, both have been for a week or two, but he is a very nervous child and he wouldn't let anyone pull them. One thing that makes me uneasy about Askew, is that his nose bleeds often, and has been doing so nearly his whole life. I think it has bled about 4 or 5 times in the past week. It doesn't usually bleed that often.

Travys went with us to Jackson and when we crossed the gin branch* he says "gin branch" and we were surprised that he (17 months old) knew the name of it. 'Tis my favorite walk and I've always carried my children there. When we arrived in Jackson we went straight to Dr. C's office and he was busy and said would be for an hour so we drove over to Dr. W. C. Bryant's beautiful home and I spent a while pleasantly with my girlhood friend, Lula, in looking thro' part of her beautiful home and at many pictures, books etc etc.

Travys ask me when I was salting butter to let him taste (by repeatedly saying "taste" "taste") and I put some in his mouth and he says "dood" "dood."

President McKinley is dead. He died September 14th about two

---

*A small tributary of Tussahaw Creek which formed one of the boundaries of the farm. See map.

o'clock. He was shot twice by an anarchist by name of Leon Czol-
gosz.

The President's last words to his wife were: "God's will, not ours
be done." And then he chanted the hymn "Nearer my God to Thee."

December 19

Three months have passed since I wrote in this book. I have suffered inexpressibly since then and tho' a *great* deal better, still a very
bad stomach trouble yet have I. I have taken six bottles of physic
from Dr. J. E. Woods and near a month ago, I ceased medicine
and kept fruit to eat and the fruit seems to help me more than the
medicine did.

Snow is thickly spread over mother earth today and two smaller
children bother me so playing around where I am trying to write that
I am so unnerved I can't *think* or write intelligently. The weather has
been extremely severe recently. The children, naturally noisy, keep
my nerves unstrung, as they can't play out from fire long. My health
being bad affects my nerves.

Travys was weaned three months ago (at eighteen months old) and
after he was weaned he had a serious time cutting some teeth. He
had the highest fevers I ever saw any of our children have, and his
head would be awful hot. He has had three serious teething spells
but since the last spell, he has better health than he ever had in his
life before and is a real fat, jolly, cute, bright, sweet, baby now. He
says many very bright things for his age. He surprises and amuses
Papa as well as Ghu and I. Papa plays with him and calls him "a
smart boy." At present he is best looking of the three and people say
he is a Wynn, that he doesn't favor the Le Guins.

Our expenses have been very heavy this year, especially this fall
and winter. I've hired good deal of sewing and quilting done on
account of my health and my fruit bill is still going on. Ghu bought
me a good stove and treated himself to a clock recently. My appetite
failed completely and we bought good many different kinds of things
to try bring it back but while still not good, I can eat one hearty meal
most days—breakfast.

I don't think I will ever have much health—am afraid I'll never be much more than an invalid. It is almost impossible now for me to keep house without help and past three months had to hire lots done. We are going to try get a white girl to live with us next year I reckon Negroes are so much of a bother—no principal—so little to be trusted and such trials.

Jim Ellis, a negro boy who came here when Askew was 3 months old or 6 (I don't know which positively) left us in good humor. He had been here nearly seven years but just would not act with any principle. His lack of principle has tried me sorely and I am truly glad he has gone and my only fear is that he will not stay gone.

If he had been mine, he would have been gone long ago, but he was Papa's hireling and my trial. I am thankful Jim Ellis left! While he had some good traits he was a sight of trouble to me. We had another negro boy (Papa did) the past two or three months who would try to do his tasks some better than Jim and who I felt I'd like to keep if it were not for having two negroes but the next day after Jim left he deliberately walked off too. Lucian Millner was his name.

We will be obliged to get some one to help around the house. I can't draw water and if we can't get Laura Edge, a white girl, guess we will have to get another negro. My health is such, and has been for 8 years that I need constant help of a girl or woman in house-keeping. I know I am not lazy but my health is so much worse all the time than any one, except Ghu, has any idea of.

Just a week till Christmas! I am not well enough I am afraid to go to town and get a few things for Santa Claus. Askew wrote to Santa Claus two weeks ago (had me to for him) and ask for a set of toy tools. He firmly believes in Santa C. I was afraid Jim Ellis would learn him not to believe in our Childhood's Saint. I wish I was well enough to go to town and select a few presents for the three little tots but if I can't go, Ghu will get them up something from little country stores, if he doesn't take a notion to go to town.

I don't know of anything that I would enjoy better than to make them happy with my selections Christmas morning.

1902

January 15
New Year!

Papa has been feeble since before Christmas and stays in doors nearly all the time. In our best days (most pleasant weather) he stays awhile at the mill.

Askew, Fred, and Travys have whooping-cough.

We do not know where they caught whooping-cough unless they caught it Christmas Eve at Mr. Maddox's store. There were children at the store that P.M. That is the only place three have been in a long time, together, and all three of them seemed to cough about the same time. Fred's cough is worse than the other two. Whooping cough is making Fred look bad and he coughs so hard. Askew has it worse (or it seems to hurt him worse) than Travys. He coughs lots but seems livelier than Fred. Fred is very quiet and weak looking. Travys, so far, has coughed less, much less severe than the other two.

Askew has his first school book, (bought it today) and he is rite anxious to start to school. When his cough gets sufficiently well and the weather gets pleasant we will send him. He will go to school where I first went, only in different houses. I went to New Hope schoolhouse (which has been torn down many years) and Askew will go in the church. Mr. Compten has opened a school in the church. We expect to build a new church this summer at New Hope and make a school-house of the old one; that is why they permitted school to be taught in the church and the old church is in rite bad condition. There are more children around New Hope than there are near the academy at Peeksville.

I have a white girl living with me for an indefinite time, by name of Laura Edge. My health is not [good enough], (nor hasn't been in 8 years) to do all the housework (ironing, sewing, sweeping, cooking) and see after the children without aid. We've needed someone but not feeling able financially to hire is one reason we haven't hired sooner or tried to. Another reason was because we were not in our own home. I feel that we are hardly able to pay her wages, yet I am willing to deny myself of things I can do without, if she will only faithfully do her work. It seems if I possibly can get help I *must*, as household work and care of children has been a burden to my overtaxed body.

Willie Wynn, my sister-in-law, sent Askew, Fred, and Travys a picture book for a Christmas present. Santa Claus didn't bring them anything particular as we couldn't go to Jackson to notify him and Mr. Maddox store was our shopping place. They had toy pistols, (A. and F. did) and I am opposed to children having toy pistols — because it might have a tendency to create a desire for real pistols and do untold harm. I've read from Mrs. Felton and other able writers cautions against by [buying] toy pistols, guns etc-the tendancy being towards desires for real fire arms.

February 11
Tuesday

Today is Fred's and Travys' birthday. Fred is four years old and cute, sweet bright little Travys Lowery is two. Fred has a kind winning disposition, speaks a little slow and long in a kind of musical tone. Travys is I think at the age to be the very *sweetest* and to get most attention. He is very mischievous, bright and interesting — the household pet. His Grandma and Grandpa ("Damma" and "Porpor") love to hear him talk and they talk lots to him and humor him a great deal. They are amused every day at him. Travys is very much devoted to his Papa Ghu and often at night wakes up and cries till Ghu takes him on his bed or comes and lies with Travys' head on his arm till T. goes back to sleep and then slips back to his bed and leaves T. Fred and Askew sleep with Papa Ghu and Travys with me.

Our cow is dry now and I did not cook T. and F. a birthday cake but made them a pudding and some syrup candy. Fred's Grand Pa gave him a chicken and sent Lucian to the store to buy (with the chicken) a knife and some candy.

Many happy birthdays may my little treasures see.

They are all better of whooping cough now, but Fred coughs real hard yet but not very often, and he stays up all day now and is livelier.

February 24

This winter has been a severe one and our children have been housed up ever since Christmas, with exception of a few days when they played about some. I will be glad when weather gets warm enough for them to go with Ghu to Sunday School. They all dearly love a ride in a buggy and they haven't had that pleasure in so long.

Well another February has come and on the 18th I was 33 years old and on 20th Ghu was 32 years old. and on 11th Fred was four and on same day Travys was two—

Night—Ghu bought me today, from Dr. Gideon, a magnolia bush to plant at our first baby's grave.

March 15

I sent Askew over to Mr. Jim Ingrams store (distance of one mile) yesterday by himself. 'Twas the first time he had ever been sent as far alone. There is no bridge at the bridge place now—recent high water washed it away. I felt a little uneasy about him before he returned— afraid he had fallen in creak in trying to cross the footlog. He told me he had walked the planked log several times by himself. He was very anxious to go the distance by himself and came back smiling over his adventure. He was very proud that he was large enough to go to the store and only six years old.

He did a nice thing too: Mr. Ingram gave him two sticks of candy and he took a small bite of each and brought the rest to Travys and Fred. We expect to send Askew to New Hope to school soon as weather will permit. I feel a dread to, somewhat, because he is a delicate, nervous, and somewhat timid boy. If I could go with him to quiet him when afraid, to encourage him when timid, to protect him if protection should be needed from larger, rougher, boys, I'd be satisfied.

He is very anxious to start, yet I think he has lots of fears about the "untried field" as he has never been away from Ghu or myself one, or the other, a whole day in his life.

March 25
Tuesday

Askew did something this A.M. he never did before, namely: he started to school. I know he feels like he has done wonders! I know he feels that he is a *bigger boy* than he ever was before. I didn't much want Askew to begin school on any day except Monday. Yesterday was the day we had set for him to start, but 'twas a rainy day. I yielded to Ghu's wishes tho' and let him go today when I had rather he had waited till next Monday. He is so young and not very stout and I've always thought best not to hurry him to school. I did a new thing too this morning! Ghu and I have been married near ten years and I made a fire before Ghu got up, for first time in ten years (when Ghu was at home).

March 31
Monday Night

Easter Sunday came in March this year. Yesterday was Easter (the 5th Sunday) and on Saturday eve while I had two lady visitors (both kin by marriage) I went in stove room and made an Easter cake with eggs (most of them were his) that Askew had been saving for Easter. With Laura to assist we put pink icing on a large cake and Sunday morning early I put on a pretty white table cloth, put two vases of fresh Johnquills on table and in middle of table a spoon holder (to answer for a vase) full of beautiful double hyacints. We had the large pink cake near center and some colored eggs in tiny glass dishes by each little fellow's plate.

Askew, Fred, and Travys had their cousin Florrie Bell with them and Travys, a baby, gave up his table chair for Florrie Bell to eat in and Florrie Bell ate out of her great-grand-mother's china plate. (A plate that came to my mother, when her mother's things were divided among her children. The plate is mine and for its antiquity and because 'twas my grandmother's I appreciate it highly.)

One of my pretty glass vases was broken in the P.M. Wind blew hard and I lost bottom part of my loved vase.

Laura painted Askew two eggs to carry with him and he kept one of his over yesterday to carry. He was the only little boy at school today with Easter eggs. I told him to give his little cousin Blanche one of his colored eggs because she had no mother to paint her eggs. Her own mother is dead but [she] has a step-mother.

Travys is sick. I carried Mrs. Anna and Florrie Bell up to Mr. Barnett's yesterday and couldn't well leave "Tabby" and I think the windy ride has caused his sickness. He is *such* a cute sweet baby! He has been cross and cried and coughed lots all day and called me several times and called me "Miss Maggie! Miss Maggie—Oh, Miss Maggie."

He is so sweet! Did I ever love a baby so before? Sometimes feel that not altogether did I love other babies so much.

April 10

Fred has ear ache a good deal and "Tabby" recently had a bad attact. "Tabby" has a new pair of Sunday shoes; he cried so hard to wear them that Mama told me let him wear them out every day. Papa Ghu objected but baby cried so I let him keep on day by day and he carries them in his arms to bed every night except one since he put them on. How he loves a little pair of new shoes! Better than anything he ever possessed. Tabby tries to do like Fred when he says his prayers and now often "tabby" says his and looks awful cute while so doing. He said his prayers earlier than Askew and Fred. . . .

April 18

Askew pulled two of his teeth yesterday. He pulled them easily. When the other two were loose he had some difficulty in getting them out—was afraid they would hurt and was a day or two getting them out. He, like all other children, was very proud when he pulled a tooth. He will be 7 years old in August, and has up to date shed four teeth. The past three nights "Tabby" has slept with Ghu. He takes funny notions; Fred sleeps with me, since Tabby sleeps with him.

Askew likes to go to school. School closes today for awhile.

All three of the little boys love flowers. I am glad they do. If I had

strength enough I'd cultivate a separate bed for each and in different ways try to increase their love for them. I always loved deeply
our modest little wild violet. Each of my little boys are very fond of
violets, and since they've opened this spring "Tabby" and Fred will
hunt for them and eagerly gather all they see. They seem to have
a decided preference thus far, this season, for the violet. I carried
"Tabby" and Fred down [to the] little creak (my favorite haunt in
spring, summer and fall) and I found a few honeysuckle open but
they prefered the little violet. Their pleasure in gathering the violet
seems remarkable to me. I love very dearly the precious violet.

April 21
Monday

Travys went with "Papa Ghu," Fred and Askew to Sunday school
yesterday. First time he ever went to church without me. We intend
for him to go on now with them when convenient. He had not worn
any Sunday clothes before since last summer (as he has been housed
up all winter) and he seems to be delighted to get on a white dress
again.

I thought, as Ghu drove off, that he and his three little boys made a
pretty picture. Ghu said "Tabby" behaved all right at Sunday school.
The lovely weather now is making the three little boys happy. They
are playing out doors and all chattering merrily—nailing and building minature bridges this A.M. They go out as soon as they eat.

April 24

Fred has put on pants today (He had worn some a few times before last summer for fun) but he has them on in earnest now. I didn't
want him to put them on till May but Papa Ghu and Fred both
wanted him to don pants today and leave dresses forever behind. I
feel sad because he will never wear dresses anymore. Just to think my
little boy Fred will never look like he has so long looked anymore—
never be happy with his Sunday dress on again and it always gave
him to much pleasure to put on Sunday dress tho' none of my children were ever finely dressed but neatly dressed and tastily as I could

make them. Just to think that even this week Fred took a notion (at my suggestion) to lay aside his cap and wear a little starched sunbonnet. (He and Tabby love starched clothes. Askew the reverse—has asked me twice not to starch his—tho' I pay no heed to that). I thought Fred looked so sweet and so gentle going around quietly playing and hunting violets with Travys and each with sunbonnets on. What a leap—from sunbonnets and dresses to pants—all in one day too. After he put on pants he seemed very proud of them and Askew seemed to be as happy over the change as Fred was. They then walked over to Mr. Ingram's store after some articles for me and Askew carried a hen for Mama, to exchange for ginger. The walk was too long for little Fred this warm April day and he cried and when came home was worn out and fell across bed and is yet asleep and hasn't eaten dinner—so tired he slept while we ate.

Lets see, Fred is 4 years and 2 months and several days old—and no more will he wear dresses after today. Sad to see babies growing from innocent babyhood to "boys grown tall" so fast. Sad to think I'll never see him look as he looked in dresses anymore. I was loathe to put pants on Askew but on account of Ghu's desire Askew and Fred both donned them a little earlier than I wished. Gentle baby Fred—in pants.

Laura has carried Travys this spring with her to hunt Ferns and other flowers. Since then a Locust tree in our yard has put on new leaves and they are a little like a fern leaf, and Travys called Laura severel times to come out in yard and give him some "ferns." He talks so plain for a two year old baby. He and Papa were handling some wood yesterday and Travys says "that's poidon! throw it out doors!" Papa was surprised to hear him use the word poison. He talks so *plain* for his age. Talks plainer now for his age than Fred, I think.

April 29

Tuesday

I have no good pens. Ghu forgot to get me any in town and Mr. Jim Ingram hasn't any.

Papa has been making Askew, Fred and Travys whistles as he has been doing ever since Askew was a year or two old, in the spring.

Goes up in woods and makes them of chestnut and chinquapin. Our roses are budding this week and each of the children are watching them like myself, with much pleasure.

We are having such lovely weather now, that the little boys love to play our in the balmy air, among green leaves and admist the sweet songs of the birds.

May 6

Our May roses are blooming profusely now and early every morning Askew, Fred, Travys and myself go around to all the bushes and gather all the old ones (those ready to shatter) in order to keep the odor as long as we can. We have now a work basket about twice full gathered. It is surprising, when one saves them, how fast they can gather and how soon two or three baskets full can be accumulated. I did that last year and this year we are going to make us a rose pillow.

The little boys love our roses and delight to help gather them. 'Tis one of the sweetest pleasures of my life to gather the sweet roses early every A.M. and put them in water in the house where we can admire them and inhale their sweet odor all day as we are busy with our work. We sit in the hall in summer and I keep little tables in hall full of flowers when we have them plentiful. Laura keeps lots of wild flowers in jars on floor. I help gather and fix these too but many times when she goes I haven't the strength to go with her. A hunt on creek for wild flowers is a genuine pleasure to me — like a trip to "fairy land."

May 16

We had rain yesterday and still cloudy and misting. Thus far, this has been a very dry May and I think the warmest one I ever experienced. Travys was threatened with croup nearly all night — Wednesday night. Good many people say he favors Mama, and sometimes say he favors Splint. There is a beautiful place some little distance down the creak — the spot is the largest sand bar I ever saw and in the bar are some beautiful water oaks and other green trees. The water oaks are lovely. Laura carried Travys in her arms and she and I went about right to this spot this week and on the next eve, a little earlier, we went again and Fred and Askew and "Rex" (G's dog) went with us this time. The visits to this beautiful spot was a sweet pleasure to me. I've been so close in doors past 8 or 9 months, except occasionally a ramble on creak or branch.

Askew helped faithfully, to set out flour [flower] plants this morning. He loves flours and seems to delight deeply in transplanting them. I am glad he likes this line of work. My strength was not sufficient to help him and Laura in yard—a deep regret too—as I am extremely fond of the work. I certainly would love to have time and strength—a little yard pailed in—and work flowers with Askew and F. to assist—to learn them to love them "more and more."

May 17

I declare Fred is a curiosity on one line, at least. He can spell ever so many words correctly and doesn't know a letter! I've never tried to learn him the alphabet—I think there's time enough yet—don't believe in learning young children "book larning" too soon.

I have been surprised at his spelling. A year ago he could spell his first name F-r-e-d—just as well as I. Few days ago I heard him spell this "w-e-l-l—well" when no one was talking to him at all. Askew usually gives out words to him, and then he spells and has Fred to spell after him and now he gives out and waits for Fred to spell those that he can.

I've been amused a number to times, since Askew's school closed (I think he went about three weeks) to hear Askew giving out words and having Travys spell slowly and distinctly each letter after him. Travys likes it for awhile.

I was surprised several days ago to hear Travys spelling Fred's name, and again today I heard him saying without being told "F-r-e-d—Fred." So they are funny little fellows I think—Fred four years old and spelling severel words and Travys two and can correctly spell Fred's name and neither one knows "B from a Bull's foot" of their alphabet. Travys has a splendid, unusually good, memory. He calls me "Magnonie" (for Magnolia) most all the time and has for a month. Sometimes he will say "Magnonie is name Mama Magnonie." Today he was begging for little nails and I didn't reply

and he says more earnestly—"dood dreacious! I want some nails!"
Papa Ghu administered to him a rite good spanking yesterday because he cried a good deal. Guess it stopped him, as he was pleasant
shortly afterwards till "shut-eye-time." He and Fred are partners.
They usually play contentedly together. Askew is, when Travys is
hurt or in need of protection, real good to Travys, (other times he
is not always patient or as kind) but I've seen Askew do some noble
deeds towards Travys. He leaves his play and runs to him when he
cries as if hurt and tries hard to passify him. Has been carrying him
like a cat carrying a kitten for about a year I think. When I was sick
last fall and Winter Askew would "tote" him some that way and he
kept it up. "Tabby" gets awfully frightened if caught in a shower
if it is ever so light. Askew brought him tagging around his waiste
from mill to home recently thro' a shower and Travys was very much
frightened and crying all the way. When they are off at play, if Askew
gets excited or frightened, he is like a mother to T. and has always
been. He will seize T. under his arms and hurry to the house—never
forgets to protect T. from all danger.

Few evenings ago they were taking one of their very frequent
walks with their Grand pa, and Askew found about three half ripe
strawberries—he gave Fred one and F. ate it up and begged Askew
all the way to the house for the other, but Askew wouldn't give them
to him, nor eat them himself—brought them to "Tabby." His Grand
Pa notices several instances of Askew's unusual thoughtfullness and
Kindness to T. Papa is one of the *most* indulgent grand parents I ever
saw in my life. Mama is greatly so too but not as much in every aspect
as he is. She thinks sometimes (not often) they need a whipping. He
says whippings *do no* good and *should not* be given them. They've all
taken almost daily walks with him in good weather ever since they
could walk.

We've been having some drizzly weather today and yesterday and
early this morning Mama said to Tabby, what do you think—and
Tabby said "I fink its rainy day" (Laura told me this. I didn't hear
and don't vouch for the exact words.)

Ghu went to Philadelphia [church] today. Askew is always extremely anxious to go such places as he can with him and was deeply
disappointed because Papa Ghu thought weather too bad for A. and
wouldn't let him go. Askew has a tooth ache today. For more than
a year he has suffered with tooth ache from two decayed teeth.

Very young (I find by comparison) to have tooth ache and shedded teeth early.

'Tis so sweet to see Tabby kneeling by bed saying "now I lay me" etc. I wish I could retain the devotion he now has for me—a regret constantly comes to me: when another comes to our home and hearts that will require all my feeble strength and time, my precious pet T. will never be just *as fond* of "Magnonie" as he is now. No one takes "Magnonie's" place in his little heart now. He loves "Magnonie" now better than anyone; is better satisfied with her than with anyone. I fear when "Magnonie" can not have time and strength to devote to him he will *never never* be so attached to her again.

Askew is a good boy in many ways. My greatest and almost only trouble with him is his carelessness. Can't trust him to pour a cup of milk or bring a dipper of water, unless he (most invariably) spills it. Is careless with his clothes and person too. I hope he will soon get to be a careful painstaking thoughtful child.

Another trouble Askew gives: he does not like to be bathed and is as fidgety as a child with St. Vitas Dance when I wash him. He is in a jerk with hands and arms and is crying and hurrying me all the time, and so my strength and patience are worn threadbare nearly every-time I bathe him. I wish I could get him to be calm at such times. May the Heavenly Father help me to be a true Christian Mother and raise my children in fear of the Lord. Hope each will be one of God's jewels and that I may not come far short of my duty as a mother to them.

May 24

When Travys woke up this morning the room was very dark (thick curtains down) and when I let up curtains he says "sun is shining; 'taint raining is it?" He says lots about rainy weather and seems so glad when weather is fair. Few months ago he would look out the window at the rain and cry because the rain was pouring down.

I have a large monthly rosebush in the garden and recently a pair of mocking birds made a nest in it. Three blue eggs were laid and then alas! the female bird came no more to the nest. The male bird makes me feel sad every day. He sits near by all day it seems and calls for his mate. I've listened and watched him; he looks sad and forlorn. I guess he didn't see the cat when she caught and ate his mate. I feel sure 'twas one of our cats that ate her. I saw "Hotema" (Travys' smart kitten) in there and our old lazy black cat stays there lots. I go every morning to the bush and cut roses and the male bird flies around me and cries a pitiful cry. This morning it seemed to want to fight me. I've noticed its distress plainer today than ever.

May 25
(Fourth Sunday)

Askew and Fred went with Ghu to church this A.M. Travys isn't very well and didn't care to go, so he has been rite with me ever since they left. Laura cooked dinner before she left so Tabby and I have done little of anything.

Last night when I was washing Travys he says "Me lub you—me lubs you." Yesterday eve he pulled up his dress and started to urinate; Papa says what are you going to do? Tabby instantly replied, "Don't you see?" He says some very unusual things for a two year old. This morning while we were eating Mama asked T. what he wanted. He replied "I ain't going to tell you." He is very mischeivous and answered her thus for fun.

Well, yesterday I carried Tabby to my rose bush in the garden to let him see how the male mocking bird would fly about us in order to protect the nest and 2 eggs of his dead mate—My surprise was great when I beheld two birds in the nest instead of eggs. The male bird has evidently been roosting on the eggs at night and we've had such hot weather all this month that the eggs hatched without a mother. Now I am afraid the male bird can not know to feed the little things. I hope he will feed and raise them and that no cat will eat them.

June 21
Saturday Evening

Tomorrow is Fourth Sunday—been a month, liking one day, since I wrote last in this book. What changes have come in my life in that length of time. What suffering! What a wearisome, inexpressible weary, times I've had day and night since three weeks ago, most of the time.

We have another baby in our family—another little boy 3 weeks old today. He hasn't been named yet. My strength has been so over-taxed since the little life has been given me that I can't think of any names I like particularly. When he gets to sleeping better and crying less, and I gain more strength and get more rest and sleep I'll name him.

Ghu called him "no. 4."

He was born on Saturday morning, about or near 9 o'clock, on May 31st '02. He wasn't weighed till the 2nd day. He weighed 8 lbs. He has been laughing few time just last two or three days. He cries great deal day and night too—some nights sleeps very well. I've worn myself completely out worrying night and day with him.

Ghu helps me some at night but I do all I possible can because Ghu can't quiet him and is always miserably sleepy and tired after a day of hard work.

Travys, Askew, and Fred think lots of him. The first time Travys saw him, I told him 'twas his baby—his brother. He so often talks of "my bother." T. can't say brother—he says "my bother." He be-lieves it is his baby. The baby grows and is improving in appearance every day if he does cry. He had sore eyes a few days. Ghu obtained some eye medicine from Dr. Colvin while at Locust Grove and now his eyes seem to be well. The medicine was good and helped first day. Dr. Thurman was here when baby was born. Telephoned for Dr. Woods and he was not at home.

This has been such a hot month and our room (the front room) had to be kept very dark and still we keep it so. We would not have suffered so from heat if we could have stood the light—the baby and I. Red curtains were up and how they caused the light to hurt us— Ghu bought me some green ones since and we have a satisfactory shade now, but can't have them up much, on account of baby's eyes.

(Maybe in four months I can go and have the two pieces of teeth pulled, and have my teeth this year. Sickness has caused me to go minus my upper teeth so long.)

June 23

Papa says Travys is one of the brightest children he ever saw. I feel sorry for the poor little thing; since the new baby came and takes all my time, little Travys is neglected and looks like a little motherless boy. The new baby is nervous and can't sleep when there is noise and poor little Travys doesn't come often, thro' the day, in our room.

The new baby has colic every day and when not crying he is unusually bright looking for a 3 weeks old baby. Few days ago, a hot evening, Ghu carried him on front veranda to cool, and he gazed on the sky—'twas late and shady—just before dark. I thought he was *unusually* young to notice as much as he did the sky.

Jim Ellis, a negro boy who came here when Askew was a few months old (three I think) and lived here till Travys was nearly two years old, came here yesterday and played with the children. Being raised together, they are great friends, tho' I am opposed to them playing long at a time with Jim, as I think he is a worse boy about some things, than when he lived here.

July 1

"Boy No. 4" was a month old yesterday and weighed 12 lbs. He weighed 8 lbs at first and hence has averaged 1 lb. a week since. He has been, since 8 days old, an awful cross baby and I have been most of the time extremely tired, weak, and overtaxed. Yesterday he did well. He has had colic, cold feet and bowels ached. I think I can doctor him better now as I feel little stronger from the rest he let me have yesterday, and since I think I understand better what has caused him all the crying he has done.

Ghu weighed him last night.

Our other babies had a name ere they were a month old.

No one had ever cut Fred's and Travys' hair except myself, till Saturday P.M. Geo. Thompson cut Fred's and Askew's. Ghu (for first time he ever cut any of the children's hair) cut Travys'. I couldn't cut their hair on account of lack of strength and cross baby.

Baby laughed (not aloud however) when 5 days old, first time, and has laughed every day since I think in spite of the fact that he is a terrible cry-baby.

Mamie O. wrote me to name him Lyndon. Ghu seems to like the two following names linked: Guy Stanton.

Baby made a low cooing noise about three times this P.M. and only a month old. He can make a noise when lying down kicking—a noise that I think indicates he is feeling good. Really he can make noises uncommonly young.

Dollie Wynn suggested I name him Athell; Mama suggested the name Raynor (after a prominent lawyer she has read of). Papa called him McKinley the first time he saw him.

July 3

We had company yesterday. Mrs. Annie Ingram (a woman I like) and Annie Bell was with her. Annie Bell brought Askew, Fred, and Travys each a candy birds nest with five eggs in each.

July 7

Our baby is one of the smart kind. Laughed out yesterday (5 weeks old). He laughs lots and notices so much. I'd rather he *looked less*, and *slept* more. He sleeps well now at night, and sometimes in the forenoon.

Della Huddleston was here yesterday and she would say of our baby "he is much a knowing baby!" and "how he laughs!" and "how large he is!" Willie Wynn wrote me to name him Paul. I have a notion of naming him after two dead brothers and call him Paul Esca (for my oldest and youngest brothers, both dead) tho' I love the name Frank and dislike to give it up. Am afraid Frank and Fred are too much alike tho'.

Askew started back to school today. Mr. Garr is to teach just today. Mr. Thurston will be the teacher this term, but has business to attend to and has Mr. Garr in his place today. Askew is anxious to be in school again.

Fred did a sly trick last week—when he thought no one would hear him and he worked on the clock awhile and I spanked him and he ran to the mill. Poor little Fred has never been well since he had whooping cough. He looks real sad at times I think and pitiful too.

He has a gentle kind tone of voice and a gentle disposition, but not always so—at time he and his two brothers are harsh, cross etc with each other.

Travys is smart. Talks surprisingly. At dinner table I asked Travys who he favored. He always answers: "I favor Grandma" and I expect him to say it then, but he spoke out loud and distinct "Favors Mish (Miss) Ann" and we all laughed. Papa laughs hearty at Travys often.

July 14

Baby grows and doesn't cry much now, if we nurse it a great deal— spoilt—he sleeps more, but is not a baby to sleep soundly yet. He can coo sometimes a little!

Travys and Fred went with "Papa Ghu" to Mr. Wilkins yesterday P.M. to eat watermellons. 'Twas a rare treat to them both. Askew went with Ghu to Phillippi church in the A.M. and he remained at home in the P.M. Travys says *very bright* things—surprising things everday, for one of his age.

Fred went to school with Askew this morning, not as a pupil, but just to be going. Askew wanted him to go. Fred thought he must have a book to carry and the poor little innocent fellow picked up a seed catalogue and was a few steps from the house and Askew discovered the seed catalogue and it was embarrassing to Askew for Fred to carry such a book and so I got Askews picture book (which has the alphabet in it) and Fred carried it proudly off. He is a splendid disposed child (Fred) and so gentle in his tones until he has little cross spells, which most all children are subject to, I suppose. With other children he quickly makes friends on account of his gentle smiling face and kind tones and sweet disposition.

Askew rode horseback, far as from here to Holder's shop twice last week. I am glad he is learning to ride horseback.

Baby isn't named yet. We have been thinking over lots of names but, while Ghu wants him named rite away and almost any of the names, I'd like to wait till I could decide more satisfactory on a name suitable to my liking. (Baby was in my lap, under this book while I did part of this writing).

Papa and Mama have 48 living grand children, 9 dead grand children, and 9 great-grand-children.

Papa hasn't been able to be about much past two or three days and lies down most of the time. Travys plays on bed with him and cuts many capers and says many funny things. Papa told him just short while ago, that he was the smartest boy in the country. Travys is a *real* bright boy for two years and 5 months old. Travys can say "Pa-Paw" and is in habit of that and doesn't call him anything else but "Pa-Paw."

Our little baby is a very bright looking young baby. Seems to know just well enough, when I give him "love licks," that I am playing, and he has a real playful eye—a bright eye—a cute, pleased expression.

Baby just stays wake past few days all day, except dozes or cat naps and I am tired almost out of my senses. We came back to our room yesterday and baby slept better this A.M. than he ever has. Baby boy "No. 4" was born in front-room and Askew was born in that room. Splint died in that room (the room opposite the parlor) and Fred and Travys were born in my room. My girl-hood room. (My room by the stair-steps). Askew and Baby boy "No. 4" being born in warm weather we couldn't stay in our warm room.

Askew has been to school about six weeks in his life and can read very nicely for his schooling.

Fred and Travys certainly do have happy times this watermellon season. They go from morning till night to the patch. Eat lots of little ones up there. They have a "gully resort" and a mulberry tree where they sit and eat. The eat more watermellons than *any body* I ever [saw] in my life and they eat *so often* and seem to be always ready for more. They certainly do look cute tugging back to the house with a little mellon in their arms and as happy as they can be. I never saw them more happy than this dry weather watermellon patch has made them.

July 25

Baby not yet named—7 weeks—nearly 8 weeks old. He has the most playful air—most playful eyes—of any 7 weeks old baby I've ever raised unless I've forgotten dreadfully. Grows—stays awake enough thro the day to worry me exceedingly—more than I can express. So tired! So fatigued! Can't express it.

Ghu says my baby has been so much trouble to me that I "may

have him for my girl" to assist me in the house. I told him I was going to write that down—that promise and have him sign it—in my book.

Travys is a great pastime to Papa and Mama. He is so bright! funny! and fun loving! He says so many smart things. His Grandpa learns him to say and do things that he and my mother think are funny. Some of them I would rather Travys didn't say or do.

August 1

Baby was two months old yesterday—we weighed him last night. He weighs 15 lbs. Haven't named him yet.

He laughs and coos and plays with his fingers, and kicks in his play. He uses his hands and feet well for his age. Seems to be a healthy baby, but nervous—can't sleep where any noise is.

He has never been out of doors yet and two months old. My strength (being overtaxed) is cause of that.

Askew will be 7 years old 18th Inst. He is going to school now, while they are building the new church at New Hope, and enjoys it.

August 2

I, Magnolia Wynn Le Guin, have five times been a mother. When 25 years and 3 months old I first became a mother—of a sweet baby girl (who died in 3 or 5 days afterwards. I was *low* and health impaired ever since).

When 26 years and 6 months old I became mother of Askew.

When 29 years old I became mother of Fred.

When 31 years old became Travys' mother.

When 33 years and 3 months old became mother of another boy.

Jane Miller col. a darkey who had lived a number of years with Papa before I married and since till this year (and who was a sort of "black mammy" for all my children except last one) came to see us this week. Askew, Fred, and Travys always thought lots of "Aunt Jane." She moved away from here 7 months ago. Previous to that time all of their lives she had lived here on Papa's place and was our help in time of need — and our wash-woman most of the time. She was always good, patient and kind to and with the children. When she left she promised Travys she would bring him a cake and she brought a nice cake.

August 7
Thursday

Baby had his first drink of water Tuesday. Fred brought it warm to him. Wednesday (yesterday) baby was carried out of doors for first time (2 months and some over) and we went to, and across, the bridge. I carried him in my arms. I never carried any of my babies that young that far before that I remember of (on account of physical weakness) so I did more than I thought my strength would permit. We came back to the lot (Fred and Travys were with me) and waited for Ghu and he brought Baby on to the house. We saw some little Edna Davis negroes on the bridge and that was why I crept on so far — thinking, without a doubt, I could get one of them to bring Baby back for me. I asked a little negro girl to help me bring him back and she impudently refused.

Askew has gone with "Papa Ghu" to Quarterly meeting at Mt. Bethel. Ghu let him out of school today because he loves to go to Quarterly meetings. Fred didn't want to go. Staying in church so long is too confining for him. Travys cried to go, but he is too little yet to be away all day from me. So T. and F. are spending most of the morning in their favorite way — playing up at the watermellon patch, and cutting the little mellons.

Lula Sullivan, the eleven year old daughter of Walter and Jennie Sullivan, is with us now. She came Tuesday. Jennie and I are warm friends and Jennie sent Lula to see me. I had never seen Lula before. I was surprised to have her come, but agreeably so. She is an intelligent, kindhearted little girl. She recites wonderfully well for her age. She has studied elocution and recitations are her greatest delight it seems.

August 9

Yesterday was Papa's birthday. He was born Aug., 8th 1821 so he was 81 years old yesterday. Mama will be 74 in a few days.

Little baby coos and laughs and notices more than any of my baby's did at 2 months old.

August 11

Had a letter from Jennie Sullivan and suggested the following names for the baby: Earl, Boyd, Douglas, Randolph, and Donald.

August 13

One day this week I bought a clothes basket and put it under the bed in my room. That night I pulled it out from under the bed and put a sheep-skin and pillow in it and told Travys it was his trundle bed and he might sleep in it. And he did go to sleep in it and slept in it all night.

August 18
Monday

This is Askew's birthday. If I can get a chance I am going to bake him a cake and put seven bird eggs (candy eggs that Annie Bell Ingram gave the children) on the icing. He is at school.

Laura, Ghu, all my boys and myself went up to the new church yesterday.

I haven't been in a buggy before since last winter. The ride and worrying with baby together certainly did fatigue me. My weak back seemed could stand no more. But I've been so close at home so long that I enjoyed so much seeing the new church and being in the old one again before it is torn down. I sat in the old one a long time, trying to get baby to sleep and had many thoughts and in my heart prayed. Felt like praying in the old church where I had been going all my life once more before it was torn down and when I got to the top step of the new church I paused some little time before entering the door. In my heart I was hoping that my little boys might be converted in the new building. I made the wish (an old superstition on entering a new building) that they would be. I did enjoy going in, and looking at, the new church, and one thing I enjoyed greatly was that Ghu was one of the main stays of the building. Ghu, Mr. Wilkins and Papa, are the main cause of the church being erected. Papa gave 100 dollars. Ghu and Mr. Wilkins gave largely and then have both worked faithfully on the building. It will be finished last of this week—not painted tho.

I have had to write like fighting fire, in extreme haste—baby crying as hard as it could and now he is in my lap while I am finishing up this. I'm doing hard work worrying myself almost helpless every day with baby and trying between his naps to do all the work I can. I am doing the work of 2 strong negroes and no health and strength. Baby wiggles so I can't write.

August 25

Baby isn't quite 3 months old yet. He has been laughing out about 8 or 10 days and this P.M. he cackled repeatedly out louder than he ever has at Travys and myself. He has no name yet, tho' Travys calls him Ralph and I like that name well. Askew first suggested the name of Ralph.

Laura left me yesterday. She married Laz Edge yesterday A.M. I certainly do miss her work. Baby takes up so much of my time and my strength it is not near sufficient for the demands made upon me. We've tried to get a negro girl but have not yet succeeded but will keep on trying. Laura had been here 6 mo. She came in Feb.

My three little boys enjoy being with Charlie and George W. Especially Askew. He will remember with pleasure, for a long time to come, the two Weathers boys.

September 1

Ralph was 3 months old yesterday. We named him yesterday too. Mr. Weathers and wife and children have been here on a visit.

Mr. Weathers told me to decide on a name while [he was] here and let him baptize the baby; suggested that I name him for himself. So yesterday I named him Charles Ralph, Charles, for Mr. Weathers, and Ralph for no one. So Mr. Weathers baptized him today in the presence of Papa, Mama, Fred, Travys, Dollie Wynn, Aunt Margaret, George Weathers, Charlie W., Fannie W., Ghu, myself and old Bill Miller.

I think Edna Davis, colored, witnessed the baptism also.

Mr. Weathers took him up and stood up with Charles Ralph in his arms, and poured the water on his head with his hand from a little bowl (just put his hand in the bowl and dipped up water).

Charles Ralph didn't cry because, I suppose, that Mr. Weathers was standing with him and the baby likes to be carried around. I imagine he thought Mr. Weathers was going to "tote" him. Well, Ralph is a baby that requires lots of attention, and we have had house full of company. I gave Jane Miller a dollar to cook three days and half for me. I liked Charlie and George Weathers.

Mr. Weathers has been preaching at New Hope since he came.

Edgar Thurston preached the first sermon in the new church.

I don't go to church when babies are very small. Strength not sufficient to worry with babies away from home, even if they did not cry. Well baby has been named and baptized at last. Charles Ralph.

The day Ralph was 3 months old he was named. The next day baptized and weighed. He weighed 16 lbs.

Ralph weighed 8 lbs at birth.

At end of 1st month he weighed 12 lbs
At end of 2nd " " 15 "
At end of 3rd " " 16 "

September 3

Fannie Weathers had Travys to say a speech every day. She would have him repeat it after her. These are the lines:

T's speech

Ann ate some cake
Ann ate some jelly
Ann went to bed

With a pain in her—(here a jesture)
Don't be mistaken, don't be misled
Ann went to bed with
a pain in her head.

Here is Askew's first speech:

Grandmother says in her quaint old way
The world wasn't made in a day—a day
The great blue cloud [sky] where the white clouds flit
Why, the dear Lord was six days painting it.
  Cheer up honey and don't you fret
  The way ain't sunny
  But you'll get there yet.

A letter came addressed to Askew today from Faith Jarrell and in it a note to Fred, one to Askew and one to Travys. Also a tiny tin box for Travys. He was proud of his box.

September 23

Ralph plays with his fingers now. Amuses himself lots with his hands. He is a pretty baby—fat and white. Askew rolls him in baby carriage every A.M. to help me while I cook. I am always rushed in A.M.s on account of the time I am obliged to take up with baby.

Askew and Fred are picking cotton. Papa pays them. Fred is real industrious in the cotton patch. Works more regular than Askew. Ghu says he is a very industrious cotton-picker for his age. Askew is now getting to be a good deal of help to me to do little things and is very nice to mind me usually. He doesn't like to be sent to many places on errands. I think on some lines he is *very* timid.

Jennie Sullivan, my childhood friend, Lula and her sweet baby Alf, spent one night here last week.

Travys is one curiosity. He talks so plain. Expresses himself well for a two and half year old. His vocabulary often surprises us. He talks no baby talk—none of them ever did that but "precious little" Travys talks plainer now than Fred—Fred two years older than he. Travys has a cat named Hotema that he is very fond of. Travys loved Laura when she lived here and he certainly does appreciate her visits now. She spent last Sunday here and Travys was delighted all day. Travys has been to see her once and came home with a bucket full of good apples. Travys, Fred and Askew think it a treat to go on a load of cotton to the gin — all have been with Papa Ghu. Travys is a very cute, sweet, bright baby. Papa and Mama are fond of him and are daily amused at his talk. He is pretty too when dressed in Sunday clothes.

Askew is getting to be more useful and a help around house — helps some by rolling Ralph in baby carriage.

September 30

Ralph is four months old today. Have not weighed him yet but I want to before the day is over. He has less hair than any of our babies ever had, but has some all over his head now. At first he was bald on top. I went to Jackson yesterday and left him here. Lil was here and she let him nurse. I have a weak back and on that account I left him. He did first rate without me. Edna stayed here to help take care of him. I went to Jackson and had some teeth pulled and if nothing prevents I'll soon have a new set of teeth — my health has kept me minus upper teeth for a year — i.e. it has been 13 months since I had mine pulled. I went down to Ann's to see her little sick baby Joe. I was so overcome when I saw the thin weak, pale, baby I went in a room and cried till I could controll by feelings before going where Anna was any more. The little sick baby is 9 months old and so tiny.

Askew, Fred, and Travys had a nice time playing with Esca, Lillian, and J. A. C. Lewis. We carried none of the children with us.

A little negro, Dola Tarpley, has set in to help me nurse Ralph and do things. She is so small that if I can do better I may change but I am undecided what to do yet. She hasn't been here long enough for me to know whether she can manage baby or not. Ralph isn't attached to her yet, and is cross when she nurses and does any thing to try to amuse him.

Askew writes (in his printing way) letters and Fred makes crooked marks and thinks he is writing and comes to me to read them often. Travys even thinks he can write.

October 2

October has a charm for me, and has had for years, peculiarly its own. Little Ralph has just gone to sleep and tho' I am real busy and just *longing* to read a package of Youths Companions sent me by a very kind friend (Jennie Sullivan) yet I feel I just must lay aside my sewing and write a little about our little boys.

My health has been better than usual the past few days—(nearly always better in fall than any other time)—and I've had more strength and more life—talk more to the children, laugh more than usual. Ghu looks both pleased and surprised at my fun with little boys. I can see that Askew is surprised too.

Ralph discovered his feet this morning when I was dressing him. He regarded them with wide open eyes and with much pleasure. He would wiggle his toes as he sat up double like a ball while I was putting his clothes on, and blare his eyes and jump and try to catch his feet, but he isn't old enough to controll his muscle yet and never succeeded. He certainly was amused and so was I—(tho' not at his feet). I laughed out to see him so surprised, pleased and playful over the discovery of what seemed a very great curiosity—two feet—toes that could wiggle and blared eyes watching them.

Jim Ellis, a negro boy, was nurse for Askew, Fred, and Travys. Dola Tarpley is nurse for Ralph—a little negro girl. Laura Edge was first who helped me with Ralph—a white girl 25 years old.

October 15

Ralph seems to be teething and oh, how he cries day and night and what I endure with my weak strength seems superhuman. My throat has been very sore—ulcers on tonsil, and I gave completely out and had to go to bed with throat and complicated affections one day this week and am creeping yet. Fan, Mynta, Pauline, RoseBud and Mynta's boy are out from La.

October 21

We had Quarterly meeting at New Hope last Saturday and Sunday.

Dr. John B. Robins, Presiding Elder, spent Saturday night with us and so did our Pastor in Charge, Mr. Leak.

Dr. Robbins kissed Ralph when he first saw him and played some afterwards with him.

He kissed Travys on Sunday and said the kiss was worth a quarter. So, these two boys, T. and R. have been kissed by a man of giant intellect—great brain.

It always pleases a mother to have her children kissed by those who stand so high.

Dr. Robins preached excellent sermon both days. Sunday he earnestly preached to parents about educating them. He is a man who educates his highly—spends money on them that may fit them for life and then ceases to foot their bills after they've graduated and reached 21.

I went to church both days. The children all went Sat. Ralph did as well or better than I expected. A negro girl helped me nurse him over there, 'tho he took a severe cold and has been real sick with cold since. Fred doesn't like to go to church as well as Askew and Travys does and he didn't go back Sunday.

Papa was sick last night—had a pain and tight feeling about his heart—had to leave supper table and go to bed and Fan bathed his feet and he rubbed his chest and after good while he seem to rest during remainder of the night. I trust my aged father will be spared long time yet to his children and grand children.

Mama hasn't been well in some time. She looks bad.

Papa talks lots to Travys to the amusement of us all, when we have company. Dollie Wynn, Joe and Fan, laughed lots at him Sunday trying to imitate in a fine voice Mrs. John Wynn's voice in these words that she said to her spoilt little girl over here "Florrie Bell, did you break your neck?" Travys is very funny. He amuses all who come to see us that notice children at all. Fan pays him lots of attention.

The first time Ralph went to preaching Dr. John B. Robins preached and Ralph was 4½ months old. Dr. Robins spoke as if he thought Ralph a promising baby—complimented Ralph more than either of other 3 tho' he kindly said all were fine boys.

Ralph weighed 18 lbs at end of fourth month. He has on his first shoes now and the other little fellows enjoy seeing him with red shoes on. I sent to Atlanta and bought him 2 for what one pair costs here.

November 1

Ralph is five months old. He has been wearing short clothes and shoes about a week.

November 2
Sunday

Ralph is fixing to cut a tooth I think—he has been biting things as if his gums were itching and been a little puny for 2 weeks. He is a real pretty, fat, playful, sweet, baby; but my! my! my! the trouble!!! He never lets me catch up night or day light and keeps me up rocking him long and late at night and sometimes (yes often times) I am up thro' the night with him. He sleeps cat naps and I rarely ever finish anything that I undertake to do while he sleeps—he wakes too soon.

I am *intensely* anxious to read some new magazines and Youths Companion I have here and *can not* for in week days at this season I'm compelled to sew when not cooking, nursing or ironing and on Sundays the little negro girl usually goes home in the P.M.s.

Heaven only knows what a mother with a weak body, and a family like ours, has to do overtaxed, and how much self denials are to be practiced; no time of my own till babies can walk.

November 7
Friday A.M. 8 O'clock

Ralph has been well the past few days and just as sweet and good "as you please" both night and day. He is an *awful* sweet baby. He is one of the whitest, fairest, babies I ever saw in my life. I take that to indicate that when older he will be a little sallow complected. When Fred was an infant he had a beautiful complection—*very* fair—white indeed; now he is a sallow, somewhat, and inherits it from Ghu's people. His people were dark, very and others sallow—one brother

of all family has clear good skin—his mother had good fair complection.

A fine rose is my favorite of *all* flowers. Ralph's face is one of
the brightest and sweetest I ever saw. He is so fresh—so beautifully
white, so smiling and has bright, laughing eyes. He reminds me of
one of the finest rose buds—fresh with dew—fragrant—delighted to
eye etc.

'Tis always refreshing for me, to look at Ralph, my rose bud when
he is well. His eyes allways joyfully lit up! His large sweet mouth
spread everytime I speak to him with an angelic smile too sweet
it seems to be human. Although only 5 months old, he loves fun.
His nurse plays with him; he jumps, squeals, and laughs with keen
delight. A sweet baby is my rare rosebud, Ralph.

His large sweet mouth is to me, a very attractive feature. I am
delighted with the shape of his mouth: so much like my brother
Charlie's mouth. And the beautiful dimple in his chin! Like Charlie
too. Blessed spotless flower!!!

I sometimes sing a little song about "P-i-g-hoggy-H-o-g-p-i-g"
and tho' haven't in some time, yet few days ago, Travys surprised me
by saying "I saw a little white pig named P-i-g-hoggy." Travys is a
very bright child—not 3 years old till Feb. He is wonderfully quick
to "catch-on"—wonderfully so! Wish I had time to keep my little
fellows clean and more tidy but I am so overworked these days I am
obliged to let them go more neglected than I ever am willing to

To Askew, Fred, Travys, and Baby

I would flood your path with sunshine
I would fence you from all ill;
I would crown you with all blessings
If I could have my will.

/your Mama

November 15
Saturday P.M.

Busy am I these days!!! Sometimes something interesting happens
in regard to the four little boys God has placed in our care, and I
will want, *oh so much*, to write it down in this book but am so situated

then that I can't and so busy and body so overtaxed makes a weak memory, that thing will be forgotten and many other things occur and are forgotten before there is any chance or opportunity for me to pick up pen and ink. "Tempus fugit"! How *fast* time does fly!! Oh, what an extremely busy life mother of four boys (and others to cook for!) has to live. I covet an opportunity to go out in this beautiful fall weather and see and be among the beautiful colored trees, the creek and gather the many hued leaves.

A most devoted admirer of Nature am I—all my life I've been. Never more content than out in woods or in the creeks and branches of fields. Oh, what a *great* loss it is to me to be denied of the pleasure of taking my little boys out and talk with them about Gods beautiful sunshine, beautiful frost, beautiful balmy weather (we've had so much of lately) and beautiful colored trees etc etc.

We've had this pleasure only once this fall—went to spend awhile at one our favorite nooks by a babbling brook we call "little creek" or "gin branch." Ralph was too small to carry before—he enjoyed it splendidly tho' only 5 months old. Ralph is teething I think. He is not well. Travys has been charming us all lately—(and all his life—since he could walk or talk anyway) he is real smart—awful sweet and cunning. Says and does smart things.

Askew has started to school again, to Mr. Levy Thurston. Papa gave an acre of land near the church for a school house and a few people of the community, including Ghu and Mr. Bill Ingram, took the old church and made a schoolhouse of it. So Askew goes to school where I first went (not in same school house, nor same spot) but close by.

Fred and Travys play sweetly together. They usually get along beautifully. When Askew is with them Askew and Fred are not as kind to each other as they ought to be and don't, at all times, play as sweetly as I'd like them to.

I do love to see Fred and Travys play. They are sweet together. Travys loves Fred devotedly. Tries to do just like Fred.

November 22

Ralph is five months, and little over, and ate some tonight for first time. He had drank a few spoonsful of buttermilk before but tonight he ate some gravy when I had steamed sweet potatoes (with small bits of potato mashed in gravy very thin like soup) and drank more buttermilk than he ever had. Ralph is such a fat, pretty baby: Strong and never still only when asleep—is a nervous baby—doesn't sleep sound—(inherits that from me.) but my! how he grows! He likes to have us hold him and let his feet be on the floor—we have our hands under his arms—and he jumps, squats and enjoys those cute capers and lots of others. He laughed heartily at me today. We've had such mild weather lately that Dola carries Ralph to cowpen to see "Beauty," (our fine calf) and to the mill and out doors long and often. Dola fell down this morning and had Ralph in her arms. I think he was hurt a little and frightened much.

Anna (Jarrell) and her little sickly baby Joe have been up a few days. She was looking after Dr. J's farming interest two P.M.'s and she came for me to let Joe nurse too. She doesn't give much milk and the little weakly sick baby will not eat but precious little. I feel so sorry for little Joe. They went home this P.M. I felt sad when I saw little sick Joe leaving tho' he left, just after nursing a big "bate" from me, in a good humor and smiling.

Travys went with his Papa to Locust Grove this P.M. Ghu expects to go to High F. tomorrow and let Fred and Askew go with him down there and let Travys go to Locust G. to keep him from crying to go to the Falls. Travys had never been to Grove since he could remember before and 'twas a treat for him. Fred has never been to High Falls and his trip will be a treat for him. He is near 5 years old (and will be in Feb.) and has never been to High Falls and I am glad he is going. I do love for my little boys to go about with Ghu. What a treat it would be to me to go and carry them to different places just for their pleasure—that would please me to see them pleased. I am denied that sweet pleasure and Ghu carries them to town—i.e. he carries Askew and Fred and has begun to carry T. a little. He said Travys was too small to carry to High Falls with him yet. Papa waits at the mill every evening for Askew to come from school and they come on to the house together. Papa had some apples and candy given him and Mama and they put it in Papa's closet and they give it out to my children. Mama and Papa are just as good and kind to the children as they can be and seem to be happy in having candy and apples to give them. Travys is such a funny talking baby and they are *very* fond of him and have lots of *genuine* pleasure with him. He is

Mama's favorite I think, if she loves one more than the other. Lately Mama and Papa both have been real feeble but they talk lots to the children and especially Travys. Papa talks lots to Askew. He always loved Askew. Most people who visit us are partial to Travys and Ralph — nearly everybody has lots of pasttime with Travys and lots to say to him. He is a smart baby and such an incessant talker. Fred talks very slow; he is an "odd fellow" from the other three — talks very slow and altogether different from other two in many respects.

November 27
Thanksgiving Day

I'm a very busy mother but tried to give one room a red letter day appearance — the dining room.

Yesterday I had Edna (a negro woman who lived with Papa this year and one whom Ghu has hired for the coming year) to cook dinner for me and in meantime I made two large picture frames and two small ones and pasted some thanksgiving scenes on them and put three of them in dining room. I also made a cocoanut stack-cake and Edna dressed a rooster for me and today we put on a company cloth and a vase of lovely roses and had a little Thanksgiving dinner. Askew was at school. Prof. Thurston is absent this week and his sister Estelle is teaching.

Ralph, my beautiful white lily, (he reminds me so much of a sweet and beautiful flower) is growing. Papa nursed him awhile one day last week and played with him a day or two before. He doesn't usually pay babies that much attention till over 6 months old. Ralph isn't quite six yet. Travys is very proud that he is old enough to sleep in night drawers just like Askew and Fred and he feels that the possession of these garments has made him ever so much larger — "a big boy."

Well, we are having a cold snap and I'm glad. We have much to be thankful for this Thanksgiving day — our four boys — each other (Ghu and I) and my parents. They are so good to our children and lately so many blessings have crowned us. May our boys and ourselves, be a christian family and a thankful family as long as we live.

December 5

Ralph is six months old. Can say "mam-mam" (tries to say Mama) and when he calls the other children he says "hey! hey!" Loves cats and sits in a box with two cats—a black and white spotted one and a brindle cat. The brindle cat is Travys' much loved Hotema—named after an Indian I read of.

Yesterday evening Fred said to me: "I like Dr. Robbins, Mamie Owens, Mr. Ingram and Mr. Lummins (Bogue) better than any body." He meant outside of family circle. Fred is more particular with his clothes than Askew. He usually has his put in place—Askew gives me lots of worry because he is extremely careless. I hope he will soon improve greatly on this line. My life is an extremely busy one, more than ever before, since another member has been added to our family and I *never* catch up with my work and I work all the time someway. Ralph is an exceedingly restless baby and I am obliged to amuse him nearly every moment that Dola is doing her chores: drawing water, bringing in wood etc etc. He sleeps so little in the day and my slumber is always so broken and we (Ghu and I) are up with him often.

Raising children, working and nursing them is a Herculean task—yet if they will just be true, honest, upright, God fearing, and God loving, I shall feel I've been doing a good work and not a fruitless one.

Papa gave (I reckon he gave it) to Askew a cheap watch. Askew was very proud of it. How I long, from depths of my heart, for leisure time to talk, walk, read, and devote exclusively to my children, but it is work, work, and nothing much but work. I love them, but these days it seems I'm too busy, too overtaxed, too downright worried lots of the time to show them that I do love them. By not keeping house [i.e., by living in her parent's home], our tasks are many more, but it is a duty that God has placed in our hands and we accept it willingly.

I hope we will be able to give our children, each, a good education, and that they will be good children, and grow up christian men, and after this life all of us be united in "Home Beyond."

Yesterday at dinner table I ask Travys who kissed him at Quarterly meeting? He answered "Dr. Wobbins"; Papa and Mama then ask him what Dr. Robbins said it was worth? He answered "he said it was 'wood a twarter.' " He is a bright 2½ year old.

Dora Wellmaker has been to see us lately. We've had lots and lots of company this year.

December 8
Monday

Company plentiful yesterday. I was so overtaxed that when night came, in trying to tell Ghu about how I suffer from daily (almost) cooking for company, and trying to sew and look some after the children and household generally, I broke down (to tears) before I could finish telling him the unpleasant things I had passed thro'. We've had company nearly every week this year and nearly every day big part of the time and while I love congenial company, yet *this is like a hotel here* — my strength fails and then I'm troubled. But if this is the place where God would have me to be, I want to do the best I can and be contented here.

This morning when I was eating breakfast, Askew took a notion to fix his school-bucket himself. My youngest brother, who is now in Heaven, use to fix his own bucket when we were school children and I told Ghu that moment (while A. was fixing his bucket) that he reminded me so forcibly of Splint. Oh, it seemed that my sweet brother was before me, a child again, fixing his bucket to go to school.

Then again up in the day while I was preparing dinner Fred came in stove room with brush in his hand for me to brush his hair "like Uncle Splint's." Well, to me, it is so strange that my oldest little boys love to speak of Uncle Splint and are always interested in him and his pictures and he died before they were born. There is a quiet way too, when they speak of him, as if his name was affectionately and reverently spoken.

They often have spoken to me of combing their hair "like Uncle Splint's." I guess they mean the way his hair looks in his picture.

December 12
Friday

Askew had a severe attact of earache last night. Kept Ghu and I awake most of the night. Little Ralph was awake lots too, laughing and playing because the lamp was burning.

Ralph is 6 mos and 12 days old and he ate some solid food this week. He had drank milk some few times in a spoon before but hadn't learned to eat. None of the other three learned to eat till about, or near, a year old.

"Ralph took the cake" last Wednesday. I went to Jackson and left him here with his nurse, another good negro besides, and Mama said he didn't cry a "whimper" and he ate biscuit and coffee and drank buttermilk and sweet milk, just like he had been accustomed to such diet. He surprised me more than a little. I was absent till nearly sundown—went to see Dr. Franklin, my dentist. Since then Ralph has eaten and drunk milk and water without a spoon—shows a keen appetite for meat—tho' I have plenty of maternal food (breast milk) for him.

Askew didn't go to school today. Weather, wet, and he having such a bad night with earache. We let Fred go to school the day I went to Jackson and he stayed over there till dinner, and then came home. Travys went with us to Jackson, but was so sick with cold that he didn't enjoy the trip as well as otherwise he would have done.

1903

January 5*

With Myriad of duties staring [at] me from Christmas to Christmas and with no privacy—none at all—children around me almost every stroke of the pen, talking to me, playing like a room of colts— with nerves unstrung—a very restless cross baby—in the face of this—more—I am going to *try* to keep a diary, this year A.D. 1903.

I've been very busy today, ironing and patching—night came and found me working hard, room growing cold and Ralph and myself growing likewise; I was so anxious to get thro' most of the patching that I neglected baby some in not talking to him and getting Dola to build us a good fire. I wish I could overcome *worry*. It overcomes me almost daily, sometimes to a smaller extent—often to a large extent. There is always so much for me to do. Ralph cries or frets rather and I have to take care of him so much of the time. He is very peart most of the time when we will carry him around our room or house and play the way he wants us to, but my strength doesn't hold out long at this way and the little negro Dola Tarpley gets tired too I guess and so we both worry together every day with Ralph.

Ghu has rented the most of Papa's land here this year (all except what Bill Kelly has rented) and now there is a chance for me to have more help in the household than any year of our stay with my parents. He has an old negro, Mary Brownlee, to wash and help me about the house when I need her.

Askew started to school again this morning. What I regret deeply is a chance of reading and writing as much as I formerly did. Since Ralph came I've been so overtaxed and at all times, with lots of work ahead. Ghu gave me a Bible for a Christmas present. I am real proud to own it—in other words, I appreciate it highly and hope to be a

---

*Beginning with this date, entries are taken from each of the two diaries which Magnolia Wynn Le Guin kept from January 1903 through February 1906. Angle brackets are used to distinguish one diary's entries from the other.

more constant reader of it this year than I have been in several years. Life has some peculiar trials for me and I need to read more than I've been doing in the Word. Hope I will so live that I can shape my life by teaching of the Bible. I want to live so that I will commit no sin—knowing it to be a sin. I want to do nothing wrong intentionally or knowingly. Impatience I sometimes think is my besetting sin. I pray the Lord to be with me this year—on thro' subsequent life—and that I may so live each day as if it were my last—that is, to live each day ready for death. But these things are what I *want* to do and be and not what I am, for what I am does not compare with what I ought to be.

‹ January 6 ›
New Year!!!

Another Christmas has come and gone. The little boys, except baby Ralph, enjoyed a little Christmas tree at New Hope academy. Each had a present or two. Then the following night *their socks* were hung and found next day with confectionaries and a present or two (simple, inexpensive ones) and I think the little chop axes have given more pleasure than any other.

Now New Year has dawned and Askew went to school again yesterday, but weather being so severe today, he started, crossed the bridge and came back home.

Dola (Ralph's nurse) let him fall of the bed today. There was a rubber rattle *on Christmas tree* for Ralph.

I have a set of new teeth at last.

Ralph is 7 months old and has no tooth. I am letting T's hair grow longer than ever before, for two or three reasons: one is, because Fan cut it off last; another because my Papa said let it grown out awhile, and last because I wish it to grow long because I have a picture of my oldest (dead) brother taken when he was small and he has beautiful long hair and T. favors the picture some.

‹ January 8 ›

Travys and Fred like to play with dolls. Fred cried because Santa Claus didn't bring him a doll. He had me write to Santa C. before

Christmas and tell him to bring him a doll. I made him and T. a
rag-doll yesterday and last night they carried their rag-dolls to bed
with them.

I am letting T's hair grow out and I twist it up every day with a
string in the longest place — nowhere long enough to tie easily. I was
surprised today at Travys: he has scissors and a stiff piece of paper
and was cutting it in different shapes and he cut one piece and told
me it was a "talking machine." He saw 2 graphophones when we
were in Jackson just before Christmas, and the paper was in shape of
a graphophone with a piece standing out like the tin horn that is on
graphophones.

Too cold today for Askew to go to school — a very cold day. Snowed
little in forenoon — sun is out now but my! how the wind blows!

<　January 19　>

Monday Night

In midst of a hullabaloo of children's noises: Askew nailing and
knocking, Travys knocking, Fred crying (because T. has broken
spring in his knife) and Ralph crying because he is sleepy — I will
try to write, but what a confusion we have every night in our room,
till "shut-eye-time." Fred has gone to bed now; he is the quietest
one of the four. He likes dolls — has gone to bed with Dola's china-
doll and will sleep with it all night. Travys has on his night-drawers
now and is looking for his rag-doll to [carry] to bed, because Fred
carried a doll. He loves Fred and humors Fred in many ways — F.
cries sometimes when he and T are playing and T. will give up every
plaything to Fred when he cries for them. Askew goes to school to a
pretty school house — white outside, sealed in and lots of windows, a
pretty school house. Askew selected a few days ago three lines in this
(Cyr's) First Reader, for his recitation the coming Friday and when
Friday came he spoke these lines:

> "Little things on little wings
> Bear little souls to Heaven."

I thought it did very well for his age and his selection. Some little
folks his age the same Friday spoke such as this: "I had a little dog
his name was Rover" and "Roses red and violets blue etc."

January 19
Monday Night

A noisy time we have in our room every night this winter. Four boys to make a fuss till one by one they go to sleep. Fred, the quietest of the four, is often first to retire. He went to bed tonight and carried Dola's doll. . . . So bye and bye Travys put on his night drawers and got a rag doll and went to bed. They will sleep all night with those dolls. Somehow I am interested in their love for dolls. I loved dolls myself and *such a sweet and great* pleasure it was till I was sixteen.

January 20
Tuesday

Last night Ghu interrupted me so I did not get to write all I wished to. There is *so much* for me to do—a mother of four children, cooking, ironing, sewing, mending, doesn't leave much time for writing and reading. All my reading is done so hurriedly the past 7 months (Ralph's age) that I can't remember well many good things I'd like to retain.

Now while I am writing my irons are hot—and I most always write hurriedly since Ralph came. I am reading a book that Laura Edge loaned me. She is a white girl who lived with me six months last year. She came over here (with her husband Lay Edge) last Sunday and brought a good book—loaned me to read. The title is "The Ideal Life." It is a good book and I am never more blissfully content than when reading a good book. I have scanned some of its pages and wish I was able to buy the book from her. I will try to find time to copy some rich paragraphs from it while it is over here.

When Laura and Lay came Sunday P.M. I was dressing to go over to the church. They have painted the church and school house and I wanted to see them in their new dress (our church hasn't been dedicated yet).

Someone broke into Mr. Ingram's store last night and Mr. Ingram sent over here after Ghu this A.M. early to go help find the person or persons who went in his store. Ghu hasn't returned and 'tis past 8 o'clock P.M. now.

January 23
Friday Night

A *busy* life! A *busy* life!! A *busy* life!!! One of my deepest regrets is that I have no time to read much. The past 7 months I've had such little leisure—a craving to read often; strong inclinations to write, and lots to do—always busy only when I just will lay things aside and take a little walk for recreation. But my deepest regret is that I can't read more. Want to read my new Bible more, my magazine and now what I'm especially interested in is a borrowed book, a large thick, good one "The Ideal Life." There are some sweet [pieces of] poetry especially to my liking in it and I want to copy some of that and some paragraphs and sentences particularly good that I wish to copy so that I might read again. I'm going to get me a new ledger if I can find time and copy it full of such things.

Now I am writing, and I have laid two garments by to sew buttons on and work button holes, but I glanced over daily paper, semi-weekly journal and read some in [Wesleyan Christian] Advocate—now I am scribbling and the little garments just as bare of buttons as when I put them by. Ghu is rocking the baby to sleep and keeps at me to do this and that and the other and I must write a letter for him. I do most of his writing.

Now this is a poor apology for a Diary. An old acct. book of Ghu's. Yet I feel so anxious for a diary that I use this and maybe by and by I'll have a nicer book.

Dola went home last night and hasn't come back yet. Another little negro girl by name of "Monk" helped me with Ralph today. Ralph was very cross, very restless and tiresome to us who had to worry with him. He is an exceedingly troublesome baby and I sometimes think not many mothers ever had such babies—such hard, worry-some, times as I do with him. Ralph doesn't like Dola to nurse him and was very much displeased with new one. Ralph is crying and Ghu is vexed.

January 24
Saturday Night

This has been one of the *most* trying days! Ralph just cried all day when awake. Dola stole a cegar out of Ghu's overcoat pocket and I took it from her as she was leaving. I guess that is why she didn't come. The new negro "Monk" is extremely dull and can't do anything to quiet Ralph many seconds at a time. I've been sick today and could hardly stand up at all but Sam Tollerson and Mr. Brand (our new preacher) ate dinner here and I had to prepare some things. Old aunt Mary helps, but she can't make a pie or biscuit fit to eat by herself so I have to do all the time even if she is here. She draws water, sets table, grinds coffee, minds the things in stove, etc.

I had a letter today from Jennie Sullivan. She write a warm letter. Her health isn't good—arm is affected and eyes too—and a *housefull* of children. I don't see how she can get along. I don't think Jennie worries anything to compare to myself. I've been so worried today that I didn't know what in the world to do. Askew is sick with cold. He has catarrh real bad. The negro nurses I have worry me exceedingly. They do not know how to move a chair as it ought to be or to do a single thing right and they don't know how to quiet Ralph. Ralph is one of the most troublesome babies I ever saw in my whole life. He worries me almost out of my very senses. Sometimes I wonder if I don't act awful strange—he tires and overtaxes my already weak strength and my other work I must always be trying to do.

How I do *crave* to read. . . . I've been denied of all recreation (except very little) since Ralph was born. Maybe there are better days ahead. May Heaven help me as a mother to be patient, good, kind one to my little boys.

January 28
Thursday P.M.

Since I last wrote I did one thing that was a sin—a big one I'm afraid. Askew dropped or let Ralph fall of bed—just sheer carelessness and I slapped him with my fist several licks on [his] back. I am ashamed to write that. I—a mother—would so utterly loose controll and whip one of my children in that style. If I had composedly used a switch I would have felt allright. Askew let [Ralph] get such a *very hard* fall. I am sorry I did not controll self and use a switch.

I made apologies to A. before night. I was so unhappy all day that I knew I couldn't get to bed satisfied without telling him I did him wrong and telling how sorry I was.

Askew and Travys went with Ghu to meeting Sunday. I was sick and couldn't go and have not been well since. Have neuralgia in forehead or rather a neuralgic headache today and Ralph slept badly last night and my slumber was broken many times at short intervals. Ralph is looking delicate—pale—and has cold.

Mr. Brand, our preacher, ate dinner here Sunday. Jim [Wynn] spent one night this week here. He left Porter Dale [Porterdale, Georgia] and rented a farm near Island Shoals. Deliver me from a factory, more on account of the low, immoral class of people, one has to live with there, than the work itself.

I've been sewing a little this week: made Travys a dress, and F. and A. a waiste a piece last week. I get along slow with such work but I'm not *pushed* now—about any work.

Am going to buy me a book and fill it with quotation. Have a borrowed book with many good things I hope to get copied.

< January 28 >

Thursday P.M.

Askew stayed out of school most of this week. He was threatened with croup. He was always croupy. Ralph and Travys are half sick with cold.

Askew is shedding upper teeth now—shedded under ones some time ago (age 7).

Little Ralph likes to play with a rag doll as well as anything. He is one of the most nervous, restless, babies I ever saw. He sleeps badly night and day. He is very white—don't look of a healthy hue. Fred is the quietest one of the four—I believe he is the healthiest too this winter. Askew has catarrh real bad of the head (not nasal).

January 31

Mrs. Penn (mother-in-law of Mr. Charlie Child's) came down here this P.M. I was very *busy* when she came trying to get out in the lovely weather—was going to walk up to the school-house, had she not come in. How I did regret giving up the coveted walk—all children going with me. Fred was keenly disappointed too. So seldom I get to take these walks; and the weather was so suitable—could have carried Ralph out allright. And how I do *enjoy* such outings after so much indoor life. I love with all my nature out of door life, but am compelled to live most of the time in doors—housekeeping and family affairs: sewing, cooking, ironing, patching etc etc etc etc etc.

So Mrs. Penn came and I had to forego my trip and so I ironed *hard as I could* all time she was here after irons got hot. And talked to her too. Now I am extremely tired, jaded, overtaxed, nervous.

The noise of the children is almost unbearable when I'm working so hard. Any work done standing so long has this effect on me.

Mama is very poorly. She says 'tis a kidney trouble. She has lots of these spells.

Mrs. Penn had three children with her and such a racket they kept up. Askew is, I think, the most unruly one we have.

Mrs. Penn spoke of the evangelist S. Dunaway. I hope I'll get to hear him preach some time. I've heard so much of him.

Well if I could lie down, undisturbed, I'd like to go to bed. I feel too tired to read much, but I was going to read a chapter or more in my Bible and I want to read more in my Bible this year than I have in past two or three years. I want to love my Bible better than I ever did and I trust my life will be regulated by it.

I will soon be 34 years old. I want to live close to the Lord the rest of my life. I wish I had redeemed the whole of my past life by living a *true earnest christian*.

‹ January 31 ›

Ralph can say "pop" and "ma-mam." He has been saying "mammam" two or three weeks ago, but about 3 days ago began saying "pop-pop." Our children learn to say Mama (as well as I now remember) first word and always before they say Papa. Ralph is eight months today. He can't sit alone. He is strong tho'. He has gotten too big for his cracker-box. He won't sit down in it — just pulls up and is liable to overbalance and fall out, so we've put the cracker-box aside. He likes a pallet — we put him down and he rolls and goes along somehow a few paces. He is extremely restless, never still and never satisfied long at a time anywhere unless 'tis when he rides in buggy or has someone to carry him in their arms out of doors.

Travys is in bed with Papa now — goes to sleep there often. Mama is real sick tho' not confined to bed.

I cooked the children some nice syrup candy, of ribbon-cane, for their bad colds. Ralph likes it. He has a rite good appetite considering his age and lots of breast milk and in comparison to what the rest ate at his age. And he has been eating quite awhile.

February 3
Tuesday Night

Well another month has dawned — this month Ghu's birthday, Fred's, Travys' and mine comes.

Mama is real feeble. Kidney affection [affliction] she thinks. She doesn't sleep much or eat much and is nervous and excitable. I hope she will be better somehow. I've had that nervous weak experience so often I know how bad it is. She has bought two bottles of kidney medicine and I trust she will be better tomorrow.

Mattie Lou Smith is with us this week. I enjoy the best kind Mattie Lou's conversations and her presence in our home. She is like a ray of sunshine on a cloudy day this week to me. We are having wet drizzly weather. Mattie L. and I (and Fred) spent half hour up at Charlie C's Sunday night. We walked out after we ate early supper. Mrs. Penn (Charlie C's mother in law) got good many pieces of shrubbery down here yesterday to put in Charlie C's yard. He has a new house close (tolerably) to us.

Aunt Mary (col) helped me plant some shrubbery in the garden this P.M. I planted some lilocks in garden. I love, deeply, flowers and if there is ever a time when I can have time and strength I want a small flower yard with a variety of flowers. I cut out some sewing this P.M.

I had a letter from Jennie Sullivan yesterday. I enjoy a letter from her and she writes rite often and I looked forward to a letter from her. She is suffering with an affected arm, and diseased eyes for now. She is about as warm a friend as I have I reckon.

Askew has made a rise. Has a "Sandford's Primary Arithmetic" and has an order in for a "Swinton's Word Primer." So he is feeling proud and *large* over it.

Last night I went with the children down to the door of two negro houses here on the hill. 'Twas drizzling rain and Ghu had brought a large quantity of rich lightwood. The children wanted to walk about with a torch in the rain and I felt like I would enjoy carrying a torch out in the misting rain and so we had a "torch light procession" of only a few minutes duration. We couldn't stay long because Ghu was keeping restless Ralph for us.

‹ February 8 ›

Sunday Morning

The sun never peeped out once yesterday—rained hard—as a consequence the mill race is again washed up.

The little boys like to see the high water. Mr. Ingram, Grady and Annie Bell came over to see high water and us awhile this A.M.

Fred has a cocoon—(a silkworm) and I've put it up awaiting spring to bring forth a beautiful butterfly. I have all my life, found real sweet pleasures in such things and wish my children would derive the same sweet pleasure and interest from the source of Nature—her curiosities.

Ralph is one of the most restless cross babies I ever knew. He can when in a pleasant humor, squeal the loudest I ever heard a baby and it amuses us all.

Askew is going on 8 years—is shedding jaw teeth, pulled out one after he went to bed last night.

February 8

At Noon. Sunday

The sun didn't peep out "a wink" yesterday and the rain never abated—not even for "feed time."

The creek is high today and the race* washed down — another expense for Papa.

Mama has been real sick this week — couldn't sleep much and had no appetite, had severe backache etc etc. She was in a bad fix. I think she is better — slept some past 2 nights.

Mattie Lou Smith spent this week here — she will spend a part of next week here I reckon. She has been, until past day or two, telling me lots of interesting things. She visits a good deal and I enjoy what she tells me of different homes she visits and different people she has made friends of. The past day or so she has been *very* quiet — no life in her many moments at a time. She says it is a nervous trouble that makes her unsociable. Alf [Wynn] is here. We've just eaten dinner. Don't know how I would get along without Aunt Mary Brownlee, Col., as she relieves me of dishwashing and lots of other steps etc etc. Mattie Lou and I have planned to go up to New Hope and plant some shrubbery in the graveyard if weather permits this week.

February 9
Monday Night

We (Mattie L., Fred, Travys, Ralph) (Dola, Monk, and Aunt Mary) went up to New Hope cemetary and planted some shrubbery.

We walked; we stopped at Mrs. Holder's and rested. Mrs. Ingram, a woman that I think a lot of — a noble, good, woman, came down and spent awhile (in fact we left her there) and Mrs. Lewis Shaw stopped in to see us awhile and also Mrs. Fran Lumus. We had a beautiful evening. Tho' we were very tired, yet we enjoyed our trip. I planted some cuttings at Charles B's grave.

We had darkies to help us dig and plant and carry shrubbery and children. We met Mr. Sullivan the mail-carrier — and I was real ashamed for him to see us with so many negroes.

Ralph is better outdoors than anywhere else. He is crying so now that I must stop scribbling. Sunday was a rainy day — and high water washed the race down.

---

*The mill race at Wynn's Mill on Tussahaw Creek.

February 11

Today was Fred and Travys birthday—Fred 5 and Travys 3.

Mama has been in such a serious condition all day that I couldn't keep my mind on much of anything else. She can't sleep and looks awful bad and I've felt distressed all day on her account and I trust that by tomorrow she will be better. Do hope she can sleep tonight.

I've been busy all day and the worry about Mama's serious health has caused me to feel overtaxed. When I get troubled it seems to paralyze my movements—my strength. I have a *large body* and *small strength*. I can not meet the demands of a family fully no way. Old Aunt Mary (col) helps me some—but she isn't always here. Now I have a pile of sewing on hand, a cross baby, pile of clothes to iron and cooking etc etc. May the hand of the Lord strengthen me to do the most needed things for Mama, Papa, and our little ones, and forgive me for all past sins and help me to be consecrated to Him fully in future. How many mistakes, sins etc I make and am guilty of. Perhaps the greatest of all, the one most often repeated, and repented of, is the sin of impatience.

‹ February 11 ›

A red-letter day for Fred (Travys is too young yet to know much about it) as this was his and Travys' birthday. Fred was 5 years old today and Travys was 3. Fred looked *glad* all day. He is very proud that he is five. Wants to start to school now—have often told him he could go at five. Fred is asleep now. Ralph, Askew and Travys are awake. Fred goes to sleep "quick as a wink" after he goes to bed. Quicker than any of our family.

Mama is *very* sick. She looks bad—can't sleep well—scarcely any. Her condition has distressed me all day. Once today she took Travys up, as feeble as she was, and kissed him.

Papa is just as attentive as he can be to her. Poor Mama and poor Papa! Both old and feeble—soon our little boys will not have "Grandma" and "Grandpa" to love them—and they have been *so good* to my children—so devoted to them. Little Travys they love so devotedly and all the rest they are so good to, and so patient with, and they never want them whipped. More especially does Papa bitterly oppose it.

‹ February 15 ›

Ralph is 8½ mo's old—can't sit alone soon falls over but the past two or three days he tries to crawl. He doesn't crawl either, but can slide across the room on his stomach—push himself with his feet. He has learned some new words (for sometime he has been saying "mammam" and "poppop"). Now his vocabulary has enlarged and he says "daddad" and when he wants *anything* he says "ninnin" and "ninniny."

Mama is in a serious condition. I am afraid she never will be herself again. She speaks and looks like one suffering mentally. She says she has been bothered about John Wynn and can't get him off her mind: Says she is mighty sorry that she can't get the troublesome thoughts about him off of her mind, but says she can not do it. She distresses me. I'm afraid, at her age (73), she will never be herself anymore. Lord grant that she may get well. My eyes fill to think of her pitiful condition. My heart aches to see her speak so pitiful. Heavenly Father, if it can be Thy will, restore her to her usual health mentally and physically.

‹ February 16 ›
Monday

Fred went to school today—his first day as a pupil, and he wears a very bright happy face over this event in his young life—5 years old few days ago.

Mama is very sick—nervous trouble. Dr. Woods came today. Papa is very feeble. He has looked so sad, so haggard and worn since poor Mama has been so sick. Papa brightened up a little when Askew and F. came from school. My children have been blest with loving Grand Parents (my Mother and Father) they are so tender patient, kind and loving to them.

February 16
Monday

Dr. Woods came to see Mama today. He says her affliction is a nervous trouble. She looks awful sad—awful pathetic. Papa is very feeble. Mama's serious illness makes Papa worse. He looks so feeble —so feeble. My heart goes out to them both in deepest sympathy. I never pitied or sympathized so with anyone before. Oh, Heavenly Father, spare them yet unto us longer. Restore Mama to her normal health if it can be Thy will.

I slept 3 hours last night; spent the rest troubling and praying for and about Mama. . . .

We looked some for Dr. Woods last night and it was about eleven when he came or near that and how anxious I was for him to get here and Papa walked to the front door and looked often for him.

‹ February 20 ›

Fred has been to school one week with the exception of one day. We had a blizzard and he and Askew stayed at home one day. Fred likes to go to school. He has worn a very bright, happy face all this week. Travys cried lots this week because he had no one to play with. A stronger devotion exists between Travys and Fred than between Travys and Askew. Because, I suppose, they are nearer the same age. Mama being sick caused me to neglect the children. Ralph has been rite sick this week. I reckon surely he is fixing to cut teeth this time. . . .

Today is Ghu's birthday— 33 years old. Day before yesterday (18th) was mine— 34.

February 20
Friday Night

Mama is in a very feeble condition. She is suffering from nervous prostration. She is 74 years old and just completely worn out, it seems like. She seems the most pitiful person I ever saw sick before.

Dr. Woods has been to see her twice, and will continue to come. Dr. J. [Jarrell] came first. His medicine didn't help her any. I was opposed to having any Doctor but the best when he sent for Dr. J. I have no malice, no prejudice, no ill will towards Dr. J but I have been an afflicted woman since the first time I became a mother. Dr. J. was my physician. He perhaps and no doubt did best he knew, but he came near killing me and wrecked my health in some respects for life, and he caused the death of our first born—a baby girl. As a Dr. he is unfit to visit human beings, I verily believe.

February 21
Saturday Night

Lil has been here two days (or day and half) and Cape and Jodie are here tonight. I have written lots of postal cards to Mama's children since she got worse. She looks less depressed than she did before Lil came. That helps my feeling more than any thing has. I am in her room now, staying with her till my time to go to bed awhile.

Papa has been snoring. Mama lies quiet but is not asleep.

My sweet little boys are obliged to be neglected since Mama got sick and baby Ralph even. My life at all times is a busy one and my nerves diseased and I've never been as cheerful and patient (long at a time) with all noise, fuss etc faults, failings etc of my little sons as I want to be. I love them dearly but seems so much of the time I'm too busy and too tired to let them know it. So overtaxed that often I can not be cheerful.

February 23
Monday P.M.

Mama slept some natural sleep last night, first in a long time. Papa thinks she slept better than she has in a month. She is suffering indescribably and tho her sleep was good she said, when she awoke, these *most awful* bad feelings came back at the instant she awoke.

Dora (Wellmaker) came yesterday, and left this A.M. Maud Wynn Hooten came with her. Lil came Friday and went back yesterday P.M.

Lil's visit was a help to Mama—a *great* help, because she had suffered the same way for several months. Lil told Papa, if Dr. Woods didn't object, to get a patient [patent] medicine called "Miles Nervine" and Dr. Woods did not object in the least. We are much encouraged since she slept and since she doesn't look so depressed. She isn't cheerful yet but looks a great deal better. . . .

I am not doing much of anything, only cooking and giving Mama attention and looking a little after Ralph. Can't see as much after Ralph as I wish to, but see that Dola is keeping him quiet and comfortable as much as she can.

We trust that Mama will soon be able to sit up and Thank God, we have some hopes now.

I expect that Dr Jarrell will be wrathy because he is in our family and because we had Dr. Woods. Papa sent for Dr. J once. Papa did not know how seriously ill Mama was at the time, [if he] had he would have sent for Dr. Woods instead, I think. Dr. Jarrell said while here that we could send down and get some medicine for her that he didn't have with him. Papa asked him back again when he passed the mill. Dr. J also said while here, that when he has a patient out in the country he would lose practice there in town. He did not help Mama with his morphine and stuff and I think with him alone for her physician she would soon have died. Papa says Dr. J is not much of a physician and that he always knew it, but he doesn't bear malice or disrespect to him and wishes him well every way. So Papa had a letter from Anna and Mary (Dr. J's wife and oldest daughter). I saw in letter (through the lines) they are blaming *me* about not sending again. Dr. Jarrell is prejudiced against me and has been for years. When I first became a mother he wrecked my health—and in some respects wrecked [it] for life. I was in a serious state for a year. Papa first got a bottle of medicine for me during time of my serious ill health from Dr. Peek and so we didn't take any more from Dr. J but even after when in need of physic for "me or mine" we went to other Drs. When we had to have Drs. we never sent for Dr. J any more and since then he has talked hard things against me and has caused some of his children at times to treat me with the greatest disrespect. Yet—I do not bear malice, ill will or such things against Dr. J. There is a death bed coming to me. There is a judgement day ahead of me—for these I want to live so as to be able to meet both "in peace with God and all mankind."

I never would have sent for Dr. J if it had been left with me. I *know* he is not fit to visit a woman who was as low as Mama was, and is now. Enough about Dr. J. I don't know just why I felt like this ought to be recorded in my diary.

Dr. Woods wife was with him last night when he came to see Mama. It was nearly night when he came and I was cooking supper. Mrs. Woods sat out in buggy and Ghu saw her out there and invited her in front room to a fire. Dola came in stove room and told me she would cook in my place if I would go and stay with Mrs. Woods. I had never met her before. She is a "big" talker, and intelligent woman *far* above the average; she has a large vocabulary. I almost envied her of her intellect. She looks young, is pretty and *very* stylish. Dr. Woods and wife are bontons and we so plain, so dull too, that in many ways I feel embarrassed when in his presence. . . .

Papa is as good to Mama as I ever saw any one to another since she got sick—just tried to do all he can and everything to make her comfortable. I am writing in the room where Mama is and it is late in P.M. and I haven't had a chance to wash dishes yet. Well, I reckon maybe I can get them done by supper. Necessity caused me to let them go and I can't carry on my house work systematically now till Mama gets better.

< February 24 >

Mama has slept some natural sleep and we believe now she is better, and now we believe that God will spare her yet awhile longer to be with us. I believe God has answered prayer. Bro. Charlie wrote how he grieved over her illness and said he could do nothing for her but pray. Papa has just come in and brought her a five dollar course of patent medicine to be taken with Dr. Woods medicine.

Little Ralph is rite puny. The morning was lovely, bright, sunshiny morning and I bundled him up with plenty of wraps and let Dola roll him about in sunshine.

Ghu bought a new cow. Travys had not been accustomed to a cow with horns (our other cow has no horns) and he went down to the cowpen to see the new cow and says "the new cow has some new hookers." Fred and Askew told me about it and told me to write it down in my book. . . .

March 10

It is with a sad, heavy heart that I open and pen these lines in my diary this morning. Mama is so weak. My heart aches to see her pale, thin and weak. If she could walk around the room or sit up most of the time in her chair but she can not step without someone to steady her. She has been in bed going on five weeks; this morning she was trying, I think, to test her strength, to walk from her chair to another and came *so near* falling in the fire. As she and the big arm chair creaned [careened] over to the fire, Ghu excitedly, almost breathlessly, caught the chair and her. I was so weak from the shock it gave me that I could only with difficulty stand up (weakened) for a few moments. Papa and I—also Ghu—have earnestly asked her never to move a step without one of us (Ghu or I) to support her but she picks a time when we step out to test her strength believing so strong that she could walk a step or two and out of one chair into another, but she is too weak to seat herself and has fallen twice before.

I trust, hope and pray, that our Heavenly Father will spare her and Papa a good while longer to us. I pray she may once more get strength enough to sit up and walk around room some. Oh, God, if it be Thy will spare my aged parents to us yet longer. If Mama lives till August she will be 75. If Papa lives till Aug., he will be 82.

Papa is very feeble—can't walk with any ease—a partial paralysis all one side—can't bear any weight when standing—weight will cause him to crean over. He seems too very sad, so heavy-hearted. I pray God's choicest blessings on them while here and Heaven at the end.

< March 10 >

Mama (my little boys' grandma) has been in bed going on 5 weeks. Can sit up a little while—just a very little. I pray our Heavenly Father, if it can be His will, to spare my parents to me and my little boys— their indulgent, affectionate, grandparents, longer.

Travys went up to the schoolhouse with Fred and Askew awhile yesterday (he spent ½ day there) and Mr. Thurston was very kind and good to him. I shall always feel a kindly interest in Mr. Levy Thurston, because of his attention to my 3 little boys. I would have

Sunday School yesterday. Prof. Levy Thurston was there; he said Travys and himself were "partners." It rained while they were off at church, thundered and haled some. Mama was very uneasy about the children. She asks so often all day long about them—uneasy when they are out of her sight. She loved them so and was always anxious or uneasy about them when they were out of her sight. I've been by Mama's bedside, or busy in house 9 weeks yesterday. [Since] Papa and Susan Tarpley were in room with her and as she is *so much* better, I carried Askew, Fred, Travys, Ralph and Dola down to my favorite haunt—the little creak—to bask awhile in Gods blessed sunshine and feast our eyes to our hearts content on his handiwork: Beautiful honeysuckles, sweet shrubs, the forest, just donning its green robe—so beautiful to behold. It was a rich treat to go down there. First time little Ralph had seen a spring out doors; the first April of his life. He loved the forest, the flowers, the babbling brook; the large rock that we sat down on and let him sit and play on bare rock—he wanted to get in the water. Ralph went up to Charlie Childs (with Dola) and Aunt Mary (two darkies living here) yesterday P.M. and spent awhile. He was real sick from then on till [to]day—better now. Had *hot* fever—hot head, hot mouth, hands etc; fretted lots—wakeful all thro' nights. Fixing to cut more teeth. We (Susan Tarpley and I) were up with Mama; she was restless and we couldn't sleep any in her room til I had to take Ralph in our room about or near 12 o'clock and Susan says she was restless all night.

< April 16 >

Ralph is learning lots of cute things (10½ months old); can pretend that he is crying—cover up his face with his hands and make a noise like he was crying. He also slaps his hands together when he sees our dog (trying to set dog on something) and many things he is learning fast *quick* (astonishingly so to me) to catch on to these little things.

Travys is lots of past-time to Papa now. Papa stays close in doors with Mama and he has Travys around often giving him candy and apples, lemonade (things he keeps [for] Mama) and has Travys to talk to Mama lots. He is an attractive child and is favorite with most everyone. So many people, (all his life and continue till now,) say he favors Mama. . . . He always says so too. Papa says Travys is the greatest curiousity he ever saw. He laughs, talks, hugs and nurses the little tot lots. Truly Papa and Mama have been the best grand Parents to my little boys. Now in Mama's affliction she is forgetful of many things but from morning till night inquires about Ralph (when out of her sight); she is afraid his nurse will let him get hurt or neglected and too every day asks where the other children are often when they are out. Papa is so tender, so devoted to Mama in her affliction. I pray God's presence and blessing with my Parents the balance of their days and that I may be all I can to them.

Askew is 7 years old (will be 8 Aug.) and can write a plain hand considering the little time he has been in school. I picked up a short composition on "Tramps" that he wrote and composed a few days [ago]. 'Twas splendid for his age. He has wrote Aunt Fannie Wynn lots of letters (never mailed them) and he composes *well*; writes a newsy letter for his age.

Fred went to school awhile—became tired and quit. He is so young we wouldn't make him go (5 years). Fred is a negroes friend. All the negroes like Fred; he is gentle by nature and they "take to" him and he makes some good friends among some of the best who help about the house or on farm. An old negro woman, we call Aunt Mary, is very good to Fred—good thoughtful and kind to all of them—but Fred is her special pet. He thinks lots of her too. Travys begs to go to Mr. Thurston's school again on a visit. Hope he will get to go one P.M. before it closes. Weather too rough now.

Susan Tarpley has been lots of help to us in waiting on Mama. She thus far has pleased Mama well.

April 23

Thursday P.M.

My chances of writing have not been good since I wrote in these pages last. Although I've written many letters and postal cards to our family and relation concerning Mama's illness.

Verily "Truth is *stranger* than fiction." For two weeks Mama lay at point of death—we kept her alive by giving her nourishment (sweet milk, whiskey, whites of eggs, liquid Peptonoid, etc etc) with a syringe thro' rectum—not swallowing medicine, water, or anything by mouth. Few days we would moisten her lips. She was unconscious and would close her mouth vice-like together and when we forced it open and put liquid (few drops) in, she wouldn't and couldn't swallow and it came out at corners of mouth. However after a few days we would force her mouth open and give her a few drops occasionally and we would hear her swallow a little. Still none of us had *any* hopes of her.

Dr. Woods had no hopes whatever. She was low so long—weeks we sat up (or I) at night. No one who came in ever expected her to be any better in this world. Hers was indeed a strange case. Dr. Woods and Papa said it was the strangest that ever came under their observation. During time she was so low she had a sore throat, hard swollen place under her throat, and that went down but for weeks after that she was low—extremely low. Dr. W. gave her up—said all we could do was to give her nourishment with syringe and make her as comfortable as we could. He expected every day for some time to hear of her death. Mrs. Ingram would phone to him every day how she was. Awhile mentally she was weak as would naturally be expected of one so low and so old. We feared, after she began to mend, her mind would never strengthen much but another wonderful thing is that her mind is strengthening wonderfully and she is miraculously improved!!! She can walk a few steps unaided. She sleeps very well, and lies quiet all night. We had to watch her all the time awhile to keep her from trying to get out of bed alone and we knew she would do so if not watched—we knew also she would receive injuries. Now her mind and body are miraculously improved and she *quit* taking medicine. Just will not take it and it wasn't medicine that saved her life altho' the medicine Dr. Woods gave her did help her awhile and she, Papa and I think Dr. Woods one of the *best* of physicians.

Papa told her few days ago that 'twas the "Higher Power" that saved her life. And verily, God does wonders and the day of miracles has not passed. No, verily; "all things are possible with God."

Well, Mama sits up awhile (short while at a time) now—She takes good deal of buttermilk (in preference to anything else) for nourishment. For the past two nights and days Papa has been sick and today both are in bed. Papa has been *seriously* sick, has rheumatism and cold—suffering excruciating pains with leg and hip. We talked of sending to phone for Dr. Woods. He said if he was no better by tomorrow we could phone for him. Never saw he and Mama both a bed at same time before. Twas pitiful too—to see such an aged couple so feeble. Mama seemed so sad and anxious about Papa. I was sorry for her—because she has suffered so long, been so low, and still so feeble and now anxious and sad about Papa's illness. Heavenly Father, Thou hast been mindful of us. We thank Thee for past and present blessings (of loved ones spared) and we would ask a continuation of these blessings to us. We would live closer to Thee, since Thou hast blessed us *so* abundantly. Our besetting sins and our weaknesses we ask Thee to forgive us of and strengthen in and build us up with thy Holy Spirit.

Bro. Charlie sent Mama a nice box of good things to eat suitable to an invalid. Her appetite is so poor that she doesn't eat much of them yet.

One thing has given me some "bother" since Mama got sick and that was that my own sister seems to be offended with *me* because Dr. Woods and not her husband (Dr. Jarrell) waited on Mama during her illness. I do feel so troubled when my brothers and sisters treat me cool or with offense when I know I had no ill will to them. I will do what I believe is right toward them no matter what they do or say to me because another life awaits us after his one: this one preparatory to the next. "If it be possible, as much as lieth in you, live peaceably with all men." Lord help me to be right, *in my heart*, with Thee and all mankind.

Charlie is devoted to Mama and so is Lil. I believe Fan is too. One of the strangest things I ever saw happened while Mama was sick. When she first became low, she had been, apparently, expiring all night—pulse growing weaker and most irregular all night and Papa said he didn't think she would last till day. So we thought she was dying and ceased pouring drops down her short while before day. At day light, or some short while after, she seemed to be gone—seemed to be out of flesh—pulse stopped, could detect no breathing. Miss Babe says her heart has not entirely ceased and let's rub her pulse with whiskey. We (Miss B. and I) began to rub her pulse, lips with whiskey and we found her pulse after so long, were beating again. After awhile we saw a sign of returning breath and I knew her head was too low, so we were excited and asked some of them standing by to lift her up higher on a pillow. Misses Matt and Babe and Lil thought they couldn't and called on Cape. He had rheumatism and said he couldn't so I was a strength (not natural) I hopped up on bed, picked her body up and laid her higher on a pillow and then she breathed more freely and soon afterwards slowly opened her eyes like one just awakened. She seemed like one whose spirit had left body for another world and come back to this. She smiles as soon as her eyes were opened—and in few moments laughed out loud enough to be heard over house—face seemed radiated—a sweet heavenly expression seemed to flood her face. 'Twas something wonderful! wonderful!

April 24
Friday Morning

Yesterday company came in and interrupted me while I was writing in my diary.

Papa seems a little better today than he was yesterday. We are having a cold snap. Frost plentiful down on creak this morning and I heard yesterday that a thin skim of ice was seen early morning.

May 5

Mama continues to improve rapidly. Goes to table (walks over part of the house—has tolerably good appetite). She says when she was low she told the Lord if he couldn't make her feel better to take her away. She told Him He could heal her without money and without price and she says 'tis the Lord's doings. She says He has spared her for some purpose.

Papa has been rite sick. Dr. Woods came once and fixed him up with some medicine. I wrote Lil that Papa was sick and she came and spent two or three days.

Dr. Jarrell and Anna are against me because Dr. Woods was with Mama. (Reckon they don't know he was with Papa.) I am sorry; it is very unpleasant to me for member of our family, or relatives to be holding unkind thoughts, words and acts toward me, when I've done them no wrong intentionally. I study about such things good deal. I am staying with my Parents from a sense of duty. Prejudice is against me from more than one at times. I think if I were keeping house [that is, living in a separate household from her parents] they would not bear as much—perhaps none—but I must try do my whole duty to my aged parents whether I enjoy these unkind people or not. I have no malice against them and have done all I could to live peaceably— returned good for evil—

Sallie Wynn is here this week. Howard Carter goes to see her. If he will be good and kind always to her I hope they will marry. She misses a mother's love.

We have more roses on our monthly bushes! I've been sending baskets of them to friends. I love those lovely roses! They are a source of much pleasure to me. I live so close at home, and have always plenty of work and to gather roses and send them off is a recreation—a positive pleasure.

I sometimes hunger to read—sometimes to write in my diary. Ere I can get the chance, the things I so much want to write have been forgotten. I wanted to make Askew some pants, but here I am writing and pants cut out—no more done towards them. Tomorrow must starch and iron if weather is suitable. Mr. Ingram sent me some chrisanthemums this P.M. I've set them out in the garden.

Olivia Wilkins, a young lady friend, sent me a pretty bouquet of cream roses by Ghu last Sunday. I like Olivia. I think the making of a good woman is in her.

Well must stop and cook supper.

< May 5 >

Askew has [written] a letter of the other side of this leaf. He is 7 years old. He likes to write. Hasn't been to school much yet, and shows some talent in writing and composing.

I didn't read this and no one helped him spell more than 3 or 4 words.

McDonough, Ga. RFD 1
Apr 25th 1903
                Wynne Lewis   High Falls Ga.

dear Wynne
I will tell you what we are doing.
We are all well but Grand-Ma and Grand-Pa.
I hirt my foot

I fell down a wall
The trees are green and pretty
and The Frogs begin to hollow
and the birds begin to sing
and the Folks begin to be happy
The wirl begin to look pretty
These prtty days would make any body happy
I will close

   Askew Leguin

Little deeds of kinds
Little wirds of love
Make this earth

like the Heven a above
Today [is] wendenday
Mr. todd is the precher now

Ralph is teething and doesn't stay well many days at a time. This coming summer, I fear, will be hard on him. The 2nd summer of a child's life is most trying. Ralph is a sweet baby—just good as you please, when well, if weather permits him to be out of doors. He glories in an out door life. He learns new "tricks" easily and lots of them. Is pulling up by chairs and jabbers—says some few words—Will be a year old last day of this Inst. . . .

‹ May 7 ›

Last week (1st day of May) in the P.M. old Aunt Mary carried Fred, Travys, and Askew up to Mr. Bogue Childs. There had been 18 children in their home that P.M. Mr. Bogue, Della and his pretty wife have been so good and nice to us all—especially since Mama was taken sick. They are so clever.

Ralph is a cute, sweet, baby. He loves dolls. Will take any garment, pair of hose etc and hug them up and laugh gleefully—thinking they are dolls. He is so young to *know* so many things—quick to understand. He plays with Dola's doll often and hugs them so cutely and then gleefully laughs his ever musical laugh.

Travys is the favorite with most people. He is a sweet, loveable, little fellow. He isn't afraid of people—likes to talk to folks and loves attention. He is always brought into notice by Papa and Mama. When company comes they have Travys to do lots of his funny talk. He is a bright 3 year old. Hope he always will be, according to his age, as now.

‹ May 8 ›

Saturday P.M.

Papa pays Ralph lots of attention now. Ralph jabbers and plays so sweetly and at his age Papa first begins to notice babies. He sent for Ralph last night to come in his room and get on bed (Papa had retired) and he played with Ralph on bed awhile and again today had him in there rolling and throwing him up etc on his bed. Ralph is my girlboy. I am going to let his silken hair stay long awhile. I sent after some blue ribbon today to tie up the locks above his fore-head. I often say he is to be my girl—my help in the house.

Ghu says he ought to be, to pay me for the amount of trouble I've had with him.

Little "tot" Travys three years old begging for pants. His fond Grand Pa wants him to wear some and today he has on a pair of Freds. I love for my little boys to wear dresses till four at least. I want to keep them *babies* as long as I can and they get "big-boys" so rapidly after getting on pants.

May 8

Saturday

We have had cold rainy weather this week; Ghu has gone off now with his overcoat—to Locust Grove.

Well we've had so many beautiful roses! How I do admire and love them. They are such a pasttime to me. I cut baskets full and send to friends and give some to every darkey that asks for them. If the receivers enjoy the roses as well as the donor enjoys sending, my mission isn't fruitless.

Little old Travys is awful cute and sweet. He is going around all
day, so far, with a pair of Fred's pants on. He is three years old; Fred
wore them at 4. He is such a smart (intelligent) little "tot." I don't
want him to wear pants till 4 at least but I expect his fond Grand Pa
and loving Grand Ma will have him in pants sooner. Papa was the
cause of Fred wearing them at 4. Askew wore them just a short while
before 5 years old.

May 10

Sunday Evening

Ghu and Askew have gone to Sunday School. Fred and Travys did
not go this time.

I heard yesterday that Leola Brown was dead—was buried in
Locust G. yesterday. Heretofore when hearing of Mrs. Leola I would
be a little discouraged or downhearted concerning my own surroundings, the little trials that beset a mother and housekeeper. Why?
It was thus that I would think: Mrs. Leola has an *elegant* home—
everything beautiful. Then she has a negro man who cooks unusually well. Herself and children can dress lovely every day while I
can't keep clean in plain wrappers—don't always have a supply of
them on account of so many things to do—have to sew for family
and can't catch up. My body so much of the time so overtaxed that I
fag out almost before getting meals ready sometimes. I *love* beauty,
orderly homes. I strive to keep [mine so]—fail sadly sometimes: so
much to do, can't keep up all corners. Well it was thus I'd compare
Mrs. Leola's surroundings with my own. Today I look at it this way.
Mrs. Leola had to leave her luxurious home, devoted good husband
and her children while I am spared to work for my family in a plainer
home—but one to be thankful for and thankful that I'm living to be
with my loved ones, and strength to do as well as I ever do. She has
allways lived a life of ease and luxury. She was kind and sweet to me
when I was about 16 or 15 and used to visit her younger sister, Allie.

We are having cold weather for 10th of May. Sallie went home
today. Howard Carter came after her; he is a nice looking boy—has
a very pleasant face.

I wish I could hear Evangelist Dunaway preach. I am so weak spiritually. I feel like his sermons would help. Lord help me to be *patient*, calm and strong—to controll my spirit: to be gentle, forebearing etc. To speak good or nothing of people more—speak of faults less.

Ghu went to his friend, Bogue Childs, last night. About 12 men met there to have past time: drank beer and ate crackers and pickles. Was it right for Ghu to go, I wonder? He has told me, I think, that he wouldn't go to such a meeting. This is his first visit. We have 4 boys. They will be apt to follow his example. They are led more by a father than by Mama I think. If they were girls, 'twould not be so I think. I'm uneasy. I'm afraid Ghu is not only doing himself wrong, but will be slack with raising boys. I don't know that it was wrong, but I can't believe he ought to have gone.

May 12
Tuesday

How weak I am on certain lines! How deeply I deplore it. On this particular line I sometimes think I have myself well in hand—under good controll when in a thoughtless hour or less time I've said *many* things (sometimes only a few, but this particular time I've said many or several) about the ugly faults of some one and have said in many words, strongly emphasized my dislike of such a disposition. How unhappy it makes me for days afterwards and maybe for weeks, before I'll cease feeling so badly over my last season of lost controll—loss of better self—weaker self predominated. How troubled I am when there are any hard feelings or ill will to the "stepmother" I said these things about, yet what I said could cause her the greatest hatred towards me and I know that facts about some things are best kept inviolate—untold to others—and the wrong things done us endured. We will never feel troubled over silently enduring ill treatment, but will feel wrong over spending our *opinions* sometimes. "If wisdom's way you'd wisely seek, Five things observe with care, *Of whom* you speak, *to whom* and *how* and *when* and *where*." Ah! had I taken that caution.

A motherless girl (a relation) was telling me of unjust treatment she received from a stepmother and I said several things. I pray to God (tho' I don't deserve it) that the things I said will never reach that stepmother's ear and Oh, Heavenly Father, forgive this erring one—this sinful one—and help me to be strong on the line of saying unkind things, even if true, in wrong ways, wrong times and to wrong people. Lord do help me to be a true Christian—so true that I'll easily forgive, quickly forgive, any such offense—whether to myself or loved ones.

A quotation from my favorite magazine (The Ladies Home Journal):
  1. "I hope to be able to reach the stage when I shall never speak evil of anyone, and will say nothing if not good."
  2. "One of the first secrets of popularity is to speak well of everyone and to be silent when you can not do so honestly. The habit will lead you to look for qualities that are sure to reward the search."
  3. "Self-denial for honors' sake will make you the finer woman."

Lil has been here one day and night. I was not well—tired, and overworked besides, the day she came and remained dull, and bothered too some, and she thought me *cool*. I could see it all the time she was here. There is another fault I lament, the one of not being cheerful when not well—and perhaps I seemed less so than I am aware of. Oh, if I did, I am so self depreciative and blue that maybe it is best that at this particular time, I can not see myself as others see me. I told her I wasn't well, but I feel that she had no idea how bad I did feel yesterday when she came, and that she took it for down right coolness. I saw that she thought I had cool feelings toward her and so I couldn't repress one of my children lest she took it to mean that I was hinting at hers, and so I betook myself away from her betimes.

Ah, how Lil misunderstands me and how often I feel it when she comes up here. She is so sensitive about anything I do or say until I don't know what to say or do at times where she is. For instance, she left some fruit jars here and I packed them up and told her that was not intended as a hint for her to hurry off—yet I could see my words were not believed and she thought I wished her to go. Ah, why is this? Is it my fault? I *know* she mistakes me and my motives— sadly, for she is ever a welcome guest and I would be glad indeed [if] this sensitiveness on her part, could forever be done away with. By the way, maybe the sermons of the much talked of Dunaway could do away with lots of ugly things in us both. That ugly things are indwelling in me largely I know, am sometimes *very* much surprised how much territory they've taken. . . .

In physical strength, how incapacitated I find myself to fill the duties of a mother of 4 children, and to aged parents etc. Mentally too, how unfitted I am to raise children and govern the careless negroes who help me. I'm not firm enough with negroes at one time and the next, I think, too impatient, etc. Now for child-raising, I think, what a bright mind, what a strong character is needed. Some of the best letters from mothers in *Home and Farm* that I ever read. How much I'd like to do as they teach, about never reproving a child or servant in anger—Be calm and self controlled all the time and when necessary to correct, always say something to encourage the offender at closing remarks.

‹ May 13 ›

Ralph is lacking a few weeks of being one year old. He can stand alone (has just a very few times) a moment or so. The poor thing fell off a high bed in my room night before last. It scares me nearly to distraction for few moments when he falls from so high and hits floor so very hard. Again yesterday eve he had a hard fall, one that pained him, climbing up and on wash-stand.

Travys is very much interested in setting hens. Set one yesterday in little backroom. Papa and the little boys set her and Travys sat on veranda with his grandPa and the same P.M. waiting for her to hatch. He lay down with Papa awhile (as is the custom of all the little boys to do often after Papa retires) and talked lots about the hen hatching. He and Fred are intensely interested in setting hens and getting eggs. Travys seems thrilled thro' when he sees the little chickens under hen when hatching. He went with Ghu and I to the cow pen last night and just thrilled with delight and exclamations when the little calf came nursing to its mammy. Travys would have a little bucket to carry; said he was going to milk his calf. It is a bull but little Travys thinks it could be milked. Fred loves to help feed the dry cattle. I hope they will love cattle and be kind to dumb brutes.

May 13

Ghu and I had a long talk about Lil's coolness. We think that she was not feeling good toward us. He said she was fickle and for me not to worry over her coolness. Said she wasn't as sociable with him as usual. Surely when she reflects she will feel bad. I think she came with "*a something*" in her heart unpleasant toward us. Guess we will have trials as long as we live here. The children and grand-children have unpleasant feelings, jealousies etc against us because we are with their parents and mine. And my parents are devoted to my children and I think more so than they are to any other grand-children. That may be what is the matter. Dora, Charlie, Buddie and Fan and Cape do not have any petty fault findings with me. Their feelings toward me are all right. Lord help me bear the troubles cheerfully, and bravely, for Thine own sake, Amen.

I've been feeling badly this week. Have a cold, cough some and troubled some with chronic complaint of several years standing.

May 15
Thursday P.M.

Rain, rain, rain!

> "Rain! Rain! Go away,
> And come again another day."

We have had a wet May so far. Maybe if sun would shine we who feel blue and bad would feel true and glad.

Believe rainy weather has something to do with self-depreciation and blues. Have been wondering, thinking and (crying), almost crying (wiping tears away) about Lil's antagonism towards me. I can't fully understand why she feels so unkind towards me and why she cares *so little* for my feelings. Wish sun would shine and I could forget all unhappy memories.

I guess troubles of this kind will fall on me as long as I live with my parents and my parents will know nothing about it. 'Tis their children—they would not or could not believe if I told them. I dare not tell unless it gets to be unbearable (then I would hate to). I pray for grace to sustain me in home of my aged parents where I'm treated cool by some members of the family.

May 28

We are having warm weather, July weather almost.

I went over to old uncle George Griscom's yesterday (an old sick negro) and carried him a jug of buttermilk and something to eat. Askew, Travys, Ralph and Dola went with me. We didn't stay there but a few minutes—stopped at Gin Branch and rested on our way back.

Well, I have nothing particular to write about in my diary this A.M. The warm weather keeps me feeling weak and any way but comfortable. This weakness tho' is the biggest bother, as I can't hold out with my work.

Ghu is working *very* hard on the farm now. The grass was getting alarming.

I am baking lots of light bread these hot days.

Mr. Brand and Alf ate dinner here Sunday. We expected Mr. B's wife and baby but baby was ailing and she couldn't come.

Mr. Lewis was here last week enroute to Locust G. after Bessie; she will not attend school there any more, Lil said—expenses too heavy.

‹ May 28 ›

Askew had earache one night this week and says he can't hear well since. He isn't healthy—has catarrh real bad and I never knew anyones nose to bleed so much, and so often as his. Askew has "spells" of helping me—Two days lately he whitewashed some fireplaces and did it well. Another morning this week he swept big space in yard that needed sweeping.

Ralph is cute. He tries to talk and has big fun with other little boys. He is very small and likes only a few days of being 12 mo's old.

May 31
Ralph's 1st birthday

Mama, Papa, and myself alone (Ralph and his nurse on premises). Ghu, Askew, Fred and Travys have gone to Sunday School. Mama,

Papa and I are lonely. We stay so close at home; know so little to talk about—children gone and no company—makes a Sunday evening quiet. Mama seems cheerful, so peaceful tho' calmly quiet since her recovery—since her return to life—her return which ever will be one of the greatest miracles. It is so sad to think of what she passed thro' and how long she lay low—and so very sad and depressed she was before getting very low—or rather getting lowest. Those are sad memories. I feel so sure that *nothing* but God's power sustained her life. Then His miraculous power restored her reason as clear as ever after all the suffering she passed thro'. I never did believe her mind would be perfectly clear again, as she is near 75 years old and her sickness so long and so severe. But God has performed a miracle— restored her life and mind. Now she seems like one ever ready for summons Home; she seems so gentle, so *sweet spirited;* reads Bible lots; seems to be trying always to scatter cheer and sunshine—so peaceful, so gentle!!

Travys talks to Mama and Papa lots and they to him. Mama and Papa think lots of my four little boys.

I am sorry that Mama hasn't used her rolling chair more, i.e. I am sorry I couldn't roll her out doors. I am not strong enough and she doesn't need it in doors as she can easily walk over house anytime. I have been weak and ailing for nearly a month. I think it is hay fever that causes me in summers to stay so weak. Freezing weather braces me as nothing else can.

Mama's recovery was a great blessing to Papa, and us all, but especially to him. They are spared to each other in their extreme old age. Mama's recovery was a great blessing to me. I feel that I never could have been reconciled to her death had she died when so low, as I can be if I outlive her now.

I hope I will never omit any duty through forgetfullness or otherwise toward her while we journey together.

Lord I thank Thee that Mama's life was spared and Heavenly Father help me to have the Holy Spirit to dwell in my heart to make me a blessing to my parents the rest of the time we are together.

‹ June 1 ›
Monday

Ralph was one year old yesterday. His first birthday was spent about like any other day, only it came on Sunday and in the P.M. I put a suit of nice clothes on him and two little negro girls (Dola and Della Tarpley) and myself carried him across the creak and up road a good piece. I took more pains in setting table than I would had it not been his birthday. Put white cloth and napkins and a vase of roses on in honor of Ralph, but when dinner time came he was fast asleep.

. . . He weighs 19 lbs. He has 5 teeth — can say few indistinct words. Can't talk like the other 3 did at his age, but talks unmistakably with his eyes. His eyes express lots of things. 'Tis amusing to me to read his meaning in his eyes. Has more teeth nearly through.

June 4

I am not well. I have been feeling real badly about a month and instead of getting better I am very much afraid I am going to feel worse. The Lord only knows the depth of my trouble over this sickness and to what heights my *fears* attain as to what the sickness may terminate [in].

I trust, hope, and pray for better things in regard to my health than what leads me to fear.

Lord relieve my distress anxiety by restoring usual health and strength to do housework and tend to my children — as well as usual — tho' that is never perfectly well.

Susan Tarpley, an old negress, raised by my Uncle and Aunt, has been down today preparing a remedy for me.

Well I feel so anxious to have my usual strength and to be able to see as usual after home and children that the fear of not being able to continue so and fears of the greatest suffering in future for me has caused me to be weaker than I otherwise would have been. I pray from noon till night that this cup will pass from me. Lord, Thou knowest the anguish of motherhood. Thou knowest how much I am needed in this home. Oh, God! If it can by Thy will I pray Thee grant that I may speedily be restored to usual strength, that my present fears will speedily be allayed — that what I most hope for—usual health—be speedily granted. Oh, I pray Thee if it can be Thy will grant this prayer speedily. Pardon me for all transgressions and help me to live according to Thy will concerning me, for Jesus sake Amen.

We are having rainy weather. Ralph is a very restless baby; he is teething and therefore crosser than he otherwise would be.

God grant that nothing will happen physically to me to prevent me seeing after him and family any less than now. Oh! how heavy fears have sunken my heart the past few days. How low spirited and weak I am! Oh, that I may never know the pangs of what I so much dread. Mama and Papa are old and feeble. I am not cheerful often. I pray God for strength to do my duty towards them. Oh, Lord hear and answer this prayer if it can be Thy will. Oh, God deliver me from such awful suffering and grant me health enough to be "up and doing," for Jesus sake Amen.

June 6 or 13
Saturday P.M.

Isn't it awful to suffer so that one can not be the least bit cheerful? So that one hasn't strength to keep tidy house and clean children, at least reasonably clean?

To be thought able to do simple housework and at same time wholly unable to do almost anything? To have company and to be too sick to cook for them? To see a one year old baby need attention and too weak and sick to give it necessary attention. To see aged parents need a cheerful person to talk to and be with and at same time be too miserably sick to have any cheerfulness about me. These and nameless other such things I fear will be my lot in course of two or three weeks.

I've never had to wean a baby as young as 12 months but I fear that will be Ralph's fate—and his second summer—the worst in a child's life.

> "Life is a duty—bear it
> Life is a thorn crown—wear it."

I fear the thorn-crown is coming to me.

Heaven help me for all the trials that is to come upon me. If it is best that I suffer this *awful* sickness, help me to bear it, the best I possibly can. I have passed thro' and am living, but now overtaxed my body has been and mind too—and again so soon—it is appalling. What I suffer from physical weakness caused from excessive childbirth, Heaven only knows. I trust I may pull thro' and be spared to my children.

Prayers and tears have not availed—it is best I reckon. Oh, God, Thou knowest what a life of suffering I am passing thro'. Lord help me. Oh, that I could when my health completely fails have a negro to cook, keep house etc etc. I could be more submissive.

< June 14 >
Sunday

Poor little Ralph! *We have begun to wean him today.* I pity, from my heart, the little sick baby, passing thro' this weaning process. Now my heart goes out in sympathy to the little one when crying for a mother's nourishment and can't gratify the little thing. He has been sick all this week—not bad off, but weak and feverish and bowel trouble. I know he must feel that his Mama, the one he loves best, has treated him awfully bad. If it were not for committing my little Ralph into God's loving care and trusting little Ralph to him I would grieve more over weaning him than I do. God bless precious baby Ralph and all my little boys. Guide, direct, and protect them all along thro' life and at last receive them into thy Home above.

My heart goes out the past several days in more love and sympathy than usual for my little boys. My heart feels a tender pity for them. Oh, God, spare me to raise my little children and help me to live humbly and obediently according to Thy will and be contented, whatever our lot, if I may be granted this, my hearts greatest desire— to be spared to my children—to raise and stay with and comfort and be a blessing to each of them for Jesus sake. Amen.

"Papa Ghu" works so hard, *so hard.* I wish he could live without so much *hard* labor on farm—wish he could do only such work as did not overtax him. He has worked very hard and is not well. He coughs and has a cold all the time lately. I am sorry. I am so sick myself that I can not do very much and have to lie down a great deal. God be with us.

June 14
Sunday P.M.

Little Ralph, my precious baby is beginning to be weaned today. He nursed before he and I got out of bed this morning the last time, and tis near 5 o'clock in the P.M. now. The little fellow has been kept away from me all day, except occasional glimpses and how he yearned to come to me those times and cried so pitiful for me.

My Heavenly Parent, Thou who didst give this little innocent baby to my keeping, take special care of him during this trying time, of weaning him. Lord, Thou knowest the little thing is not well; that he hasn't been in several days. How glad I would have been to have kept him at the fount of Nature (the mothers breast) until this, his second summer is over, because he is teething and likely to be sick all summer but this can not be and as it can't be, Heavenly Father take my dear precious little Ralph into Thy special care all summer and on through my baby's life and when his race has been run and ours, receive all my children and my husband and myself, an unbroken family, in Heaven.

Again Heavenly Father I ask Thy special care over little Ralph and help me to be a true Christian a devoted mother, a blessing to my children. Forgive me for all my sins and blot them all out of Thy book of remembrance and help me to strive daily to live as Thou wouldst have me live, for Jesus sake Amen.

Little Ralph is off now with old Aunt Mary and Dola. . . . I sent him up to their neighbors with them, to prevent him from crying so hard for me to let him nurse.

Ordinarily I would not have consented for Aunt M. to have kept him more than an hour, off at another's house out of my sight, but my eyes can not allways be on little Ralph and I must trust God to take care of him and my other 3 little boys.

Ghu has gone to S[unday] S[chool]. Travys and Askew went with him. Fred didn't want to go and Ghu wasn't well and let him stay here so that there would not be so many to wash and dress. I am so sick too that I can't do very much but have dressed Fred since he left. And so Mama, Papa, and I get lonely on Sunday P.M.'s. I think it well enough for Fred to be here with us this P.M.

Ghu has been working *very* hard and has overtaxed his strength and hasn't been well lately. He is a *very hard* worker — has too much energy for his strength. I sometimes fear he will shorten [his] life by too much hard work on farm. He hurries so and does much more work than any man he has hired.

Bro. Jim and Alf ate dinner here today. One of Jim's neighbors, a poor man, had the misfortune to get his house and all it contained burned up this week. I gave Jim, for them, a sheet, pr. pillow cases, and a nice dress for a small child.

August 10

I've been so miserably sick all summer that I ceased to write in this diary or to be interested much in anything in the world. Had to send for Dr. Woods; he visited me 3 times. I continue sick, sick, but Drs. can't *cure* anything tho' when I sent for Dr. W. the last time I couldn't sit up. I think I must, with other ailments, have asthma. I sent today, for a dollar box of Dr. Blosser's catarrh remedy; have been troubled last few days with asthma (I reckon it was) and have fresh cold. Askew is crying so I can't write. He has a stone bruise.

Papa was 82 years old Saturday.

< August 10 >

I've been sick all the Summer, and consequently have written nothing in this book. Too sick to become much interested in anything in the world. Ralph has been sick too, all the Summer.

Askew has started back to school (to Mr. Thurston at New Hope).

Fred had light attack of fever in early part of summer and we didn't send Fred. I think there is "time enough yet" for Fred as he is only six.

Travys is well—full of life—lots of talk and a loveable little fellow. He is more of a favorite with people generally, than the other two.

Ralph has pretty hair—enclined to curl. He was weaned in his 13th month. Has been awful poor—thinner than any of our babies ever because and I've been at times this Summer, very much afraid we could not raise him, afraid he couldn't live thro' the Summer. He is again better and now if he has no serious backset I think he will get thro' tho' be puny till cold weather. He is cute when he gets better.

He has some new bonnets and he thinks them very pretty and wants to wear them all the time nearly.

< August 31 >
Monday

The last day of Aug. seems to have a breath of fall. How glad I welcome the coming fall—having been so weak and sick all Summer! Fall is my favorite season.

Ralph is 15 months old today—can't walk—been sick all summer. He is doing well now. I dressed him up this P.M. and Ghu carried him, Travys, Fred and Askew all over to Mr. Ingram's store.

Yesterday Travys says "this is my left hand" (then held up right hand and hesitated a moment and then said) "this is my *front* hand." He didn't know that one was left and the other right. I was surprised that he knew so well his left hand. He says funny things but I am *so* busy, and *so* tired, I have no chance to write them down, tho' I regret *deeply* not having the chance to do so. Having a weak, tired, body, I naturally have a weak memory and forget them quickly.

Dola Tarpley, Ralph's nurse, left yesterday morning. She wasn't good to mind me and was a little sassy yesterday A.M. I slapped her a few times for her wrong doings and she threatened to go home. I told her to go right away; that I would not object. She was troublesome on some lines, and couldn't be trusted far. While on other lines she did very well. She had been here nearly a year.

Askew's school is out. Mr. Thurston, his teacher, spent one night here recently. Askew is getting large enough to be some help to me now. He can amuse Ralph real well and that is a *great* help. He has learned—within the past few days—to draw water, but can't pour it out or bring it in.

Fred is rite fond of an old negro woman, Aunt Mary, who lives here. She pays him marked attention and saves him fruit etc etc.

August 31

The last day of Aug. has a hint of Autumn in it. How glad I am too the weather is a little cooler. How I love Autumn because I am always weak in Summer and grow stronger in Autumn. I am diseased in a way that cold weather makes me feel better than any thing in the world. Warm weather nearly prostrates me. The past summer has been a trying one on my strength. How sick I have been—words can not tell. A negro "Aunt Mary," cooked 2 months and wouldn't cook any longer. I was compelled to go in and do the cooking and could hardly stay up long enough to cook the meals many times and some times compelled to lie down between cooking one thing and another. No one could ever know, without some experience, what I've been thro' this summer. A cough, and something like asthma, and fresh colds are becoming chronic. I've had them all summer. Ralph has been sick too all summer—has lots of spells and high fevers.

I love to sew (on children's clothes and Ghu's shirts) and many other things. I love to cook in cool and cold weather; I love to iron starched clothes. I love to work when I can, but what a burden when one is not able to work but very little to be compelled to keep strength overtaxed heavily. I am thankful cool weather is coming. I have not been anywhere in a long time—not since last Winter and not but a few times then. Evangelist Dunaway is conducting a tent meeting at Locust Grove now. I want to go one night this week if I can.

My! at the crowds of folks that do come here every summer! from beginning to end, not many days, not many meals, pass, unless company is in the house. Hardly a day but someone is here. So many kin folks; lots who are no kin come—and no health in the world to do for the people—to be genuinely overtaxed, body and mind. If I had health, and a good servant, how much less burdened all this would make my poor weak (always tired and aching) back and body. But I am glad I am as well as I am. I never expect much strength; and I could be worse. May the Lord be with me in all troubles and help me bear patiently all that I am called upon (by Him) to pass thro'— But how I do need a good negro to help me always, and especially thro' summer.

‹ October 19 ›

Friday

Well, Ralph is 16 months old and can't talk. None of the others were least backward about talking. Some time ago, Ralph made some effort to talk and I thought he was going to be bright on that line. He is bright—shows his intellect in many ways and amuses us all greatly. Papa . . . says he has lots of sense—Papa and Mama play with and amuse Ralph every day. Mama gets him to sleep often and puts him on her bed. They pay him great deal of attention and think lots of him.

Ralph has been trying to walk about 3 weeks. He isn't healthy (indigestion and bowel trouble) and that prevents his walking. He tries hardest to walk of any baby I ever saw. He walks several steps—goes too fast—falls down and tries it over repeatedly until he is tired out. Ralph can say "Baa! Ba! Ba!" (trying to bleat like a calf) and Mama and Pop-pop. [That's] about all. Says "me" when he wants anything given him and "mine."

‹ October 21 ›

Wednesday Night. Shut-eye-time

Ralph walks at last. At 16½ months he walked. More backward than any of the others. Still slow to talk. He is cutting teeth—has 11 or 12—and isn't well—indigestion and diarrhoea. He is smart and cute tho'.

Papa . . . says for me to let his hair remain uncut for a long time; that it is too fine and silky to cut off. I cut all my babies' hair in their 2nd summer, except Ralph's, on account of hot fever in their heads (caused from teething), but Ralph's hair grew thin and I didn't feel it necessary to cut it. Now I am just as proud of his silken hair as I can be and enjoy combing and tying it. Bought him some ribbon this week for his hair. Put new pair of shoes on him today—he was very proud of them and walked more than any day of his life. He was the *gladdest* baby I ever saw when he found that he could walk [a] few steps. His face would beam with joy and he is still joyous when walking. Ghu pays him more attention than he ever did any of the others at his age (tho' was always attentive enough to all), but he seems to be more attached to Ralph than he was to the others at Ralph's age.

Ghu carried Askew and Fred to Atlanta today to the Fair. 'Tis Askew's and Fred's first rail-road-ride. Askew is *very nervous* about a train. Always has been *very* much afraid of a train, and tho' 8 years old, he *dreaded* getting on train, tho' he [was] anxious to see Atlanta and the fair. Fred was never afraid particularly of the train. They may come back tonight and they may not get back before tomorrow. Fred wore his first "bought ready made" suit of clothes today. Ghu bought him a suit this week. He is very proud of his suit.

Travys didn't cry to go with them. He wanted to go but when told he could not he was perfectly reconciled to staying here. Travys is so devoted to Fred — more so than Fred is to him. His love for Fred is beautiful. All his brief life he has loved Fred more than he did Askew.

Papa . . . is certainly devoted to all of them. He loves them so tenderly. He devotes some time to them all every day and all their lives they have lain on his bed at night after supper awhile with Papa. Papa retires early and they all pile up with him awhile before going to their own beds — oft times some of them going to sleep and Ghu has to bring them out asleep. Papa has a deep love for those children — he has been a kind affectionate Grand Pa to my little boys all their days and has always made me think so much of Bill Arp (Major Charles Smith — now dead) in that particular respect. He certainly has been a devoted Grand Pa to my four litle boys.

Ralph loves Mama (his Grand Ma) and Travys does too. They think lot of her and she is good to them and to all.

November 7
Sunday Eve

Ghu and three of the little boys have gone to Sunday School. Ralph and I are alone in our room — weather cold and I have to keep hall-door fastened to keep Ralph from getting sicker — by staying out in cold — either in yard or back porch. He is very hard to keep in doors. All of my children, from baby-hood up, allways were, and are. Ralph and all of us have bad colds and I have to shut him in to prevent real sickness. Now, while I am writing R. is driving pins in between planks of floor. I gave him these to keep him amused.

I haven't been as lonely this Sabbath afternoon as I usually am. I have enjoyed the quiet calm evening, it has seemed *so sweet* to me. Usually I am so lonely I don't enjoy much of anything till Ghu and children get back, usually feel so completely worn out from trying to amuse Ralph, but he has been real sweet and amused himself with playthings and kept contented all this P.M.

This calm cloudy still Sabbath eve is so sweet to me. So calm, so sweet! so sweet! I can't help but *long* to get out and view the beautiful scenes of nature—the woods in their perfectly lovely colors! How they fill my soul with admiration! The creek and branch I'd love to behold awhile. The waters are so clear and still in creak and clear and beautiful at the branch that I love to go to at all seasons, especially fall. Fall is the sweetest season of all and approaching winter has such charms for me.

Nearly Christmas! How inexpressibly sorry I am that I can not go Jackson and buy the children a few Christmas things. How, with all my heart I would enjoy doing that. I believe in making Christmas just as bright and happy as we can—especially for the dear children. Childhood comes but once. Oh, how I would love to buy a few (we don't feel able to buy many) Christmas presents—simple tho' they would be. Askew is only one knows who Santa Claus is—learned at school.

I am in bad health tho' and in a condition that I can't go out in the crowds this coming Christmas and Ghu doesn't enter as heartily as I do in the spirit of Christmas and Santa Claus. I just feel happy over thoughts of approaching Christmas and am working extremely hard every day and some (when strength will possibly permit), with my sewing, in order to get necessary winter clothes done a week before Christmas so that I will not be so greatly worn and overtaxed—that I may have strength and time to cook some pretty cakes and have house cleaned and cedars to decorate etc etc.

The Lord is good to give me this much strength. I crave to live with my children and work for them. I am so glad that I can be up— that I am not a perfect invalid.

‹ December 13 ›
(Sunday P.M.)

Nearly Christmas and the little boys (Traviss and Fred) talk so much about Santa Claus and are so anxious and impatient for Christmas to come. Askew is anxious for Christmas to come but alas! some thoughtless person told him there was no Santa Claus. I am sorry too, for such a sweet pleasure to be destroyed is such a loss to childhood. I reckon when Fred starts to school (which will be soon after Christmas) somebody will destroy the belief in the beautiful myth for him. Traviss is a good innocent child—he tries harder to please me than either F. or A. at present ages of the three. A sweet spirited innocent baby—nearly four years old. He is anxious to wear pants but likes new dresses and aprons that he has this winter too. Askew is getting large enough to be of much help now. He keeps Ralph, grinds coffee, draws water and brings in wood for me. T. and F. help about bringing wood and all three help set table, carry dry dishes in from stove room. Askew has one fault that is annoying: [he is] careless and thoughtless. Hope he will soon be more careful about his personal appearance, his clothes, and be more particular to do his little jobs well. Fred, Ralph and I are bedfellows this winter. Fred is rite good—and a little more quiet than the others. Ralph is a mischievous baby—cuts up pranks all day—is foolishly fond of his Papa—likes very much old aunt Mary Col [colored]. He is very slow about talking but the past week made effort to add new words to his short list.

1904

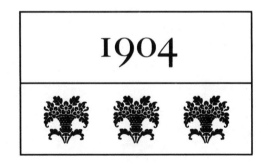

< February 8 >

Mama has been in bed since 2nd day of January. She doesn't improve. She was such a warm, loving hearted "grandma" to my 4 little boys. The last time she was ever out of the yard she went below the buggy-house and brought Ralph in out of the cold. Her back had grown so weak (she had been feeble 2 or 3 weeks) she could not pick him up in her arms as she was accustomed to doing, but she picked him up by his arms and brought him to the house that way. She looked after Ralph a good deal – I believe more than she did any of our babies. Would often put him in a rocking chair on a pillow (that she and Papa sat on) and rock him to sleep while I was busy preparing meals. She and Papa have always loved our children and have been such good grandparents.

I don't believe Mama will ever be any better than now. Last Spring she was *very* low and got up but I don't think she will get well any more. Her mental vision has been clouded since Christmas day.

Askew is in school. Fred started but not being well hasn't been much. Traviss considers it a treat to go over to the schoolhouse. He went awhile one P.M. last week. Ralph is not well much. He cries good deal and has inflamed eyes, caused from teething I think. I crave health enough to be cheerful, and not by overtaxed strength to cloud the lives of my children. I crave enough health to make home bright and cheerful for husband and children.

Ghu's mother died [in Louisiana] the 12th of last month. Our children never saw their grandmother Le Guin.

< February 13 >

Lena Wellmaker (Dora's daughter in law) wrote me that Cliff Wellmaker accidentally shot and killed himself on 10th Inst. Pistols do such untold mischief that I hope my boys will not carry them unless absolutely necessary. Dora's favorite child dead – what sorrow! no words to describe that mother's anguish.

Thursday was Fred and Travys' birthday (Feb. 11th) both on same day of same month. I cooked them a little birthday lunch and syrup candy—much as I could do with my little strength and Mama's sickness. Mama has been growing some weaker past few days. Travys comes in and talks to her occasionally tho' she seems pleased yet she doesn't know any one many moments at a time. Travys was 4 years old on 11th Inst and Fred 6. Fred has been puny for a week. Ralph learned this week to ask for peas. Aunt Mary eats lots of them, and now during Mama's sickness she stays here and Ralph carries a tin pan to her and says Peas! Peas! His vocabulary is exceedingly limited. He, when finding any garment with buttons on it, says "corl, corl, corl" (means good schollar, bad schollar, worth a dollar dunce; I've gone over those words with his clothing that contained buttons). He never sees a button without trying to say repeatedly "Corl" "corl." He loves shoes—will play with his old ones and Travys' and any one's he can find. He had lovely hair and I was forced to cut off above his eyes close because my strength has failed and he could cry so that I couldn't keep it combed and tied up.

"Papa Ghu" is half sick with a bad cough. Travys is a favorite with most people, and by most people said to be best looking child I have. He has a sweet disposition—tries to please us and very obedient all times. He is so very thoughtful—most thoughtful one of the children so far.

< February 14 >

Sunday Night

A little cricket is chirping merrily tonight, in our room and the good cheer it has aroused has prompted me to scribble. 'Tis the first cricket I've heard this year. I'm going to take that the chirping of that tiny little insect is an omen for good—the chirping is always so delightfully pleasant to my ears. Hope my little boys will be interested in all harmless insects and will not take the lives of these little things that our Heavenly Parent has created.

Travys went with "Papa Ghu" and Askew to Sunday School this P.M. Travys loves Prof. L. M. Thurston—Mr. T. was at Sunday School this P.M. and T. came back and told me "Mr Thurston picked me up in his arms and I showed him my locket (a little cheap per-

fume thing) and he ask me if he might smell it." Ghu carried Ralph
to ride this P.M. and brought him back asleep. He is now about 19
or 20 mos old and has a decidedly short vocabulary, learning to say
a few words, such as "peas" "War-war" (for water) "hot" "doll" etc
etc. Fred is puny [mildly ill] and didn't go to school. Fred and Travys
are much easier for me to controll than Askew is.

‹ February 18 ›

Another birthday I (Magnolia Wynn Le Guin) have lived to see. I
am 35 today. Papa was surprised when he was told — he didn't think I
was that old. Ghu will be 34 on 20th Inst. At 35 years of age, Askew,
my oldest living, is little over 8 — Fred is 6 the 11th Inst, Travys 4 the
same day and Ralph 19 months old.

Yesterday Mama was propt up in bed and talked lovingly and tenderly to Travys (her favorite and the one who favors her) and to
Fred. She ask for T. to come to her arms; she hugged him warmly
for some moments (pressed him so warmly to her bosom) and kissed
him over and over and cried and talked to him. She hadn't noticed
anything before to count in a week. She smiled when he approached
the bedside. How Mama did love Travys and Ralph and all [the] rest,
but especially T. She will notice Travys and Ralph now quicker than
anything — will notice Travys' voice quicker than anyones. There is
something strange about it and *so pathetic.*

Papa thinks she might possibly get up again if her mind would return, but her mind doesn't clear perfectly, even for as short a time as
10 minutes. Her disease is Nervous prostration — has a Kidney and
spinal affection.

February 18
Thursday P.M.

My birthday! 35 years old, and have been a mother 5 times and will
be one again, if nothing prevents, *quite soon.* May be before another
day. (The torture is so great I shrink with all my nature from the
trying ordeal.) I ask God to help me bear this suffering that is in
store for me. I ask Him daily. He has brought me thro' 5 times. I

trust Him again. Mama has been in bed since Jan 2nd. Her disease is Nervous Prostration and a Kidney and spinal affection. Her mind gave way Christmas and has never cleared up since. Susan Tarpley, col., Papa has hired to wait on her. Suse came here on 5th January. Mrs. Bartie Marsh is staying with us awhile now. Papa told her if she would stay he would pay her.

Cliff Wellmaker shot and instantly killed himself on the morning of 10th Inst. The family wrote us it was not a suicide—but an accident. Am sorry for Dora. Her favorite son, her idol. He was a model, from a moral standpoint. Her first trouble in life. Tho' trouble was late in calling on her—yet what A GREAT one came at last.

Papa thinks if Mama's mind would clear up that she would get up again. Her sickness is so pathetic. She loved our children so tenderly. Her and Papa's devotion to them has been great. She, at times, talks to them yet—when she notices anything at all. I don't get a chance at my diary often. What I may pass thro' before writing in this book again would fill it, I expect.

I pray the Lord be with me, with Papa and Mama and [the] children. Especially do I pray for Ralph. He is 19 months old and I dread to be helpless in bed and unable to wash, dress, and keep Ralph dry and clean. Have asked God to take care of him—give me some one to dry and see after him.

< March 19 >

Saturday P.M.

Since writing last in our home and life changes have taken place. I have no mother now—my little boys—(and my little girl)—have no grandmother. Mama died the 1st day of this month—was burried the 3d. Her corpse was a pretty one, for her age. We can't realize that she is dead. Everywhere we miss her so. She was such a warm-hearted woman. Her devotion to our little boys was beautiful and what an irrepairable loss to ours! The rich love of grandma is theirs no longer in this life. (My body isn't strong and my time limited and I can't write as much about Mama's "going away" as I'd like to— a cross baby keeps me *so* occupied that I find almost no chance for anything but to attend to her.)

About 10 or 11 days before Mama died a baby girl was born to
us. We are proud of a girl and hope her life will scatter sunshine
and much happiness in the world. Her name is Mary for Mama. She
has never been weighed. I think at first her weight would have been
7 lbs—not over. She looked smaller than any at first. She was born
on Saturday morning, before day light. Dr. Woods, a good physician
and perfect gentleman, was here. (He was Mama's physician.) Our
baby was born two days after my 35th birthday and born on Ghu's
34th birthday. We said she was Ghu's birthday present.

Travys is more proud of his little sister than any of the other children are. Ralph has grown so spoilt last 4 weeks—is *devoted* to Ghu.
Baby Mary is 4 weeks old today.

< March 20 >

Sunday Morning

How sad to think that my Mother . . . is no longer in our home.
The tears roll down my face when sweet sacred memories of Mama
come over my mind. How inexpressibly sad for Papa. I believe that
my children had the best Grand Ma and Grand Pa that most children ever had. The devotion and patience of each of them toward my
little boys has been remarkably beautiful. All of their lives they've
lived with their grandparents—all of us in same house—yet Mama
and Papa was so good and patient to and with them—as much so as
I—sometimes more so—and they so old! Mama 75 and Papa now 82.

Papa and Ghu have gone to see a sick man this A.M. . . . tho' [Papa
is] afflicted and has ridden little in 3 or 4 years, yet his loneliness
and grief so great, that he bought a horse yesterday to try [to] ride
about a little. He misses Mama so, and grief so great, that it seems
more than he can bear. What is home without our mother? How
distinctly every thing proclaims her absence. No one fills her place
at head of table. She always sat there and poured coffee. As yet Papa
hasn't gone back (only to pass to and fro) in the room that he and
she stayed in for past 33 years. He can't make up his mind yet to go
in there to stay or sleep without her who stayed with him 56 years—
(married life). He sleeps in room that I always called "our room"
and Askew sleeps with him. Papa has always loved Askew and Askew

seems to think more of his "Grand Pa" than of myself. I am glad he loves Papa—Papa deserves all the love (and more I'm afraid) that he will ever get—we all are due him much love.

‹ March 21 ›
Monday Morning

Papa went to High Falls today. Mr. Lewis came up here last night after Papa, and he went back with Mr. L. this A.M. It has been severel years since Papa went to the Falls. Having been afflicted the past severel years, he didn't feel able to ride so far; and if Mama were living I am almost sure he never would have taken that trip again. 'Tis because of his sorrow for her that he has gone now. Seems so strange that Papa is away—Papa nor Mama at home—so strange. They both never went away at same time. We are going to miss him strangely. He has gone to stay till Saturday. We will till then miss him strangely and go on missing Mama sadly. Everything brings her to memory.

> "Into life's calm, the wind of sorrow came
> And fanned the fire of love to clearest flame."

Yes, fanned the fire of love for Mama to clearest flame. We didn't know how much we loved her till she was taken forever away.

‹ April 6 ›
Wednesday

I, today, mail Mama's obituary to the Wesleyan Christian Advocate. She had been a subscriber to it for many years—constant. Splint subscribed for it (i.e. he paid her subscription and had it sent to her) for about 2 years, I think, before he died and she was ever afterwards till she went away a constant subscriber.

Mama went to Heaven March 1st, a month ago Sat. I believe she was homesick for her loved ones gone on before her. Just before taking her bed she spoke of her mother, her twin-brother, her first-born (Sunny he was called) and her last born, Splint. She told Papa (just before taking her bed) that she had friends (loved ones she meant) in a better world and it would not be long before she would be with them. Papa is so sad and lonely without her, after journeying o'er life's pathway about 57 years, together. Papa has been very bad off since he came from [High] Falls. Dr. Wood was with him once. Askew sleeps with Papa and Papa talks more to Askew than he does to any of us I believe. Papa is quiet, sad and thoughtful, reads Bible a great deal every day.

Fred was 6 years old in Feb. and shedded his first teeth today. Ghu pulled two for him.

Mary, (the new baby) is nearly 7 weeks old. Laughs great deal; coos more than any baby I ever knew—coos so loud for her age; she has been cooing since 4 weeks old and laughing too. She is a very nervous, wakeful baby. She sleeps well at night but worries me awfully in day time.

Fred is learning real fast at school. He surprises us all (Ghu, Papa, and I) about learning. He is smart too, about making fires in stove and doing little things that helps me about cooking. Travys is willing to help too but so little he can't help much. He loves flowers and today he, Askew, and Fred gathered me a bunch of violets, wild, and Travys talks lots about flowers. Is delighted when he gathers a bunch of wild ones. At present Travys is very much interested in a gang of little chickens. He loves Mary better than any of the rest does. Ralph is deeply in love with Ghu. He doesn't pay me scarcely any attention since Mary came. He is perfectly devoted to Ghu and cries after him when he is at work and Ghu often spanks him, on this account (sometimes too much I think) but Ralph is perfectly devoted to him. Travys was Mama's favorite and he talks till tears run down my face about going where grandma is. Travys has taken 2 rides with our mail-carrier—a rank stranger to him—Andy Castellow is his name.

< April 15 >

Baby Mary is one of the most nervous, wide-awake babies I ever saw. She worries me nearly to prostration almost every day of her life. I am rocking the cradle now while I try to write. She allows me no past-time. She sleeps only cat-naps, some days no naps—and I am worried almost beyond endurance. So much going undone. Sallie [Wynn] has been here nearly 6 weeks. She and I together get three meals a day—baby is so awful cross that oftimes Sallie cooks a meal alone. If she had not been with us the past 6 weeks things might have been worse than they are in the housekeeping line.

Mary is extremely nervous—at 5 weeks old a loud thunder-clap caused her to scream out quite loud—so loud as to be heard down in other part of the house. She is 7 weeks old now and I never, in all my experience with babies, saw one at her age laugh and coo so much. It is almost strange how loud and how much she coos. I almost get uneasy at times—fear it is an omen of ill to her.

Ralph, poor little thing, is so neglected since Mary came. My heart goes out to him but I can't do any more than I am doing with my cross baby and weak strength. I sometimes fear Ralph will be so neglected that sickness of serious nature may occur. Today he is very sick—taken suddenly with high fever and pale. What ails him I do not know. He was out in wind bare-headed too much yesterday I think. On colder days tho' he was out and no serious effects afterwards. Poor Ralph—how I do wish I could devote more time to him.

Askew has the mumps—as yet they have not given him very much trouble. He was very proud of them the first day of his sickness, but next day he looked sick and had fever and wasn't at all proud of them.

Travys is anxious to take them. He is a big Interrogation Point! Travys claims all the roses that are opening now and is stingy with them. When I made Fred a bouquet to carry to school this A.M. and 4 or 5 roses in it, Traviss complained and said he only gave me permission to pull 2 for Fred and later on in the forenoon Misses Babe and Mat and Meetsie C[hilds] came by on their way to family burial ground and went to the rose bush and Travys objected and protested. The rose bush is a famous one for its size. It is the largest one I ever saw in my life. The house protects it. It was Mama's bush for about 11 years. We brought it to her when we moved here. Now it is a wonderfully large bush and the tallest one people who visit here ever saw. It is commented on by all who see it. I call it Mama's rose bush, as I did in her life time.

Fred is going to school this week by himself—(Askew has mumps and can't go) and he is a cute little boy. He learns *fast*. He carried a ginger-cake man with him today. Sallie made it and called it Sir McKibben. I made T. and A. one.

‹ May 6 ›
Thursday

Traviss put on pants this week and bid his dresses goodbye. He felt that he had suddenly grown very large and was of much more importance when he put on pants. Travys has been taking rides with our mail-carrier Mr. Andy Castello. Yesterday Mr. Castello brought him a little sack of the best kind of fancy candy.

Mary is little over 2 months old and has never been weighed. We weighed the others, except first one, at birth and occasionally afterwards. Somehow our only girl (living) has been neglected on that line. She is an exceedingly spoilt baby—never lies down unless asleep without crying as hard as she can, (except just occassionally a very few moments) and she tires me beyond description. It is such confinement, as well as bodily fatigue, to nurse little babies; I keep her nearly all the time in a dark room, i.e. with light suitable to her eyes, and so don't get much fresh air.

Mary will never know anything about a grandmother. My Mama died 10 or 11 days after Mary was born. Ghu's mother died about one or two months before she was born.

‹ May 9 ›

Mary is over 2 months old—a very sweet baby, except that she is so spoilt that she cries all the while, unless someone holds her on their laps etc. Sometimes no one can pacify her but myself, hence I get on slowly with household tasks. She is a healthy baby; has good use of herself, laughs a good deal—almost a perpetual smile. Has been cooing nearly all her brief life and laughs out loud.

Ralph is awfully spoilt—seems to think, ever since Mary came, that he belongs very little to me and very much to Ghu. Ralph follows Papa around a good deal—to get up eggs and around the yard and stays very close about him in the house. Papa pays Ralph great deal of attention. Papa calls him Charlie all the time. It is an interesting picture that I see daily; an aged man (nearly 83) and a little boy, not quite two years old, walking about and daily companions.

Traviss talks *great* deal about setting hens and chickens generally. One day Papa told him that he had some choice eggs (PR's

[Plymouth Rocks]) in his closet and as he talked so much about setting hens, he believed he would set (Traviss) on a box of those in his closet. Then he asked Traviss "what do you suppose you would hatch?" Travis answered "a crowd of little boys." We all told Travis not to set them as we had a plenty of little boys already. Later on Travis said he would hatch some little girls too and that he would not have to set but 2 days; that all the little boys here were Papa Ghu's and that he would hatch me out some little boys. He talks as if he thought he could set on the eggs and hatch out little boys sure enough. He has seen 3 winters; was 4 years old in Feb. last.

Ralph will be 2 years old last day of this month and can't talk, but is learning rite fast past week or 2 to say words. He can't connect more than two—the other children talked as plain at 10 mo's as Ralph now talks. He is very devoted to Ghu—especially so since Mary came—goes to sleep with his arms around Ghu's neck nearly every night. He is so cross that Ghu very often spanks him but he clings to him all the same.

< May 29 >

Papa stays out this warm weather around or near buggy shelter most of the time. I think he grieves so over Mama not being with him in the house, is why he does it. My little boys stay with him most of the time; Ghu has made Fred and Askew chop a little cotton. Askew doesn't like to chop—Fred does well at it. Sallie made Fred a pair of gloves today to wear when chopping and Traviss cried because she didn't make him some. Traviss talks about birds very much—calls a female jay—"the mammy Jay-bird" and the male "the old daddy bird." He watches them feed their young with much interest. He hunts birds nests—never harms them. He has been talking "birds" from morn till night last week. Papa procured an empty nest and put it up in an apple-tree in front yard and fooled Traviss. Fred found out that his Grand Pa had put it there and "let the cat out of the wallet." Sallie . . . stays here now and she and all the little boys went strawberry hunting this P.M. Traviss sleeps with Sallie most of the time. She is somewhat nervous about sleeping alone and glad to have him share her bed.

Mary was 3 months old last Friday and for first time in her life, she was weighed (that day) and weighed nearly 15 lbs. I ordered her a baby carriage last week but haven't received it yet. She is spoilt — cries so hard when I put her down to do any work most of the time.

I had my Mama 35 years. Was 35 not many days before her life ended. I miss her so. The home, without her presence, seems sadly liking. How strange that she is never more to be one of our household number! How short the last year of her life seemed to us. She had been low a year before she left us and was spared a few short months to us. How we miss my aged mother! How lonely Papa is without her. No one can tell. She was one of the best of mothers: a sacrificing, true helpmeet as a wife — a gentle, devoted grandmother — yes, such a beautiful *deep* love was hers for children. I trust each and all of us will meet her in a Home Above and all of us be reunited there where no separations come. Her nature was so sunny. Her love for children so deep. She was a great lover of flowers too. Her chief work was raising and caring for chickens and just few days before going to bed (never to be able to walk again) she caught her pet chickens that she had so tenderly cared for, put them under a basket (Christmas was almost here) to kill during Holidays for her children and grand-children. She talked lots in her last days of going to see Anna. She had a great desire for Alf (her grandson) to carry her to see Anna.

< June 1 >

Ralph was 2 yrs. old yesterday (Mary 3 mo and a week) and he is small to his age. Has big feet, legs large enough, but not proportioned. He is learning to talk — connects two or three words now. Travys is cute and bright now, as a little boy — don't know how he will be as he grows older. Travys and Fred will repeat their prayers after me when convenient for me to see them off to bed, but am sorry to think that Askew doesn't say his — if so I don't know it. All of them used to, but Askew was not as easy to become willing as other[s] were. Hope each one will be Christians even while children. Ralph is more trouble than any of our children — has always been. Yesterday he spilled my ink (making 2 bottles of ink he has upset) — pulled a chair up to table and got in chair and blackened things generally where my ink stand was.

‹ June 14 ›

Travys was first one to put flowers on Mama's grave. He put water in an oyster can and filled it with yellow lillies one Sunday A.M. and in the P.M. put them in buggy when he started off to Sunday School; after he arrived there (in company with Ghu, Sallie and other children) he carried them to graveyard and put them on Mama's grave.

Ralph can say words much better now—join a few. He hurt himself (trying to carry it) with an iron this P.M. and said "heavy," "heavy" (meant it was too heavy for him to carry).

‹ June 25 ›
Saturday

Papa had a tomb and monument put at Mama's grave today. Mr. Middlebrooks put it up (bought it from him) and I'm to go over tomorrow P.M. to see it. How her presence is missed in this home! What a self-sacrificing soul she was! How homesick I feel for her presence!

‹ June 27 ›

We (Ghu, Charlie-Ralph, "Mary-baby," and myself) went over to New Hope cemetary yesterday P.M. The monument at Mama's grave is *very* pretty—the prettiest in the cemetary. How I've missed her today.

Papa sits out under the shade trees, below buggy shelter most of the time during the day. I never knew him to stay there in her life-time. I think he misses her so sadly, that he prefers to stay out doors from such loneliness in the house where he spent so much time with her and where she was so accustomed to staying. She stayed indoors more than most people do I think.

We went up to Mr. Ingram's awhile after leaving the cemetary. Mrs. I is a good woman—a friend. She has a baby 8 days older than Mary. Walter I. rolled Mary and Mrs. I['s baby] good deal—both together—in Mrs. I's baby carriage.

Mary was 4 months old few days ago. She weighed 15 lbs. I weighed then 152 lbs. Mary is a plump little thing—fat enough but small frame—the smallest for her age and at birth of any of our little brood. She has only one name yet. I like the name of Woods (for Dr. Woods), Wynn, Jim, or James (for Papa) or Vashti for Mrs. Leguin, but so far have decided on nothing but Mary and that was decided on before she was born, if the baby was a female, to be named Mary.

Mary has on long clothes yet—today, for first time, she has on only dress and napkin, and she kicks, gets her feet bare (first time I ever let them go uncovered many moments) and she enjoys kicking splendidly.

< July 2 >

(Saturday)

Mary has been wearing short clothes few days. The first town Mary ever went to was McDonough (at 4 mo's old). She wasn't a good baby in town. "Papa Ghu" kept her while I traded and couldn't keep her amused. Today is a red-letter day for Travis and Fred; they have gone to High Falls with Ghu (Sallie went also) and it is Travis' first visit to the Falls and Fred's second. They talk more of going to the Falls than anywhere. Askew is anticipating a G O O D time at High Falls next week with his Grand Pa. (Papa will go next week if well enough to make the trip). Papa calls Ralph "Charlie" (for Bro. C) and Askew does it too. Ghu says he wishes we all had begun calling him that and he and I would like to call him "Charlie" just because Papa does; and Papa is so fond of Ralph and so good to them all. When Papa gets sick I can easily detect an inexpressible sadness in his manner toward the children—thinking of leaving them; he doesn't want them whipped—feels sad at thoughts of a time when he will have to leave them.

Poor Mama! She manifested a like feeling, when just before taking her bed (little over a year ago—her next to last spell) she knew that she was going to get down and never expected to get up again and one day picked Travis up in her arms (as she sat by fire in big arm chair) and kissed him tenderly with quivering lips and eyes dimmed with tears; then pressed him long and warmly to her breast and the meanwhile saying some endearing words to him. But that precious Grandmother has left little Travis. "Calm she sleeps beneath the stone" while "Grandpa" wanders here without her, sighing for her companionship. He was so constantly in her thoughts. I wonder if her spirit doesn't often visit our house? Some days I miss her sorely. The clock in her room seems to speak of her absence; she had wound it up and set it for so many years. I think of her often when I hear it strike.

Ralph is 2 yrs and 1 month old. *Very* backward about talking. Ralph tries to talk but doesn't talk plain at all. Travis talks of birds, their nests etc and of chickens, eggs, etc. He picks up most of the eggs and puts them in a box in "Grandpa's closet" to keep me from cooking them and buys candy with some of them from a chicken peddler who passes here each week. (Papa makes him think he can buy candy with all the eggs but when peddler comes on I buy needed articles with some that he has collected). Travis is a very sweet, inno-cent, little boy. Easy to make believe things—He is easily controlled; has a warm heart, a sweet, sunny disposition. He was his grandma's favorite. . . . Askew is his Grandpa's favorite. Askew is thoughtful and good to his grandpa; sleeps with him and waits on him and stays around him so much. It is a beautiful trait in dear little Askew (Askew is 9 now). Fred is a clever little boy too—minds very well—all of us.

< July 16 >

Saturday

Ghu carried Sallie, Askew, and Fred to Sardis today to "Children's Service." They told Travis that he couldn't go and so he stayed sat-isfied. While he would have been glad, yes delighted, to have gone, he contentedly stayed, knowing all could not go. Ghu carries them often, but not all together, they divide. Recently he carried Askew, Travis, and Ralph to Locust Grove on a waggon. He went after meat. He had a great deal of trouble with them—lost the gate in back of waggon going in, and on way back home lost sack of meat. When he would be compelled to a get a little way from Ralph, he would get excited, thinking his Papa was going off and leave him, and my! how we would cry. Otherwise he said Ralph was real sweet and that he enjoyed having Ralph with him if he did have trouble. Ralph cries

good deal and isn't old enough to make mind and two babies are
a great deal of trouble—with much else to see after, it is at times
very overtaxing, but I pray God's care over us and His help with the
management of our little ones and my work. Sometimes my body is
so tired (Chronic backache and nervous) that the days drag wearily
(from being overtaxed) but there are pleasures too, mixed, and blessings always if we only look for them. I love to work for them. I
delight to sew iron etc etc, but until precious little Mary gets older
many things will be overtaxing. Ralph is learning to connect words.
Doesn't call words (not many at least) plain, or distinct. He is funny.
He follows his Grandpa daily. Papa . . . is so good to all the little
boys. Ghu often carries them all in bathing—that is a treat to them
all. Askew and Fred started to school at New Hope Monday. I think
Fred will learn rite fast. He loves to go over his lessons with "Papa
Ghu" at night and we see that he is learning.

< September 22 >

What a summer we've had! Sickness since June. Ghu, first, had a
spell of bilious fever. His attack was bad. He had some strong symptoms of typhoid fever and I was never more uneasy in my life! So
afraid he would take typhoid fever and die; but one night (late in
the night) he told me he thought he was going to have a bad spell
of fever, and gave me directions about a negro to wait on him and
told me to charge some things to the hands they had been getting
[free?] etc etc. Then told me "not to worry about him" (in a voice
that bespoke emotion) that "the good Lord was not going to let him
be taken away from me." Well he spoke so *assuring* that a load was
lifted, but I had another worry—my strength was fast giving way
and I wondered what I would do! I feared I couldn't possibly stay up
and nurse him thro' and nurse baby too. I didn't have any nurse, but
Aunt Mary was cooking snacks for family and I waiting on Ghu and
baby. I lost so much sleep and worried so over Ghu's illness that the
trouble was heavy—Sallie went home while he was sick. Protracted
meeting began while he was sick. What a load of trouble I had! The
heaviest I believe I ever experienced. Next I had a light attack of bilious fever, and before I could sit up, Travis was taken; he was sick
longer than Ghu or I, but the greatest trouble and deepest was when

Ghu was sick. I feared when I was sick that my sweet baby would be sadly neglected. We had, during my illness, a bad negro girl (about 16 or 17) to nurse Mary; I hired Susan Tarpley (or rather Ghu did) to take care of Mary and feed her 3 days. We could not keep her longer. But God was good to us and my sickness was not more than 17 days in bed and little Mary got on better than I expected and quite soon sufficient milk from maternal fount provided her. She is 7 months old now and very peart—a very good sweet baby. Travis is getting better fast. Ghu has suffered with neuralgia and other things ever since he got up—yet he is working *awful* hard and I am so uneasy at times about him yet. He works so hard and not physically able to work but very little.

< October 4 >

Baby's Name

What sweet name to fit our pet,
Dorothy or Margaret,
Alice, Gladys, Susan, Joyce.
Katherine, Jean, or Rose for choice,
Faith or Phyllis, Helen, Grace,
Which fair name to match her face?
Mildred or Penelope?
Ah, a puzzled group were we.
Long we chatted, wondered wrought,
Racked our brains in solemn thought,
Scanned the poets one by one,
Knew no more than we had done.
Then, we said, the little elf
Surely yet will name herself.
But, again, what was not fair,
And with many wistful prayer,
We picked out a name of love,
Sweet all other names above,
And, to suit our winsome fairy,
Chose to call the babe, Mary.

(Margaret E. Sangster, in Every Where)

Mary is smaller than any of our babies ever were at her age (7 months) but she is well and very playful. Fred helps me with her for 25 cts a week. He and Travis roll her out about the cotton house and bales of cotton every P.M. lately and she sits still in her carriage and watches them play. Ralph thinks he is as large as Fred or Travis. He is learning to talk, but slowly. Papa is such a good "Grandpa." He is so kind to them all; he notices little Mary's cute ways now occasionally. He says these children are as near to him as his own—that he sees no difference (All born and thus far raised in his home) and not long ago I had a bad character (a negro girl) to nurse for me. She spoke of slapping Ralph over and Papa overheard her and he came and told me and he, as well as I, gave her a *straight* talk. She left the next day. I would have dismissed her ere then but sickness—so much of it—in the home, and I, unable, to see after baby.

These are busy days. Ghu as busy as can be from dawn till dark. We get up about 4 every morn and retire early; both busy and tired out. He and Askew picking cotton—I cooking, nursing, sewing, sweeping etc and how the days glide by and I get such little time to read and how *hungry* I am, so often, to read; most that I do read, is when so tired I can't retain it much. Maybe when Mary begins to walk I can have some leisure. Askew picked one hundred and nine lbs of cotton yesterday. Ghu picks nearly 200 every day—he loves picking cotton. He has to work so much this fall when sick because he had only 2 negroes to help him gather his individual cotton crop. . . .

< October 12 >

Mary is 7 months old (and little over) and when I say "pat the cake" she will so cutely pat her sweet little hands. She looks so inexpressibly sweet when she does that little trick. She is an unusually pleasant baby—smiles and has a bright face—laughs lots. She is most always bright and laughing until near night; I have more trouble with her then than any other time of day. She is not easily pacified—no one can successfully quiet her then except myself. She loves "Papa Ghu"—cries after him. She has begun to watch Papa . . . now when he is near her. He thinks she is cute and often says something to her and sometimes "chuckles" her chin. He doesn't become warmly attached to children, usually, before they begin to walk. Fred helps me better with Mary than I thought for. Askew and Travis are fond of picking cotton and pick well—Travis remarkably well for his age (four) and Travis sticks to it well, says he is "picking for money." Ghu pays them. They are going to take care of most of their money and buy something that they need with it.

It is a funny sight to see Ralph toddling along a-w-a-y behind Ghu (when Ghu goes to milk), with a small tin cup and a wee basket of cotton seed. When he gets there he gives his favorite cow, "Beauty," the seed, pours water out of the cup on the ground (will *not* go without water) and then has milk from Beauty put in his cup; drinks as much as he wants and then brings cup as full as he can bring without spilling to the house.

A chicken peddler . . . comes by here ever Friday morning and always stops here. All the little boys look eagerly forward to "the peddler's day" and Papa . . . for past-time, saves them eggs in a wooden box in his closet, to buy candy from the peddler with. Papa enjoys the pleasure they have in buying and eating candy.

We (Fred, Travis, Mary and I) went down the gin-branch yesterday eve and stayed an hour or more. My strength isn't sufficient in warm weather to take these walks which I love so much. Mary never rode so far in her carriage before—would always cry before when pushing her only a short way. Yesterday we used a parasol that belongs on her carriage for first time (she little over 7 mos) being the first time we had ever needed it. She enjoyed the ride splendidly, and the trip was pleasant—she loved the woods, the water rippling over rocks.

October 16

Many changes have taken place since I wrote in my diary last and tho' it is a pleasure for me to write—I have such little time for it.

My Mama died since I wrote in this book last. How we miss her—no words can express. How precious the memory of her. Everything seems to speak of her. *She never went from home much* and so strange her room and our home seems without her. How lonely Papa is: he sat out under shade trees most of the time this summer; when she was here (the last few years) they were almost inseparable and I suppose the house without her seem lonelier than to sit out in open air. How every change of the seasons bring forcibly to memory thoughts of Mama! Every flower about the yard (she loved them so!, watered and tended them) and the chickens (which were *all* hers) were her special care. How they remind us of her. When people come to see us, especially kinfolks, how we think of her. Her aged and bent form, her worn hands, her sad, sad face—all come so vividly to memory (after she was taken sick this time her face look so inexpressibly sad.) God help me to live in discharge of my whole duty and sanctify the tender and painful memory of Mama to the good of my soul is often my prayer—and farther I pray often that the painful memories may make me especially good to others to atone for any unthoughtfullness toward her.

Mary, my only girl (except first born in Heaven) came to brighten my life just about 10 or 11 days (or maybe 12) before Mama's life went out. I named Mary for Mama. How sweet she is!

How my life is Filled and Overflowing with cares. No time to *think* [or] *read* much or write much. I have a chronic weak back that pains me so much when I work—in fact *all* the time only at night. Two babies to care for! While I love them, yet my cares nearly run me, as the saying goes "wild" often times. Back aching allways and Ralph cries *so* much all this year and is so self willed and so many demands made upon me that I can't fill for lack of strength and for a little while "blues" almost overcame me today.

This is Sunday and I am so tired—can't write or read without being disturbed.

Sallie . . . stayed 5 (five) months here this year. She came rite after Mama left us. Sallie agreed (with Ghu and Papa) to come and help me with my household work and Papa and Ghu were to clothe her. She wasn't willing to help me with all of it, and so I troubled myself almost into sickness because she would be offended about our work, with me.

Ghu was taken down with fever and Sallie went home in about 2 days after he took his bed. I was so sorry that she had unfriendly feelings toward me. I have seen trouble, and a good deal of it, about it. Ghu's sickness was one of the darkest and hardest places I ever passed thro' in my life. He was so sick that he and I both thought he would have typhoid fever and I thought he would die, if he took that kind of fever untill one night (away late) he told me (in a trembling tone) he was going to have a bad spell of fever and for me not to worry; the good Lord was not going to take him from me; he seemed to have such assurance from the Lord that he would not die, that helped me—but other troubles during his sickness nearly prostrated me. I thought I was going to get down before he got up and was so afraid he would be seen after properly but tho' I was weak indeed, I *drug* along and gave him every dose of his medicine, attended all the while to Mary and all by myself to him. The strain mentally and physically was one of the greatest of my life. After his sickness I had a light spell of same fever, but not near so bad as his tho I was longer in getting out of bed. Before I would sit up Travis had a spell and his was worse, a good deal than mine, but no trouble to compare with Ghu's sickness came with mine and T's.

< October 23 >

Sunday

What a G-L-O-R-I-O-U-S month October is to me. How it thrills me and fills me with joy and life, as perhaps no other month in the year! I have no strength (comparitively speaking) in warm weather and how gladly I welcome the s w e e t month of October. It *always* fills my mind with happy thoughts and my heart is thrilled with joy when this month enters. When a girl I experienced the same preferance for the lovely October month. I feel as different as if I were another person when warm weather passes and October comes in. Thank the Giver of all good and perfect gifts for the month of October.

I went with Ghu to church yesterday, and today Askew, Mary, Travis and I all went in buggy and Ghu rode horseback. Askew persuaded Ghu to let him ride horse back home and the horse is a very swift footed one and Askew soon fell off, horse ran so fast he couldn't possibly stay on or check the horse. I was badly frightened—afraid he would get killed. He wasn't hurt much however.

Papa Ghu kept Mary so that I could hear the entire sermon, both yesterday and today. I have had no chance to go to New Hope before in a long time and I enjoyed the sermon and seeing and speaking—handshaking with my friends.

Travis has his first "bought suit" (as he calls it) of clothes; this summer when he had fever Ghu and Papa gave him some money which he kept by him in bed until his recovery. Papa . . . gave him a dollar and Ghu remainder. Travis paid two dollars for his clothes — Ghu adding 50 cts. T. is very proud of his first suit of ready made clothes. . . . Such an everlasting talker is Travis! And such an interrogator! None in family (of the children) talk so much as he or asks so many questions. He is a big ?.

< October 31 >

The last day of my favorite month. Farewell October 1904. You brought me more happy thoughts than any month of the year. My life is such a busy one. No time to think, to plan; no leisure (to amount to much) no day. Read a *little* occasionally; seldom write this year. Never catch up with work but maybe when Mary gets to walking I can *think* more and plan more. Tired! Tired!! Tired!!! Such a weak back — all the time, more or less weak (and now have a new brace to try strengthen it some) but I guess this is something like the experience of every mother — no rest till baby can walk. A nurse we have not — Fred and Askew help amuse her some but only when I'm busiest — they can not render help that I need with Mary. Too small, I don't care much for a nurse either as I would be compelled (if I possibly could) [to] sew for them and they are all more or less troublesome and somewhat expensive.

Mary is bright and happy if with me — is naturally a sunny baby — almost always laughing when with myself or "Papa Ghu." She is the pleasantest baby we've ever owned; she is also the most animated one so far. She is in motion all the time when awake.

Travis asked Papa this question, a few days ago: "Grand Pa, why does Mama call you Papa all the time?" I guess he thought I should call him Grand Pa. Mary is crying so much that I can't write.

< November 3 >

Papa is not as well as usual. I am sorry to see him feeling worse; he feels badly all the time, never free from pain — rheumatism and something like a partial paralysis, (which for severel years he has suffered with) with difficulty that perhaps none of us think how great, that he walks. He is the *best grandfather!* How unexpressibly good he is to all my children! How he loves them, Oh, so tenderly. He says he loves them as well as he did (and does) his own—said he didn't see any difference in them and his own. God gave my children two good friends—their Grandma and Granpa Wynn. When both are lost to them and us (one, Mama has gone) we will never find any to care for us as they did—no other one (except Papa Ghu) can approximate their love for us. Heavens choicest blessings rest upon my dear Papa—my little boys devoted Grand Pa—the remainder of his life and I pray God to spare him yet a long time with us, for life would never be the same without him. Something sweet went out of my life when my poor Mama went beyond. There is an empty place in our hearts and home since Mama went away that seems sadly strange and without her life seems something like a dream. How deep and beautiful was her love for my little children and for all childhood. How warm and tender her love was for us all—no one can love us just in the same way she did.

. . . Little Mary is a sunbeam shining daily in my life since Mama went away. I think I will add Wynn to her name. Then she will be Mama and Papa's namesake—both.

Ghu, Mary, and I went to Jackson this week and Mary took cold and is a little sick yet. Tho' 8 months old, 'twas her first bad cold. She has been a healthy baby. Dr. Butner, Johnnie Settles, and Lee Smith paid little Mary some attention that day. Dr. Butner told Ghu to take the "little lady" to a fire; that she was cold. Mr. Lee Smith tried to take her in his arms and show her something but she didn't like the stranger well enough to go to him. Papa Ghu has been in McDonough on the Jury for three days and last night, tho' late in getting away from McD. he came all way home in dark cold rain to see our little Mary who was rite sick and restless the night before. Papa Ghu is a devoted Papa and husband too. He is so good and thoughtful to his "sweetheart" (he calls me that) and little ones.

Askew and Fred, perceiving that if Papa Ghu came at all, it would be late, went with a lantern and fed cows and hogs. The bravest thing I ever knew Askew to do. Fred is a brave boy—for a year has at times slept willingly off in a room alone in dark (tho' only 7 yrs old). Travis is a great chatter box. . . . He is pretty, most people think him best looking one; he is loveable and sunny natured always, in a crowd, received more or less attention. Fred is a good boy in many respects; all are rite good children so far. I pray they will always be. Askew is remarkably good, kind thoughtful and obedient, to his Grand Pa. Askew is Papa's bed-fellow—and I declare the devotion that exists between the two is beautiful. (My) Papa has told me twice that he was going to give Askew his watch, that was my brother Splint's in his lifetime. One thing noticeable Askew does every night: just before getting in bed with Papa, he carries him a drink of water. Askew certainly loves his Grand Pa devotedly and his Grand Pa is certainly devoted to him.

Papa, recently, gave each of his children 50 dollars apiece (9 of us) and a few years ago he did the same thing.

< November 13 >

Sunday A.M.

This has been the dryest fall I remember ever knowing. More dry wells than I ever heard of. Farmers had no intermission in gathering crops—no rain to prevent constant cotton opening hence they were very busy. Seems to me that Ghu was busier than I ever saw him, and for a longer period.

My household cares (increasing family etc) has caused this to be the busiest year, in some respects, of my life.

Mary is 9 months and half old. She has no teeth, can't crawl but has had a bad case of measles—is just getting over them. She was a very sick baby until they broke out good; had awful hot fevers—from head to foot. She had taken violent cold from the exposure Papa Ghu gave her in Jackson and had been sick before taking measles, hence they "went for her."

We dread for Ralph to take them—he is obstinate and we fear he will suffer from exposure.

When Travis had fever this Summer, his Grand Pa and Papa Ghu gave him money occasionally and he told his Grand Pa, yesterday, that when he took the measles he was going to keep his pocket book in bed with him, and asked me how much money I thought he would get when he took measles?

‹ November 23 ›

The day before Thanksgiving! Askew has broken out with measles today—has been sick about 4 days. I don't think he will enjoy our Thanksgiving dinner tomorrow.

Mary is looking well, since she recovered from measles. She is real lively—always laughing, jumping and kicking. She is the liveliest baby we've ever been blest with—a veritable sunbeam. A *very* sweet baby is she.

Ralph—now two years and half old—has learned to talk. He has just lately learned to talk in a sentence or to connect words. He was the only slow one in that respect, and Ghu and I began to be afraid he would be long time yet, talking.

Travis corrected Papa yesterday. Papa spoke of his ears and called them "years" (said he didn't think Travis would know what he meant, if he called them years) and Papa was amused at T. correcting him and told us (Ghu and I) about it. Papa told T. not to correct him before company. Papa said T. was a rite smart of a curiosity.

Papa says Fred is the best boy here. Says he has known it sometime. Papa is a devoted Grand Pa and a dear Parent. He loves devotedly our children; while he is inexpressibly fond of all—yet I think Askew is his favorite. He is wonderfully attached to Askew and Askew is more careful to obey Papa and more attentive to his wants and needs than he is to Ghu's or mine and we are glad that he is so attentive. Papa gave each of his children 50 dollars this fall.

Papa says "Mary is a mighty good baby." Says "she is mighty like her Mammy when she was a baby" and says she is now "like her Mammy."

Fred is good to keep Mary—while I eat—at times—when he hasn't eaten himself. Sweet little Fred. I hope to possess and retain the love of each one of my children, long as I live.

All of our children are deeply attached to Papa Ghu. He is an affectionate parent and they love him apparently more than they do myself; i.e. Fred, Ralph, and Askew do; Travis is more devoted to me than they are. Mary loves me best now, but my! how she loves him and cries for him to take her, and she is perfectly satisfied with him unless hungry. She loves him—like the other children—dearly.

November 25
Friday P.M.

My Diary:

I haven't time to write — am leaving sewing undone to scribble now — needed sewing too. I *love* to write.

Yesterday was Thanksgiving day. How many memories it brought to my mind of my dear Mama, who was with us last year at this time. I felt all day that Papa was thinking of her too. She was strong on my mind. How I missed her. Our first Thanksgiving dinner without her. How the change of seasons do remind me of her; sad, sad, sad. Nothing is sweeter than the memories of her. Now that she is gone; the depth and warmness of her hearts affection for me . . . stands out so clearly. *No love like a mother's love.* No one can love me as she — just in a mother's way.

I so often feel, if she were only back that I would do many things to try to cheer and brighten her life, that I did not think of before she went away.

God forgive me for neglectfullness of such a treasure as my old time-worn weary Mother. Do, oh God, blot out all my sins of omission and commission toward her as far as east is from west and help me bear patiently any neglect I may encounter from relation or friend; because of what I now so plainly feel was my neglect of her. And help me to be a special blessing to Papa during rest of our sojourn together. It would have been her wish that I see carefully after him. Thus did she — yes anxiously did she see after his welfare for years — always — I believe — since they became man and wife, but so much so since each became old. And too, to atone for what I see was neglect of my poor love hungry mother, I would like to be a comfort, a warm friend to all old ladies. . . .

Well, to return to Thanksgiving day. I asked Miss Babe and Miss Mat Childs to eat with us. They were among Mama's warmest friends. Mama wanted them to eat with us so badly last year on Thanksgiving day. She was anxious for them, but some how they didn't come. So in memory of Mama, or for love of her, they were invited yesterday. I wonder if Mama's spirit wasn't with us all yesterday? I almost felt like her presence was here. It seems so strange for Mama not to be here when Miss Babe comes. And about the time the first table finished eating Anna (Jarrell), Mary and Faith drove up. It was another strong reminder of Mama. She would have been so glad for them to have come on that day, had she been living. Anna was so much in Mama's thoughts. She loved her and sympathized with her so warmly.

The last two years of Mama's life, she seemed to study more about Anna than any of her children. And the last 2 years of her life she craved to go there—didn't talk of going anywhere else except there, only once, and she went with Miss Mat up to Mr. Bogue Childs, just a short while before she was taken sick. She talked often of "going to Anna's" and planned to go. She stayed away on account of Papa—did feel so anxious about him couldn't get her consent to leave him; sometimes weather was too rough when wanted to go and for a good while she was waiting for Alf [Wynn] to take her. She looked week after week for Alf to carry her to Anna's; he promised to do so, and when she was taken sick she asked time after time, "I wonder why Alf did not come and take me to Anna's." For two whole years she craved to go there, and planned to go and talked of going. Mama put up a jar of muscadine hull preserves—cooked them herself—she put up two, but one of them she put out time after time to be eaten here on table; the other jar she never opened. I think she was saving to eat from when her children came or maybe intended giving it to Anna—just like Mama's hands left it. In loving memory of Mama I am going to try give Anna some little things as often as convenient. I am sure Mama would have liked me to do so. In loving remembrance of Mama and in Mama's stead I want to save Anna some milk and butter and other little things when convenient. Dr. J doesn't feel kindly towards me because I live in house with Papa and he is afraid I will get something and because we have Dr. Woods to do our practice, but when I can I am going to do what I know Mama would have liked me to have done toward Annie.

< November 27 >

Sunday

Little Mary has a T-O-O-T-H, an under one—a very new one—just discovered last night at supper table. Papa Ghu took Mary in his lap to relieve me while we were eating supper (I had been busy and had a back ache—very tired) and he was giving her buttermilk

from a tumbler and everyone at the table except Papa . . . heard a
little tooth hitting against the tumbler. When Ghu put the glass to
her mouth she would bite the rim so we heard a little tooth "tink"
"tink" against rim and Papa Ghu heard the "tink" "tink" first. She
was 9 months 7 days old and this is her first tooth.

Another new occurrence in the little Girlie's life—she sat alone
2 days ago quite a good little bit, on a pallet; first time she had ever sat
alone. She sits in baby carriage so much that she has been backward
about sitting alone.

I can't leave the room satisfied and leave her with the little boys,
unless she is in baby carriage where she can't get so cold, or get near
the fire. She can crawl or slide a few ft. now when left on a pallet.

Ralph says and does funny smart things that I'd like to record here.
Papa pays him much attention.

Mary is very much in love with Papa Ghu. How could she help it?
He is a good Papa and tho' we've been married 12 years he doesn't
forget or lay aside some of his love-like ways; he brings me a sack of
fancy candy often and a bunch of flowers.

< November 29 >

Last Sunday (Fourth Sunday in Nov.) was our 12th year of married life. I love Ghu stronger each year and now with all these little
folks, I am *so dependent* on him. Time flies. In 12 more years we will
be on the shady side of life. 'Tis so sad to think how fast these twelve
years have passed.

Ghu is *all* to me, except Papa. I have Papa yet. I wish to do my
whole duty by Papa and be a blessing to him in his last days. To Ghu
I wish ever to be a helpmeet.

Little Mary is 9 months (and a week over) and is learning to eat
just a wee bit, just began to eat a tiny bit [a] few days ago.

December 6

These are peculiar days I'm passing thro' now. My dear Mother
has gone—no mother to walk life's way with us—to keep our home
sunny—to cheer Papa. Papa is feeble. He feels and shows a depth of

sadness. Blessings brighten when about to depart. How sad the time will be when there is no longer a father to go on life's pathway with us. Yet on these things his thoughts dwell much, I am sure. Only yesterday he handed Ghu a large envelope and told him to go where I was and for Ghu and I to read it. We read his will. How sad, how sad! To think, that at longest, he can't be with us long. I trust tho' that for some years yet God will leave him with us. His children and *my* children (who've been born and reared in his home and with him all their life so far) will receive such a loss—a loss—a loss. He seems sad and so lonely without Mama. I pray daily God's spiritual blessings on his soul—and for him a home in Heaven.

Askew and Mary are over with measles and just now Fred, Travis and Charlie are very sick children—measles thick on them but they seem to have good deal of fever and are so sick they can't sit up much.

< December 6 >

Fred, Travis, and "Charlie-boy" are three sick children. Measles are *thick* on all three at once, but they are so sick they can't stay up—can't eat. Lying about, grunting [complaining] and sleeping some. They are what I call sick children. Coughing good deal and all look sad, quiet, and pitiful.

"Papa Ghu" is a dutiful parent—helps me with children more than almost any father that I know of. He waits on them quite as much as I—with their measles.

Ralph always says he is Papa Ghu's boy or baby and that Mary is mine. Little sunshine Mary loves Papa Ghu wonderfully now and cries after him.

< December 7 >

For about a week (going on ten months) Mary has been trying to tell the dog to get out. She makes a noise like this "Dout D-out." Travis, my sweet loveable little boy, is very sick with measles. He is the most lovable one of my little boys—a general favorite with friends and relations. He is a *very* innocent child. . . . I am sorry to see the little "Sunshine" so weak and feverish and quiet. He and

Fred and Ralph had them at same time and all three were very sick children but Ralph and Fred are up today walking over house, and my poor little Travis is very weak and sick and feverish—can't sit up in bed. Poor little Fred was very quiet and pitiful when at his worse—little Ralph was very sick and very cross. Ralph is extremely cross and so hard to keep in doors—out of draughts and by fires. We expected this as he has always been so obstinate. I am afraid he will expose himself until he will relapse.

Mary sits alone at last—9 mo and a little over. She is a bright baby—always laughing, jumping and playing antics of some kind. She seems so full of life—such a promising baby. Mary did a bright thing this P.M. for one her age—(for a 9 month old baby). I left a newspaper on her pallet, till a more convenient time to put away, and when I got thro' nursing Mary I put her down on top of news-paper and busied myself at something, when I was surprised to see her over on her stomach looking *intelligently* at a ladies picture, and laughing at it. She would look at me with her expressive eye to indi-cate that she saw a picture. I have never shown her a picture, and the news-paper just happened to be lying with a good size picture up-most (an advertisement for Pierce's Favorite Perscription). Fred was present and was surprised as well as I and exclaimed "She's looking at a picture!" I then had a Child's Picture Book brought to me and we (Ralph and I) showed her page after page and she looked at each. I *do hope* she will love pictures as well as I and that she will love to read as well.

< December 20 >

Little Mary is a very attractive baby—people are compelled to notice her. She attracts so much hearty laughter. I never saw any-thing her age to equal her. Nine (and little over) months old and laughs so heartily and loud that she can be heard all over the house. Papa . . . said she was so much like me that he wished he had a picture of me, when I were a baby; that no one would know that it was not Mary's picture. Papa laughs at Mary when she spreads her mouth and crackles so loudly and merrily. She laughs at pictures and tho' we began only last week to see her love for them, yet this week, she cries when the picture book is taken from her. She delights to have the little boys, or any one who will, turn leaves and show her the pictures. She crows, jabbers, jumps, and laughs gleefully over the pictures. She has two teeth now. Papa Ghu discovered each first. Papa Ghu says he is afraid I am going to idolize my baby Mary.

Ralph is getting more and more interesting—talks better—joins words—makes sentences. Shows a bright mind—a good memory if he was backward about talking.

Travis is a very gentle, innocent child. He is pretty. . . . He talks, talks about Santa Claus and says it is only 12 days now, till Christmas.

Askew thinks lot of Mary and of Ralph too. He helps me great deal with Mary although he or Fred soon tire of nursing and wouldn't help with her as much as they do if I or Ghu didn't make them.

1905

January 1
New Year. Sunday P.M.

Another New Year has dawned. O, what will it bring, joy, sorrow, sadness or sickness to me and mine?

The year that has just closed was one of a good deal of sorrow for me, much sickness and trouble in our home. Sallie stayed 5 months in our home and seemed so often to feel unkind toward me and I had to stand alone in need of one to take my part — when she proved false — Ghu took my part in one sense, but I felt that hunger in my heart for one who would take a bold stand for me when a friend proved false. Sallie has caused my heart to ache several months this year. And Papa while not taking a stand out right against me, sided with Sallie. Sallie was in error, but my Papa is encouraging her to treat me cool and unkind by giving her (soon he will give it) some nice furniture. The One above only knows how my heart aches and how I loose sleep on account of the coolness from Sallie. I was afraid for her to come over here to stay knowing she was prejudiced against me and prayed that if it was best that she would not come but Papa asked her to come and I've had to suffer ever since. This P.M. I went behind the garden and gave vent for a moment or two to my feelings — cried somewhat aloud and then prayed a few moments for the Lord to help me bear all the unkindness from that source as He would have me bear it. I haven't always been as thoughtful and kind to everyone as I should and I pray to bear all rebuffs and all unkindness and pray to be able to return good for evil and try to atone that way, for my shortcomings. Well, whatever this New Year has in store for me I pray the Lord to help me do his will with my life more perfectly than in years gone by.

Lil left here today — she, Esca and Leone — the new wee baby. Esca is a smart good child. Lil is very kind to me and I think will be on thro' life and I think a great deal of Lil. I believe she is my favorite sister tho I love Fan and rest. There is something more of a confidante between Lil and I than any of the rest of the family now — Fan is so far away (in La.). Lil is to move down S.W. Georgia, to Unadilla next week and we will be separated then and I am sorry. I've lived close at home for 8 years—Papa is feeble and I stay close—he doesn't have any idea how much I would enjoy going and is not on my side in trouble, but he believes he is right. Lord help me to do my whole duty—help me walk the lonely way—the way of sacrifice—the home concealed life—help me to live nobly.

January 2

Monday

"Be patient with your cares and worries. We know it is easy to say but hard to do. But you must be patient. These things are killed by enduring them, and made strong to bite and sting, by feeding them. A little while and you shall leave behind you the whole troup of howling troubles and forget in your first sweet hour of rest that such things were on earth. Never lose confidence that matters will come right in the end. The world is governed better than any of us could govern it. If we wait and labor we can not suffer beyond remedy."

I came across these helpful words today. I had copied them perhaps 3 years ago—they are words in season—as I had been brooding over "bothers" and I think these lines and other fine things in Home and Farm (which I've been reading this P.M.) are going to be a great help just now.

January 10

I feel, and have felt ever since day before Christmas blue, or depressed, so much so as to give way to tears some times. I work steadily and am so tired and never get through what I see needing to be done and I get nervous and overtaxed. I am not just well, and I reckon that is why I am more depressed than usual.

My thoughts constantly dwell on Sallie.

The One above, only knows the heartaches that Sallie has caused me—how prejudiced she was against me—how unkind were her feelings toward me. My ill health, my hard work, for the sons, daughters, grand children, relatives and friends (who visit my father now—and my parents in past) and the prejudice some had against me (they believe Papa gives me things or money) has made my life often times like climbing a mountain.

Papa does not give me anything only when he makes a general gift to each child—only then do I get a thing but none of the prejudiced ones believe that.

Sallie, I tried to be good and kind to, tho' I knew she was prejudiced. How unkind she treated me. I wonder if this New Year holds as much bitterness for me as the receeding one did?

Sallie said she would marry soon after Christmas.

Mattie Lou Smith said some cutting things when here day or so during Christmas. She insinuated that I tried or did *boss* Ghu. She never dreamed how she hurt me or what a mistake she made. I've never tried to "boss" Ghu—don't want to "boss," but have tried to influence him in ways that would add to the happiness of each of us. Then she referred to a book Ghu had given away as if he had unbeknowing to myself, given Olivia W[ilkins] a book—she seemed to think it all right if he did, and that it was because I would have objected, had I known—just blaming me—not Ghu. Ghu asked my permission to give Olivia the book and I assented readily—but book was given in Ghu's name.

I've known Mattie L. nearly all my life and she never hurt me so before. Three or four times during her short stay she by words and acts accused me of being "boss" or trying to "boss" Ghu and took what she thought was his part. She made my heart ache and Ghu was surprised at her view of me and he was displeased with her tho' we both treated her as though she had said nothing unkind.

Time after time, have I heard her take such views of married ladies, and known her to rebuke or disapprove of the wife and take husband's part or approve of him; in so many cases she speaks of husband as ruled by wife etc. when I do not see a thing to make her say so. I've often said she was not as true to her sex as she ought to be and her remarks were most unkind on this line, about other folks and I've always thought she made a grave mistake in this particular thing but so long as she didn't come to my home and to my face and insinuate these things against me it didn't hurt but my! how she stung me this time! I've prayed to overlook and not dwell on it. I've prayed much that I would feel no wrong toward any. A heart of peace with God and all mankind I want daily, hourly, all ways.

‹ January 13 ›

Mary is sick—has been for two or three days and nights. She is teething. Mary is nearly eleven months old (liking about seven days) and did her first real crawling today. She is very weak, fretful and quite sick; I thought it so strange she could crawl at all being so very weak. She had been sliding on her stomach a few steps, for some time, but today she crawled half across the room. She has fallen off good deal and looks weak and pale but makes attempts at playfulness for few moments now and then. Her nature is sunny and cheerful, bright and playful but poor baby—how she will suffer now on, occasionally, and maybe all this Summer—till thro' cutting teeth. The 2nd Summer is generally considered the hardest in life—deaths occur more during 2nd summer than any stage of life, I think I've read that from Mrs. Felton.

Ralph was threatened with croup last night and Fred the night before, and Mary *so* sick both nights, and Papa very sick night before and I too, with cold. So many of us sick at one time is a rare occurance. I am so weak today I can scarcely keep up.

‹ January 15 ›
Sunday Morning

Little Mary still not well, but cheerful tolerably. Papa was in bed yesterday and I was real uneasy about him. Am glad to see him up this morning. I thank Him who has prolonged his life so far, that Papa's strength is returning. This time last year my dear aged, mother was down in bed and in March left the home and us all; she had been such a home-concealed person—we miss her and feel strange that we are to go on thro' life without Mama—my little boys have no longer their affectionate, fond, Grand Ma. While she loved all, she was particularly and deeply attached to Travis. Travis favors her and Splint. How fondly she pressed him to her bosom with tears filling her eyes, when she got sick a year before she died. She thought she was soon to leave him. The picture I will carry thro' life of that scene.

And a year after, then only a few persons were know by her, in her last illness, she was aroused to consciousness by the prattle of Travis at her bedside talking to her—and again she clasp him over and over to her bosom and spoke endearing words to him and kissed him and cried out. Oh, what a picture—a sad picture that is hanging "on Memory wall": Another memory: not but a few days before she died she roused to consciousness enough to ask "Where is Mag?" and the nurses told her that "Mag is down in front room with a young baby." How the tears flow down my face when now I see those dear sad pictures on "Memory's Wall." How I miss her today. She was too good for us I know—us older ones—and what a *deep* devotion was hers to my little boys. May the memories of Mama be sanctified to make my life a better and more useful one while I go on without her—till united again where we will forever be together.

Papa . . . is a devoted Grand Pa. He is afflicted and 83 years old but patient and loving toward our children.

Little Mary never had a grandmother but few days. I think about 10 days after Mary was given us, her grandma died. Her Papa Ghu's Mother died awhile before Mama did, in La. Mary at present is devoted to Ghu for one so young; cries after him and sits so still and for a long time in his lap. He is mighty good to nurse her and often eats with Mary in his lap, because she pulls away out of my lap and crawls to him.

We have a picture of eleven kittens of many colors—one is buff or yellow—Travis calls that one a buff-cochen kitten.

The past few days Papa has been sick and Fred will untie and pull off his shoes for him without being told . . . and Papa appreciates it and compliments Fred on his thoughtfullness. Says "Fred is a good boy"—"the best boy here except three more."

Mary, I fear will be backward about talking because she is tongue-tied. Although her tongue has been clipped once, but was not clipped sufficiently. Dr. Woods thought it would take after being clipped when she cried and would not clip it enough to make bleed.

Memories of my Mother; "To Mama the voices of children were the sweetest music." She was always depressed when a little child cried. What a deep love she had for little children—all sizes of children. Her soul was thrilled at the sight of flowers. She loved Flowers passionately, although we never cultivated very many—her strength nor my own, being sufficient to work them and my time taken up with necessary, unavoidable duties. She loved bright sunshiny weather. She dreaded cold weather and snows—because her blood was so thin. She delighted in raising chickens—feeding, watering, and setting them and gathering eggs. This was her chief work the last few years of her life. She enjoyed sweeping yards around doors—this she did as long as she could get out. She could draw well—a natural talent— never cultivated, and she often drew pictures of boys, girls, houses, flowers, and birds for our children and the other grandchildren. She would often cut boys and girls from papers quite awhile to amuse grandchildren.

January 19
Thursday night

With a tired back, yes a tired body, I try to write in my diary or journal tonight. To write is a real pleasure to me, something I love deeply—were it not so, I would never try to write under these trying circumstances, namely: Mary pulling up by me and Ralph and Travis cutting such didoes around me. But my time is all taken up! My life is such a busy one, that unless I just write anyhow, I will never have a quiet leisure hour. . . . I love my work if I only could have a reasonable amount but my strength is so overtaxed almost every day that I am not the light hearted happy woman I would be, could I just have enough work for my strength. I long to be cheerful—pleasant etc etc but my strength is so overtaxed that I can't be the blessing to my children and husband that I otherwise would be. I *love* work— but my strength is not sufficient for the demands made upon it. I feel thankful for many things tonight: that my aged father is still with us; that husband and children are tolerably well and all in this world yet; that I am in the land of the living and able to do as well as I am. God help me to do the best I can and trust Him with all. (Now Mary and Ralph are tearing up everything in tray of my trunk) but I am so anxious to write awhile. I find my sweetest pleasure and only pastime in reading and writing. Somebody sent me two small monthly magazines called Family Doctor that are fine and I need the wholesome advise contained in them so much that I feel that Providence ordered them to me. One thing it teaches is to strive to be cheerful and think pleasant thoughts etc; to keep temper under controll, be calm etc etc.

I received a letter from Miss Delia Smith yesterday. Miss D's life and mine are so different—she having had (and still has) so many advantages that I never had that I have always felt that I was so *plain* that Miss D. could not be interested in me. Howsomever, she cared much for my brother Splint and I am going to answer her letter soon as I can. I enjoyed her kindness in writing to such a plain hard working home-concealed woman as I. I have felt since Christmas that I was somewhat snubbed by Mattie L. Smith and Olivia Wilkins. I wrote Olivia two (I believe) friendly little notes and sent her a new Delineator. She has not by word or note acknowledged the receipt of either notes or Delineator. Then when she was here Christmas I thought she acted as if I was of no interest to her. From now on, or at least the next time I am with her or M. L, they will be sociable toward me, if I do much toward sociable talk. Not that I am mad, but after so many of my advances being met with such apparant rebuffs, I will feel that they have enough of me—don't want my friendship. I shall not bear malice or act cold toward them. I wrote and sent each a pretty card during Xmas and no response tho' Mattie Lou is visiting Olivia now—ever since Xmas.

I reckon Lib is lonely since Joe and Alf married. Blanche Wynn spent last night here.

‹ January 20 ›
Friday Night

Mary was eleven months old today. She tried and succeeded in pulling up (and holding to trunk) and standing by my trunk today and once fell; bumped head hard, trying to stand by Ghu's; the lid was closed and she had nothing to hold on to.

Askew has begun to study Geography and enjoys it very much. I think Askew advances nicely in all his studies when I compare him to Hines and Owen Wynn, who started to school before he did—they are now in second reader; Askew in Fourth. Neither of them study Geography. Askew studies a book called English also. (Askew was 9 years old in Aug. last.)

Fred is learning to write a little; studies first reader. Fred is six years old—will be 7 next month.

Travis tries to do everything (that he can) that he sees Fred and

Askew do; they use tablets and today he had 5 cts and bought him one. Makes marks like this: ∿∿∿∿ and calls it writing. Travis wants to go to school very much. Fred reads well.

Papa pays Mary good deal of attention. He says often that Mary is pretty. Up to date Travis is prettiest one in our family; he has red cheeks, clear blue eyes and fair complection and favors my Mama and my brother Splint. He is the most innocent, trusting child of all (to his age), takes everything in dead earnest. He loves me better than the other little boys do; he is the only Mama boy among them. Charles is a decided Papa Boy. He often says I am Papa Ghu's little man.

‹ January 27 ›
Friday

Askew went to school today, after staying home two days on account of *very* cold weather—as cold as we generally have in this country. Askew isn't a healthy child, but learns fast. I've always been somewhat uneasy about him, because he has had catarrh nearly all his life. (Catarrh of head and gets hoarse, somewhat croupy, often; I suppose that is caused from catarrh too.) He has a pale face this winter. He advances nicely in his studies, I think. Compared him last Sunday with his cousin, Faith Jarrell; she has been in school much more regularly than Askew—is three months older—had all her school-days, advantages of Jackson Institute—and she and Askew are in same studies (except a different kind of arithmetic) and we've made another comparison; Hines Wynn (about 8 months older than Askew) started to school before A. did—and Hines is away behind—in 2nd Reader and A. in 4th. Askew is 9 years old; studies 4th Reader, Arithmetic, speller/word book, and Geography.

Ralph looks different from any of the children, acts different. He is the crossest, i.e. cries most—is bowlegged and falls almost "40 times a day." Never saw a child his age fall, such head-long, hard falls! He is neglected and that is why he cries I think—for more attention, more humoring or petting. I have two babies and a host of things to do—no one to do them but me, and can't, just can not give the children the attention they need often times, which I deeply regret.

Mary is a sun-beam! Her face is almost habitually wreathed in smiles. She is as fresh as a rosebud sparkling with dew.

Travis is pretty. He is a general favorite. He has pretty eyes, complection and hair. . . . He pays me more attention than any of the little boys so far.

Fred doesn't like to go to school and doesn't like to take care of Mary while I cook; in fact, none of the little boys like that job.

Papa gave Travis 5 cts. yesterday, to sit still 15 minutes. Awhile before Christmas he gave Askew 25 cts to sit still a certain length of time.

< February 1 >

February is here again! How many changes wrought in our home since this time last year. My Mama dead! My baby Mary here now— a namesake of Mama's. Mama left us March 1st. Mary came us Feb 20th on Ghu's birthday and in 2 days after my 35 (thirty fifth) birthday. How many sad memories we have on account of death's removing my aged mother. She, at this time last year was in bed and almost entirely unconscious. . . . The last time she recognized me she looked really glad to see me and seemed as tho' she felt it had been a long time since she had seen me. Her face lit up and she said "why, howdy Mag! it has been a long time since I saw you." But didn't know me many moments. If I mistake not she shook hands with me then. May we strike hands in a "Home Beyond" where there are no more partings and no more "Goodbyes." Oh, my heart aches when I think I might have been more to her—I didn't think often times of trying to help her over life's rough way and making her pathway as smooth as I now think I ought. I can now look back and see wherein I did not make her burden light as I now believe I could, and should, have done. No doubt her heart ached and longed for a warmer hearted companion that I proved to be. I lived too much absorbed in my own cares and worries to have been the sunshine and help to her that I believed her whole nature craved and longed for. My God, forgive me for not giving her a full share of love and sympathy, all the way our path was together. I think, now, that I understand the feelings of home-concealed old people, or old ladies especially better than I ever did before. The memories of my mother are sweet and sacred. I went in cemetary at New Hope last Saturday P.M. alone to be by my dear mother's grave. God help me to be kind and thoughtful to all old people and to patiently endure indifference from any who may treat me with such—to atone for what I failed to do in adding good cheer to my precious sweet Mother's life.

Mary is not well. Will be one year old in 20 days—has 2 teeth. She will not be well this year I'm afraid long at a time. The 2nd Summer is always so trying for Babies. I dread the coming of Summer for her. Poor little Mary! I fear there is much suffering in the year 1905 for you—for us both, but you, oh, little Mary, will suffer so before you cut your teeth—the 2nd Summer of baby's life is so trying—so much suffering to be endured. I trust little Mary will pull through, that I may have more strength than I usually have in Summers to nurse her with.

Askew cried this A.M. with toothache. His teeth have given him good deal of trouble. Fred too complains with tooth ache. Travys will be 5 yrs old soon and begs to be allowed to go to school.

< February 12 >

Sunday

King Winter has reigned this month! We've had two hard freezes —one following the other—before first had all melted another was on. Trees and everything covered with thick, hard ice; rain frozen on them. The vision as far as eye could see was one of loveliness and splendor to me. I imagined our country resembled those countries nearer N. Pole. Well *I* enjoyed it; 'twas a season of some rest for me, as I didn't cook meals "on time" and didn't have to rush with anything. One of the freezing days I gave most of my time to the children—cooked them ginger cakes and syrup candy and Papa Ghu popped a whole lot of corn, after supper, for them. (He is a dear fellow and helps me much when in doors. He often wipes dishes and helps get breakfast most every morning. He has done this ever since we were married, when I have no help. Then he wears a bright face and I feel more cheerful when he is around if I am blue.)

Yesterday (Feb 11th 1905) was Fred and Travis' birthday. Fred was 7 and Travis was 5. I baked them a birthday cake, a rice pudding, and a small rice custard (in old saucers) apiece.

Travis is very nervous. About 4 weeks ago he carried a negro woman a letter and a bad dog came near biting him thus scaring him nearly to death. Ever since then he has been extremely afraid at night to walk across the hall, or to go from one room to another. Ghu killed the negro's dog that frightened him so; the owner came rite on and told Ghu to kill it—that they could hardly prevent dog from biting Travis. When Travis came back from negro house he was crying and weak and his heart was beating wildly.

Well, we are still having Weather—a cold rain today and last night. Little Mary has a cold nearly all the time—a cough too now. I didn't think nursing babies ever had the croup but she has croupy coughs—and gets awful hoarse.

"God gives us but one mother." How true. How I miss the one He gave me. How unworthy I was of such a mother. I think of her daily. I miss her all the time. I miss her worse now than I did the first six months after she died. How sad to think she will never be with us again. She loved my little children so strong—so tenderly. Her heart was so wonderfully soft and her humility and meekness was manifests. Her worth I never fully realized till she was gone—gone forever. Life will never be the same again.

< February 13 >

Monday

This is a month of birthdays in our family. Ghu will be 35 on 20th and Mary 1 on the same day. I will be 36 on 18th and Fred and Travis celebrated their 7th and 5th on the 11th. Askew will be 10 next Aug. and Papa will be (if he lives) 84 in Aug.

'Tis a sad thought to me that I am in middle life now and going on the down-hill side. Sad, doubly sad, because I have not lived the 36 years in just the way I ought—a goodly part of it has been lived out of harmony with God's will. Had my life (the past) all been lived in sweet submission to God's will; had my spirit been sweet—had I always been patient, and my tones always kind then I would not so regret that I was going down the rounds of life's ladder. But the time

(35 years) is past—I can not recall none of those things—may God blot out all sins of my past life and may I, by his help so live in future that there will be no deep regrets, no remorse. I feel that I am not worthy of a home above, even tho' I live to be old and "do good" the balance of my days, but I trust the Lord will pardon and when life is over, that I may live a more perfect one in Heaven.

Ghu weighs more this winter then ever before—weighs 146. I weigh heaviest I think too! I weigh 170.

‹ February 20 ›
Monday

Mary is one year old today and Papa Ghu is 35 today (and I was 36 Sat) so we had Ghu's, Mary's, and my birthday dinner all in one—and had it yesterday. We had a large hen baked and pudding with sauce (flavored with nutmeg), 2 favorite eatables of mine. Papa Ghu weighs 146 at 35 yrs. I haven't weighed Mary, but she is a "teeny" girl, the smallest child we have ever had at 1 yr. old. So far she has no other name but Mary. Sometime we add another name. I weigh, at age 36, one hundred and seventy (170).

This month has been the roughest February I remember ever knowing. We have had some *Cold* Cold weather! But the coldest weather I ever experienced was 6 yrs ago; Fred was about a year old and snow was deep and the coldest wind—Whoop-ee-. The wind blew the snow up in drifts and banks against out-houses and garden pailings. Papa Ghu would nearly freeze going from house to lot to feed horses. That was the coldest cold weather that has ever been in my life.

Ralph has always been the most obstinate child we've raised at his age—2½ yrs—but because he was nearly dead the whole summer (last Summer was a year) and because he has always been cheated out of his rights by Mary. It makes him rebellious. For instance he is a baby, but she is a younger baby. I am obliged to see after her—haven't the strength necessary for demands of the family—necessities have to be done and poor little Ralph doesn't always get his share of attention; he knows it and cries about it. Ralph seems very different from the family to me—no two seems alike—but Ralph is something of a curiosity to me. He has the best complection of all—

the *clearest* blue eyes—pretty blue—pretty eyes, pretty skin, pretty soft fine hair—the finest hair of any. He has the biggest foot of any (to his age) and I think the largest framed one according to his age. He has the biggest mouth of all and how he loves Papa Ghu! He doesn't think he belongs to anyone but Papa Ghu or didn't think so till lately; he begins to love me now and called himself my boy sometimes. A long while he loved me little, and Papa Ghu devotedly because my Mary came in his way.

Travis is a nervous child. Cries so much in the night from fear of mad dogs. He talks more than any child I ever saw about mad dogs and dreams of them. He was scared nearly to death by a dog and it did him great harm. I let him sleep with me sometimes on account of his scare of dogs in the night. Travis minds well; tries to be obedient, usually wants to do as we wish him to—he is easily controlled. Hope he will continue to be as he grows older. Askew is rite good boy in many ways tho he and Fred are sometimes very cross with each other.

Little Mary—one year old. Well, the little Girlie has gotten on rite well, most of the time, of the first year of her life. A little doll-looking thing she is. Short and chubby—small but plump. Sunshine. Always smiling. Devoted to Papa Ghu. Just ready for a frolic every time he takes her. She is so bright—so pleasant, so cute. Today I saw her pushing a child's chair half across the room and walk after it (by holding to, and pushing it) and she can't stand alone. Has only 2 teeth (two little pegs just in front—lower one). I wish I could weigh her but weather is wet and cold and I can't carry her to the mill. My Papa . . . says "Mary is the prettiest one of the bunch." He often says she is pretty. Papa is very patient and affectionate to all of the children. Call all of them "honey" nearly as much as by their names. He calls Ralph "Charlie" and we all ought to, because he does, Ghu and I think. Mary is a good baby and has been a good sweet baby ever since she put off long clothes. She always wants company—won't play in a room alone. She seems to love Askew—prefers him to nurse her of the little boys. She loves to play with Travis; he makes her laugh lots. She likes Ralph but he is too little to play with her without hurting her or taking her toys or playthings. He isn't old enough to know how to amuse or give up anything to her. One year ago today little Mary came to our home and hearts—in our lives to love, to brighten and to add to our cares too.

‹ February 28 ›

The last time February 1905 will be written in ye pages and a sad thing I have to record. My best Brothers are dead—Buddie is dead. John wrote Papa that Buddie died on 22nd Inst, with pneumonia—had been sick about two weeks. Wrote the last half hour of his life (if I understand his letter right) he spent in prayer and that he saw our Mama. . . . John writes that he told them he saw her.

He was a favorite son of my parents—(a favorite brother to us all, he and Splint) and now Mama and her best children, Splint and Buddie—oldest and youngest are all together. To me it seems like a dream—to Papa I know it was awful.

How uncertain is life. Lord help us to so number our days that we may apply our hearts unto wisdom and live always ready. Buddie is gone from this world to another! Splint gone (about ten years) and Mama been away nearly a year. All were Christians and are reunited we fully believe.

February 28

Buddie is dead. How sad. Buddie was such a lovable being. So gentle, kind and sociable. John wrote us he prayed half hour before dying (I suppose he meant the last half hour of his life) and that he told them he saw Mama—our Mother and two favorite sons (and two favorite Brothers) reunited. Mama has been on the other shore nearly a year (—lacking a few days) and Splint has been gone about 10 or 11 years and now Buddie has joined home. Papa loved Buddie so deeply, so warmly (and always did Mama the same) that I know it must be unspeakable sorrow to Papa!

Papa feels (and signifies it) that his time is short here. Lord be with us and help us to be up and doing (Thy will with our lives) with a heart for any fate.

‹ March 3 ›
Friday P.M.

I had a letter this evening from Fan telling me the particulars of Buddie's death. He was taken with la grippe and it went into pneumonia; they had three doctors with him. He suffered greatly and during it all, he would say "The Lord's will not mine, be done." He would say "it is severe suffering but is all for the best." Told his loved ones that he would soon be among the blest with a harp to praise God with. Prayed much during his sickness and just before dying called out loud and distinct "Ma! Ma! There she is Mollie! Why don't you go to her!" Marvin (Buddie's youngest son) is hard of hearing but Buddie spoke loud enough for Marvin to hear and understand him. "There is no death. The stars go down to rise upon some fairer shore."

He was so submissive to the will of God in suffering and in death. He was one of the gentlest, sweetest spirited men I ever knew. He retained throughout his whole life a child-like simplicity different from any man I ever knew. He was always affectionate towards his parents and devoted to them deeply and a marked devotion to his Bro's and Sisters, wife and children. His wife is a true sweet soul herself and so like an own sister, instead of sisterinlaw. Buddie was the most affectionate, kind hearted child my parents ever raised unless he found an equal in Splint.

Splint, Buddie, Mama — all reunited. Would to God my heart was as clean as was Buddie's.

Travis, my gentle, obedient, innocent little (five year old) son went to school today — a visitor — but is to start as a pupil Monday. My little white souled Innocent going to school! How sad. He is remarkably innocent and trustful. He is an affectionate little thing — a lovable child one who receives more attention than others from people in general. But I do hate to think of a time when he will be less innocent. Askew and Fred have learned ugly words, *ugly* ones, at New Hope School and I know Travis will hear those black words too. Fred and Askew used one or more of the ugly words they learned at school and Travis came to Ghu and I and told us what words he heard Fred and A. say. Fred's words were so bad that Papa Ghu whipped him a little. I hope that Fred nor Askew will ever use another bad word.

Travis has all the five years of his little life been warmly devoted to me and I carried Mary in my arms half way to mill to walk with the little fellow on his first day in Miss Nellie Maddox's school. I cried and laughed too. The thoughts were happy and sad ones mixed. I stood and watched the trio [Travis, Fred, Askew] until they turned the curve across the creak and the hill obscured them from my sight. 'Twas early but I gazed at the picture they made and had to tug Mary back up hill to do my multitude of little things in the house. That picture I think will stay a long time in my memory. Askew looked back oftener than any of the little fellows. Askew is very kind to me in many ways and feels more for me (my tired body) than either of the three, may be, because he is older. He is kind and thoughtful of me in many ways and helps me greatly. He is very kind and thoughtful of his Grand Pa. Askew and Fred are dear little fellow. Travis favors Splint and he reminds me of Splint when S. was a little boy. Travis' face was all aglow when he hung a book sack over his shoulder and marched off to school. So full of anticipation that he didn't give me much thought this morning. He has been a real sweet little nurse — helping me to amuse Mary. I missed him that respect today and in others. He is a talker and an interrogater, and every day lately when I cook dinner he brings Mary in stoveroom. I missed him there. He, Mary, and Ralph eat some of my dinner every day, before they go to the table.

I've been baking birthday cakes recently and today cooked a pudding and Ralph says is that my "everyday-cake." I replied yes, this is not a birthday cake, this is an every-day-cake.

Our clever mail carrier brought Travis' first School Book yesterday, sent out by our kind friend Ed Peek of Locust G. Travis was "*dee*-lighted." His eyes danced with joy. I read him some pieces and I never saw a child listen more eagerly or more interested. He was overjoyed on reception of his book. I believe he will earn fast. I always have called him "My Boy" because he seems to love me more or at least pays me more attention of a certain kind than the other little boys do. I told Ghu, for fun, to just wait till "My Boy" starts to school, and then you will see a boy who will learn fast. Travis speaks more correctly than Askew or Fred and is much more careful to speak correctly than they. He is indeed a surprise to me on that line; as far as he knows, he is careful to speak correctly. Since I've been scribbling Ralph and Mary have torn my trunk "topsy turvy," scattered a jar of buttons over the floor, turned half dozen boxes and the contents bottom upwards in my trunk and on the floor and Ralph has whined a good deal. If I did not love to write I'd never do so under such circumstances.

, Quotations from Fan's letter, of Buddie's talk during his last illness: "He said, time and again 'Thine will, oh Lord, not mine' " and would say "it is all for the best." About twenty minutes before he breathed his last he looked at Little Sis and said "we were married in early life but will have to part. I will soon hear the shouts of the holy land and play on the harps every day." . . . "He was conscious to the last." "Talked lots just before he died; called us all by name to his bedside. He prayed much during his illness and prayed half an hour before dying."

< March 7 >

"Maidee" (Mary) fell off the bed today—a high bed—and 'twas the first time she ever fell off a bed and I think 'twas the hardest fall she ever had. I left her asleep and went away in stove room to cook dinner. So now she has a blue spot on her "noggin" and at first a red swollen place. A year (and week or two over) old, but never fell off before.

Papa . . . says often that Mary is pretty. Sunday night at supper table Papa said "Mary is the prettiest one or best looking one." Said she was pretty and "hard to beat." Misses Babe and Matt Childs say she favors my sister Fan very much.

Ralph is more trouble to me than Mary since all three of other little boys have started to school. Sometimes he is very troublesome indeed; he does things that causes Mary to be more trouble to me.

I am pardonable now if I do "feel as big as my Daddy" because he told me the other day I had his weight now— 170 lbs. My! ain't I big? Feel as big as my Daddy (don't look as big).

Well I don't get to do much but cook and see after the wants of babies: Ralph and Mary. I nearly live in cook room. Wish it was a cosier place and I'd enjoy it better. "Maidee" is sick with cold—and I think teething. Year old and two teeth only.

‹ March 11 ›

"Maidee" is just now (as Papa Ghu expresses it) "cutting hair." She has been very scarce of hair all of her life till rite lately. While not a bald headed baby, she had just a wee bit of hair and none on top of her head. Papa Ghu began to be uneasy about her delay in "cutting" hair. All our other children were born with plenty of hair.

Travis is a nervous little boy, afraid to go out in the hall after dark to get a drink of water. Our baby carriage stays in hall at night and Papa Ghu often tells him (when he goes out after a drink of water, peering down the hall as if something was going to grab him) to "look out! The baby carriage will get you!" Ghu says many funny things.

Travis awakes far in the night and is so frightened he can't sleep and keeps Ghu and I awake. There is a popcorn parcher hanging on wall by the bed T. sleeps on now and Ghu told Travis one night this week that if he didn't look out the pop-corn popper would catch him. One P.M. this week T. was afraid to go out doors and play by himself with a new ball that Ghu had made him (from an unravelled sock) and kept asking me to go out on veranda so that he wouldn't be afraid and Papa Ghu told him he was afraid the old Plymouth Rock rooster would eat him up.

‹ March 21 ›

Ralph is rite cute and at time is rite cross. Always falling and getting bumps. As the spring weather stays with us, I leave my household work a short while nearly every day, for a walk of a few moments in sun and was planting some lilies today in a little spot where my dear Mama kept some plants and we called it Mama's flower yard. (The children called it Grand Ma's.) Today Ralph remembered hearing them call it Grandma's and he doesn't understand their meaning. He was so young that he has entirely forgotten her I think (and she was so good to him, so mindful of his welfare) and so he will say "it is Grand Pa's flower yard."

Mary is thriving in this bright weather. She loves out door life and we carry her out when weather permits awhile each day. She is learning new cute tricks; is so lively—so light hearted—jolly. Travis enjoys going to school. Isn't learning much in his book but learning many games etc. from associating with other little boys. Fred and Askew are not as smooth in disposition as they were formerly. They talk harsh and cross and are quarrelsome. I am sorry, and hope the habit will *not* grow on them. I read, a few days ago, that ill temper was more contagious than almost anything.

I miss Mama sorely. I miss her now much more than I did last Spring. Every new plant that blooms is a strong reminder of her. The peach trees and fruit trees in bloom bring thoughts of her. The garden speaks of her—the rose bushes and flowers especially bespeak her. How desolate my heart feels because I no longer am with Mama. Her presence was the warmth and light of home—how much so I didn't realize till she went away to stay. How Spring does stir up memories of Mama! And every change of seasons do! The warm bright days—how they do bring forth memories.

I gave Miss Babe and Mat each a piece of glass ware that was my mother's because they were so good to Mama and Mama thought so much of them—I gave to them as a keepsake from Mama. 'Tis nearly time now to cook supper. Don't know where my pen staff is and I do not like to use a pencil. My little boys *loose* my things so!

‹ April 7 ›

Mary is 13 months old. She weighs 20 lbs. Mary is not well and not apt to be anymore soon. Warm weather will disagree with her so; she is teething. We've had an epidemic of croup in our family lately. Fred, Travys, and Ralph, all had it. Travis didn't get relief as soon as R. and F. did. Travys coughs badly yet and is not well; he is quite thin and so often cries in the night from fright.

We are having cold weather today; some ice, and frost this morn. All three little boys are at home from school yesterday and today. T. sick, and Askew has toothache.

I'm busy trying to sew—Spring sewing. Will have a busy week next—Spring cleaning and cooking for Quarterly meeting and expecting the PE [Presiding Elder] with us—and Mary sick and quite cross.

< April 10 >

Monday P.M.

Mary has been real sick — bad off; took a violent cold — we all knew she was very sick. Papa was as uneasy as rest of us. We all feared congestion of the lungs. She is much better now, but so hoarse. She can't cry so as to be heard. For a few nights and a few days she was so sick and had high fevers and so long before fever would subside. Her face was scarlet — high fevers caused from lungs — she came so near having pneumonia. My work (except that which *had* to go on, cooking etc.) had to stop and Mary isn't well enough yet for me to take up any work besides cooking and sweeping. Papa Ghu helped me night and day. He waits on all the children wonderfully for a man, when they are sick. I sometimes feel that he has much more love and tenderness for his offspring than many, so called, good mothers have. In fact, at times his tenderness makes me feel that my own pales in comparison, after the children get out of babyhood.

Mary is tongue-tied and at present, the ligament under her tongue is swolen and very white like it was extremely sore and festered. I am real uneasy about it and wish I could see Dr. Woods about her tongue. I am sorry it had not been clipped more (the ligament) for I've always felt uneasy about it and feel so afraid it was not clipped enough in infancy to do her any good. We phoned for Dr. Woods last Saturday while she had such high fevers but he was gone, so on Sunday she didn't have high fevers and we decided to continue doctoring her without a Dr. unless she failed to improve rite soon.

Travis is not healthy. He is the thinest one of them (of the boys) and never gets much flesh on his bones. He is the sharpest featured one. He coughs great deal and so does Fred, although Fred is the fattest one and eats more of anything in general (when well) than the balance. Askew is peculiar about what he eats — more so than any of our family. Doesn't eat much game, chicken, or meats as we, nor as many vegetables.

This will be a busy, busy, week for me if Mary gets well enough. Our Quarterly meeting comes off. So much cooking and cleaning for me to do.

Mary is very devoted to Papa Ghu and could he stay with her I could work on. She is so contended with her Papa, so in love with him.

< May 19 >

Am amusing a sick baby and can't use pen and ink. Mary has been real sick for 3 days—lying in baby carriage or in our laps, but today she plays on floor. Diarrhoea is her trouble. Mary will be 15 months old tomorrow; she is very delicate, a doll like little thing. We (Ghu and I) have been weaning her the past two days and nights; this will be the 3d night. She was remarkably easy to wean. Didn't cry much. How sad is made our hearts to have to wean the little sick delicate baby in her 2nd summer—a time so trying to a baby's health and strength, but it had to be done and we pray God to be with us in our troubles and cares. I pray to abide under His wings till these troubles are past. Have prayed much lately that I might have my usual strength and be able to see carefully after little Mary and my aged and feeble Papa, but my strength has failed and I pray God to be with us all.

Ghu is having a terrible time with his farm; rains have caused so much grass and laborers are few and he works so hard and my strength calls for his aid in house. I am sorry for Ghu and all family. If I get too weak to keep us all will suffer from various neglects.

< June 1 >

Yesterday was Ralph's birthday— 3 yrs old. I was so very sick that I could not prepare anything for Ralph's birthday. Dr. Woods stopped by today and left me a tonic that I think will be helpful to me. He is a nice man. I certainly do think a great deal of him as a man, as well as physician. He is kind. I wish there were more men who hold high positions with his fine traits of character. He came by here today too—but never mind recording it—I shall always remember the kindness he manifested.

Mary is better the past few days. She is awful little for 15 months! Can't walk—has 6 teeth. Can't talk—not a word—but tries, jabbers. We know when she means kitty, chicken, etc. When she wants sweet milk or anything to eat or drink she makes a noise like "oggle-oggle." She is looking brighteyed again and is playful.

Askew is a good boy to amuse Mary; he can do more with her than any of the children. Askew seems to love Mary and Ralph fondly.

Askew is more thoughtful this year than either of the children; I guess 'tis because he is older. He is very good to help me wash dishes. Fred and Travis are helpful too. All three are good sweet boys. Mary lives on (principally) boiled sweet milk. Fred has gone to Mr. Kelly's most of the time for the milk. Our cows were dry, tho' now we use milk from our own "Beauty." Beauty and Mag each have new calves and Ghu had his hands full milking them and so much of other work.

Ghu has been working awful hard but has his crop of grass somewhat conquered now, altho' he is still digging, but says he is not so pressed and worried about the grass now. Askew is a fine fellow with a hoe. He works manfully and daily. He is certainly a deserving boy; he has worked *so* steady and hard for his age. Fred hoes some too and does well for his age. Fred and Askew and Papa Ghu have a hard time bringing water so far. We have none in the yard and it is tough on them indeed.

Travis isn't well. . . . He is sick good deal. Papa . . . told him today he had pretty teeth, too pretty to pull—not to have his pulled. Papa is awful good to each one of the children; he talks to Mary everyday. God bless our home; and spare him to us and to our children. We all love him and he is good to us all. Bless each member—and help us do Thy will with our lives. Forgive us for all past sins, be with us in all the changes of future life and eventually receive each of us in the Glory World, for Jesus Sake Amen.

< August 20 >

Sunday

Mary is 18 mo's. old today. She is well and lively. One of the merriest little creatures I ever saw! Never still except when asleep. Such *quick* motions and movements! She fairly runs when going over the house. She is the sunshine of our home and hearts (a little corpse passed here just now—Arthur Kelly's little Jeff—and I know their hearts are saddened). Papa pays Mary great deal of attention. (My! she is crying in pain now—has turned herself, chair and all over.) She has learned past few days to climb up in a high chair and take a seat. She never cries long, has hushed and gone to playing with Askew's rubber types (letters and figures and the way she is scattering them!) Mary's Grand Pa . . . thinks Mary the sweetest baby in the world.

Natural for him to love her, because he seldom sees other babies and she was born and so far raised here and she plays around and with him — at nights sometimes gets on his bed with him and just smacks her mouth to kiss him. Sometimes she gets up in his lap and talks to her and laughs at her. He often says she is a funny baby and a smart baby. She is slow in walking. If I mistake not she was nearly 17 months old before she walked. She was weakly but lively cheerful and playful. All of Mary's life she has had such animated eyes — when a tiny baby she had playful mischievous eyes.

I have been sick ever since April and could not on these pages record many things that I so much wished to. Mary is climbing in and out of a chair now near me and I'm so uneasy I can't write well. I am so *hungry*, so impatient to write. I have written only one letter since April. I would lie down when not compelled to be doing absolutely necessary things in house for the family when not engaged trying to entertain company. (This is 3d time I've moved since I began to write from Mary. I've just had to get up and slap Askew for worrying Fred and Fred may have needed the slap worse. I do not know. I rarely ever chastise them and when I do, I often do it in wrong impatient manner. And oftimes I do not know which one is in fault. I feel sure I slapped him too severe. I ought to have used a hickory instead of slapping.)

Askew was 10 years old Friday. I cooked him a belated birthday cake — we had it today. Mary ate good deal of it — never would eat cake before. She is very fond of peaches and eats many. She can't talk much. Calls "Mamma" and "pop-pop" and says "pie" and when she wants biscuit with sugar and butter on it she says "chee-chee-chee-chee!" Her daily diet and that which she most relishes is buttered biscuit with sugar on it. This is "chee-chee."

I am sorry I slapped Askew. A child should not be slapped strong about the head. He told me this morning he had a swimming of the head. I am sorry I did not use a hickory to punish him with for nagging or worrying Fred. I was so anxious to write — too anxious — and my impatience overcame me.

Ralph cries good deal — has all his life. He calls himself "Your Putty Boy" — can't say pretty.

A little stray kitten came here this week. Mary went into ecstacies over it — hugged, jabbered and lay down on it and squeezed it terribly. She was disappointed when the owner carried it away. Never saw her manifest such devotion to anything before. We roll up a small garment and she hugs it up and says "daw" "daw" (means doll). She loves dolls tho' I've never bought or made her one yet. My health is not good and not having any help I can't sew only necessary things and don't go anywhere to buy her a doll. I reckon Santa Claus will bring her one next Christmas.

Nellie Maddox has closed her school at New Hope. She is a fine girl—a queen. Her worth is superior. Travis went to school with Askew and Fred. Travis didn't learn fast.

We've had lot of company this summer so far.

> Dollie and Joe and Ruth day and night
> Callers:
> Foot peddler Hillman took dinner
> Mrs. Ida Childs one P.M.
> Kelly family often
> John Carter and son one P.M.
> Mr. Allen Crumbly and Meetsie one P.M.
> Sam Tollerson, wife, and Sarah one day.
> Blanch two days and one or 2 nights
> Sweetie Wynn one P.M.
>   Hay Wynn one night
> Sarah and 2 children one day and one night
> Joe Wynn occasionally.
>   Aunt Margaret Wynn 2 days and one night
> Mollie Hooten and grandson one day and night.
> Cape and Walter Wynn 2 nights and days.
> Olivia Wilkins one day from church.
> R.S. Le Guin and little girl Kate, Dubach, La.
>   August 21st, 1905.

> Our kinfolks who died this year.
> Buddie in March (22nd) 1905
> Little Sis in Aug (21 or 22nd) "
> Jodie in Oct (near 1st) "

Papa: 84th birthday passed on the 8th Inst. May he be spared to see many more. How we would miss him were he called away. He is not childish, nor any trouble as most old people are and his mind is so good. He doesn't want to be any trouble and is not a childish person. May the Giver of all good gifts, spare him a long time yet to us and make me a blessing to him. Askew is powerfully good to him — and so thoughtful of him and associates closely with him and sleeps with him. Papa is so kind and indulgent to *all* the children. He is a powerful kind, loving grandfather to my children but I think he is especially so to Askew. If any of them get sick he gives them a dime or something even if just a penny. He feels for them so tenderly, one and all.

August 20
Sunday

I've been sick since April—have had no time to write and too sick to write. Wasn't able to do housework, but not having any help had to do what I possibly could and let lots go undone. What a calamity I felt had befallen me as I suffered so with a weak body and *miserably* sick stomach.

It was so bad! so bad no words can picture my sufferings. But now I am better, stronger and can eat. While still sick and weak, yet ever so much better. We've had a lot of company so far this summer. I am not able to keep things as tidy as I wish too and am often miserably embarrassed on account of somethings being unkept or untidy and haven't strength to do any more than what I am doing.

Anna Jarrell spent a few days here. She helped me with my work and was not trouble for me on the contrary she was a pleasure and I was real sorry when she went home.

Allie Jarrell and Grace spent two weeks here and they helped me to my necessary work—cooking and sweeping and I was sorry when Grace went home. Susan Tarpley helped me cook a week and tho she charges high we had so much company I was obliged to have her. Mr. Clark, Mynta, Baby Fannie and Pauline were here and also Cape and Walter. Emma Jinks and husband and a peddler one day and one day Olivia Wilkins and one night Bro. Millican.

The summer isn't over yet and other company is expected. How I do wish I was able to hire someone to help me but am not and must peg on—drag along.

< August 22 >

Mary is learning new words (18 months old). She is a tiny little thing but not bony—has enough fat. Askew is something of a carpenter. Helped Ghu cover the buggy house today. Learned how to place and nail shingles at once, better, Ghu says, than many grown people.

< September 1 >
(Friday)

Hot! Hotter! Hottest! I will be thankful when cool weather comes. This had been a trying summer to me, but I hear gleeful Mary running, jabbering, laughing and squealing, and she out doors; if it is sizzling hot, she is as pretty as you please. That Baby Mary is ready for fun at any hour—a merry little bit of humanity. I don't know how much the little thing weighs, but there is a sight of animation and *sense* about her. She has always expressed so much with her eyes! She always (since a tiny baby) *talked* with her eyes. What a good recollection too! at 18 months old she is *smart*.

Ralph goes with the other little boys (Fred, Askew, and Travys) to cotton patch. Picks ½ lb sometime, wants it weighed. All little boys went with Papa Ghu to the gin today. They *so much* enjoy going to the gin. Askew and Fred have to churn now—a job they very much dislike and they do the job badly.

Mary is saying lot of new words but don't say them at all plain and doesn't connect any. . . . Tho' little Mary never knew a Grandmother's love, yet her Grand Pa (Wynn) thinks a lot of her. He watches her cute doings and is amused at her and interested in her daily. He says she has lot of sense, and is funny lively baby. She is the dearest little girlie in all the world to myself, Papa Ghu, her brothers and Grand Pa (Wynn). (She has never seen Ghu's father nor has any except Askew and Fred; Askew was in dresses then and Fred was 6 months old [when he died].)

My Mother loved the other children so much that I know she would have loved "Maidee." Mary is named for her. Mama loved Travis deeply, fondly, and I have a picture fresh in memory of her hugging him warmly to her breast, kissing him, and crying. Crying at thoughts of leaving him. She knew she must die. A sad picture! How warmly devoted she was to that child and on her death bed how she would notice a child's prattle or cry quickly when she didn't notice other things. How warmly she felt *for children*—What a warm friend to childhood.

September 1

This is a terrible hot day! I just can't rest noway. I am glad that summer is ending—time for cooler weather close by. This past summer has been such a trying one for me. My health failed in Apr. Not a well hour have I seen since. How hard it was to be reconciled to the calamity—that which seemed a calamity to me, but I trust the life that is to be, will be after so much suffering be a sunbeam to brighten my own, as Little Mary's life is. When I feel the pulsations of another life (which we expect to see in Jan 1906) I feel a fear that my little Mary will never get her share of my attention—as strength will be so weak and my cares so many that I will be crushed—no words describe such a multitude of cares, responsibilities and overtaxed strength.

Mary is so bright so jolly! Such a *rare* "girlie." The sweetest little "girlie" in this world to Papa Ghu and I—her brothers and her grand Pa Wynn. He loves little "Maidee." I believe the Creator will do what is best and I will be satisfied with whatever sex the Lord gives us next, but Mary is the cutest baby that has ever been here.

How sick I've been since April! Oh, how hard it has been to keep up! to cook! to make beds! to sweep floors! to care for babies— Ralph and Mary. How I've dragged around doing absolutely necessary things! How I've prayed when strength failed for help to get the meals done. Summer is ending. I am glad. All summers are trying to me—weakening—making strength easily overtaxed, and cooking and entertaining the crowd who visit us—it is always overtaxing to my strength but summers when I have a deathly sick stomach and eat almost nothing—'tis worse.

If I just could have a good negro to help me with my work—then I could be worth more to my family and my friends and relation who visit us. And it is awful to try to cook and do housework when one is suffering as I have been this summer. Yet there was no one I could get—we were not able to pay a great big price—and I had to do all I could, but so much went undone and I was so embarrassed because so much went undone or untidy. I've prayed about it and cried. I would be a clean tidy housekeeper if I were able to hire help. I love a tidy home and tidy children. I deeply regret not being able to have these any more than I do. These things bother me *much* and trouble me deeply. My greatest ambition is clean home, clean premises—good meals, tidy clean children and myself to be so. I trust the Lord to be with me and with the life that is to be, and with those already entrusted to our keeping. The suffering, the sorrow, the labor, the pain, the worries, the cares, the responsibilities that are yet to come upon me I pray Thee Heavenly Father to help me to bear and sanctify all to the good of my soul.

‹ September 8 ›

Mary is the least trouble of any baby who has ever been in our home. In day time when she wants to go to sleep, she doesn't fret or cry, but just lies down on floor and goes to sleep. I always find her and put her in a comfortable place. Sometimes though, I don't find her till she has been asleep awhile. I found her yesterday out doors, on ground, in sunshine partly, fast asleep. She is truly a good baby— so playful, so jolly, so easily amused and seldom ever cross.

Ralph is the crossest, most disobedient, little one we've ever had in our home. He is also the noisiest—loudest one. So far Askew is most industrious one and more willing to help me I think, altho' all despise churning and don't enjoy wiping dishes.

‹ September 19 ›

"Maidee" is a curiosity. She is 19 months old tomorrow. She is very fond of candy and one day Ralph was playing that he was a peddler (Mr. Crumbly he called himself) and was pretending that he had some candy. For a moment Mary thought he was in earnest and that he did have candy and ask him (in her grunting way) for candy. Ralph put his hand (empty) into Mary's. She caught on then to the joke *at once* and carried it out, by putting her hand up to her mouth and smacking like she was eating and laughing pleasantly at same time. She has a jolly disposition. Ghu says that I am too partial toward Mary; that I pay her too much attention and the others too little. Sometimes he says he is afraid that *we* think too much of her. Papa . . . says she beats anything he ever saw. She asked him, or commanded him (in her way; tho' she can't talk much she can easily make her wants and wishes known) to clean up an ugly place on the floor and gave him a piece of paper to wipe up floor with. To humor her, although he can stoop only with difficulty, he wiped up floor.

Ralph has many small festered sores on him. He is rite cross and more or less troublesome. He has always been more trouble than any of the rest, tho' at times he is just as good "as you please."

Travis can beat Fred away yonder, picking cotton; can pick easily 28 lbs. by dinner and more if he stayed longer. He doesn't pick much, only as he chooses, and goes and comes when he gets ready.

Askew is an industrious boy—in field. Picks sturdy for his age and lot of cotton. He has a patch this year. He often reminds me of Splint, when Splint was a little boy. Askew helps me better in the house than Fred does tho' neither like the little jobs I give them in housework.

I went to Mrs. Fran Lumus to get some sewing done yesterday and carried Mary and Travis with me. She gave us all a slice of cake as we were ready to leave and Mary and T. enjoyed being in her cozy little home. She is a model of a housekeeper and is so neat in her dress. How I do love to take the little ones with me when I go but sometimes I don't carry them because I am weak and 'tis good deal of trouble for me to bathe and dress myself and one or two of them and see after them after getting to my destination.

Ghu is working hard—picking cotton and hauling it to the gin. I have to lie down sometimes 3 or 4 times before getting my A.M.'s work done. How I do wish I had a good woman, white or black, to help me do housework and how badly I need help!

< September 20 >

Mary is 19 months old today and lively and bright as a sunbeam. The household joy! Papa has talked and played with her a good deal today. She went out on front porch three times today and ordered or asked Papa up out of a chair that Mary likes. He would become amused at her and give her his chair. I am going to Suse Tarpley's this P.M. to carry clothes to have ironed and am going to carry Ralph and Mary to ride.

Mary has 2 jaw teeth. Papa Ghu found them first. Travis says they were not lost. They didn't make her sick (to cut them).

< September 29 >

Friday Night

We had rain today after a very dry dusty season and *hot*—the hottest Sep. I think I ever felt and the hot weather sapped my strength so that it seemed almost utterly impossible some days (most of them) to do my necessary housework. I was truly glad when I felt the sprinkling of the rain. I was so glad I couldn't content myself indoors washing dishes, sweeping floors, making beds, etc. etc. so I just postponed those things and churning too awhile and betook myself out in the misty rain with a new brushbroom and swept a lot of this large yard and inhaled the sweet air scented with rain-settling-dust. I longed for rain to refreshen us and settle dust and cool atmosphere and I felt new life as it were when it came so it is cooler tonight. We had little fires at times today. I didn't feel the need of any, but Papa did.

I reckon 'twas the first fire little Mary remembered (she is 19 mo's old) ever seeing in fireplace as I have been weak all summer and did not kindle fires to iron clothes with but hired them ironed away from home.

The little boys enjoyed kindling up fires—for a change and they also popped some pop-corn which all enjoyed. First pop-corn too Mary ever saw and she liked it. I think it was a big treat for Ralph.

Today Papa . . . was telling of something that happened years ago. He was talking to Ghu and when about halfway thro' with the narrative little Mary walked up to him and began to smack-smack-smack her lips—she wanted to kiss him. He stopped talking, picked her up in his lap, kissed her some and she kissed him and he said she was a mighty sweet little thing; he put her down, took up the thread of his narrative and finished relating—but not till Little Mary had been taken up, kissed and she had kissed him.

Ralph or Charles or Charlie (he is called by 3) feels very proud of new drawers and feels bigger because he wears them. I was sick all spring and summer, unable to make and put them on him until quite recently—he is 3 years and 4 months old. He is very nice with them and gives no trouble.

< October 1 >

Sunday P.M.

Askew, Fred, and Ralph went with Ghu to Sunday School this P.M. Travis stayed here. Ghu leaves one of them nearly every Sunday to keep Papa from being so lonely.

The little boys have a tricicle (among them) and I have never seen them so carried away with *anything* before. They have not tired and keep it going only [except] when they eat and sleep so far. I never did see them so carried away before with anything! It cost 2.25 I think. Papa paid [some] and Ghu .70 and they picked Ghu's cotton for rest. He pays them for picking cotton. They rode up and down the hall on the tricicle last night till bed time and were up early this A.M. and Fred locked it up in closet while we were eating dinner and put keys in his pocket so that he would be first one to ride after dinner. I declare! They are carried away! Away! Mary and Ralph are not interested much but they ride when Papa Ghu holds them on and Mary hurt her foot on it her first ride. She has lot of sense—expresses so much with eyes, jestures etc. etc. and is learning fast to say many new words. She says a whole lot of stuff all in a jabber just as fast as she can and with it all asks questions and laughs heartily. These funny talking spells no one understands but her dear little self, but she is *so* funny when she goes on so rapidly with a long "rigamarole." Fred went to McD. with G. yesterday. Ghu had for me Papa's [medical school] diploma nicely framed. It is nice now and I can keep it a life time as a keepsake. Papa gave it to me when I was a small child.

< October 4 >

Have been sewing hard this P.M. and will sew in P.M.'s till Christmas and then not get through (if health permits). This October weather must affect birds (with new life) like it does myself, for past few days a pair of animated mocking birds have been staying around and in, and near, our back yard—and such sweet singing they've done! I've watched and listened to them with interest. I love mocking birds and wish they would never decrease in No., but increase—wish no one would catch, kill, or cage them. My pet cat, Hotema, killed one one night recently and wasn't hungry for him either, because she just ate one foot and no more of the sweet and graceful song-bird.

(I am cooking supper now and writing too, so must hurry.) Little "Macy" came to me while I was washing dishes today and wanted a spoon. I gave it to her; she, (by herself) found a dish towel and wiped it and wanted to wipe more dishes and then picked up broom and tried to sweep some in stove room. A smart 19 month old baby.

Ghu and Askew had a race with a heifer—one Ghu bought and was trying to bring home—drug Ghu few yards and they had an exciting time with her. The little boys had a goober [peanut or ground-pea] patch and they with Papa Ghu and Clyde dug and picked them yesterday and today. All little folks are continually eating them. I enjoy their groundpea and popcorn gatherings.

< October 7 >

Saturday Night

Ghu has gone to prayer meeting at New Hope. Papa is snoring. All little ones are asleep.

Ralph has been sick two or three days; he had rite smart fever two days and two nights. One night he was scared almost into a spasm—had hot fever. I do not know what caused him to have the fever. Today he is much better and I am glad; I asked the Lord to grant that he might not be stricken down with a spell of fever. I feel that the Lord answered my request. I am not strong—have lot to do—am considerably overtaxed—but if little Ralph had taken fever things would have been worse. No one to help me and how much I do need help. I can't be near the mother to my children that I want to be and would be if I were not so overworked—strength is so overtaxed.

Mary is a rare baby, a sweet, attractive baby. Papa . . . said this eve that she was a sweet baby—a great curiosity to him. He said she came to him this P.M. and smacked her lips, wanted to kiss him (she often does him thus) and he kissed her and Askew kissed her, and she wiped her mouth good—wiped Askew's kiss off.

Travis is the prettiest child in our family up to date. He doesn't favor Le Guins. He was often said to favor Mama . . . and I think he does and also looks some like Splint did.

Fred is the quietest one of the family—talks less than any. Mary is the funniest one. We all say daily "She is a funny baby." She is a fun-loving baby too. She is a dainty made little creature—shapely limbs—beautiful legs, arms, hands and feet. She is so merry! Sunshine all the time. Ralph has best complection of all—is the noisiest and cries more than any of them ever did. He is a fine fellow tho'. He talks less plain than those older did at his age.

Ghu says I am partial to Travis and Mary. I don't want to show partiality. Some are so disposed that they naturally get more attention than others I think. Askew is enclined to help me more than rest and does more for Mary—well he is only one old enough to be any help scarcely. Askew is a very good boy and I think Travys and Fred are too, for their size. Our children have the name of being good children by every family who know them I think. People so often speak of them that way to us.

October 7
Saturday Night

I have so much to do between now and January 1906 and I don't see how I can do it all—so many little garments to make and such little time to sew. I've no help and I'm cooking most of the time. I've already hired more sewing done than I ever did one season before (4 dresses for self 3 coats for boys) and must hire about 6 little prs of pants made yet I guess—and then a whole pile of cloth to sew myself. How I am *ever* to get it done I don't know. I don't have no chance some days to sit down to the machine; some days I'm tired out of reason—no strength so overtaxed. Ghu has been to town today and bought good deal for me to sew. He buys all of his clothing ready made this year. I use to make him shirts. How I'll ever get through before the stork's visit I don't know. Would that I didn't have to live in such a strain—my strength so overtaxed! If I had enough leisure and less strain I could and would be a better mother in many ways.

I have not the time to be a companion for my children and am to tired to talk with them much of the time. I often fear Mary will be neglected when or after the stork's visit. I do not know now who will cook for me then. She is a remarkably sweet baby. If I could have time to devote to her and strength.

I don't see how I can do with another addition. If I just had help! Lord help me! Thou knowest, my frame, my frail body, and many cares. Be with me in all and if it can be Thy will, when another life has been given us, that we may have useful help, to run household work. Help me to trust Thee for help and for strength and not worry so.

We heard Friday P.M. that Jodie Cape's wife was dead. She was burried Thursday—her death was sudden. I am in the land of living and ought to be more thankful and worry less. I wish I could be patient about my work and absence of strength and cease to worry. Lord help me to draw nearer to Thee and cease to worry.

< October 12 >

October is always a month that I look forward to. I think I enjoy it better than any month in the year (when as well as usual) and it is a month that I nearly always seem to take on fresh vitality in. Tho' I am busy—exceedingly busy this October—lot of sewing must be done and a thousand other things to do—all by myself—and I not strong—tho' better than I've been since April.

I killed a highland moccason today in the house—in the hall—going toward my room. I was in front room sewing and heard Travis call Fred to come and kill it. A hammer was lying near me and I picked it up and had to hit the snake in a hurry to prevent it getting in our room where I feared I could never kill it. 'Twas not a large one, but long for its size. I didn't know what kind of snake it was but Papa knew and told us. Travis, Mary, and Ralph were all close to the snake and Travys excited. Mary wanted to go rite to it. Mary is the funniest baby I ever saw in my life—cuts so many funny capers all day long every day. The healthiest teething baby we've ever known among ours. . . . She is extraordinary cute.

Poor little Ralph is afflicted with enough sores to keep him feeling badly. He looks pitiful too. I'll be glad when the poor Little thing's sores heal. So often he (when well) would pull little waggon around house and call himself Mr. Crumbly but too puny now to play that he is a peddler. Poor little sore footed and sore fingered and sore nosed boy. I trust he will soon be well.

Fred and Travis helped me real well today. Askew picked cotton all day. "Papa Ghu" went to Worthville to Quarterly meeting.

‹ October 16 ›
Monday Night

These are busy, very busy, days with me. Almost *all* days are busy ones with me (unless so weak I can't keep going) but besides other work, I am doing good deal of sewing trying *my best* to get our winter sewing done by Dec or 1st of Jan and Mrs Lumus doing good deal for me too. Ghu is always busy too—seems to me he does more than any man I ever saw, or knew of. Askew and Travis picked cotton away from home today—first time any of the little boys ever picked in any crop but Ghu's. Travis picked 12 [pounds?] this A.M. and 7 this P.M. and says he isn't going back tomorrow but Askew will go and I think Fred will go with him. Fred doesn't like to pick as well as Askew does. Fred helped me nicely—willingly and cheerfully around the house today while all were gone but himself. Ghu isn't very well; has a little boil on his neck—is looking little thin. Little Mary played around Papa's chair all A.M. He sat out in the warm sun near severel bales of cotton and he said Mary cut many capers, made many faces—said she beat anything he had ever seen yet. Ghu has one shoat out and Mary stays indoors unless Papa or the larger children are out with her.

How I wish I had time to get out in this beautiful October weather! How I would love to take a stroll on creak or in woods with my children! But work! work! and all indoors, except when I'm brushing yards. Am going to try to get away from home one P.M. this week (go to Matt Groggin's Col.) and buy some dried fruit. I enjoy every little outing I get, if I do go away each time on business.

‹ October 21 ›
Saturday Before 4th Sunday

Yesterday was a very busy day—I did work outside ordinary household work—pasted paper on stove room and little room walls, and
baked a cake. Mary played all day—was so good—but rested badly
all night. Now, tho' not eleven o'clock A.M. she is asleep—not well
I think. Papa . . . said yesterday eve that Mary got . . . a wet rag two
or three times during the day and washed up dirty spots on the floor.
And 19 months old. He told me of other funny things she did, but
my body so overtaxed that I didn't retain in memory what else he
told me. I am so tired and feel that I have no time to rest—so much
to do today.

November 9

I am tired, so tired! I long for a short quiet from children's talk,
questions and noise. I've worked and worked but not at the work
I most wanted to do. Today has been more trying than some days
are. Twice have tears rushed to my eyes. Ghu has been gone all day
and will remain away till in the night. Today he has been at a school
election or election for Local Taxation—from there to Worthville to
Masonic lodge. Little boys (3 largest) gone all P.M. and I need help
so bad. I need a good negro all the time (if there are any good ones)
our wash woman and her children give me trouble—some clothes
missing and some not clean and she owes for things I let her have
just to please her (a nice little bonnet that I wanted to keep) and to
be good and accomodating to her I let her have it for her to make me
four brooms (I furnish the straw) and she to scour 2 water buckets. I
asked her twice to scour the buckets last week and no buckets scoured
yet. Ghu's gone—no milk from cow—hogs go hungry and stayed so
late I will have to churn at night and have late supper. They have to
get me water from away from house to do things with.
    I went to Fred Groggins', colored, to pay his wife for dried fruit
(she sent here last week) yesterday. The road was worse I ever rode
over in my life and I had Ralph and Mary in buggy with me and
I think Providence brought us home safely. A rotton bridge was
very dangerous—horse broke a plank and fell slightly. A good negro,

Fred G., led horse across when I returned and 'twas then the plank broke. Road was so awful bad in places I just held Mary with one hand and held to buggy with the other and let Fred G. lead the horse. How Ralph held in I do not know, only that it was Providential, as I asked the Lord to be with us while we were gone. In heart I pray thus whenever I leave home. I am so tired, so tired but must go on and cook supper and churn, wash dishes, cook pumpkin and go to bed.

< November 11 >

Saturday Night

I hardly can content myself tonight without work as I've been doing good deal of work at night but this is Sat night, so I will rest. Saturday, after sundown seems a part of Sunday to me.

I have been busy as people can be (it seems to me) since latter part of summer or beginning of fall—was not able to do much till then since April. I *LOVE* work, but to be rushed, and *crushed* with it, is so bad on a weak woman. But I do love work if I could take some past time or have some leisure along with it and could feel that I had strength sufficient for the tasks awaiting me. Yet I am *glad* that I am as well as I am.

Went to Fred Groggins this week one P.M. to pay her for dried fruit and Ralph and Mary went with me. Fred and Matt gave me small table peas to bring home and Fred gave me 4 pumpkins and I appreciated the kindness. . . . We stopped awhile at Bro. Jim's. We went to Miss Fan Lumus' first to pay her for sewing done for me. . . .

Ghu went to Worthville to Masonic Lodge one night this week; I sat up late and did lot of sewing that night. Some nights I am so awful tired I can sew but little. We had a cold rainy day yesterday; we slept late and had only 2 meals that day. Papa went to bed after dinner (at 3 o'clock) undressed and remained in bed till this morn at usual hour of rising. I could get on nicer with my sewing if we could do that way oftener. I liked it—sewed good deal. I've been making picture frames and am going to try make home look brighter (as far as I can) by Thanksgiving Day.

‹ November 12 ›

Sunday

Thanksgiving Day isn't far off and I don't feel like I could cook a Thanksgiving dinner. Hope I can, and will try unless I just know I haven't strength for the undertaking. Have been writing letters lately for Ghu—he always gets me to do his writing and calls me his secretary, to Miss Ruth Jenks to get her to teach New Hope School. She has accepted and will begin Monday week. Next thing is who will board her? I have no help and not enough strength to do for our family and *can not* take a boarder. Ghu will try to get Claud Peek to board her awhile. Ghu received severel letters applying for the school from different ones. Miss Ruth had been elected when he received one, or two, I might say that we were favorably impressed with; one from Miss Jennie L. Hill of Irwinton, Georgia. She wrote a plain hand. I judge lot of people's character by their handwriting. I judge her to be a superior woman—a fine character—a strong intellect. We received one from Miss Ada Camp, State Normal School, Athens. I believe she would have made a good teacher. Others we received I imagine would not have suited. I enjoy looking over the letters of application and mentally judging the character of each. We had one or two applications from other states. One from California; I believe one from Miss.

Sunday Night: I went down to see old Aunt Mary (Brownlee) this P.M. She is crippled—her foot is awfully swollen and will have to be cut off or [it will] kill her, I think and so does her Dr. say. I was lonely and anxious to get out of the house. Tonight I sent her and Monk something to eat. Ghu went to see his Aunt Sarah Mason this P.M. She has been sick a good while. I love to ride and so do all the children. Ralph, Mary, and I rode up to Suse Tarpley's (col) yesterday. I carried her clothes to iron for me. We all enjoy just that little ride. Mary has been cross today all day—is teething I am almost sure. I've been lonely all P.M. and bodily fatigued. I was too tired to bathe and dress neatly, till late in P.M. and would have been so embarrassed had company come in and found me in a soiled wrapper.

Ghu will bathe all the little boys tonight. I so much wish we all could bathe on Saturday night and present a neat appearance on Sunday morning and then should company come in unexpectedly we would feel free and easy—but some Sat. nights it isn't convenient for us to do so. I know Papa has been lonely today. No company dropped in all day. Must quit, but I love to write.

November 16
Thursday Eve

Oh, so tired! Headache too. Have just taken in pile of starched clothes and cleaned up a *great* many soiled things in dining and stove room.

It is now time to cook supper and I have headache and feel so tired for anything. Weary, weary. I feel weak when I begin the day and work on and soon become weary.

A negro by name of Will Stewart and his wife, Mandy, moved here this week. She helps me some—a little help is appreciated when one has so much to do and so little strength, tho' she doesn't seem to be an industrious negro and I don't think will ever be much help. Must stop and go cook supper. Seab Sloan and boy are at work here on the well and I have to cook more. They are blasting the well in the yard. Lord be with and help me each weary day of life and guide and direct me thro' all pleasant days. Be with our little ones—our aged one—us all and Thy wings of protection and blessing be over our ark-home.

Night: Supper cooked—dishes washed. I seated.

I've been busy past few days preparing things for a stork's visit (clothing) and now I am thro' with that sewing but have some starched ones to iron tomorrow if I can do so. A *job* off my hands and now there is no particular sewing ahead—none to be anxious about. I will sew up part of a bolt of homespun and perhaps make me a bleaching underskirt between now and Jan 1906—(a time for a stork). Well, what noise Ralph does make. He is the noisiest one of all. Travis is the most attached to me of any except Mary. . . . Mary is quick in her moves and acts. A funny lively baby. I pray that when I am not able to take care of her that somebody will be provided to keep her dry and reasonably clean; that food and necessities be very well prepared for the balance of the family. How I hate to leave my post and retire for a season. How I regret to be unable to do for the family. How I fear for their neglect. But I trust them all to the care of One above and that gives me freedom from worry about their needs etc.

‹ November 20 ›
Monday Night

Made Maidee a wee little dress today. She is teething and isn't well but plays. She is a little cross—unusual when well. I love to sew children's clothes—simple ones. I especially love to make Mary's little things; she is so little and short.

Ghu went to McDonough today. Miss Ruth Jenks will open her school next Monday. I know I will miss the little boys dreadfully. Mary will call Askew in vain many a time. She loves Askew and calls him often to take her, when she is with me. When she is sick she wants to stay almost all the time with him, even calling him sometimes after she goes to bed and she always has slept with me. It is strange how attached she is to Askew. Askew pays her more (and better care he gives her) than the other children do. Many times a day she calls "Askew" when he gets out of her sight. Well I must stop and sew a little before shut-eye-time.

‹ November 27 ›

Miss Ruth Jenks opened school and New Hope today; Ghu was up there with little boys (Askew, Fred, Travys) when school opened and talked with Miss Ruth concerning what kind of school desks to buy. Not many days till Thanksgiving day and I am afraid I can't do much towards cooking a good, nice dinner, on that day as I haven't been able today to do much of anything. Suse Tarpley helped me yesterday get dinner. She may come and help me again the day before, and on, Thanksgiving. . . .

I miss the little boys. . . .

Magnolia Wynn's parents, James A. C. Wynn and
Mary Ann Settle Wynn, ca. 1900

Magnolia Wynn in 1892, at age twenty-three

Ghu Le Guin in 1892, at age twenty-two

45.

Jan 9th 1902

J D Carter Dr To G G
  Cash Lanend   92 00
  at 8 per cts   17 75
                                  23 75
Settled by Note

would naturally be
expected of one, so low,
so old, we feared, after
she began to mend her
mind would never streng
then much but another
wonderful thing is that
her mind is wonderfully
strengthening and
she is miraculously im-
prooved!!! She can walk
a few steps unaided.
She sleeps very well, & lies
quiet all night. We had
to watch her all the time
awhile to keep her from
trying to get out of bed
alone & we knew she
would do so if not watch-
ed — we knew also she
would receive injuries
Now her mind and body
are miraculously improved
and she quit taking
medicine. Just will not
take it and it wasn't
medicine that saved
her life.

126 Ralph is 2 yrs & 1 month old.
very backward about talking. All others
talked very early & so plain. Ralph tries
to talk but doesn't talk plain at all.

Travis talks of birds, their nests &c & and
of chickens, eggs &c. He picks up most
of the eggs & puts them in a box in "Ing
pa's closet" to keep me from cooking
them & buys candy with some of
them from a chicken peddler who
passes here each week. Papa makes
him think he can buy candy
with all the eggs but when ped-
ler comes on I buy needed articles
with some that he has collected.)
Travis is a very sweet, innocent little
boy. Easy to make believe things —
He is easily controlled; has a warm
heart, a sweet, sunny, disposition.
He was his grandma's favorite.
Many said he favored her & he
often told her she favored her & she
appreciated his telling her that so
much. He is 4 yrs old & gone to High
Fall on his first trip then. Askew
is his grandpa's favorite. Askew is
thoughtful & good to his grandpa; sleeps
with him & waits on him & stays
around him so much. It is a beautiful trait in dear little Askew [Askew
is 9 now.] Fred is a clever little boy too —
minds very well — all of us.
Saturday July 16th, 1904. When carried
Sallie, Askew and Fred to Sardas today
to "Children's Service." They told Travis
that he couldn't go & so he stayed satisfied.
while he would have been glad, yes delighted
to have gone, he contentedly stayed, knowing
all could not go. When carries them often,
but not all together. They divide.

Samples of pages from Magnolia's diaries
(Magnolia Wynn Le Guin Collection,
Hargrett Rare Book and Manuscript Library,
University of Georgia Libraries)

Magnolia with her three youngest children, Maggie,
Frances, and Trella, ca. 1918

Dorothy Le Guin (Phillips) in front of Le Guin's Mill, ca. 1925

Ghu in front of homeplace, ca. 1940

Magnolia still writing in 1946

November 29
Wednesday Before Thanksgiving

Tomorrow is Thanksgiving Day. I am so worried today that I don't know what to do. Ghu has gone to McDonough. I have no one to shoot my Thanksgiving rooster for me, nor to do other things. A negro woman named Mandy came up for her breakfast and after milk and was so impudent that she wouldn't sweep dining room and stove room after she got it. I wanted her to iron—she gave me to understand she would not iron this A.M.

Oh, how unsettled, and *nettled* it made me! How badly I need help the Lord knows, and I ask Thee Lord to calm my spirit and help me under such provocation to keep calm—preserve me gentle in my commands when darkies are insolent. Oh, how agitated I have become over the impudence of the negroes this morning. Oh, what physical and mental suffering it has caused.

Lord help me to be right in Thy sight when the negroes are provoking me. I feel so bad, so hurt and tears spring to my eyes.

I wanted so bad to fix up something for Thanksgiving.

Ghu worked yesterday over where Howard C[arter] and Sallie lives. Howard insisted on Ghu taking dinner with him. Ghu carried dinner with him and took dinner with Howard. Sallie sent me samples of her winter clothing. The first time she has shown a friendly act towards me since last Christmas. God knows how my heart has ached from the coldness she has shown me but I forgive freely and am glad she sent the pieces. I hope she will speak to me when I see her again.

Here are a big pile of roughdried clothes for me to iron. Here it is 9:30 o'clock. Here I sit writing, weak, and tears in my eyes. No one to help—lots to do—and I so unable. Lord be with me today. Would that I could see Suse Tarpley today. She has her faults but is kinder to me than any negro on our premises.

‹ December 1 ›
First Day of the Month

The first day of Dec. 1905 has dawned *cold* and cloudy. I like cold weather, tho' I am cold natured—but I am always stronger in cold weather and take on new life as it were when winter comes and collapse when weather gets hot or warm. Yesterday was Thanksgiving Day. We [had] company in P.M. . . . Just at night fall I walked down to see old afflicted Aunt Mary and Monk. Sent them some dinner yesterday on a waiter. Ghu went hunting in P.M. and sent Aunt Mary all the game he captured—Three birds.

We have log-heap fires today. Oh, what a treat! Freezing weather— bright log-heap fires! Life is sweet in such weather to me.

Ralph annoys me greatly. From dawn till bedtime he knocks or cuts with a small hatchet—has been at it 2 weeks. When weather was balmy he was afraid of a pet shoat that stays in yard and wouldn't go out doors unless other boys were with him. He doesn't mind— obey—and is too young to whip much.

Weather is so severe we kept Travis home from school today.

December 2
Saturday Night

The last month of the year has dawned. How busy I must be as this is the only whole month I can be up before a trying ordeal will be mine. How many things there are for me to do, and *so much* of each day is spent cooking. Another life to be added to our family in January—about middle I think. I fear a hard time awaits me—a weak body, a large family, and the additional care of an infant. Not but that I love to work and will love and give my best possible attention to another infant; but so much to do and no strength—what trying times! My health is always bad, or strength weak—and bodily fatigue great for about 7 months after birth of the little ones. A chronic weak back and a trouble feminine sex is sometimes given to.

And little Mary has always been such a sweet, good, baby. Just to know she will have to be neglected is sorrowful thoughts. She is such a winning lovable baby. Oh, God, be with her—send someone to see after her when I can't. Lord protect my little Mary always when her mother can not be with, and see after her and help me to trust her to Thy care and to worry not. I hope each one of our children will have a pleasant Christmas.

Lately I've busied myself trying to brighten the cook room where I spend so much of my time. I've pasted newspapers over the dark, dingy walls to a good height. I've put few pictures about on the papers to brighten room and for past-time for myself and children. Little Mary notices them and tries to talk to them. I've put few pictures in dining room and few in our room and some in front room (where the stork comes) and I am so pleased with the bright cookroom, that I feel thankful for the papered walls.

We have in our room some wandering jew (2 little boxes) and one fern. I wish I could keep them alive all winter.

I am told that Papa received a letter from Nina Wynn today, saying that Marvin [Wynn] was *thinking* of coming here this winter. My family is large; my strength is small. Papa furnishes no provision. I am not able physically nor financially to board him. Yet I reckon I can tell no one so except Ghu and and the One above, without being misunderstood and giving offense. So I will ask the Lord if it can be His will, to prevent Marvin coming in our home to stay.

I was disappointed lately because C.V. Weathers had a charge [church] at Locust Grove. His family and himself have put upon us when my health was bad. Because we are in house with Papa we have many people to feed and cook for and expenses to foot when the people do not come to see us at all—claim to come to see "Uncle Jim" or "Grand Pa" etc. etc.

It is so hard for a weak woman like me to wait on them—cook for them. Lord to Thee only can I look for any relief: grant if it is Thy will, this Weathers family and Marvin Wynn will not give me trouble by staying on us. Lord prevent these mentioned ones from intruding on me if consistent with Thy will.

December 5

Tuesday Night

I am tired!—tired! tired! Darkies, Ghu and I have been putting away fresh meat—I didn't do much about it, or with it, but nevertheless, I am awful tired tonight. Ghu helped Gordon and Ebb cut up lard and sausage. I cooked dinner, helped them some and sewed some and washed thro' one water 25 napkins or more and my back aches yet. Would be sewing now instead of writing were not my back too tired.

I can stand only little while on my feet and I am afraid it will be impossible for me to fix up a great deal of cake etc. for Xmas. If I could I would make several cakes and will do best I can anyway.

December 9
Saturday Night

Mary, Ralph, and I are all alone — in our room — Papa is quite alone in his room. Ghu, Fred, Askew, and Travys have gone over to Tom Holder's to a rabbit stew. I ironed a big ironing this P.M. — more than I felt like I ever could finish, but I think the Lord helped me, as I ask Him to. I didn't know of a negro who would do it for me tho' I pay well, I always feel, for anything the negroes do for me. I was surprised when I got thro' ironing that I wasn't more tired and weary — until I remembered I asked the Lord to help me get thro' with the clothes. I believe He did help me, and I believe that is why I feel as well as I do now. Well Christmas is about 16 days off or 15 now. How time will fly those 15 days! I will, if strength permits be very busy those 15 days. I hope to get my preparations all done by Christmas Eve and trust I will not be rushed and strength so overtaxed that I can not enjoy the King's birthday.

I am going to try to get thro' and not be so overtaxed when Christmas Day arrives. How well do I remember last Christmas Eve and Christmas Day. I was tired awfully and very nervous. Didn't get over it in several days. Didn't enjoy Christmas day or any of the following holidays. Had company but was so overworked that I felt no pleasure in their visit.

Lord help me get my Christmas preparations all done and be somewhat rested when the day comes and enjoy it as I ought.

Mary is crying now to get in my lap. I think she is sleepy. I want to get her to sleep and take a bath before I retire.

December 10
Sunday P.M.

A cold day. I enjoy cold weather tho'; yet I am cold natured — have cold feet allmost all the time only when in bed — yet I love cold weather. Yes, I just love it. I have a husband who does, with help of the little boys, out door jobs, so I live indoors and enjoy winter.

Housework is so much lighter in one respect in winter (we do not have so much company to cook for) and nearly always I have more strength to do it with. But how my strength fags in warm or hot weather. How burdensome is my work then. Sundays are not near so lonely for me in winter. In summer Ghu and part, or all except baby, go somewhere on Sundays. I have to stay here to keep Papa from being alone. He isn't able to often get in a buggy. But in winters, Ghu is at home some Sundays all day and all the children rarely ever leave at once, and anyhow, the very weather is company and time doesn't seem long on Sundays in winter, as a general thing.

Now, while I write Ghu and Mary are asleep, the little boys at the wood-pile in sun—Papa alone by the fire in his room. Ghu is a "sleepy-headed" fellow. It doesn't take near so much sleep for me as it does for him but no doubt I would be better off, physically, if I slept as much as he does. He retires earlier than I, unless it is in seasons when my health and strength are such that I'm tired and worn out.

Jim Atkinson is sick now, with pneumonia. I use to be with Lora (Lora Childs, before marriage) and from childhood to young lady-hood was associated. I liked her always. She is a neighbor this year, but I've had no chance to go to see her. Ghu sat up with Jim A. one night. Lora's mother, Aunt, and sister-in-law were there the night Ghu went. I am glad Lora has relatives and Mr. Jim has, who care, and will be with them in sickness.

When Ghu and I get sick—how different. No one to do any thing for us except a hired negro. I am not complaining. I am just making a comparison. How thankful I ought to feel that none of our family are down on sick beds—what a blessing to be able to keep up. But soon I must be down on a bed, helpless. Soon I will be too weak for two months to see after the needs of our family. Soon I must suffer the terrible pangs of child birth (unless my sufferings are lighter than in times past). Soon another care, another life will be added to my many many cares and what then? Who will wait on me? Who will cook meals and make beds for family? Who will see after little one till I have strength to sit up? Who will see kindly after Mary when Ghu is out?

I do not know who.

The Lord has brought me thro' the pangs of childbirth six times.

He can as well bring me through seven times. The suffering is so great, we shrink from it and seems too great to bear, but what has been bourne, can be again I hope. Tis nature to dread it and shrink from it. I have asked the Lord to send us some one and we will, Ghu will rather, go see who he can get to help him with household affairs. Some one has always been, and we've made out somehow; sometimes help was badly needed for me and the infant, but we are living yet— I trust the Lord for some one to help. Suitable, satisfactory help we do not expect, in many particulars. How helpful it would be to have a good conscientious woman with us awhile—say two months, but not our luck I guess. May the One who watches over all, take care of, and be with us all; thro' those trying times which are not far away. Jan 1906 will bring a change in my life, in our home. May His Wings of protection be over our ark home now, then, and on thro' our residing here. Lord do be with us and help us to trust Thee for all absolute needs. In the name of Jesus we ask these things. Amen.

December 14
Thursday Night

All are in bed except myself. I am not sleepy—drank coffee for supper. Travis and I will sleep together tonight and he has a bad cough, so I guess I will not sleep much. Mary has gone to bed with Ghu. She is so fond of him that she will sleep all night with him lately. Mary is learning to talk fast. Often exclaims: "I declair!" She was doing so a week before we knew for certain what she was saying. "I dekare" is the way she says it, and she talks fast. "Come in—Hogs get you" is the way she calls and calls to them when they are outdoors.

(I hear Ghu snoring now.)

Fred and Askew are learning fast in school. Miss Ruth Jinks is the only strict teacher they ever went to. They had been to Prof. Levi Thurston and to Nellie Maddox only. Travis being so young we don't send him in worst weather. He doesn't learn very much, but there is time enough for him to learn—he is young, little, and not very stout and we don't care for him to go in severe weather.

Ralph asks me to make him pants so that he can go to school. Thinks he can't or must not wear dresses to school. Ralph and Mary are playmates.

Our little boys are all interested in the Christmas cakes I've been making this week. I've baked three nice ones this week and when they get home each day from school they soon ask "Did you bake any cake today?" The smaller ones (Askew knows who he is) talk good deal about Santa Claus especially does Travis.

Mary is a cheerful little thing—all life. Quick in her movements—talks fast—laughs much and prattles gayly from morn till night. She is an unusually *sweet* and good baby. She is 22 months old.

< December 14 >

Thursday Night

All in bed some time ago. I am not sleepy much and decided to sit up awhile after they retired. Have been writing. Wrote to Dr. Woods for Ghu, asking him to be at home or rather to come, when we phoned for him in Jan—

Ghu told me to write to him.

Mary will not be quite 2 yrs old before another baby will be here. She will be 2 in Feb. Another expected in Jan. Old Aunt Mary Brownlee, col., moved from here yesterday. She had been here about three years. I felt sad to see her go because she is not likely to live long—been unable to walk ever since Spring. Poor old negro—and Monk lying helpless—moved lying—'twas an unusually sad sight to see two helpless ones carried away in a vehicle. Don't think Aunt M. will live but short while.

Christmas is nearly here. Ten days off. I have baked three cakes—*real* pretty cakes smooth, even and perfectly cooked I think. I wanted if possible to not be so overtaxed this coming Christmas as I am nearly every Christmas, so I'm trying to get all my cakes done and everything else I hope to finish without rushing greatly by Xmas Eve—and be rested so as to enjoy the birthday of our Savior or King.

I want to enjoy it this time. I think it wrong to be so worn out and weary on Christmas day that one can't enjoy any thing; I can't always plan and get thro' tho' with my work like I am this time. Ghu is hurrying me to bed. The light is keeping him awake. I haven't read a chapter in Bible today and must quit writing and read it. I feel uncomfortable when I fail to read some each day in Bible.

December 15
Friday Night

Another drizzly day. Another cake baking half day for me. I made a raisin cake this P.M. Guess I will not bake any more cake now for Christmas except a quantity of tea-cakes. I have now one cocoanut plain cake, one cocoanut stacked cake, one plain cake, one raisin cake—all good size. Next comes tea-cakes, custards, baked chickens—then I'll be done with kitchen work. Then comes decorating with holly, cedar, mistletoe (provided I can get these) and a primping of two front rooms. Don't I enjoy fixing up for Christmas! Indeed I do. I think the Giver of all good gifts has given me strength to make Christmas preparations so far because last week I could scarcely do just common cooking any day.

December 22
Friday Night

I want to write so bad tonight. I love to write but Mary may be somewhat troublesome and prevent my writing. Don't know when I may write again maybe soon—maybe late—and knowing this only intensifies my desire to write.

Papa is sick tonight—has been sick ever since last night and has been lying down good deal today. I hope he will be better by morning. He has a cold, headache and rheumatism.

Old Aunt Mary the negro woman who lived 2 or 3 years here, and who moved away from here a week ago, was buried yesterday. Poor old negro—how pitiful she did look when she left.

I am not able to get around much, to do my domestic affairs. I have my house tho' nice tolerably. Ghu and a negro scoured some today—I've worked hard one day this week tidying 2 front rooms and changing pictures and furniture and fixing beds—had some help too for all that. I will be busy tomorrow I guess—baking custards etc; want to put up cedar and holly. Cedar is plentiful, but I may not get any holly and mistletoe.

Well another year is closing—a new one will soon dawn. I ought to have lived better in this one and pray that some of the wrongs I

do now I can overcome in the next—the sin of impatience and iri-
tableness with my children I speak of. I say cross words oftener to
them than is right. I loose patience daily; Lord forgive me for these
sins. I've spoken ugly in tones and words to Charlie boy tonight. I
do something of the kind almost daily to him—I am sorry always at
nightfall for my impatience with him.

‹ December 22 ›
Friday Night

Miss Ruth Jinks closed her school this P.M. (till Jan.) with a small
Christmas tree. This has been a very bad week—rainy—and tho' she
had a nice little tree—she had only 7 schollars. Askew, Fred, Travis,
Alice and Della Kelly, Annie Thompson and Olin Mason—were the
pupils. Ghu Mary and Ralph went over there. Mr. Kelly and 2 more
children and Ollie Mason were all who were present. Miss Ruth
put good many fruits and confectionaries on the tree for the whole
school (for those absent as well as those present) (I can't half write
on this book on my lap).

Ghu is to go to McDonough tomorrow and carry Askew, Fred and
Travis to see Xmas toys and a Carnival is there for a few days too—
the carnival begins tomorrow.

Papa isn't well at all today. He was sick all night and has been all
day—lay down good deal today. Has headache and rheumatism. Very
feeble.

Old Aunt Mary (the negro who lived with us 3 yrs and moved
severel days ago)—was burried yesterday. Lived a week after moving
from here.

‹ December 23 ›
Saturday Night (The night before Christmas Eve)

All are in bed and asleep unless it is Ghu. He retired last and may
not be sound asleep. I am going to bathe—I have almost *no* chance
of bathing in day time. Tomorrow is Sunday and we expect our new
preacher to take dinner with us—Mr. Stilwell is his name. Ghu went

to church today and met and heard him preach. Our 3 oldest children went somewhere nearby today and cut down a beautiful little cedar tree for Santa Claus to tie their gifts on. We put it in the hall. It is a lovely cedar. But Fred seems to prefer the old way—to hang up his stocking. Late this eve Askew, Fred, and Travis went up the road, nearby, and cut down cedar limbs for me to put over pictures and looking glasses—to decorate for Xmas. Tomorrow being Sunday we couldn't do it on Christmas Eve. How Travis does talk and talk about Santa Claus. Fred too. Travis says "come on Fred—let's go in here and talk about Santa Claus."

Papa . . . seems to be better today than he was yesterday. I am glad that he is better. He is such an old man that we get uneasy when he gets sick.

It seems strange to me that old Aunt Mary is dead—the old negro was here this time last year—I baked a cake for her—she furnished material. She was here 3 yrs., and in the house often—almost daily till her health failed last spring.

Little Mary loves a tiny hammer and has been saying that Santa Claus was going to bring her one; Ghu and I are both sorry she can't get one—he couldn't find one in Jaxon without getting a tool chest and intended going to McD. today but a rainy morning prevented. He went over to Mr. Maddox's this P.M. Askew went too— for confectionaries.

I feel that I have more than I deserve for Christmas. Ghu gave me a good and pretty rocking chair (and I wanted one so much) and because I love pictures so, he gave me a pretty oval shaped picture. Not long ago I bought a new one, and few days ago we paid for the picture of Papa and Mama enlarged. I like it—think lot of it. Then I have a new pretty cake dish—got it this week and will renew my subscription soon as convenient, to Ladies Home Journal. That is a rich treat. Then my room (maternity ward) is better fixed than ever—3 new pictures in it and some real pretty (tho' not expensive) curtains and some of the children and I ordered some small bright pictures and so we have brightened up the home and I have more than usual for Christmas, counting all these—and yes the maternity ward has a nice new wash stand—not fine but roomy and useful— and I appreciate it too. I ought to be grateful. I want to be. I love nice things, pretty things—don't crave very expensive things often, because I guess that I know I am not able to have them.

1906

‹ January 1 ›

New Years Day, 1906

Another New Year has dawned upon this world. Another year of troubles, trials, cares, sorrows and joys. I feel that I'm likely to have a full share of cares and I trust some joys and pleasures may be mixed.

Fred, Askew, and Travys went back to school this morning early. Mary and Ralph are quite noisy playing with each other. Mary is devoted to Askew and calls for him often when he is out of her sight. Mary had a pretty doll on their pretty little Christmas Tree Christmas morning and on 3d day broke its head. She loved her doll dearly, tho' played roughly with it. Since I've put a rag head on her doll— she likes it yet—but not as devoted as to its original beauty.

The little boys had a rite pretty tree—nothing expensive—Tablets, pencils, fruit, and candy, each a pair of gloves to wear to school etc. etc. etc. Now the little fellows are off to school for severel months.

Ghu is deeply interested in their education and helps them at night with their lessons with much pleasure. Ghu is a great help with the children. He is my prop and I fear myself and little ones lean too hard sometimes. What would I do were it not for the help he renders me in many things and above all with the children. He bathes the three oldest—I help to dress those who need help—and he nearly always bathes Ralph now—I of course, bathe Mary. He is always when well, cheerful and joky—he says he doesn't bathe girls. Ghu isn't rite well—eats hearty—but doesn't sleep well, complains of indigestion and weak heart. Something new—a weak heart—for him. Indigestion is an old trouble of his. Mary is so devoted to Ghu that she clings to him all the time nearly when he is in doors and insists on continually climbing in his lap to frolic and keeps him tired, but he is so fond of her that he has spoilt her about his lap. He plays so much with her! I do wish we had a good negro with us who would help us along all year with our *big* little family and household cares.

‹ January 6 ›

We've had company today: Mr. Tucker Childs and Mr. Bogue Childs, Sarah and 3 children, Joe Grant and Frank, Alice and Della Kelly. Meetsie Crumbly came Saturday P.M. to see me and today one week ago too. I love Meetsie very much. She is always so friendly towards me. Well surprising things do happen. Mr. T. Childs has been gone 12 years from family and wife and now returned. He looks a rite smart older and dressed *well*.

And another event in our home—Jan-1906—a telephone in our hall! Ghu had it put in last Tuesday. He had it put in for 3 months—he may keep it longer and may not. Says he doesn't feel able hardly to put $1.50 a month on the 'phone.

Travis, Fred, and Askew are very much interested in the 'Phone and talk sometimes to Olin Mason. I too, enjoy it very much. 'Tis past time to one who stays so close as I. Papa often goes to the phone to listen. Takes more interest in it than I thought he would.

January 7
Sunday Night

The New Year is 7 days old.

We have a telephone in our hall.

Mrs. Bartie Marsh was to have come here today, if Ghu had gone after her. Ghu and I thought if he went for her today she might not stay with us as long as we would want her and we decided to wait till nearer the *eventful* time of the visit of the stork.

Ghu carried Sarah and 2 of her little ones home this P.M. Mary went too, with him. She is coughing hoarse—has been threatened with croup.

Ghu and Fred have gone over to Mr. Kelly's tonight to a singing. Mr. Kelly has a new organ. I ordered it for them from Sears and Roebuck.

< January 14 >

Sunday P.M.

Ghu has gone after Mrs. Bartie Marsh this P.M. Papa is sick with a cold—not in bed, but ate *no* dinner—drank a cup of coffee. Said he didn't sleep well last night. Askew, Fred, and Travis are looking for Jim's boys this P.M. and Olin Mason (A little 3d cousin of theirs that they think well of). I must stop writing and bathe Mary, Ralph and myself before Mrs. Bartie gets here.

Askew and Travys have been sick with colds this week. Each have been part of the time out of school. Miss Ruth has about 40 on roll, and about 30 or 35 on good days but she has taught two or 3 rainy days with 3. Two of our boys and Olin Mason.

January 14

Sunday P.M.

I am weary—tired. Would lie down and rest, but 'tis Sunday P.M. and I haven't bathed and changed my clothing, so I'll rest a little while writing till my water to bathe in gets warm or hot.

Ghu has gone down near Fincherville for Mrs. Bartie Marsh to stay awhile with me. I wonder if I will be up and about this time next Sunday?

It is with worry that I think of future. I have a chronic weak back and after delivery I am always weak and nervous worn out and tired for about 7 months, and more or less so, as long as a baby nurses. An affection [affliction] peculiar to my sex I have suffered with for a long time, and more or less all the time. Dr. Woods has ordered me an abdominal supporter that I hoped would help me bye and bye. It has not come yet and I think it has been ordered long enough to have been here. I fear I'm not going to get it.

We are having a drizzly day. We have lot of wet weather. Children have bad weather to go to school but Ghu carries them and goes after them on rainy days.

Well, I may not have a chance of writing again in this book in a long time. Much suffering, trials and sickness may be my portion before I again scribble in here. Lord be with me thro' all that I must pass. I've been thro' much already and am still spared. My cares are so many now and our family so large that I feel afraid I can never again meet the demands made upon me physically in future as well as in past without constant assistance. Lord I do trust in Thee. Help me to trust Thee daily—hourly. Amen.

‹ January 22 ›

A rainy day—a very dark, gloomy, rainy day—warm for this season and thundered good deal. We've had such unseasonable weather for some time—or severel days.

Mrs. Bartie Marsh has been with us a week. She has been a great deal of pleasure to us—helped to pass off many pleasant hours.

Papa has been sick a week or more—with cold. His cold has broken but he seems so weak. Papa read in daily paper—[Atlanta] Constitution—today of the death of D. C. Brown. He was our preacher severel years ago—he united Ghu and I in bonds of matrimony 13 years ago.

Old Aunt Susan Tarpley is here tonight. She will spend awhile here—to assist me.

Askew, Fred, and Travis all went to school this rainy day—Ghu carried them and brought them home too. The children like Miss Ruth and are learning.

Hope Papa will soon be better or as well as usual. I pray God's wings of protection to be over this ark-home and that the inmates, the aged one, and the little ones will be seen comfortably after, when my strength fails. Lord be with and abide with us, and help us to seek to do Thy will all the time. Be with us in sickness and in health. Abide with us, watch over us thro' the days that are in near future— for Jesus sake. Amen.

January 25
Thursday Morning

Am not as well today as usual. I expect before the day ends that I shall suffer, suffer, suffer—

Suse Tarpley is getting dinner. Mrs. Bartie is assisting her some.

Mrs. B. is so kind that she sympathizes with Suse and will help her. Suse has rheumatism and is getting somewhat old.

We are having disagreeable weather today. I fear Papa will get worse when weather is bad. I hope he can stand the winter. I feel so sorry for him—feeble and aged, lonely and oft-times sad. Lord bless him, comfort him and sustain him—and if it be Thy will spare him yet to us. . . . My aged father and my little children will soon (I think this very day) be without my attention for a month or more. I trust they will do well and have all necessary attention. Heavenly father be with them and be with me. I am suffering some now—Oh, Lord be with me thro' every pang and afterwards. Be with me oh, Lord.

February 18
Sunday Night

Today is my birthday— 37 yrs old and the mother of another little girl who was born on 25th of January about 3:30 P.M. The suffering was great—would have been greater but for use of chloriform and the mercy of the Lord. Dr. Colvin was here. Our physician, Dr. Woods, was off. Dr. Smith was next phoned for—he was in Stockbridge, and Dr. Colvin came in good time. I might have died if no physician could have been present (child born breach-foremost) so the Allwise One had a Dr. to be on hand and one who did his part well I think. Ghu calls the baby Maggie Wynn.

Now my book is full. . . .

< February 18 >
Sunday Night

My (Magnolia Wynn Le Guin's) birthday— 37 years old. (Ghu will be 36 on the 20th Inst and on same day Mary will be 2 yrs old. Fred and Travis' birthday came both on 11th Inst—Fred 8 and Travis 6 yrs old).

We have a new baby—little over 3 weeks old—born on Jan. 25th— 1906. Ghu named her Maggie Wynn. She is rite large to her age. Wasn't weighed at birth—tho' larger than Mary was. She is rite long and will make a larger woman (if both live) than Mary will. She has a head full of hair and on back of her neck her hair is long (long all over, for a young baby but longer there). Her hair is very dark or black—eyes blue—skin seems to be fair. At first she favored Charles Ralph but now (at 3 weeks old) she favors Fred. Baby's change *so much*. Mrs. Bartie Marsh spent three weeks here, left when baby was over a week old. Old Susan Tarpley col. stayed 2 weeks to do for baby and I. Now Mary Watson (Col) is cooking for us and I have been doing for baby since she was 2 weeks old. The Lord has been good to us and baby and I are getting on very well. I thank the Lord that we both are living and the ordeal is over—tho' I am not as strong as many and do not expect to be, but am doing fairly well.

Expenses are very heavy for Ghu now. Trust our necessities can always be supplied, wish I was able to hire a good negro girl to help me all the year. Heavenly Father, be with me and help me as I struggle on, if struggle I must, for our family; or if it be Thy will grant that I may have help so that my work will not be so overtaxing. Help me to be cheerful and not so worried over my work and weak body. Lord do help me for Jesus sake, Amen.

Papa has been feeble over 3 wks and remains about the same. Hope he will get no worse and can stand the winter. Papa gave Askew 2 dollars "for waiting on him" he said; he gave Fred 1 dollar (last week) and some time ago gave Travis a dollar. They are going to take care of the money he gave them. Askew is very good to Papa. He is the most thoughtful boy or child I ever saw for his grandfather's comfort. In some respects Askew is an exception—a noble boy. His Grand Pa thinks so and speaks of Askew's kindness to him. Papa said that Askew was the closest student for his age that he ever saw in his life. He thinks Askew remarkably bright in his studies. Askew, Fred, and Travis are getting along nicely with their studies. Miss Ruth Jinks advances her pupils. She is a good teacher—a hard worker in the school-room. I think we were fortunate in having our boys in her school.

Old Mr. Mobley is very low. His son-in-law while drinking beat him and it may kill the old man. Ghu has gone up there to sit up tonight.

Little Mary has gone to sleep sitting up in rocking chair and I am not strong enough to carry her to bed, to do myself justice and I don't know how I am to get her there. I guess Askew is asleep.

Lots of folks came in to see little Maggie Wynn and I when she was only a few days old. . . .

< February 21* >
Wednesday

Yesterday was Ghu's and Mary's birthday. Ghu was 36 and Mary 2 yrs old. Little Maggie Wynn will be 4 weeks old tomorrow.

Maggie Wynn notices very much for her age. Yesterday she watched Mary and Ralph severel times with manifested pleasure as they came around her when she was in my lap. Her eyes would lighten up as R. and Mary would walk up to her. 'Twas a noticable thing—so young (2 days under 4 weeks) and such a pleased expression would come over her face when Mary and Ralph would come up to her and prattle.

Poor piteous Maggie Wynn! She had colic this P.M. about 2 hours. Her little face looked pained and piteous—her cry was so piteous, as if trying to call me or beg me for relief. Poor little sweet soul. How I love the tiny creature. God be with the baby all of its life long.

Poor little Mary! How my heart went out to her this P.M. I felt sad enough to have my eyes wet with tears. It was this way: Little Maggie Wynn baby was up and cross and little Mary was sick sorter with cold and sleepy and as was her wont before baby Maggie came, she came to me and held up both hands crying piteously for me to take her awhile and let her go to sleep in my lap. I could not because I was obliged to keep the tiny baby. The poor little thing then went and dragged a chair by the bed and climbed up on my bed. Now, tears fill my eyes because poor little Mary is so often denied real necessary attention since I have to devote most of my time to the little baby. I knew, and regretted that such would be the case before little Maggie came. Mary has been such a *good* baby, such a sweet baby and required so little unnecessary attention all her life, and that makes it sadder, to be compelled to neglect her at times and oft-times now. I paid her all the necessary attention before hand and devoted at times, lot of attention to her—now the sweet soul looks at me in wonder and surprise at times that I can't do by and with her as I've always done all her sweet brief life. Heavenly Father, protect, comfort, guide and be with precious sweet white souled Mary all thro' life, and Oh Lord, be with me, her mother, and help me to be a good mother, a patient, tender, loving mother to little Mary and each of the other children.

*Beginning with this entry, Magnolia confines herself to a single diary.

Ralph is different from the other children. I want to be a tender patient mother to him. I fall short of it, I fear, often. Lord help me to do my duty by Ralph and each of the little boys. Ralph is not so bad; he doesn't mind like the other children did.

Today Hester, Grace, Allie, and Faith Jarrell came. By the way, when I first began to sit up, Mr. Boe Childs came in my room. I was alone, combing my hair, and felt very much embarrassed for Mr. B. to come in—and appreciated his friendly call very much. While in the room Maggie Wynn began to cry (Suse was in stove room) and Mr. B. went back to the bed and brought her to the fire and nursed her on his lap till Suse came in the room. He is such a friendly man. I appreciate his kind ways or attention to us all (all our family). Mama liked him.

Della Childs wanted me to name the baby after her. Georgia Welch told me over telephone to name it for her.

< February 27 >

The little baby was a month old Sunday (25 Inst) and I never saw a baby grow faster. And she is growing pretty too. I think she favors Fred more than any one else, now, but young babies make so many changes (some of them); at first, I thought she favored Ralph more than anyone else. She is a sweet baby. Has gotton so she sleeps well at night; some days she sleeps lot and some day very little, but am glad she rests all night now and lets me rest too. At one month old (and few days prior) she began to notice very much for a little thing—notices Ralph and Mary, Ghu, and other children. First children she noticed were Ralph and Mary. She began to laugh a little, before quite a month old. At one month old she is a very nice size baby—full faced and plump. Much larger than Mary was at one month old. She has a larger, longer frame too, than Mary had and at birth was a little heavier than Mary was I think. . . . She is a sweet baby and if I just had some good help to run my household affairs I would think my baby not much trouble. A rite good deal of trouble she would be now, if I had not help. A negro woman will be with me till 10th of Prox. and then I don't know how I will manage.

Askew stayed home from school today on account of toothache. Fred and little Travis went on. Travis has a new acquaintance (a third cousin) Olin Mason, by name, whom he has become attached to. He is T's favorite schoolmate. Olin thinks lot of Travis too. Askew and Fred think lot of Olin too, I think.

< March 4 >
Sunday

A darky, Mary Watson, will be with me one more week and then my hands will be full: a spoilt baby and 2 more babies (Mary and Ralph), cooking etc. etc.

Baby Maggie Wynn grows. She is a good baby when in my lap— she is well, only nearly every day she has colic—just about every night. She is a little over 5 weeks old and has not been weighed yet. She is a very nice size baby—all says that who see her. Some say "what a big baby!" She is just begging to get up, out of cradle now and if I do not stop and take her she will cry.

< March 7 >
Wednesday P.M.

Little Maggie Wynn has white thrash [thrush] I suppose. Her tongue is thickly covered with white bumps. She has colic nearly every night. I telephoned to Dr. Colvin, to send me by return mail, something for the colic, and he sent a bottle of Paregoric. Papa nor I believe in giving babies paregoric much so I 'phoned yesterday to Mrs. Woods, to tell Dr. Woods to fix her a carminative, which he did, and left it at Mr. L. Atkinson's and I will get it sometime tomorrow I suppose.

< March 17 >
Saturday P.M.

Little Maggie Wynn still has the thrash but not near so badly as she has had it. She coos out and so young for that. She is seven weeks old. Everyone thinks she laughs more than is common for a 7 weeks old—has been laughing nearly all her life. She sleeps well usually at night, and is not so bad in day. I am doing well the past few days—got a negro girl 13 years old and she give much promise of being real good help for me. I feel thankful that Providence has provided help in this needy time. I was so worried—trying to cook and nurse too. The girl (Fannie) is a good nurse and is so much help in many other ways—in short I believe she is best help I ever had before in my life up to date. If she continues to do as she has done the past 3 days.

Fred and Travis are learning fast and so is Askew. They certainly are fortunate in having Miss Ruth Jinks for their teacher. She is a tip-top teacher indeed.

Mary and Ralph play beautifully together from morn till night. They are almost no trouble. Mary has a lovable disposition and makes friends with all who come—all attracted to Mary. She is truly an unusually sunny and sweet baby. . . .

Ralph will not be 4 till last day of May. He is pettish to some extent and timid—won't talk to strangers. He visited Miss R. J.'s school Friday P.M. with "Papa Ghu" and saw Miss R's Guinea Pigs and as he has never been much from home he had a treat.

Travis doesn't seem as strong as the other little boys. He is thin and bony—age 6—in Feb. Fred is the "chunkiest" one. He is fat. Fred eats heartier than others—eats almost anything. Askew never did eat like rest of us. Many things he will not eat.

‹ March 20 ›
Tuesday P.M.

We had a little snow this P.M. Cold weather for this season.

(Have lost my pen staff and do despise to write with a pencil.)

Baby is spoilt. I am worried. Hired a negro girl and let her get in debt to me for a pr shoes and tobacco—she was nearly barefoot. She helped me 2½ days—went home Sun. A.M. Now 'tis Tuesday P.M. and no negro yet—and Quarterly meeting is to come off next Friday and I'm looking for company and a whole lot of cooking for me to do and no one to help now—I try not to worry, but I can hardly cook a meal unless baby cries and cries. Haven't washed my dinner dishes yet on account of baby, tho' it is three o'clock liking 10 minutes. Guess I could get Dell to stay with me but she can't nurse much and doesn't wash dishes nice, so she would expect and contend for big pay and be almost no help. When I had no little baby I could get work out of her by helping each thing she went at and by showing her, but now I have to be with baby so much and those who help me don't do things in a very helpful way like they would, if I were working rite with them all the time. The negro who left owes me $1.40.

Askew, Fred, and Travis went to school yesterday. 'Twas an awful unlikely forenoon. Ghu carried them to school in the rain. There were only 4 pupils — Olin Mason and our boys.

‹ March 27 ›

Baby Maggie Wynn has thrash yet. She was 2 months old last Sunday. She's had thrash about 3 weeks, and I doctor her mouth daily. She has not been out of doors yet, only once, and then just a few yards from door step. She slept all night long (and on until breakfast was nearly done), last night in the cradle by my bed, without once awaking. She usually sleeps in a cradle till after midnight and then awakes hungry. We put her in baby carriage and rolled her in another room last Friday, for first time. Did that to give her a little fresh air and also to air out bedroom. All the airing our room gets is by covering baby up in cradle with quilt or sheet and leaving windows up while I sweep. Weather is so bad we don't leave them up long.

Mary has been sick ever since last Friday — 2 or 3 nights had fever — no appetite hardly yet. I think she is cutting teeth. . . . Mary was somewhat delireous one or two nights and would laugh musically all thro' night. She is indeed a sunbeam. I never saw a child with so much sunshine in their disposition, that I know of. She is so good when even at the sickest she's ever been. Sweet, precious little Mary! I can't do for her like I wish to — with another baby and housework too. Now I have a good negro girl named Fannie to help me. Hope I can keep her till cotton chopping time — and wish I could keep her all this year. She is not one bit impudent, altho' 2 of her sisters are. I like her disposition and when I'm rite by her she does her work well — at times I can't be but nevertheless, I like her so far better than any negro I've had in last few years. I believe I'd rather have her, if I could be up all time, than any I ever have had. I am thankful that Providence has provided her so far to help me.

Askew wrote a very good letter, for his age, to Henry Co. Weekly, a few days ago. I copied, changed it some and corrected and mailed it. Askew composes well. Fred is best singer in the crowd. He has manifested some talent for singing for about 3 yrs. Traviss is a "sugar tooth Dick" or "Sugary Sam"—craves sweets—candies etc.

The telephone would be "oodles" of past time for me, had I the time to devote to it. I talk some tho' nearly every day, and enjoy the phone very much.

Old Mr. Lee, Mrs. Maddox's father died last night. His death makes me feel sad—he and Papa were nearly the same age. Papa is very feeble. He has been all this winter—more than ever before. He looks weak, weary and jaded now. Doesn't talk much. Loves all the children very dearly—thinks little Mary a curiosity—bright and winning.

Some low principled person opened school house windows Sunday and pulled Miss Ruth's beautiful hot-house-plants—the blooms. It was a *low down* act.

< April 1 >

Sunday

Ghu, Askew, Fred, and Travis, have gone to New Hope to Sunday School. Fred takes more interest in getting his S.S. lessons than any of them. He reads more in Bible than Askew does. Neither one reads much outside of that they read in school room, in Bible—so far. Maybe when Fred grows to manhood, he will be a preacher. When Fred was not over 5 days old it seemed he would be likely to die and I prayed earnestly for his life to be spared and told the One Above I'd try to raise him for Him or in other words gave him to the Lord then. He didn't nurse until 5th day after he was born and I was very uneasy about him and was so happy when he began to nurse, and was so thankful to God that he could nurse and was likely then to be raised. I hope never to forget how I prayed the Lord to spare Fred's life and how thankful I felt when he first nursed the maternal fount.

Little Mary has been sick a week, cutting teeth I guess. 2 yrs old in Feb—hasn't cut stomach teeth yet. She has come in room near me now, tired out from play and fallen asleep on the floor. I must cease writing and pick her up and also quiet little Maggie Wynn.

‹ April 12 ›

Thursday night

Askew is wearing shirts! He will be 11 in August. I meant to have kept him in waistes until he was 12, but my chances for sewing is bad with so much of my time taken up with Maggie Wynn, and shirts are easier and more quickly made than waistes are. Then too, Askew wanted shirts and Fannie Mathers told me she was going to make Noble some soon, and Noble is a few months Askew's Jr. Anything to help me to get on faster or easier with my sewing!

Miss Ruth Jinks school will picnic Saturday at or near Cedar Rock at a place she called "The Mountain Rock" and they are to have an Easter-Egg-Hunt at "The Mountain Rock" — Have to go Sat — Wish I could join them.

There surely never was, in this world, a cuter baby than our little Mary! She is the liveliest jolliest baby I ever saw in all my life, I think. She sends forth peals of silvery laughter from morning till night. She laughs *so* merrily and *so* much. She is sunshine. Every body who stays here long falls in love with Mary. Her little head now has thin hair on it, long enough to tie a piece of ribbon on, (on top of her head) and Papa and Papa Ghu, and the little boys think she looks cuter than ever with her hair tied up with ribbon. I think so too. She does seem so delightfully cute — she is so amusing, that we *never tire* of watching her numerous didoes. *She is a very unusual child.* She is *so* refreshing. *So* lovable and *so* captivating. The Creator was good, *so good*, when He sent us two precious little girls to number with our dear little boys. Lord help us to raise these for Thy Jewels.

Little Maggie Wynn is so sweet, so precious. Such a dear, darling baby — coos off and on all day. Began cooing when 8 or 9 weeks old. She makes such heavenly music to me when she coos. Such a wonderful thing is my little infant. Oh, how I love infants! Such blessed innocence! How blest I feel to have for my own, my precious little innocent infant. How thrilling to me is the life of my infants. How I do *love* infants. A negro infant I find interesting because they are *infants*. I thank the God above for adding the precious little soul of Maggie Wynn to our life, and I pray Him to help us be means of saving their souls and raising them all for Him.

Fred was sick with headache one day this week, and had to stay home from school. Askew stayed one day. Travis is learning rapidly.

He is a good speller, excellent for his age. Fred is a splendid speller too. Askew is also a good speller. Askew is bright in some of his studies and all three are progressing nicely and satisfactorily to Ghu and I. Miss Ruth is a born teacher. She says to teach as one ought, one has to have the calling to it, the same as to make a successful preacher—I believe she is quite right and we've been fortunate and I think blest, in having her teach our children. I wish they could go on to her for a few years. She is a christian—a Baptist—and such an intellect! 'Tis bed time and little Maggie Wynn has been asleep most of this day and I sewed and did good many things. Fannie is a rite good negro—and I thank the Giver of all good gifts for her help.

‹ April 14 ›
Saturday. Night—bedtime

All are in bed—(Ghu is undressing) except Ghu and I. Askew, Fred, and Travis have been to a picnic and Easter Egg Hunt today at Cedar Rock on a beautiful spot called Mountain Rock. Miss Ruth Jinks carried a crowd of her school children there today. They brought some beautiful moss back with them. (Baby is crying. I am loathe to leave off writing just now.)

Poor little Mary went to bed hungry. Little Maggie Wynn was crying and I had to pacify her and by that time poor little neglected Mary had gone to sleep. I've had a trying day and poor little Mary and Ralph are often *sadly* neglected and my heart is sad because I can't give them more time and attention. I always have trying days when a wee baby and a larger baby etc. etc. are all on my hands. My strength fails—I am sorry I can't see after Ralph and Mary more and sorry I can't devote more time to the other 3 older ones.

Heavenly Father, help me in my cares or worries—help me in raising my children. Help me to redeem the time—all that is to be given me hereafter this time on.

< April 24 >
Tuesday A.M.

Miss Ruth Jinks closed her school last Friday. I was to have gone over there but could not get off. Miss Ruth is a good teacher—that expresses it too mild. She is an unusually good one—a conscientious and painstaking worker in the school room.

Travis surprised us all in his advancement this year. He is a bright speller—excellent for his age, and reads well. Fred and Askew are getting on nicely with their studies. There will be no summer school. I hope we will be fortunate enough to get Miss Ruth back again for our next term.

Little Maggie Wynn will be 3 mo's old tomorrow. Fannie, the negro girl who stayed a month has gone home. She was to stay this week here, but a sick brother has detained her I suppose. I certainly do need her or some help. My strength fails me every day, more or less. Emma Jinks and her father came here yesterday. I wrote for Emma, Miss Nannie McKibben's obituary. I loved Miss Nannie. I love Mrs. St John and Emma. I like each member left in that home. I appreciate friendship. Mr. St. John's people are *so* kind hearted. Miss Nan was such a loving mother to every one there and so warm hearted to all. How I do appreciate the friendship of those warm heated, good people. 'Tis getting late now and I have little time to read or write. Lord be with me thro' all this day and help me to patiently toil on. Ghu has gone to McDonough. Askew is lot of help and very kind to me.

< April 26 >
Thursday P.M.

Precious little Maggie Wynn was 3 months old yesterday. She is a fine baby—never was weighed but a fine baby. Grows nicely. Has a sweet soft eye—the expression is very gentle. She favors Fred more than anyone else. Poor little Mary! Poor little Ralph! I wish I had time and strength—more to give them. And poor little Travis, Fred and Askew. I wish I could be with them, free from cares—more. My time and strength taken up and poor children neglected some. I pray the Lord to help me be a warm hearted good mother to my children and to help me after I've done best I can to not worry so because so many things are undone. I pray God to bless each one of my children and help me to gain and retain the love of each one of them.

< May 4 >
Friday P.M.

Cape spent two days with us this week, accompanied by his little son, Butler. Butler is a very innocent little boy—just like a baby, yet not spoilt. So girl-like! His mother idolized him. His devotion to her was ideal.

Little Maggie Wynn, pure white souled infant—was weighed about 2 days after she was 3 months old and weighed 15 lbs. She was never weighed before. She began to drink water (I gave it to her, luke warm) rite early—after first few weeks of her life—I think before she was over 3 weeks old. I commenced giving her a little buttermilk, rite fresh at 3 months old. She relished it and I now feel sure I made a grave mistake in not giving water to my other babies while they were young. On warm days I think my little 3 months old Maggie Wynn feels refreshed after a few sips given her from a tea-spoon.

I was all run down—*awful* tired yesterday and couldn't do anything well—so completely broken down—and neglected my sweet baby some—(seemed to me I could not help it) and last night she had a severe cold. She always coughs when she has a cold. After a dose of oil and a bath she has slept well and long naps so far today.

My negro girl Fannie came back and stayed 7½ days and left again yesterday. She was kind to the children and saved me steps, tho' she gave me trouble in washing dishes *so* badly lately and wouldn't do some of her work at all well lately. I needed help so bad tho' I hated to see any kind of help leave me, and felt some relief too about the bother she gave me. Askew and Fred and Travis are doing small things and bringing some water. Papa Ghu brings water, most of it. I miss Fannie about the baby and bringing water more than anything. She could quiet and amuse baby rite well. Don't know how I can sew any now, but trust I'll get on at least tolerably well.

Mary was sick this week and is looking thin yet, but playful as a kitten. She is the liveliest little creature I ever saw in my life. Yesterday she found in my work box a drab piece of silk and she came to me and ask me (in her way) to pin the silk up at her neck. She can't join words—very few—and her vocabulary is *very* limited for her age—but I think for no reason only that she is tongue-tied.

Poor little Ralph has discarded dresses and gone into pants. 'Tis with sad feelings I see him out of dresses into pants. Poor little soul. He loved pretty clothes—loved trimmed underclothes, but my health and many cares caused his outfit all his life to be cheap, and not much of anything, but plenty for all the going he did tho' not as nice as 'twould have been had I had time and strength for his clothes. I feel sad when I think how he loved pretty clothes and what a few pretty things he ever had. He had one pretty garment made (his nicest) and sickness on my part caused him often to stay at home and whooping cough this spring kept him and Mary close and now he is in pants and the pretty skirt he thought so pretty he never wore. He would just laugh when he saw me making him a pretty trimmed one, and always talk lot about his best clothes and be so pleased when they were put on him. He will be 4 yrs old last day of this month. Poor little boy—the care and attention that was his share never came to him after he was 14 months old—my health and care of other babies since then made poor little Charlie oftimes neglected. Poor baby boy—in pants. Divine blessings be upon him.

< May 15 >

Baby Maggie Wynn went down (with Papa Ghu, Mary and himself [myself?]) to Alf Wynn's Sunday P.M. It was Maggie Wynn's first buggy ride. She liked it and was perfectly good all time we were away. (First buggy ride 3 mo's and two weeks old) and she never wore a starched garment till 3 mo's old. I didn't visit and the soft ones were more comfortable.

Travis was 6 yrs old in Feb. and shedded his first tooth today. I put it away in my watch case. Fred also pulled one of his teeth today. I think it was an eye-tooth.

So little Maggie Wynn enjoyed her first buggy ride. We stopped to see Mrs. Sarah Mason on our way home. Ghu wanted her to see Mary and Maggie Wynn both and I wanted to see her; she has been ill so long—not expected to ever get well. Little Maggie is awful cute—a blessed baby. One of the best that ever came to bless our lives. She slept till after 10 o'clock this A.M. She was awake when I rose to get breakfast, but I made her comfortable and left her laughing and wide awake so she fell asleep and remained so a long time. She is now cooing and laughing gleefully at Travis.

Askew is a real bright boy in his studies. He is not like other children his age. Sometimes they have company and Askew will read the Daily and Weekly papers and Fred and their company fish and frolic. In the field Ghu says Askew is the most industrious child he ever saw in his life. In the house he is kind and thoughtful to help me. He, Fred, and Travis dry dishes, draw water, bring in stove wood (and in bad manner sweep the floors some times). They amuse baby and are a great help to me. Fred and Askew are very much help to Ghu in the field. Travis works there too, when he gets tired he quits. He is smart tho'. Our children are *all* a great satisfaction to me. I love them and prize them deeper lately than ever before. I guess it is because motherlove is expanding. I know that we have sweet intelligent, good children. I thank Our Father that they are such. We've been richly blessed. I've had to work so hard—overtaxed my strength so that at times I did not realize how blest we were with such a number, but *I am glad* we have a large family.

< May 23 >
Tuesday Night

Maggie Wynn is not rite well—diarrhoea. Mary is awful cute. She has some slippers, white stockings and a new cap. When she gets these on she cuts up many antics. She is awful sweet—never saw a cuter child in all my life. She is so brim full of sunshine and so doll-like. Her face is round—her limbs beautiful proportioned. Beautiful feet and legs and hands, but quite dark. A sweet dimple, more of a dimple in one cheek than the other. She is winning. She is lovable and attractive—by all who love anything.

My pen will not work.

Fred cried a lot because I would not give my consent for he and Askew to drive the horse to McD. to spend tonight at Mr. Ingram's and attend the commencement exercises. Ghu told them they might do this if I consented. I couldn't give my consent. I do not want my children to *spunge*. I was also afraid for them to drive the horse by themselves. I wish they could have attended the exercises indeed I wish it very much but couldn't let them spunge or go alone. Trust they can go to commencement next year. I am truly sorry they could not attend this one.

I was never at a commencement in my life. Wish Ghu had carried these little boys tonight but it was so far and he was so tired.

‹ May 31 ›

Today is Ralph's birthday. He has been in pants about 3 weeks I think. Little Maggie Wynn was 4 months old last Friday. She has barely gained a lb. in this month. When 3 months old she weighed 15 lbs. Now at 4 months old she weighs hardly 16, but very near 16 lbs. Little Maggie Wynn isn't well. She had a fever night before last. She was sicker than she has ever been before in her life.

Askew is a good boy to help me with the baby. Nursing the baby tires he and I too—makes my back ache, but he is the only one of the children that can quiet her, or carry her in arms well. I get weary and tired—doing all I have to do and nurse baby too. Askew helps me but how weary I am before the day is done. I don't talk out of family about my tired feelings much. We can't get our washing done regularly. I've washed good deal last week and this, for baby, Ralph, and Mary. I know not how I'm ever to do my washing and the negroes here will not wash, last week or so far this. I don't know what I will do. I am having a time with my weak back (etc) and all to do, but I am thankful to be up and going, but hope some negro will be provided for us as a wash woman. Lord help us with our work.

‹ June 7 ›

Little Innocent (Maggie Wynn) is in short dresses. She was perhaps 2 weeks over 4 months old when she donned her first short dress. 'Twas yesterday P.M. that I put her first short dress on. She was so sweet that I laid aside my work for awhile and *just loved her*— just basked in the bliss furnished by the life of little Maggie Wynn. She is a sweet, good, baby. Sleeps well, and long. Amuses herself by watching and playing with her fingers. I believe I get more rest from nursing Maggie Wynn than from any baby who ever blessed our home (at her present age). She has the *gentlest* expression of the eyes of any of our family. She certainly is a wonderfully sweet baby.

Little Mary is happy and joyous all the time. Has a wonderfully expressive face. Looks at our faces to know whether we are serious or joking. Scans us closely and is quick to know our moods and our real feelings or meaning and acts accordingly—if we are serious she is too—if we are joking she cuts up all kinds of antics, or didoes. She rarely ever cries. Seems always so happy, so jolly. She danced a job this P.M. over the joy of holding in her hands one of her Sunday slippers. Just danced a regular hornpipe I say—just because she came across her Sunday "shoe" she calls it. She will laugh merrily every day when I talk with her about wearing her Sunday shoes. She gets up the subject by asking me "where my shoes?" and then to make her joy run over I go on a rigamarole about her going to S. School and riding in buggy.

Cape came today—pop call. Boyd, his son, in Fla. very low with typhoid fever—Cape in trouble. I was sorry for him.

Mr. Stilwell, our Pastor, and wife and 2 children gave up a pop call yesterday P.M. I had been hard at work and children and yard around door was untidy—Lizzie Mason told me over 'phone that the preacher and wife were on their way over here. So I jimed around and tidied up some. I was somewhat embarrassed at untidy things, but it would take 2 *strong* women to do all I want to do. I do all I can and regret keenly and deeply that I can not at nearly all times have time and strength to keep everything around us tidy and pleasant to be seen. I would be a nice housekeeper, "yard keeper" and "child keeper" if I had a chance. Ghu said something like that to me one day recently, when I was working hard to clean things and strength overtaxed and when he knew I had not strength equal to my undertakings. Yes, I would be a clean housekeeper had I strength and assistance, but no one woman could keep all corners up in my home with all 9 of us and no more strength or help than I have. The older I get the nicer I am—more industrious, or more painstaking—as a housekeeper. Yet I don't reckon anyone can understand that because they see untidy things now that they did not see when my family was smaller. The reason is this: there is so much more for me to do and the children are all the time undoing what I do. One reason that I know I am more industrious, or a better housekeeper is that I work harder on my cooking tables and utensils than I did say 6 yrs or even 3 yrs ago. What I left undone in my cook room then is a surprise to me now—and I work hard on those things now that I once had some more time for. But my health has certainly been so bad most all of my married life. Neuralgia 8 yrs and other troubles that were so weakening at same time. And must drag tho' life with a much weaker body than any can realize, all because ——— I won't say that now about the Dr. No relief to be obtained unless I am operated on—and then I might be very little benefitted. I can't believe an operation would benefit me greatly. I find much relief in a brace—can't hardly sit up 2 hrs. without it—I feel like I don't think I could go without one. People have no idea how overtaxed my body is daily. I am large. People think I have strength to match my size.

My heart goes out to little Ralph because so many of his clothes are "left overs" (from boys older) and he doesn't look neat in them, and I have such a small chance, such little time to sew. I pray for strength to cook, to sweep house, and yards, to sew, to scour buckets, to make beds, to see after bathing little ones etc. etc., and I think I would get on worse than I do, if I didn't pray for help to do all I have to do.

< June 8 >

Friday night

The clock has just struck 9. I feel so tired—so weary, and Ghu does too. He is working hard in the field or farm—plowing. Summer has come and has robbed me of my strength as it always does, in a large measure. It seems I never get thro' and so many things from dawn till dark and the precious darling Maggie Wynn to nurse too. She has been for over a month a splendid baby—the best one ever in our house I thought, in some respects, but since June came in, the warmer weather causes her to cry. She is a very warm natured baby and her head just drips with perspiration, and she cries often when so hot. So I feel so tired daily that I feel like I could not continue creeping, going, doing, or nursing till supper dishes were washed, but tonight I drank some coffee to brace me awhile, and now little sweet Innocence is playing in cradle and I just *hunger to write.* I'll have to get up early and ought perhaps not try to have the past time of writing this. Have weakened so that I can't turn off work fast and can't get thro' and so I'm thinking of having Ghu to let Mr. Bridges take our telephone out till fall. How I regret the past time and pleasure it would afford—yet I have not the time to devote to it, or the strength after working to stand there and talk—I can't stand well from causes best known to myself. Baby crying. I must quit. Work, work, work—Goodbye to past time till next fall, when I'll have if I live and am not prevented, my telephone put back in. How keen the pleasure of talking to friends has been. How I regret to give it up, but lack of time and strength forbids my keeping [it]. Work, work—but I must believe it best to give up pleasure of 'phone and spend all my strength in housekeeping and rearing children.

We have lot of company in summer that I am not able physically to cook and do for them, being 9 of us in family and we (Ghu and I) are not able financially to have them. but we have to make the best of it. Many of them claim they come to rest and save their own expenses—sorry to say.

‹ June 15 ›

Mary's 3d summer and she is 2 yrs and (about) 4 mo's old and she has just cut one stomach tooth and has no eye teeth, and no jaw teeth. So I fear that Mary's 3d summer will be a trying one for her. She is so very backward about teething. She is sick now—has been for 3 or 4 days and has falled off some but she is the *cheerfullest* sick child I ever saw. Mary is of a remarkably cheerful joyous disposition. She is so winning—so lovable—all who come in contact with her are attracted by her. She does do many unusual, unexpected things. She amuses us all from morn till eve. Ghu is perfectly devoted to her. He says daily that "she is the *sweetest* thing I ever saw in my life." He said last night that in his heart Mary, only, came next to me. He loved me best of all in the world and Mary next. Little Mary and Papa have lots to say to each other. . . . Mary can't talk much but is learning fast. Her tongue is so tied that she can't speak her words plain. She calls milk "wiff."

Maud Wynn Hooten and her 2 children, Annie B. and Dovie Wynn, and Butler Wynn came one day this week and went back the next. They seemed to love little Maggie Wynn very much and exclaimed "What a pretty baby!" They said a good deal about her being a pretty baby. One of them said she was the prettiest baby they ever saw.

(June 15 continued) When they said Maggie Wynn was the prettiest baby they ever saw . . . Papa said they were not story telling. He said he thought she was an unusually pretty baby. He said he didn't think she could be improved. Every one says she is "flower of the flock." She is so sweet — so good. Little Travis has a pure innocent heart. He is so gentle, so sincere. So innocent. He is somewhat frail — thin — suffers from indigestion. Askew is lot of help to me and seems to *know* that I very much need help. He gathers beans for me this summer and many other things. I believe I have rite good boys. I don't say they couldn't be improved.

Mary wants to cook. Two years old and a cook — ha! She presents a comical picture rolling dough and making out biscuit. She enjoys it very much. I let her have rolling pin and dough every day lately. I also let the little boys have dough and rolling pin. They also use a thimble to cut biscuit. At times sometimes they cut their biscuits square, with a case knife. Blessed little children. How I wish each of you would always be as pure and innocent. My book is full. May our Heavenly Father keep each one of you on thro' life and when life's chapter is ended may each one's name be recorded in Heaven.

‹ June 24 ›

New Hope protracted meeting now in session. Am sick today and have not been yet. Papa has been sick. Mary has been sick but is better. Maggie Wynn is well again and would be a good baby if weather was cool. The children take it turn about in going to church. Askew went last night. Fred today. Mr. Weathers and Mr. Bowden have been with us some. Mr. Weathers and Mr. Stilwell are expected here tonight. Fannie Weathers and Noble tomorrow. Lora Atkinson and Meetsie C. came last Sunday. I was glad to see them. They are my old school mates and good friends. Little Mary is cute but since she got sick her disposition is not as sweet as formerly. Ebb Grier (Col) is helping me cook this week. Mary, Maggie Wynn, Ghu and myself went over to Mr. Maddox's last week. Nellie and Bessie amused the baby all time we were there. Ghu bought us an ice cream freezer over there. Mr. Maddox keeps ice all the time now. If we were able we could have ice cream often. We've been buying ice on Sat. P.M.'s last three weeks.

< July 25 >

Thursday Night

Maggie Wynn went to church today for her first time. She was 7 months old yesterday. I wanted Mr. Stilwell to baptize her during this meeting, but his wife is sick and he has been detained by her illness and I think the meeting will close tomorrow. Mr. Weathers is assisting in preaching and he will go to Mt. B [Bethel] day after tomorrow I reckon. I dreaded household work during this meeting, but so far things have not (since Sunday) been so bad on me. Ebb helps to cook very well so far. I've been to church twice. Today was children's service. All my children were there except Travis. He stayed with Papa. Was so willing to stay. He is a dear, gentle, low voiced sweet disposed little boy. He was his Grandma's . . . favorite and her blessings were upon him. I'll never forget her kissing and pressing him to her bosom o'er and o'er and crying when she thought life was soon to be over for her. I'll never forget it. And may her bright spirit be with Travis thro' life and guide him up to Heaven's bright stair. I believe her spirit is with us here in her old home where so long she associated with Papa and us all. How she would always become anxious about the children when they were out of her sight. How often, oh how often she would anxiously ask "Where are the children?" And in her spell of sickness one year before she died how daily and through out the days she would want to be assured that the children were not out of sight. Oh, Heavenly Father, help me to become a mother such as she was. Build up in me a warm heart like hers—a deep abiding, tender love of my little children. She loved them so! Beautiful, yea strikingly ——— (I was necessarily interrupted here and can't remember the sentence now.)

< August 8 >

My father's . . . birthday. He has lived to see his 85th birthday. I am thankful that he has been spared thus far. Maud (Wynn) Hooten spent yesterday with him. Dolie came with her. Maud seems to think a great deal for Papa. I think Maud is a very true-hearted woman. Very true to her Wynn kin. She certainly does standby them and resents anything unkindly said of them. She is a true good soul in another sense. I notice that she always speaks of the *good* traits of people and appearantly does not see the bad side or faults of any one. I think it is noble to be like her. She has a spoilt (very badly behaved) grandson with her. He made things unpleasant for all here—unless it was for herself. The troublesome little grandchild was Roy Hooten. Our little boys found him to be the unkindest little boy they ever had to visit them.

Our baby, Maggie Wynn is 6 months old and can get off her pallet (on her stomach) after anything she sees and wishes to get. This warm weather makes her fretful. I know she must feel badly. Poor little baby.

We've had a good deal of company this summer. The past few days I could hardly cook. Ebb Greer helped me some—in fact was rite good help—for 6 days. Mandy Stewart helped the day Maud and Dolie came and I baked a pie and put some salt in it. I suppose one of the small children had put some salt in the sugar bowl.

Charlie Wynn and little son, Henry, spent 6 days with us. Henry was a lovable little boy. Good, quiet and kind. Mr. Weathers, Fannie and Noble have been out. Noble was kind to our little boys but very spoilt and his parents didn't correct him but very little. He was in some respects unpleasant, but his parents don't tell him better and they don't seem to be annoyed while every one (of the grown people) in the house are annoyed.

Mynta Wynn Clark is in Ga. Her husband and baby also. I was sick all time Mynta was here and she helped me do the cooking just like she was at home. Her health is bad—she is taking this trip for her health. Her baby is a very sweet baby and very pretty. Mynta is a good kind woman. I think lot of her. Mr. Clark has good traits too but is loud, noisy; uses big words, and I don't feel at ease with him. I am not physically able to cook for our summer company. My strength fails in hot or warm weather. I can hardly keep going but there is no remedy. Ghu says we are not able financially either, but we do the best we can—struggle on, uphill, maybe there will be better days by and by. Maybe I will have help some day, some time, somewhere. Mary and Maggie Wynn, I hope, will be good help in household affairs.

< August 10 >

Saturday

Papa . . . took a ride to the bridge and back one day this week, the day after his 85th birthday, I think, for the first time in a long time. He wanted to see the old mill where most of his time has been spent for many years, now "so silent and lone" — dam and race all gone, no grinding. He had not been in a buggy before in a long time and that little ride made him sore. 'Twas sad to see him after he came back — returning from his place of years close association. . . . Sad I know must have been his thoughts now that he is so close to the spot and rarely ever sees it — can't walk and painful to ride.

Little Maggie Wynn can crawl just a little and tries to jabber at Mary and loves Mary and is gleeful over Mary often, daily and Mary loves her dearly.

Ghu, Travis and Fred have gone to Indian Springs, to camp-meeting.

Ghu's sister Stella is visiting Mrs. Emma Jinks. She and her little girl Thelma. My children do not know their relatives well, on their Papa's side, as they've lived in La. since before any children came to our home. Stella phoned to Ghu to come and bring them to our home Monday. Of all of Ghu's relations his sister Elsie and his Mother were my favorites. I never was with them enough to count for anything (with exception of Stead) until married. We lived near them first year of our married life and after that [they] moved to La.

Little Mary has been puny about one month — diarrhoea — teething. She looks pale, sallow, and so small — so tiny, but plays all day.

My father is weary and jaded with 85 years of age. I hear him sigh as if very weary. Poor old man. How weary he feels. How a house full of company does make him weak and faint like. He loves to have company. He loves for friends to call and loved ones (home folks) to spend a day or so but in summer so many visitors and some staying some time and so many of us already around, is worrisome to him, and to me — the cook — the housekeeper, the worn out mother of 6 children, the housekeeper daily for 9 — I have a not very strong body at all times, and a very weak body oftentimes. Tho' I may love people very much, I am not able physically or financially to have them visit me long and in crowds and often. I sometimes feel that I have no time or strength to cultivate friendship, tho' we have lot of company. My poor little children do so often go sadly neglected. I've been ailing good deal this summer—in bed 2 days. Over worked, fagged, weary, tired. I live *close* at home. In 8 yrs there have been few meals I've taken from home. Few places I've visited.

Little baby Mary (2 yrs and 6 months) has brought 3 tiny flowers and placed them by my ink-bottle for me. She has begun now to bring me flowers as all my children have done.

< August 13 >

I am tired—more than I can express. We have oodles of company and I have no help except that a negro washes breakfast dishes and makes up 2 beds—sometimes more than 2 beds. I am not well and so weary. Cape and Butler came yesterday P.M. and are going home this P.M. Winnfrey Wynn and Jno' Wynn came in today before dinner dishes washed, and Jno' is going away this P.M. and Winnfrey will go away tomorrow A.M. I was glad to see Cape. I think his little boy a real good child. I feel sorry for him; he is such a pitiful little fellow—looks sad without his mother and he was so devoted to her. Cousin John and Cousin Winnfrey are good nice men. I like them well enough. I am just not physically nor financially able to have such a crowd to cook for during the hottest months of summer and I've been off physically ever since beginning of New Hope meeting [in July]. My feelings overcame me today and in presences of Della and Nannie May Kelly I just cried and could not help it. When Coz. Jno' came in and asked me why I was not going to camp meeting I could not controll my feelings again and cried and told him "there were nine of us—six babies—I had no chance to go." Two babies wearing napkins and no one to help and company—continued company.

Help me My Creator or I can't struggle on. How hard it all seems to me. What rough time I do have. What a life! Sometimes it is rough indeed. I am so tired now I must go and try rest a few moments.

Names of people who have visited here this Summer. . . .

[A list of 116 visitors.]

< August 14 >

Tuesday

I am so weak—back of head feels unpleasant and seems to weaken me.

No, I just need rest. I need it oh, so badly. That is the very thing I can not get. Baby is not well—quite fretful today. Cousin Winnfrey Wynn has left to go to Will W[ynn]'s. Said he to would come back. He is a nice smooth good man. He is cultured, refined. I fell in love with him.

I feel cramped, embarrassed with Cousin John. Cousin John is a good man tho', I think, but has peculiar ways. His presence makes me ashamed of my own shortcomings etc. etc. and he was an inspiration to me. Caused me to wish to have his christian graces and to resolve to try harder to cultivate them—to pray more—to trust more. I feel rebellious once in awhile at my lot—so much drudgery and so much company to cook for and in meantime my own affairs, my own children, my little baby—all going neglected. My aged father is to be cared for and seen after by me and most of this company are kin who say they come to see him. I an not physically nor financially able to keep it up and it is a *severe trial* to Ghu and I both and there is no way out of it. My father wants us here—we can't leave him to go away. We have nothing given us from him to keep us this company with. He doesn't even pay for his clothes being washed. I love my father. I want to be faithful to him and to my Maker.

Travis wins from almost all of our company, compliments for his gentle ways and kind attention to visitors. He gave Mynta a copper. Wanted to show his feelings (kindness) toward her I think. He gathered eggs and tomatoes for "Uncle Charlie" long before he came. "Uncle Charlie" said several nice things in praise of Travis. Travis favors Splint and Mama very much. Am sorry he was not named for Splint. Little Mary looks odd. I bobbed off her hair this week. I had no time in world to keep it really platted and it was thin except close to her head. Ghu has gone over to Mr. St. John's after Stella and her little girl. Stella is a *ton of talk* and an *ounce of thought*. I would be glad to see Cousin Winnfrey awhile, again.

< August 17 >
Friday

Stella and little girl spent few days (2 or 3) and Ghu carried them over to Mr. St. John's yesterday P.M. I found Stella very bright on some lines and could express herself wonderfully well—has a wonderful vocabulary. She is somewhat fickle, not a strong character. Seems to have a very good disposition—pleasant.

Ghu and Askew have gone to Indian Springs to camp meeting today. They may spend tonight at Cape's.

This is awful hot weather! Dog Days! Rain often! Wonder who will come next? How severe some trials I have encountered this summer. How hard to do so much cooking with such little strength.

My little Maggie Wynn and little Mary will feel better when cool weather comes. I asked Dr. Woods to send some physic for them both today, by mail. I have had *severe* trials this summer. Maybe it is chastisement for wrongs I've done in God's sight—maybe for sins— that I suffer so—that these trials are by me to be borne. I wonder if next year will bring us many of the same kind? I dread the next year. Mr. Kelly will move away. Some one may move there that might in some ways (by children associating close with each other and in other ways) be bad for Ghu and I and our children. "God holds the key of all unknown and I am glad." Oh, Thou who didst create me and who has kept life within me so far, be Thou my comfort, my guide thro' another year and thro' life.

How lonely I am when Ghu's away. How I do wish we (Papa and us) could leave this place and be more comfortable in another place for Ghu and I predict trouble, *keen* trouble next year from those whom I've heard were going to move close by. Were it not for my father I could not live here; it does seem to be almost impossible for me to try [to] live here under some existing circumstances. Lord help Ghu and I—help our children to be shielded from evil influences.

‹ August 18 ›

(Saturday)

Askew is eleven years old today—1895. I have been so busy (that I am sorry to record) that no pudding or anything was made for dinner in observance of his birthday. I wish I could, on each one of my children's birthday prepare something pleasant for them to eat. I am going to try give them something tonight to celebrate Askew's birthday—for supper. My life is so full of cares that I can't do many things for the children that I wish to do. I've canned three cans of fruit today and washed little "Maidee's" head. She is a high-tempered little miss. Have a job, usually, when I go to clean her head.

I am 37 years and a few months old. Today I am wearing my first glasses. On Askew's 11th birthday I donned my first spectacles. Ghu found them yesterday P.M. at Indian Springs, and gave them to me. He said that he and I both would use them, but gave them to me. I am grateful of them because for a year or two, at times I've felt the need of some. I appreciate them very much.

Ghu looks handsome with them on. My Sweetheart (Ghu) looks better this summer than usual anyhow. His health has been better this summer than in a long time and I am thankful. Two summers ago when he had fever I was scared and trouble was worse than ever before in my life I think. I never shall forget that summer. Papa Ghu grows dearer to me as the years go by. He is my prop and a fine one he is. He helps me in many ways that lot of husbands do not help their wives. His love does not grow cold. Often he and I both are too overworked to manifest our real love toward each other and often times we are so tired, or I am, that we are not gentle to our loved ones in home circle, for a little while, as we should be. I regret that I have to work so that I can't be calm, gentle, and loving at all times toward each child and each inmate of the home. Ghu is preparing now to go to Jenkinsburgh to Masonic lodge. We are so sorry to hear of the deep trouble that our good friends Mr. and Mrs. Jno Wilkins are in. Ghu's heart and my own go out in sympathy to Mr. and Mrs. Wilkins. Mr. Wilkins has been a special friend of Ghu's and I pray the Lord to help them bear their great trouble.

‹ August 19 ›
Sunday P.M.

Folks in this community have gone to Indian Springs camp-meeting. Telephone line quiet. Can't talk to many. Ghu is with us today—didn't want to go to camp meeting on Sundays—crowds to immense. Oliver Jones is spending today with Papa. I like for Papa's friends to call.

Little Maggie Wynn just squeals shrill when she plays with the other children. She crawls well. Can't sit up at all without a support but is 6 months and a half old or about it. Little Maggie is awful sweet, but a baby of her age is always troublesome. Some one has to nurse, roll baby carriage, and amuse and how tired we get—worn out and weary. Askew gets very weary and sometimes little impatient but does well for a child his age.

‹ August 24 ›

We have received the sad intelligence of Lil's death. My favorite sister is dead. She died in Unadilla, away from all loved ones except her own household, her husband and children. She sickened, died, and was buried away from us—away from her aged Father, her sisters and brothers—away from Ghu. Ghu loved her like I did; Ghu was a brother to her—she a sister to him. To me she was almost at all times a confidante—I confided in her, she in me. We told each other our joys and sorrows—we exchanged literature with each other. We wrote often to each other. To us all (here in this home circle) she was a good friend—proved her friendship. To my father, words fail me—she was his favorite too—a great *help* to him—always was. Lil was a great comfort to her parents. She had them in her thoughts and did much to brighten their life. How astonished we were when Mr. Jno' Gardner of Locust Grove called us up over 'phone and told us of a telegram he received Tuesday P.M. The telegram said that Lil died Tuesday Aug. 21st, at 11 o'clock A.M. Would be burried on Wednesday at 2 o'clock. How strange we felt to tell others that "Lil is dead." She had fever about 2 weeks. We had 2 letters, one Mon. the other Tuesday from Bess. Both written on Sun. Bess' letter made brief mention of Lil's illness, said two of the small children were sick and that Mr. Lewis got up from sickness that day and went to the store. Bess wrote a very cheerful letter. Her letter came at noon and in early P.M. of same day (Tuesday) came announcement of Lil's death.

Lil had done a very unusual thing. Since taking the fever she had written me a very cheerful letter with her own hand, "lying flat on back." In the letter she told me about buying a new pianna, and said in her queer natural way, "I wish I had bought one 40 years ago." She described the new home, the home yards, china[berry] trees etc. Wrote a real cheerful breezy letter and I think she fully expected to recover. This letter was written in beginning of her sickness. She told how many closets they had (9), how many halls (2) etc. and said if it was not in Dooly Co. she would like it better than any place she ever lived in her life. She was charmed with her new home. How short a time she occupied it. She even wrote of a neighbor coming in and bringing her the prettiest bouquet of roses she ever saw. She spoke of coming up and staying a month but said she did not think she would come, because she felt like 'twould be best to let that much money go on Dr. bill as she knew the Doctor bill would frighten her when presented—they had so much sickness and Dr. came so often. She mentioned that lot of sickness were in the place and an infant had just died. I answered Lil's letter. I wrote perhaps 12 pages. I guess it reached her day before she died. I wonder if it was read to her. I think from Bessie's letter she must have gotten worse suddenly. Bess wrote so cheerful on Sun. and she died on Tuesday.

I want to hold myself in readiness for death. I pray so to live, after this, that I will have no doubts about being ready.

Anna and Grace Jarrell went to the burryal. Wish Ghu and I could have seen her face again and Papa too, if he could have stood it. Ghu wanted to go down there so bad, but couldn't leave then. Am glad Anna and Grace went.

> "The fountain of joy is fed by tears,
> And love is lit by the breath of sighs,
> The deepest griefs and wildest fears
> Have holiest ministries."

Mr. Morgan Castellaw, a friend of Bessie Lewis is carrying mail for 15 days now and Bess wrote and told me so and said she wished I would meet him. When we heard of Lil's death I put a note in box telling him about it and today I had a real nice note of consolation from him. He must be a noble boy to have written such a note as he did. He spoke of Bess to one of the children—Fred—the day we received intelligence of Lil's death.

Little Mary ties or pins rather, paper and rags on her feet and they are her imaginary shoes. She is a quick-witted child. Her moves are quick. She takes in things quick. When I reprove her she runs away fast, tears in her eyes and gets on bed. Always says "I go to bed!" when she has been reproved, and always goes to bed in hurry if one hurts her feelings. Many funny things she does that I'd like to record but I don't have time, and I forget, when I do get time.

Anna and Hester Jarrell and Big Sis O'Rear spent last Monday night here and before they reached Jackson Tuesday, a telegram had been there announcing Lil's death. We, Anna and I, were speaking of Lil Monday night. I was telling her that Lil had fever and of Lil's sunny letter written in bed, and of Bess' letter received that day. And Ann didn't know Lil had fever. She told me Lil had written Dr. J. a card not long since, telling him to send her down there on a visit and she talked of going. She did go—to her burial.

Maggie Wynn falls off the bed more than any baby I ever saw in my life. While I am busy, she wakes and climbs up over the wall of pillows (I fix to prevent her falling) and topples over on her poor little head and such bumps! How awful loud they do sound. How swollen her "noggin" gets—especially how swolen it was when she fell in the night. Poor baby! six months old and such falls—so many of them. She is warmest natured baby I think we've ever raised. How perspiration pours from her day and night. Mary is learning to talk fast—by far faster than Ralph did, although she is tongue tied, and he was not. He was very backward about talking. Mary [is] 2½ years old. Ralph is the noisiest child we've ever raised. Can't learn him to talk in low tone. Talks loud in house, at table and is very noisy—also cries lot. Also gets dirtier than any of them.

Mary stands by me in a chair and watches me starch, cook, etc. and has to have piece of dough and pan and has me put her biscuit in stove every day. She says every day: "Cook a biscuit! Cook a biscuit!" She means for me to give her a piece of dough and a pan and flour and let her roll and roll a biscuit.

‹ August 28 ›

Baby Maggie Wynn is sick—has not been well during Aug. but worse yesterday and today and had symptoms of spasms. She has been asleep long time now and yet asleep.

We feel uneasy and hope she will be better when she awakes and not alarm us with those symptoms. One action that passed from her had a sunflower seed in it and I'm afraid more of those seeds are in her stomach and causing those symptoms.

Little Mary went with Papa Ghu yesterday to ride—he was off on business in regard to the gin he is to run this fall. When Ghu got in buggy he gave Mary a large apple and she went to sleep eating it. When she awoke she asked "You eat my apple?" Ghu answered "No." And gave it to her and she laughed aloud gleefully—so glad to find her apple after she awoke. And she awoke and remembered that she did have an apple but did not know whether Ghu had eaten it or whether she had, or what had become of it. Papa Ghu thought it very bright in her and so does "Mama Mag."

We had on our table some fig preserves, Papa's . . . favorite preserve to mark his 85th birthday and Askew's 11th birthday. I had no chance to fix something for them on the days their birthday fell and told them I'd give them a jar of fig preserves today before Aug.— their birth month—expires. Mary and Ralph are chummy. Ralph is mischeivous. He is cute, if he does cry easily and often.

Travis gathers up all figs he can, without being told for me to make preserves. He is a sweet, obedient, kind-hearted gentle refined boy. A fine little boy—Askew and Fred have good traits too. How fast they grow. How, from my heart I wish I had time to be with them; to converse with them; to read good things to them; to be some *real* help towards making *good*, noble, men of them.

Mary is learning to talk fast despite the fact that she is tongue-tied. We were fearful that she'd be very backward for one to be tongue-tied. Little Mary is very devoted to little Maggie Wynn, Mary is a "wee woman." She plays with Maggie Wynn as if she thought herself ever so much larger, but Maggie Wynn is not far behind—Mary is such a doll-like baby—so little—so cute—so sweet; so bright, so jolly, so sunny, so cheerful, so tender etc. etc. My vocabulary is exhausted.

Little Maggie Wynn is 7 months old. Yesterday, for first time to my knowledge, she raised herself up in sitting posture and sat that way without a prop, on pallet on floor, for a few moments. She crawls flat on stomach—fast, but can't sit up. Poor little baby. I hope she will wake up feeling better.

Papa . . . looks weary, weak and jaded—more so than usual since Lil died. Lord in Heaven, be with Papa in his last days. Be with Askew, Fred, Travis, Ralph, Mary and Maggie Wynn. Help each of them to grow up *honest* in *words, thoughts* and *acts*. Help each one to fear to do wrong—to love God and try to please Him. Help each one to give themselves, their lives to their Creator in early life and on to life's end to try every day to be good. Lord bless, help, guide and be with Ghu and I all along thro' life—be with each member of this family on earth—may the tie between us be strong—between Grand Pa—Papa Ghu, Mama, and each child. All love each other and all love our Heavenly Father and all live so as when this life is over—all to be united in Heaven, for Jesus Sake. Amen.

‹ September 2 ›
Sunday

What a dark A.M. we've had! Heavy rain—good deal of thunder. I became so weak, so nervous, that I had to lie down. Papa . . . went to his room and lay down too. He and I nearly always lie down when heavy rains and thunderclouds come up. I get so weak and nervous. Little Mary, when in a hurry for anything speaks out loud and commanding "'Kase! 'Kase!" She means "Make haste! make haste!" She is cute. Little Maggie Wynn has a new sleeping place, instead of a pallet: a clothes basket with quilt and pillow in it and how precious she seems to us sleeping in that. Something that angels may love to look on. God bless that baby!

Papa seems very feeble since our Lil's death. He looks more feeble, jaded, and weary than ever since Death so suddenly carried our favorite Lil away. How I miss her! I always wanted to tell her everything of any interest that happened here in the old home—what I am doing—who visits and especially, always wrote to her when any of our relation came. How Papa Ghu, and I do, and will, miss her. Her letters we three always looked forward to with eager interest. How we are going to, as long as we live miss her letters and miss writing to her. What an empty place her removal from earth has left in our lives. I am sorry for Papa. I wish I could be especially helpful and useful to him in his last days.

Ghu is calling me. I must go to cook dinner now.

< September 3 >

Monday

My sister's death has made my heart so heavy that I can't forget it while I struggle on to do my work which is beyond my physical strength all the time. My heart is heavy. Lil dead. I never saw one that seemed more likely to live a good while. She seemed usually so strong, so energetic! So busy! Allways at work.

Lord have mercy on us—her family and close kin left behind and may her death cause us to ponder the path of our feet. To order our conversation aright. To have kind words for all, Kind feeling toward all—to get ready and keep ready, for death. To so live that at a moments warning we will be ready. Heavenly Father, pardon me for all transgressions and help me to strive daily to life in perfect peace with Thee. If it can be Thy will grant that I may be spared to raise my children. Oh, have mercy on me and forgive me for careless life I've lived; help me to redeem the remainder of time given me. Help me to redeem it—to live earnestly for Jesus sake, Amen.

Askew is learning to drive a horse to the buggy these days, by himself. He has been trusted off few times and has gone this A.M. to carry clothes to a darkey to be washed.

John Wynn and Florrie Bell, his little girl, came last week. Ghu and I went up [to] Charlie Childs' awhile yesterday P.M. Misses Mat and Babe were there; Mr. Bogue C. and family were there too. Askew came awhile after I got there and brought baby.

< September 5 >

I wish I could own a keepsake, my father's clock. For these reasons: It belonged to my Mother and Father. My Mother always wound it up and they were so closely associated that it makes the clock something sacred to me. When it strikes now it so often brings memories of my mother. When it strikes I almost feel her presence. It brings forcibly to my mind her form, her face, memories of her when she was in this home. The tone of the striking seems in someway as if my dear old feeble aged Mother was speaking. If I live long I'd like to own it (as a keepsake—something so long associated closely and owned by my Mother and Father). My Father looks so sad and lonely since so many of our loved ones passed away. We all feel heavy hearted at Lil's sudden and unexpected going away.

Our children are picking cotton.

‹ September 6 ›

Papa is sick in bed today—sat up a short while. Had no appetite—has rheumatism in both arms up to the elbow. He looks weak and pale. I am sorry, sorry that he is sick. He didn't eat a mouthful of dinner; just drank cup of coffee. Has pulled off his pants now and gone back to bed.

‹ September 14 ›

Maggie Wynn is some over 7 months old and can't sit alone. She is a queer baby: can stand up by chairs, pull up by them, can crawl (or rather slide on stomach—but can get up on knees and crawl too) but can't sit alone but few moments without falling over. Maggie Wynn's favorite posture is lying flat on stomach with head up—generally something in her hands—and mouth (as babies put everything they get in their hands in their mouth). Maggie Wynn, going on 8 mos old and can't eat—doesn't know how to swallow. She drinks good deal of buttermilk. At night we sweeten the buttermilk because by that time it is sharp. The children are making so much fuss that I can't well collect my thoughts. They are now on back veranda and I'm alone in our room. This is (or was) Mary's third summer and she isn't thro' teething yet and has been puny all summer—diarrhoea—but lively gay—cheerful. She looks pale, dark, and thin.

I hope to be, I pray to be, a better mother to Askew, Fred, Travis, Ralph, Mary, and Maggie Wynn, in future than I've ever been in past. I want to be a good christian mother to them—a patient, unselfish, loving, gentle, firm mother. I want to be instrumental in Divine

Hands in leading them Heavenward. May we, Papa Ghu, myself, and each child live here doing our whole duty (doing what we believe our Heavenly Father wants us to do) filling the niche He has just for us to fill, and then when this life of probation is over to go to mansions prepared for all who try the best they know how, to live and do in this life.

Travis likes best of all for me to talk to him about Heaven. Fred is more accessable than Askew. I can talk to them and hold their attention better than I can Askew's. I don't think Askew is as docile in religious training, but it must be some kind of timidity because he is good and thoughtful of his Grand Pa and oftentimes more so than any of the rest for me. Well I must stop and bathe Maggie Wynn. I've cleaned up Mary and Ralph. Fred and Travis also have put on fresh clothes.

Had a letter today from Fan written about Lil's sudden death, and the poor little Motherless children she left. Poor children. Heaven help me to be truly grateful for being spared to my children. Lord help me strive to do right in all things and at all times.

< September 15 >

It is with sad feeling that I pen these lines: Papa got up this morning unable to walk. He looks so sad, so pitiful, sitting in chair and can't walk. He lies down awhile and sits in chair near his bed awhile. I think he cried when he was telling Ghu at dinner that he could not walk. He looks so sad. Heavenly Father have mercy on him, bless and be with him, comfort and cheer him. Bless and be with us all.

Not long ago Askew was trying to hitch up the horse by himself and Papa, tho' very feeble, went out to help him — thro' sympathy for Askew. About a week, or maybe over, after that Askew hitches up by himself — the first time in his life; Papa spoke of not being able to help him. My poor father has many heartaches and sorrows I know, but he never talks trouble. Perhaps he fears it would be unpleasant or burdensome to others. How sad he feels or must feel today and always since Mama, Buddie, Lil and Splint went away, but he keeps his sorrow to himself — God only knows of the depth of my poor old Papa's heart. God bless him for Jesus sake. Amen.

‹ September 17 ›
Monday P.M.

Papa is better. I feel like I wanted to show my gratitude to our Heavenly Parent for granting my father strength to be up and to walk again, by trying to do just as near right as I know how the rest of my life. I am so glad that my father is so much better; can walk in yard, even, today. Lord I thank Thee.

Sunday morning when I got up and went in his room and ask him how he was and found that he was better, I went out beside the garden and to closet where I could give vent to my joy and give thanks to God. I was so thankful that he has been spared to get better. I prayed earnestly that he might be spared to us — to our home — to our children. Askew waited on him faithful when he comprehended something of his feebleness. Travis would go in and ask him if he needed anything, too. Bless the boys and may their "Grand Pa" be with them longer yet.

Poor Lil's children are on my mind lot. They have lost their best friend. No one at home to see after them and they are to be separated. Poor little 2 yr old Leone is at Dr. J's sick. Esca is there with her. They (the three youngest Jarrel children and Esca) came here yesterday.

‹ September 24 ›

Maggie Wynn and Mary Vashti were baptized here at home in guest room by Mr. Stillwell (our pastor) yesterday evening; no one being present except our family: Papa, Ghu, myself, Askew, Fred, Travis, Ralph.

Maggie Wynn will be 8 months old tomorrow. Mary is 2 yrs and 7 months old. Mary didn't understand why he poured water on her head and she being so timid became frightened and wanted to run across the floor to me excited. She was by Ghu and I across room with baby in my arms and all standing when she became frightened. "Uncle Stillwell" (as he called himself when talking to Mary) is a good old man; his wife is now very low. I feel very sorry for "Uncle S." He is a good pure old man. My heart goes out in sympathy to him.

‹ September 25 ›

Papa is helpless in bed. Yesterday he seemed to be doing very well, could walk over the house, and over back yard, a space. This morning he made several efforts to get up but can't raise himself up. He could not raise up enough to eat or drink coffee, but raised head up but couldn't drink but ½ cup of coffee in the position he was in.

Baby Maggie Wynn is 8 months old today.

It was 10 days ago that Papa could not walk, but could sit up next day and take few steps—since then until today he continued to walk and seemed to be doing very well. Askew has waited on him faithfully and lifted him or helped to pull him up, rather, beyond his strength. The way Askew waited on Papa today was noble and unusual for one so young—just turned 11.

‹ September 25 ›

Night

Papa has been in a serious condition all day; has no use of himself—can't move feet, legs, or right arm. And yesterday he seemed as well as he had for a long time. Maggie Wynn was playing and trying to gallop on all fours like Travis and Papa thought 'twas very smart of her age and was telling me about it late yesterday P.M.

Today as bad off as he has been and tho' he talked little he spoke two or three different times to Mary and told her to come to him. She went close to bed two or three times and once carried him a handkerchief and asked me if Grand Pa wanted handkerchief. Askew was noble to him. Askew has always been devoted to him. He has been an affectionate Grand Pa to all of my children.

Not long ago he said Maggie Wynn was just like I was at her age. He often said she was a sweet baby, a good baby and always hated so bad for her to fall hard. She has had many falls.

Dr. Woods is to come tonight to see Papa; it is raining now. Bro. Jim, Joe Wynn, Alf Wynn, Prun and Jack Shaw are here tonight.

Last Sunday, when Mr. Stilwell baptized our babies, I thought Papa was interested in it. He spoke to me two or three different times about having them baptized this summer. Uncle Stilwell prayed for each and all—personated the grandfather. I was glad my whole family and Papa with us could all bow together once more in this life in prayer to our Heavenly Father. It was a sweet privilege to me. Sweeter because Papa was present to see the little ones baptized that he loves and has been rite with all their lives. I pray our Gracious and Merciful God to spare my aged father to me longer yet; to spare my little children their good and loving Grand Pa yet longer if it can be His will. In Jesus name. Amen.

< September 27 >

It is now about or near 3 o'clock A.M. Ghu and Brother Jim have been up all night with Papa and they sat up last night too, so now I'm up and Papa is asleep (under influence of a drug) and I am up. Papa is helpless and restless and I know Jim and Ghu are broken down. Dr. Woods was here yesterday P.M. a while. He said in some respects Papa was better. I do hope he is, and can get up again. He has had another stoke of paralysis and can't use his right arm at all. Askew is so thoughtful for a child of his age. It is just remarkable how Askew waits on him and how often Papa calls on Askew. Heaven bless them both and spare them to each other.

I awoke (from noises made in Papa's room) this morning at two o'clock and lay in bed till 3 or near four before I got up and my thoughts were on my past life and I felt the biggest sin of my life had been for lack of love: Not *loving* enough, not loving all my close relations with a deeper, firmer, broader love. Charity (love) is greatest of all. The sad lacking in all my life has been I did not love enough — Love God and love loved ones more deeply, more tenderly, more gently. Many lives are cut off early. God has spared me to be 37 yrs old. I pray Him to help me to love Him more than ever before and to love my loved ones that he has given me deeper than ever before. Heavenly Father help me to *love* more constantly till day of my death: help me to waiste no more time in sin, or unloving or carelessness. Help me to love more and have a broad loving, warm, gentle heart for Jesus sake. Amen.

‹ September 29 ›

Papa seemed better yesterday. He seemed worse today. He said, when Ghu was insisting on his eating more breakfast: "I give it up." And said he had decided to leave off medicine as it would do no good. How sad! How sad! Oh, how sad to give up my dear old father. How sad for little children to have no dear sweet affectionate Grand Pa! Heavenly Father for Jesus sake blot out our transgressions and as we leave this world go with us thro' "valley and shadow of Death" and unite us all in mansions above. God be with my poor, helpless aged Father from now on, and when his soul leaves here save it in Heaven for Jesus sake. Amen.

Papa has always had such a bright strong mind. Now, a helpless and aged paralytic—helpless as a baby, has dictated this A.M. an order to Hammond Packing Co—Atlanta G. for meat and had his name signed to it and then had his glasses brought and read it before it was sealed. And talks in clear mind about things to us all.

He tho' can't read now enough to take a paper in his hand; takes an interest in having them relate news of Daily Constitution to him and discusses news some., altho' he doesn't talk fast, or distinct. Never was one who spoke very distinctly. Mary goes to his bedside and fans flies off and he talks so pleasantly to her and talks lot to her. Says she is so smart, and a whole lot of such things. Talks of little things that she wants to prattle about and he loves her so. And he talked to little Maggie affectionately to and she laughed sweetly at him. He keeps Askew close by. He talks to Travis, Fred, and Ralph affectionately ever time they go near his bed. He remembers things so clearly to be so helpless—about the children. He was keeping their money for them (some small change) and he sent Jim in closet to get change and two or three times carefully told Jim which was his and not to bother the boys' money; and told him what kind of purse the boys' money was in and what kind his was in. And today sent after them some candy. Mary carried him a pomegranite this morning that Sara brought her. Mr. Bogue Childs has been kind to him; came down and brought Papa some apples and persuaded him to let him give him an enema and Papa let him do so. I appreciate Mr. Bogue's kindness.

I love my dear old Father. Oh, God be merciful to his dear soul. Pardon and receive him in Heaven for Jesus sake Amen.

Just after dinner.

Just now Fred and Travis were too noisy and misbehaving some and Ghu hit them with a switch (but lightly) and Papa said very feelingly: "Don't whip them. Don't whip them," and turned away his face from me and just *wept*. It was deeply pathetic; he continued to weep (at thoughts of leaving these children, whom he is so deeply attached to). I never saw such a tender devotion. He loves my children with a beautiful love. What a depth there is in it. How they and I've been blest to have him with us. How blessings do brighten when about to depart.

He sent to the store today after some candy, telling Mary it was hers and every time he would give the other children any he would (just to please Mary) say "Mary, Charlie wants some candy. Must I give him some?" Or "Mary, Fred wants some. Must I give him some?" Once in awhile—often, calls Mary, Travis, Ralph or Fred to him to talk to them.

Yesterday Fred was strolling in our pasture . . . on banks of the creak and found a fish basket and drew it up and took out 3 rite nice cat fish. His thoughts were on "Grand Pa" at once and thought it would please everyone and Grand Pa to bring the fish for sick Grand Pa to eat. We (Ghu and I) talked with him of the *wrong* of taking some one else's fish, but Ghu paid the negro who owned the basket for the fish and we cooked them nice and brown for Papa and he ate some of them for 2 meals. Now I am so glad we had them for Papa. Fred just cried when we told him that was stealing but we told him we were not mad and that he didn't know any better and that time it was not wrong but next time it would be.

Papa appreciated the fish because Fred wanted him to have them, and laughed a little and teased Fred some about them. Askew is now reading the Daily Constitution to Papa and Papa is manifesting much interest. Askew is a noble boy in some respects sure. He is an exception in his deep devotion for, and obedience to, his dear Grand Pa.

All of our little children's lives, and even of little Maggie Wynn's brief life, when either of them get sick much Papa would tell them: "Grand Pa is mighty sorry you are sick; Grand Pa would rather be sick himself than for his boy, or the sweet baby, to be sick."

‹ October 1 ›

Monday A.M.

Papa is some better Dr. Woods said last night. Dr. W. said it was probable that he would get so that he could be rolled in a rolling chair but he did not think he would ever walk again. Cape, Anna, Lil's little Leone (2 yr old motherless baby) and Faith J. came yesterday; also Sarah. All went home except Cape. Ghu waits on my father faithfully as he would his own. Does things that no else has done for him; uses ———, gives medicine, carries ———.

Little motherless Leone is a beautiful child! Papa says "she's a pretty thing." Ghu said he just wanted to kiss her over and over! Said he'd give anything if she were his. He thought she was one of the sweetest creatures he ever saw in his life. Mary was charmed with her. Delighted to lead Leone around. Mary is *all* life. A great curiosity! Attracts attention when folks come here, they usually pay Mary attention. Little Maggie Wynn is sweet and good. Papa keeps candy for my children and has them come in for it. He often gives them (if they are in the room) some fried or baked apples off his waiter. Papa has lot of people to come in to see him.

‹ October 5 ›

Friday P.M.

Papa is better. He slept refreshing sleep last night; no medicine of any kind was taken and no one sat up. Ghu was up till late bedtime and went in to see about him 2 or three times, but it was not at all necessary last night for any one to sit up. And he slept refreshing sleep. Today he is resting well.

Thank Heaven! I am so glad that he is better — that his life is still spared to us. Dr. Woods said he was a good deal better. Dr. W. said he would soon be able, he thought, to be rolled around house in rolling chair but he didn't think he would ever walk again. But I would be thankful if we could have him spared to us, around fireside and in our home. How desolate our hearts would be, were he no longer our associate in life. I thank our Merciful Heavenly Parent for leaving him with us yet longer. A loving Heavenly Father has been good, very good, exceedingly good to us.

Little Maggie Wynn has learned this week to eat a little. She has had so many hard bumps. She fell off a high bed last night. Askew had her on bed in front room. She has fallen so many times off the bed. About one month ago I hit upon a plan to keep her on bed: I use a large safety pen (sometimes two) and whenever I leave her on a bed, day or night, she is pinned to bed. She has fallen more than any child we've ever raised. She climbs up in chairs, trunks and even the wall, and falls. She is greatest climber to her age we've never known too. I think she will talk earlier than any of the babies who've preceeded her. She began to eat I believe earlier than most of the others.

Dollie Wynn's telephone has been taken out this week. I'll miss talking to her. I am sorry.

Minnie Knot and Fannie Weathers came out here this week. Minnie went right ahead like she was at home—churned, helped get dinner, and helped wash dishes. She is a good woman. Such a warm heart—a good Christian I think.

Ghu has been shingling all 4 of the boy's hair today.

Sallie and Howard Carter came to see Papa this week. Lot of other folks came. Dr. Woods is such a nice man. Who, that ever had sickness in family and had him with their loved ones, could help but love him? Lil said when Mama was sick, "I just love Dr. Woods."

< October 13 >

Frost the past 3 days and ice one of the days—maybe more than one day. Cold weather for this time of year. Papa is better Dr. W. said 2 evenings ago, but he . . . does not think Papa will ever walk again. He lies quietly—doesn't talk much. Sits up long enough to eat and once in rocking chair each day long enough for us to make his bed. I am so glad he is that much better and still spared to us. Ghu has a lot of cares now. He has to stay close and lift Papa, carry out decayed portions etc. etc. He is a noble man and waits kindly and patiently on Papa and his own Father is in La. low now. He might (and I think would) go to La. now to see his father could he leave here—my father. He is noble and isn't complaining. Ghu is sick now tho'—cold and fever last night. Bro. J[im]. still stays at night here.

Mary is the *greatest* (incessant) talker that has ever been in our family. She wears one of my combs in her hair now. She is a sweet bright faced merry joyous, gleeful child—age 2 yrs and 8 months old.

Little Maggie is cute—stands well by chairs now—doesn't fall so much. She is nearly 9 months old—has no teeth—can eat a little.

Sunday P.M. Weather still cold. Windy too. Papa seems about the same. He did not rest well (i.e.) he did not sleep much last night. He gave Askew his watch yesterday; he gave it to him before he was old enough to understand his meaning. He has often told him since he has been old enough that "someday you may have this watch." So yesterday he gave it to him again. He gave Jim and Ghu 20 dollars apiece, for waiting on him yesterday. Poor Papa! How sad it made me feel when he gave Askew the watch he had worn so long. (The watch my sainted Bro. Splint owned.) How sad to feel that poor Papa will never wear it about the house again. He may get well enough to wear clothes but he feels it doubtful. He doesn't sit up long at a time. Heavenly Father be with him. Own, sanctify and save him. Oh, merciful God, be with my old afflicted father helpless on bed and help his trust in Thee to grow stronger and comfort him in his age and helplessness and when life is no longer his, be with him thro' valley of death for Jesus sake. Amen.

< October 16 >

How strange it seems to read in todays paper that Sam Jones, the evangelist of worldwide fame, is dead. Sam Jones dead! How sorry I am to read it. Such a man! Such a wonderful man. Such a soul win-ner for Heaven. How he will be missed in this world. How strange! How strange! So many unexpected things are happening in our lives. Sam Jones was Papa's favorite preacher. Papa had two books of his sermons and read them over and over. He has been so long a strong admirer of Sam Jones. And I told Askew not to tell Papa that Sam Jones was dead. Papa's feebleness and extreme age—I felt that the death would render him extremely sad, depress him I feared. Some one I fear, coming in sick room will tell him. We would not tell him of old Uncle Billy Philips death (buried yesterday at Philippi) but some one else came in and told him. Old Uncle George Gresham (an old negro Papa has long known and liked) died this week. Some one came in and told him that. Papa liked old Uncle George, gave him lot of things and Mama was kind to him too, and his family. Now, Papa lies a helpless paralytic, age 85 and his much loved Sam Jones has died. Lil gone—a favorite and useful daughter. So suddenly snatched away from us and her family. Heavenly Parent help us to live better daily—strive to be more patient, more gentle, more tender with our loved ones while we are together. We know not how soon more separations will come. We ask in Jesus name to pardon, blot out our transgressions and help us strive to be gentle patient, cheerful and sweet to our loved ones and to do our duty in Thy sight during rest of our stay in this life. Amen.

Mr. Morgan Castellaw, a young man of Locust Grove, friend of Bessie Lewis' called here yesterday—an agent for pictures. His face looks pure. He seemed so friendly, so cordial in his manners—I fell in love with him; he gave Travis a picture. I'm to buy one soon from him.

< October 17 >

Wednesday P.M.

Little Maggie Wynn has her first pair of new shoes—age nearly 9 months—pretty little things—tan tops, black patent leather tips, black buttons, tan tassles. Little sweet Mary is delighted more over Maggie Wynn's shoes than Maggie is herself. Mary's shoes are not so dainty as Maggie's and little Mary is charmed with shoes of almost any kind and especially pretty ones.

All the little fellows have new shoes and this is a red letter day with them—"new shoe" day; they put them on and pull them off over and over. Travis, Fred and Ralph have real angry sores—T's on his knee, F's and R's on their foot and we tell the sore footed ones to wait till his foot gets well. I told R. and others not to put black rags on their sores; to bandage them with old white rags. I went in room after that and Ralph had a black hose on his well foot and a stocking almost long as himself on sore foot—a light grey—said "I haf to have this white stocking on my sore foot." Mary is sweet—cute—original— always saying things and proving them by me. "Didn't I, Mama? Didn't I, Mama?"—all day long—Didn't I, Mama? And the children and Papa Ghu laugh at her and tease her about it. Mary has been in doors going on 3 weeks because 2 small black pigs are in the yard running loose. One is very tame and comes in door sometimes and scares her nearly to fits, (excites her very much I mean). She is a rare bird—an unusual little thing. Sweet, bright, all life. Such a talker—but tongue tied.

Yesterday was a trying day with me. I had a severe cold, and when I'd go to my work I'd feel like I'd never get thro'. Have two babies—both wear napkins and in one way are to be attended to the same and each have diarrhoea most of the time, and sometimes I feel surely this has been the busiest or most uphill year I've ever lived (outside of times when health was bad).

< October 19 >

October! Glorious month—the sweetest times of all the year. This I've felt since girlhood—now I'm 37 and the dear time—October—casts spell over me—always does unless I am very sick all during that bewitching month. O, that I had words to express the spell, the good feeling, the rest, the enchanted, the bewitching feeling, that loved October casts over me—night and day. Sleep is even sweeter. I do wonder if it affects other folks like it does me? I thank my Creator that He has spared me to enjoy another beautiful October—another grand and glorious October. Would I could express how this month charms me, but I can not—brain too small—vocabulary too narrow. O, how the month of October gladdens, fills and thrills me as no other month. How sweetly rested oftimes I feel in this month. I'm so in love with this October weather that I can hardly settle myself to study work. Thank God for such a perfect gift—as October is to me. I just rejoice all the time in this bliss that October has poured in my soul. I've laughed more, talked more light hearted talk than in a long, long time since blissful October began to reign—Oh, for words to express what I feel! I can't command them.

By the way, little Mary received a funny souvenir card from Charlie Wynn today: an automobile in shape of fish full of pretty small children. She, and all the children enjoyed it hugely. After looking at it to their hearts content, she put it in parlor.

Papa seems to be doing as well as we could expect today. He lies very quiet—gets tired lying, and tired and weak if he sits up long, but is very uncomplaining. Bears his helplessness so patiently.

Saw a good piece in Henry County Weekly today of Mrs. Stilwell's death. She said to Rev. Weathers short while before her death:
"Bro. W. preach to people to get ready for death while they are in
health for after they are stricken on a bed of suffering I don't see how
they can get or put their minds on Christ." Her death makes me feel
that I want to put forth stronger endeavors, more courage, in right
living—Christian living. What a good woman she was. I was never
in her company but once but I felt sure she was a thorough Christian. How the very wind that is so briskly stirring the trees, does sing
songs to me as I sit out here on back porch and write. Household
work claims my time now.

< October 23 >

Tuesday

Papa is feeling worse this A.M. 'Tis 9 o'clock now and he has not
been to breakfast—drank little coffee. He has always tried (and was)
to be as little trouble as possible. He has always been so very little!
He would not even let little boys do scarcely anything for him before
he took to his bed—"didn't want to trouble anyone." "Did not want
to be a bit of trouble."

Now, while helpless he often expresses deep regret that he "is so
much trouble." He seems to think, (and says so), that he is troublesome—to be lifted in chair to eat and to occasionally be lifted—but
he is as little trouble as anyone could be to be helpless. He is so little
trouble—so little—for his age and helpless condition he is remarkably little trouble. Now, his chief regret seems to be that he is so
helpless that some one has to lift him and wait on him. Oh, how sad
it is to see him wipe tears from eyes, and to see him cry because he
feels that his helplessness makes him a trouble to someone.

His one wish was that if he was to be helpless long, that he might
be able to get to fireplace and back to the bed—without aid—so that
no one would have to be bothered to lift him, but he said this A.M.
(or yesterday) he did not expect to ever be any better than he is now.
This morning he said he was nearly dead and that he would not care
if he were dead. I think the reason he added that he "would not care
if her were dead" was just because he so deeply regrets "being helpless and someone having to lift him—just that great dread of being

some trouble to some one." Heaven be merciful to the dear old man. Lord, comfort him and make him be at peace and rest during all his bed of affliction. Thou knowest how good he has been to the poor all these years—and in 41st Psalm Thou givest a promise to such. Lord bless him! Pardon all transgression—all shortcomings—be with him on bed of affliction; comfort him to the end; and lead him gently down to, and thro' valley and shadow of death and receive him in heaven and help all live so as to after awhile, join him in courts above for Jesus sake. Amen.

I heard today that Mr. Robert Sandifer was dead. He was an intimate acquaintance, a friend of long years standing of Papa's. Mr. Sandifer was 86 years old in Sep. Celebrated the anniversary with a family reunion, speaking, big basket dinner and his daughter married also on that day. Mr. Sandifer was one year older than Papa, and now since Papa has been stricken, Mr. S. has taken sick and in very few days after has died. Seems so strange that Papa's acquaintances are passing away since he has been stricken—but after we saw a noticeable decline in him. He was so feeble after Lil's death that we hated to tell him the death of anyone and now, we've never told him of Mr. Sandifer's illness.

‹ October 28 ›
Sunday

Oh, what a busy day—full of drudgery—I do not complain particularly of that, but how embarrassed I feel when real intelligent people come in and find me worn completely out and children and house more untidy than when no one are here but homefolks. (When no one are here except homefolks I have more time to sweep, re-sweep, wash and rewash, wash faces) but when the house is so full of company I have to cook so long and so much and talk with company some and much is compelled to go undone when only one overtaxed tired woman is to do it all. Oh, how weary and fagged I do feel! Oh how jaded! Just after washing dinner dishes (about 2 o'clock) I fell on bed to rest—had just gotten comfortably settled when Ghu came to my door and told me Judge Reagan and wife were at door. My! I felt like I never could pull myself together, dress and go in where such intelligent, high standing people were. And I had never seen them before either. But I felt that I just must because they had come here to my aged sick father out of pure esteem they (or Judge) had for him. So I went. I felt embarrassed, but it was a duty to my father's guest. I am glad I met Papa's friend that he esteemed so highly. . . . I am glad I came in touch once in life with his noble, broadminded wife—a woman of rare Christian graces—wonderful character. My own life would be broader could I come in contact with such ladies oftener. I was embarrassed tho'. My time has been *so* fully taken up, not only today but all last week—my housekeeping was not at its best—Travis and Ralph were not cleanly dressed (from my heart I regret that I can't have time to keep them clean) and they came near the parlor door and whispered. I heard them; they wanted to come in and hesitated; so I went out in time to prevent their entrance—and to save myself some mortification. Heaven help me keep my children clean and house neat—help me to have a body and mind more rested, less jaded, so that I can enjoy others, and others can enjoy me, more—so that I can give more pleasure (more good cheer) to those who come within our home. I'm worth so little to my own family and to relatives who come in our home, (in a cheerful, sociable way) all because I must drudge and overtax my strength so far that I'm fagged out mentally and physically. Lord help me to do my best. Mr. Weathers is here now. Cape has just left. Anna Jarrell, Faith J., Esca and Leone Lewis spent last night and left before dinner. Cape came when Anna did. Esca spent two or 3 days here—sick very. Chills and fever. Mother dead. He certainly did look like a bereft orphan. Leone was a dream of loveliness. A perfect beauty—one of the most beautiful babies I ever saw in my whole life. Ann and I sat up till 12 o'clock last night. I am sorry for Mr. Lewis' motherless children. I do wish Bessie would see, feel and realize her duty to her little brothers and sisters and would keep them in their home—away from homes where there is no tender, deep, love for them.

Heaven help me to be at heart friendly, warm and tender toward all in need of a friend. I feel sure that Esca needs a friend. Heaven protect poor sick Esca.

Supper time. I must go to cooking again. Company for supper and I expect Mr. Stilwell will be here for breakfast.

Backaches! Chronic backache. Must go and cook and wash dishes till bed time. Heaven help me! Is it right for me (by my lonesome) to cook so much for company when I've never been strong enough for endless cooking and nursing babies and working other ways. Help me *never* to murmur, but to trust in Thee.

‹ October 30 ›
Tuesday P.M.

Yesterday was Monday and Mondays are allways busy days with me. Company came in the P.M. 'Twas Mrs. Susan and Miss Rosa Peek. Enjoyed their visit; they came to inquire about Papa and to see me too. They were kind, clever, entertaining. I enjoyed their visit. Mrs. Peek seemed so kind to me and Rosa seems to be such a pure, sweet, true girl; she is good, sociable girl, intelligent too. I love her and felt drawn to her mother. I think it is so nice for them to go about together—to church and to see friends and enjoy others' companionship as they do.

Papa slept very well last night and feels better today than he has in severel days. I am glad he is better. He is a lot of comfort for me, even if he does have to be confined to his bed. I ought to feel very grateful to my Heavenly Father for prolonging the life of my earthly parent as He is doing. I thank Thee Lord for Thy goodness to me.¯

"Papa Ghu," Askew, Travis, and Ralph are digging our crop of potatoes this P.M. I've been sweeping yards some. Fred is helping me nurse and amuse baby Maggie Wynn. Mary is chattering away as cheerful as a ray of sunshine and yet she is not very well. She has a cold and has had poor appetite for several days. But my! how cheery (cheerful) lighthearted, joyous and happy she is. I *never* saw one so merry when sick, as she is! She has a real bad cold, and looks *real* bad. Poor little sunbeam! She is so small, so delicate, color very bad—a tiny mite, but so cute, so *busy*, so quick, so sweet so loving and gentle to us—especially to her parents.

Papa . . . told her, few days ago, she was so pretty and smart (and so little) that she ought to standup in a chair when we had company and let company see her well.

Night or so ago, Papa said that Maggie Wynn was a pretty baby—'most as pretty as anybody's baby—that she was just like her mother —a nice compliment for me from my aged, helpless, afflicted father. He paid Maggie lot of attention Sunday night while he was sitting up—wanted to know if Judge Reagan and wife saw her. This P.M. he has been talking to her. Fred has her in his room while I am writing and Papa is talking some to her and seeing that Fred takes good care of her.

. . . Oct. 30th, Maggie Wynn . . . put on her shoes for first time, and her first pair of shoes. She is 9 months and 5 days old. She can't stand alone, but stands by chairs — pulls up well — is strong — doesn't eat but very little food — hardly enough to say that she eats.

2 or 3 days ago I trimmed Papa's fingernails. First time any one ever trimmed them for him since he can remember I expect. Papa had a pencil brought to him little while ago to see if he could use his hand and fingers well enough to write, but he could not. He tried that once before since he got so that he could use his right arm and hand but he can't write with it.

‹ November 3 ›

(Sunday A.M.)

Somehow I feel sad this morning concerning Papa. He didn't sleep well the past two nights. Oh, how sad it is to see him lying help-less. God be merciful to him, comfort and abide with him on his bed of affliction. Help me to *do* my duty every way — to neglect him no way. Help me Lord to grow deeper spiritually in ministering to others. Give me strength to do patiently, kindly, and cheerfully all unpleasant tasks all along life's pathway.

Askew, Fred and Travis are to start to school tomorrow. What trials I anticipate: baby to see after — no little boys to help me do that; no little boys to save steps for me by setting table, wiping dishes, etc. etc. "Papa Ghu" will here most of the time to wait on "Grand Pa" but he and "Grand Pa" will both miss Askew in that room. I fear the trials for me are going to be very heavy — baby to see after — three babies.

‹ November 8 ›

Thursday

Papa is worse, weaker, appetite poorer, rest not so well, talks less; can't turn over without help, now. We started Askew to school and Papa wanted him here, so we've just let him go to school one day this week. Papa *loves* Askew so. Askew has remained in sick room close with more contentment than it seems possible hardly for a child. He *never* eats a *single* meal without having to get up once, generally twice, to do something for Papa. He calls Askew to remove waiter when he gets thro' eating and to get and light him a cigar. Askew has never murmured—even said to Bro. Jim at breakfast table this morning, that he did not mind it. Jim was saying Askew had to jump up so much each time he went to eat. So Askew has proven to be a noble grandson—noble, to nurse his aged afflicted GrandFather as he has done.

Papa didn't want Askew to leave him and we (Ghu and I) was afraid he ought not to loose anytime from school. We don't know what to do. Seems sad to take him away from Papa just now. Askew sits closely by him, reads, makes toys of corn stalks etc. etc. 'Tis wonderful how Askew waits on him; how constant and patient Askew is in sick room.

< November 11 >

Sunday

Papa slept better than usual last night and ate a little more supper and breakfast than he has within past few days. (We had fish each meal—mullet.) He seems a bit more cheerful this A.M. He told me this morning he was sure Mr. Hooten (Bill, he called him) would have come to see him yesterday; he said he and Bill were cronies; that he was a good man. That Mr. Hooten use to come to his home in Monroe County etc.

Brother Jim plays with and teases Ralph lots. He picks at him every day. It is real amusing the way Ralph looks and does and the funny things Jim says and does to him. Bro. J. put Ralph on Fred's pet calf's back this A.M. R. protested, but Bro. J. held him on and he rode half 'round the house. I saw Bro. J. going down hall with Maggie Wynn in his arms this A.M. He plays with Mary and she talks to, and about, "Uncle Jim" but she is nervous and don't want him to take her on his lap.

Someone rang on telephone this A.M. and Mary went running to 'phone; said "it is our ring!" I told her to talk and told her what to say. I took receiver down and she said: "Grand Pa is sick. Uncle Jim is over here. Maggie can crawl."

Maggie eats now. She is strong. Crawls fast. Climbs up quickly to a chair or anything she wants to climb by. She is growing sweeter, more *amusing, cuter* every day. Is learning so many new tricks. Yesterday she said "pretty" or a noise like she was trying to say pretty. She did that yesterday and laughed gleefully over a bright colored picture on back of my magazine. How gleeful she was over and over again when looking at that picture. Did me good all over to see how delighted and gleeful she could be over a bright picture. And she said "pretty" and laughs the very sweetest laughs in the wide wide world over flowers, pictures, kittens and outdoor exercize. Little Maggie Wynn is the sweetest cutest, smartest baby I ever saw. She put *new life*—enthusiasm in me. We put her outdoors on ground this week. She crawls on ground; sits down some, quietly gazing at chickens and the objects around her. Yesterday she crawled up to top step on front porch, Fred standing by to keep her from getting hurt. She gazed long and with deep interest at chickens going to roost one P.M. this week. Maggie clings to Papa Ghu. Follows after him and cries after him and clings lovingly to him. She loves me best yet—they all love me best till they are weaned, or just as long as they sleep with me, but I've always just slept with *one* of them at a time. Ghu says Mary is the sweetest child he ever saw in his life.

Lonnie Crawford, our next door neighbor's child, was bitten by a mad-dog night before last. Travis has to 2 or 3 or 4 yrs been so nervous (from a fright old Aunt Mary's dog gave him) over mad dogs that he suffers extreme fright—now since Lon was bitten he will not stay in room at night with other children unless door is buttoned. Once since Papa has been sick he has been frightened into almost unconsciousness at seeing a stray dog one night after supper. I greatly fear his nervousness over mad dog scares will greatly injure his health.

< November 16 >

Friday Night

Papa seems to be about the same: he eats about the same, (not much) and sits up nearly as long, or about the same. He seems more cheerful some days than others. He seems more cheerful today than yesterday. He looks thinner and is thinner now than when he took his bed 6 weeks ago; looks thinner in face and looks weak. I hope he will be spared to us long time yet, if it is the Divine Will. I have a better chance to stay in (room) now; Suse Tarpley is here.

Papa said today that our baby Maggie Wynn was one of the prettiest babies he ever saw; that he had always thought so. Bro. Jim said she was pretty. Papa gave Ralph a nice pretty bordered handkerchief today that some of the La. relation gave him. Ralph donned a new pair of jeans pants today that I made for him; he was delighted with them and felt that he had suddenly risen to more importance and was a larger boy. Picked up Maggie and toted her a few steps and was gleeful over that—overjoyed to know that he was large enough to "tote" baby. So bye and bye he kept displaying the new feat and fell over (baby on top) and came near hurting himself and the baby badly.

This week, one day, I was trying some new dresses (gay colored ones) on Mary. I noticed Ralph was eyeing them closely and quietly, even sadly. I divined his thoughts and desires. I says: Ralph doesn't like to see Mary with pretty trimmed clothes and he has nothing that way. He broke down then, sobbed. I was sorry for the poor little boy. So today his joy was unbounded. He had new "jeans pants, made and bought for him; like Papa Ghu, Askew, Fr. and T. wears," and remembered that he had coveted Mary's gay colors and trimming but says "I don't want no trimming and things like Mary's now." I had told him while I was sewing on his pants that he would look like a girl if he wore trimmings and colors like Mary. And his jeans pants were pretty and they were boys' clothes. He was contented—delighted. He stood around me all time I was sewing on his pants and as soon as one pair was finished I put them on the dear darling little boy. Heaven bless him and abide with him all thro' life and may his soul always be clean and white and a home in Heaven be his at life's end. God bless little Ralph.

Poor little Mary is sick, but up and all that. But easily made to cry and cries often, feelings so easily wounded. I think she looks pitiful. She is such a little child—such tiny little wrists and hands. She is not like her natural self and I feel uneasy about her. She seems *so frail*— so sallow too. Poor little sunshine is not well I know. I trust the little darling will soon grow stronger.

Maggie Wynn can say "pretty!" and is noisy—cute—her laughter is sweetest music; her ripples of laughter is music to the household. She is a picture of loveliness— *innocence*, such gentle eyes, such meek expression. She has expressive eyes and we understand much those eyes say. She points forefinger at pictures and objects and says pretty and is often making a noise of trying to *sing*. Maybe she will have a talent for music.

‹ November 22 ›
Thursday night

Papa begins to look real bad—pale and weak. He looks weary—feeble—so pale and has fallen off a good deal. I feel sad in my heart as I look upon him. Oh, how sad it is to see him leaving us—to see him so weak, so helpless. God be with him all through this and receive him in Heaven for Jesus sake. My dear father. My dear, dear, aged, feeble afflicted Papa. God be with him. Amen.

Papa has been in bed 7 weeks. Ghu has been lifting him 7 weeks by himself. Ghu has lifted him up to a chair and back to bed three different times tonight since supper. Ghu is holding out well, tho' back aches from it.

Papa took Maggie Wynn in his arms last night while he was sitting up by the fire. He held his arms out to her and she wanted to go to him and he took her. Tonight he said she was a pretty baby (he often says that) and said she was going to be chubby—wasn't going to be like little Mary.

‹ November 25 ›
Sunday Night

Maggie Wynn is 10 months old today. She is sick—teething—head seems to pain her. She's been cross and restless—had some fever 2 nights. She has a bad cold, cries some. Has no teeth yet but is cutting one I think now because she slobbers. Her cold affects her head; eyes run water and seems to pain in head or ears.

Ralph has a small purse. We did not know he cared for money. We are so busy we don't observe or read our children as close as I wish. Ralph never expressed his desire strong enough for a purse and money for us to know he cared for it. Jim . . . told him he'd give him a copper or two to sleep with him. Ralph did not want to sleep with

him at all but wanted some money. So he slept with "Uncle Jim" —
the first person in his life, he ever slept with outside our family. He
got the coppers and his face *beamed, glowed* with pleasure. Ghu gave
him one or two; I gave him one copper and others who've been in
here to see Papa have given him some. Mr. Ingram gave him one
copper today. He is just as proud of a copper as he would be of a
5 cts or 25 cts. How he appreciates his 12 coppers! What a pleasure
they've given him. And how little we understand their little hearts.
If they could express themselves how surprised we would be. Sweet
little Ralph. "Uncle Jim" has gained his friendship to a larger degree
than anyone outside the family ever has since he was a baby and
loved old Aunt Mary (a negress) so much.

‹ November 26 ›

Monday P.M.

Anna and Allie Jarrell came Sat P.M. and spent the night. Anna
has been having chills and fever and looks like one up from spell of
typhoid fever. She looks very thin. I feel uneasy about her. Allie is a
sweet, good girl. She has always and at all times been kind and very
sociable towards me. I think a lot of Allie.

Made Askew 3 pr jeans pants. Askew 2 brown shirts. M. and M.
(in Nov) 6 gingham aprons (all together 6). Dora made 8 homespun
waistes.

‹ November 27 ›

Night before Thanksgiving

A sad night. Papa has been bad off all day—the most restless day
he has spent. He is unusually more quiet in day and more restless at
night. He has had 2 bad nights in succession and this has been a very
bad day. His mind is clear for which I ought to be very thankful. I
am glad that his mind is clear—that he knows and talks to us all. So
glad his mind is so remarkably clear.

It has turned cooler by a good deal. I think Thanksgiving day will
dawn crisp and clear.

Suse, Ghu, and I have been confined to Papa's room close at times today. He is so much worse. We may all be up tonight.

Mr. Weathers has been sent back to Locust Grove for the coming year and it is presumed Mr. Stilwell will be our pastor again. Ghu and I are somewhat disappointed Mr. Stillwell has not been in here to see Papa but once and then he stayed short time—did not have prayer. I thought he would have done so. I wish we had a preacher who was earnest about soul saving as well as about what money they are to get—yes I wish more.

No mail tomorrow. We have a large young rooster for Thanksgiving but our presence and work in Papa's room will not permit of any extras for the table tomorrow. We have much to be thankful for: Thankful that Papa is with us yet; thankful that I am spared to them—all spared to each other. Thankful that none of us except Papa are in bed of affliction; thankful that Suse Tarpley is here to help me and to wait on Papa. These and many more things we have to be thankful for. Heavenly Parent be with my earthly Parent thro' his sickness and on thro' valley of death and receive his soul in Heaven. Help Ghu and I to live earnest prayerful lives and help each one of our children to give their lives to our Savior and all of us to be united in Heaven with loved ones gone on, for Jesus sake. Amen.

< December 3 >

Monday P.M. 4 o'clock

Papa rested quietly most of last night; he slept some sound sleep. First rest to amount to anything much he had in 3 days and nights. He is weaker today than he has been perhaps since he first took his bed, but he is quiet and rite cheerful. He has been playfully talking to Mary, Charlie, and baby Maggie. He seems this P.M. to enjoy seeing them around his bed and in his room. He is very weak—talks slowly and not very much but more than he does some days. I feel so glad that Papa rested last night. I am in his room now, and it seems such a sweet pleasure to be in here near Papa; it has been a sad sweet P.M. I've spent in here. The sun shines brightly softly in the window—just homefolks and Bro. Jim and Suse. Everything so quiet. Papa looks tolerably cheerful nearly all this P.M.

Bill Boatner came in to see Papa this P.M. and told us that Cape
had moved to Atlanta.

Mr. Weathers came to see Papa yesterday and read 46th Psalm and
had prayer. I was very glad of that. I've been so sorry that no minister
had been in to pray with him and read Holy Bible to him. He read
Bible *much* till he took his bed. Mr. Weathers told me over phone
awhile ago, that he was coming back to see Papa again soon. I wish
our new P.C. would come and read and pray with Papa. Papa told
Mr. W. that he lived every day for eternity; that he loved everybody.

Just after Mr. W. left Papa talked feebly and said he bore no malice
toward none — would forgive any enemy — that D. Mc—— was perhaps the bitterest enemy he had and that for 2 years he had wished,
earnestly desired Mr. D. Mc—— to come to see him and he wanted
them to be friends. Then spoke of Dr. J—— and broke down and
cried so he couldn't talk any more *so* hurt because Dr. J. is unfriendly
toward him.

It is night now — Messers Will Cowan and Ollie Mason are here to
sit up. Papa thinks lot of Will Cowan; Mr. W. is a good nurse, nice,
good man. Papa said Mr. Will would be an honor the community he
lived in. Ralph is deeply in love with his Uncle Jim; Ghu said tonight
that since Bro. J. had been staying over here these 8 weeks of Papa's
illness, that Ralph had had more attention (from Bro. J.) than Ralph
had ever had in his whole life — all put together. Jim's attention to
Ralph has transformed Ralph into a different child. I always said he
was cross and a cry baby, because I had so many babies and cares that
he had always been neglected, had never had his share of attention
and I feel that was why he cried. Could he have had more attention
he would have had a sweeter, more contented disposition. Am sure
he would, for Jim plays with him, nurses, carries, jumps him; gives
him coppers, 5 cts etc. and talks up for Ralph and gets others to add
pennies to Ralph's purse and goes hickory nut hunting with Ralph,
cracks and picks them out for R. and ties and laces and unties his
shoes and Ralph is Jim's shadow — follows him; hollows for him. Jim
plays many ways with him and plays many pranks off on him. Mary
loves Jim too and Bro. Jim nurses Maggie baby often and is *so* kind
to her; keeps her long time in his lap, and has kept her by fire on
cold days when I've been so busy etc.

‹ December 11 ›
Tuesday Night

I felt sad tonight on leaving Papa's room for the night's rest. Sadder on leaving Papa than any night yet. Did not intend to come out so soon but Charlie Childs and Jim Mobley came in. Poor Papa! He is so weary, so tired. The nights are more weary some than the days. Poor old father. He has been in bed 10 weeks today. Oh, merciful God, be with him; bless him; comfort him and "make all his bed in sickness." Papa talked good deal this A.M. of dying — he's been sick so much longer than he expected to be; said he wanted to go — he feels *so sorry* that he is so helpless and dependent on others. Says he wants to go because he (he thinks) is so much trouble to be waited on night and day. I fear my dear old father will not be here in our home circle but little longer and what a sad thought it is to me.

Mary has been sick. A rising in ear — now deaf in one ear. I am afraid she may thro' life remain so — but hope for better things. Had we bought an ear syringe sooner better hearing might have been restored. We did buy one — sent for it 2 days sooner than we could get it. Mary's deaf ear has made her seem so much less intelligent than before — deafness always *seems* to detract from intellect. 'Tis natural for one who is deaf in one ear to appear dull even tho' ever so bright — don't answer sometimes when called — don't obey sometimes when told to do a thing — can't hear requests.

‹ December 12 ›
Wednesday

I feel very unpleasant tonight. Have felt so all day because I had to reprove a grown negro boy about drinking out of the dipper. It excited me to deal with an impudent negro and I feel as if I had been sick all day. Oh, how excited I become over any impudence from darkies. I treat them all with kindness just as long as they are respectful to me. I never feel right when I get excited and say thro' excitement as much as I have today. Trust the Foster negro will behave from now on, and that I will not have to reprove but I will reprove if he manifests any impudence toward me. The good ones are where? Scarce to be sure. God forgive me for all I said today that I ought to have left unsaid and give me courage and preserve me calmly to say to the impudent ones what I ought to say.

Papa didn't rest very well last night. He has talked lot today. Heard me reprove the negro for drinking from dipper we drink from. He spoke at length on that subject—the negro's impudence. Papa seems to be some weaker. He has been in bed 10 wks. His mind up to the present is clear.

< December 15 >
Saturday

Papa is very quiet this A.M. and very weak. Ghu has gone to Jackson. Jim is here. Suse is not well. This is a beautiful bright day; warm enough to have windows up in my room (I have a good fire however and fixing to iron).

Maggie Wynn has a tooth—Askew was first to discover it. She is 11½ mo's old. . . . We did not know she had a tooth till last night. Maggie doesn't eat much. Learned to eat more than a month ago but has never eaten only by spells. Am sorry when Ghu goes away and Papa so low, but he felt that if was necessary to go. I had a comforting dream of my dear Mama a few nights ago. Seemed so plain that she was standing by my bed with a look of love toward me in her eyes and at some times as if she felt sad, or a yearning toward some one else; Papa I thought.

Papa spoke yesterday of dying calmly. He often speaks calmly of death. He said he was disappointed in being here yet, so long, but he would try to be patient; that for some cause it was for the best for him to stay on.

< December 20 >
Thursday Night. December 20th or 21st

Maggie Wynn can say "'an me! 'An me!" when she wants anything. She means to say: "hand it to me!"

Papa is weaker. He has been resting quietly 'most all day. Messers Will Cowan, Joe Wynn, Jim and somebody else are here tonight. I did not think there was any chance for me to bake a single cake this Christmas on account of Papa's sickness, but looked like when I'd speak of it Travys was so sad and seemed that he could hardly keep back tears—so disappointed. So resolved that I must not sadden the children. So today I've baked 3 cakes—went off in dreadful weather yesterday and bought 1 doz eggs for 30 cts and 100 (one dollar's) worth of sugar. So the children will have 3 cakes. They bought me 2 pkgs of grated cocoanut (no other kind at Ollie M's store yet and I didn't have time to wait). I told Travys and rest of children that as Papa was sick I reckon I wouldn't have chance to decorate house with holly and cedar. Travys replied that he and the other little boys could do that. So if I can get a chance I'll fix up the holly, missletoe and cedar for them too.

Fred has been in bed since Monday. Had some fever each day, but today he is better; had some appetite today. We were uneasy about him—afraid he might be taking pneumonia but today his fever was much lower. I'm to have fancy candy, holly leaves and holly berries on one cake after I ice it—just to please the children. Am not fixing up for anyone's sake but the children's this time.

‹ December 25 ›
Christmas Night

This has been a cold day. Daily paper says coldest spell of weather we've had in 2 yrs. Little boys enjoyed Santa Claus. Mary did not manifest much interest as she did last Christmas; this time she has a china doll; last year a bisque with natural looking hair and natural looking eyes. She loved her bisque dearly but doesn't love her china doll much.

Papa has been very quiet the past few days—not talking much. Messers Will Cowan and Dave Wheeler sat up here last night. There is no one tonight—not even Bro. Jim.

The little boys all had a purse in their stocking that they appreciated, perhaps more than any other present. Askew and Travis went to Philippi to the Christmas tree. Fred was not well enough to go. Travis and Askew enjoyed it. Miss Meetsie Crumbly sent Mary, Fred and Maggie Wynn a pretty little sack of good wholesome candy. Askew and Travys had a pretty little sack apiece also. 'Twas awful cold but they went. Mary and Charlie are sick with colds; Charlie was threatened with croup last night. Heaven bless each child in the Ark home. Heaven bless each inmate in this home.

Maggie Wynn was eleven months old today and the night before Christmas Eve stood alone for first time. She knows she is doing something smart and we all praise her and she laughs and stands alone little bit often.

This is the last Christmas we feel sure that we will ever spend with my father in this life. Heavenly Parent, help us to so live and trust in Thee that we may be reunited where partings are no more. No Lillie (my departed sister) to write to or communicate with this Christmas—we are going, we are parting—Help us; our Master, to strive to be loving, gentle, patient, forgiving, cheerful and kind. Help our little children to cultivate these Christian virtues.

1907

January 3
Thursday

Goodbye 1906. I feel like saying with the poet:

It seems to be the custom
Of the folks to sit about, on New Year's Eve
To watch the clock, to see the old year out,
To make merry of his going, and never heave a sigh,
As out across the shadow line, they see the old year die.

And maybe there's nothing in it, but it always seems to me,
Like some old friend had headed for his eternity;
And there's something sad and touching in parting
With the year, although a new one takes
His place, *the old one was so dear.*

It has had its ups and downs 'tis true like the others
Gone before; disappointments, loss and pain, some tears
Been shed, some hearts been sore; yet those that look with
Lifted eyes, beyond the strife the days have sent
Will skim the joy from sorrow's broth
And bless the great omnipotent.

Yes. I look upon the year that has gone as "an old friend" — a particular friend — my good old father was with me, close by me, all thro' the year that has passed away and today he is very sick, weak and low; he can't be with me without a great change thro' this New Year 1907. Papa is miserably sick — deathly sick at stomach — growing paler and weaker day by day.

Yesterday he was some more quiet, and little Maggie Wynn was by his bedside in my lap. Papa can't talk hardly above a whisper but he whispered to her and held his hand to her and she put a toothpick in his hand and he kept it a good while in his mouth.

It seems that an impending sorrow [i.e., pregnancy] was hanging over me past few days. I prayed very earnestly, and the anxiety

I felt, or the dread, lessened, almost ceased after earnestly praying and today I have the *positive* knowledge that this calamity is overpast or otherwise ordered. Answered prayer—I feel thankful—I should feel thankful, humble, submissive through ever day of this New Year because this dreaded sorrow is not to be mine.

Maggie Wynn has been sick, very sick with cold—she is better.

January 6
Sunday P.M.

Papa grows weaker but mind is clear except few moments at a time. 'Tis seldom that it is cloudy even for a few moments. I hoped Mr. Marks our P.C. would come this P.M.

January 13
Sunday

Papa is worse. Seemed to be rite smart worse ever since yesterday. He has taken cold and will not eat anything. As sick as he was yesterday, he spoke lovingly to Maggie Wynn; she was in his room and he thought it was Mary and called her to him. Then a day or so ago Mary came in talking sweetly, and he remarked something about her talking sweetly.

Mr. Marks, our P.C., and wife came to se Papa Friday and I am very glad he came. He went in and talked consolingly to Papa about God's goodness in letting him linger long—to give him time to think, pray etc. etc; told him that so many were suddenly taken away. He read 91st Psalm and then we all bowed down and Bro. Marks prayed a *good* prayer—it was a comfort to hear him pray and read the Psalm. I was afraid if Bro. M. did not come Friday that Papa might not know everything any later as he was growing worse. Then, too, Papa had expressed a desire for Mr. M. to come again. I am sorry that Papa does not take any more nourishment than he does. Heavenly Parent be with him—comfort him.

We are having a long spell of the warmest weather I ever remember for Jan. We've had this unpleasant warm weather for about 15 days or near that. Exceedingly warm for this season. Ghu says he never knew such a spell of weather in Jan. before. I fear we are going to have a lot of sickness from this weather.

I was thinking this eve of some cool treatment I had received and felt somewhat bothered and picked up Bible and opened at Job 5th chapter. I read it thro' and found it comforting. The 21st verse was *especially* so, and seemed to stand out for me: a promise it seemed, for me, suitable for the occasion. Here is the verse: "Thou shalt be hid from the scourge or the tongue: neither shalt thou be afraid of destruction when it cometh." The first clause is what helped me, comforted me and I ceased to worry.

January 26
Saturday A.M.

Papa is worse than he ever has been. He has taken almost no nourishment in 2 weeks—nearly 3 weeks. Drinks little coffee, little dram. Takes no medicine only that which produces rest. Bowels have not moved in severel days and he will not take purgative medicines nor allow us to use enema. His mind, which has been remarkably strong, in not clear. Not many days ago he told Suse to bring the baby to the bed. He smiled and talked to her about her flat nose etc. He loved her and all the children so tenderly. He cautioned Suse the same time about letting baby get hurt. I was out busy and left baby in Suse's care, in Papa's room.

Well, I do wish Papa had taken his medicine, bowels had moved and his stomach would have been better and maybe he would have eaten, or taken nourishment. It is distressing for him to lye here day after day and these things, necessary things, not being done. But he refuses them; says he is extremely anxious to go away—because he has been sick so long and can be nothing but helpless—here for others to sit up with him night after night etc. He can't bear resignedly to be what he thinks "is nothing but trouble and in the way." Do wish he could have left off the constant *dread* of being a trouble to others. All of his late life he has avoided every way being *any* trouble to others—has earnestly avoided having one unnecessarily to do *anything* for him. Was never childish like most aged folks are. He was such a good gentle indulgent warm-hearted parent. It is such a pity that we can't *do* everything that we feel ought to be done for him as

long as life lasts—and we would if he would let us. We can't persuade
him to take nourishments or physic.

Maggie Wynn arrived at her first mile stone yesterday. She had
her first birthday. She was 1 yr old, Friday Jan. 25th, 1907. Maggie
is learning to make the sound of words. Can make sound of several:
"Han me!" (means hand me!). She doesn't join any that I can think
of only those two. She has 4 teeth. Doesn't eat much food—can
push a chair over room little—stand alone. Is awful cute—nods her
head away over successively and says 'owdy! owdy! (means howdy!).
Blessings on the little "Tot." Many happy birthdays may she see.

Someone is coming. Little leisure have I

Night.

Dr. Woods came this P.M. He said nothing could be done for
Papa now only to give him something to keep him quiet; that he was
very low and pulse bad. How sad to think that my poor old Papa
will soon be gone. How dark all seems to me when I think of living
here in their home and Mama and Papa both gone. Poor suffering
Papa! Oh, how *gentle* and devoted he was to all—especially to Askew.
Even yesterday, when talking at random he asked for Askew to come
do something for him. Yesterday, when at himself, he smiled at little
Maggie Wynn and tried to move his hand toward her in a playful
way. Oh, God, our Creator, receive my dear old Father in Thy Home
above and help me and my children to live pure Christian and meet
with Papa and Mama—their loving devoted Grand Ma and Grand
Pa again. Papa loved them Oh, so tenderly and so did my sainted
Mother. What devoted grandparents my children had.

Ghu said tonight Papa had *always* (since he and I married) been
good, truly good, to him; he said he believed Papa would be better off
when life has ended—Home in Heaven where there is no sickness,
no sorrow, no dying, and where Mama, Buddie, Little Sis, Splint and
Lil are waiting to welcome him. Heavenly Father, help me to live for
the Lord. Help my children live for the Lord and may we all meet in
Heaven, for Jesus sake. Amen. Saturday Night. Jan. 26th, 1907. 11:30
o'clock.

January 29
Tuesday Night

My precious father, who has been so good to me all my life long is fast going away from me. Poor Papa can not speak; he has lost his speech — he aroused to clear consciousness this P.M. and made three efforts to call me (in a whisper) to the bed; I was standing close by, and he was conscious — his mind clear and from expression of the eye and repeated efforts to speak to me there was something he wished to say. He offered his thin hand to me, so weak he just could raise it and when I took his hand he seemed to be trying *so hard* to say good bye! good! bye! Good bye! And he had tried off and on all day to tell us something; has tried *so hard*, but we never got the message. Oh, how my heart aches for the message he struggled and struggled off and on all day to say to us. Askew came to the bed. He wanted to speak to Askew and *could not* and tried to raise his hand to tell Askew good bye but Askew to keep from breaking down left the bed without telling his much beloved GrandPa good bye. He tried to call Jim to bed all day and tried to call him and I. Reckon Jim stayed at fire to prevent breaking down in tears. He tried to talk to Ghu too. Told Suse good bye too. How I do hate to give up Papa! How good I've felt ever since Mama went away to have poor feeble aged Papa in house with me for company and he was so good to us and so devoted to the children.

Oh, God, comfort, soothe him in each remaining moment left to him here on this earth and go with him thro' valley of death for Jesus sake, and oh Merciful Heavenly Father, blot out my sins and help me to be made better from this day on to my dying bed — Oh, God, sanctify my precious father's death to good of my soul every day I stay in this life. Heavenly Father guide my children, Askew (Papa's much loved), Fred, Travis, Charlie, Mary and Maggie, along the right way all thro' life so that Thou can, when life is over take those sweet children that Papa loved so well to their Grand Ma and Grand Pa in a Home Beyond where we can never be separated again. Help us, oh Father to all be made better by the gift of such a father, such a Grand Pa for Jesus sake.

Oh, God, we may not have the love of Papa bestowed upon us after this night. He looks now as if he couldn't not last another day.

January 30
Wednesday P.M.

My dear, dear Papa died this morning about 8:30 O'clock.

It is a dark time in my life. How dear my precious old Papa was to me. How heavy my heart is today just to know we can't talk with him and he with us. His love and sympathy for us was so strong. No mother could have loved more tender than he—his children and his grandchildren—my children were his children—he loved them as his own—said so and lived for them, as it were. No mother it seems to me, could have been more tender with her children than my poor aged afflicted Papa was with my children. Especially was he strongly attached to Askew.

I have one regret all day—I did not reach Papa's bedside this morning before he lost consciousness. I think I saw a gleam of consciousness for a few moments. I had been up in fore part of the night and lay down—never undressed to go back to his room and see his precious face and to be in his presence known by him once more before he waded down the valley of death, but I did not wake in time. He bade me a sad goodbye yesterday and would have done so again I think had I been in the room. He gave Suse his hand this morning before he lost consciousness.

He had the strongest mind I ever saw in my life for his age and long affliction. It was remarkably bright beyond a doubt. His reason would at times on some things, and just little while at time, be clouded. The shortest length of time I ever saw for such a long and awful spell of suffering. If he had taken purgative medicines by direction I have no idea his mind would have been at any time as much clouded as it was. It was a wonderful strong mind he had.

I never saw many people die but did not know that it was possible for anyone to go as softly as he did. All who witnessed it say they never saw anyone in their life, go out easily, so gentle like a babe on mother's breast falls asleep. His eyes were half closed—mouth open—had been breathing thro' his mouth most of the time 2 or 3 days. Mouth didn't move unless one slight tremor. We who were by bedside looking on didn't know when last breath went as it went so gently. The men examined him after waiting to see him breathe, to know whether all life had gone. I firmly believe Papa had prayed to die easily. Awhile perhaps half hour, he suffered and groaned piteously, in latter part of night and could not swallow the quieting medicine. I gave him some water about 12 o'clock—he drank 3 times—a little each time in a teaspoon—seemed to be thirsty. Then as he tried hard to talk and make some requests to me, and couldn't, and seemed to be suffering I asked him 2 or 3 times to take a tablet to give him rest. He was conscious and knew what I said, but let us know he seriously objected to taking it, for some cause that he could not explain to us. What a pity he was speechless. He was a father and mother too to me since Mama went away and I loved him dearly and tenderly and I am lost without him and *no one* can fill his place in my heart or our home. I don't believe anyone can take Grand Pa's place in the hearts of my little boys—Askew especially. He loved them *all* so devotedly but was partial to Askew. Words can't express his love for his loved ones. Now his form lies in his room. I have not seen it since just after the sweet spirit winged its flight this morn. Heavenly Father be with us—his loved ones left desolate.

February 1

Friday Morning

We are alone this morning—Ghu and I—and our children, for the first time in this home in our life unless once when Papa spent a few days at High Falls after Mama died.

Anna, Faith, and Hester came home with us from the funeral of precious Papa—and they left this morning. 'Twas raining when they drove away. Anna sat in front of surrey and drove. She was exposed to the weather and I did hate to see her leave in the rain. She does not seem strong—I feel uneasy about her—I fear her health is rite bad and I fear the ride thro' rain will make her sick. I went in Papa's room after we came back from funeral. I went in after something last night at bed time. How sad it looks. How *loud* and *strong* every thing in there proclaims "Papa has gone." The old clock that for so many years has stood in one place and ticked off time—maybe for 25 yrs—seems to say "Papa has gone!" The clock always associated itself with fresh memories, daily of my mother. Now of Papa.

Mary came in the room this morning when I was taking up ashes in Papa's room and looked all over in corner where Papa's bed stood (the bed has been removed and the corner where it stood certainly does look unspeakably desolate—makes my heart ache not to see my Father in his room *no* where) after Mary looked all over room for Papa (one bed is up) she would look over there and seemed to think he must be in the room and with a surprised or astonished expression in her eyes she asked quickly "Where is Grand Pa! Where is Grand Pa? Say, where is grand Pa?" I told her he had gone. She went to the window and looked up the road as if she was looking to see him go up the road that instant. I told her had gone to Heaven. She asked "Somebody bring him back? Somebody bring him back?" No wonder she can [not] realize that Papa can not be gone to stay, as she never knew a day when "Grand Pa" was gone to stay all day. Oh, what a gentle loving heart he had. No mother could have been more tender and sympathetic than my dear Papa was to my children. He lavished love on them *daily* all their lives. I will miss seeing the tender caresses and hearing the tender words of deep love he spoke to them daily.

'Twas a *very* bad day for the funerel. Papa had said he hoped the weather would be pretty for the funerel but the weather was very bad. The ladies did not go to cemetary. We did not see the cold wet earth put over sweet Papa. Oh, such a sweet man—such a loving tender sympathetic heart. Oh, may I by Divine aid, thro' the blessed sweet beautiful tender memories of my dear Father be a better woman than I've ever been. May I be, tho' now he's gone, worthy yet, or more worthy of ever having such a father for myself and such a "Grand Pa" for my children.

Papa looked so life like in his coffin. Most natural corpse I ever saw in my life. A sweet smile seemed to be over his whole features. It was so life like that in one sense 'twas comforting to be near it and look at his dear sweet face and his dear hands that had ministered to me and mine in love all our life long. Oh, God, chisel me into the vessel I should be. Help me to be always ready to go, always at peace with God and man.

Papa was to have been burried masonically—he gave his demit to Ghu, just calmly as if he had been carrying on a business transaction about 2 months before he died. Just as calmly was his words as if he were speaking of a useful note. He asked Ghu to bring to the bed a box from his closet and he could find the demit in the box of papers—and did, I think. I came out of the room, before seeing him get it. The weather was so extremely bad that only a few masons came, not enough to bury him masonically.

Papa said in the last years of his life he had lived for eternity. He said he was ready to go, wanted to go; impatient to go during last of his illness. I believe Papa is in Heaven. That belief helps me bear the separation. And another help is this: his sufferings were so intense, such long spell of sickness. I expect one day to go where Papa is and I want to see all my children there with Papa and Mama again. I feel that never again will I feel at home in this world—Papa was a mother and father both to me after Mama went away. He was left for me to love and to cheer our home—but now Papa has gone—and it is the saddest going of all the loved ones to me. As long as he was left to me I could feel at home, but no Papa now. He had been with me, rather I with him, for nearly 38 years. I will be 38 on the 18th Inst. As long as Papa was here I felt at home, but now Earth life has grown poorer— Heaven dearer. My thoughts I feel, from now on, will be of loved ones and my home in Heaven. I feel too that death has lost much of its terror since I saw Papa die. Papa had been living such a careful life the last years of his life—kind to all—black and white and keeping his conscious clean—watching and praying—keeping his heart void of offense in sight of God and man. Reading Bible daily—some times much and long thro' the day. He gave no one his Bible. He gave Askew his watch and gold collar button. He gave Will Stewart some clothes he needed to keep him warm this winter. He gave Susan Tarpley an almost new coat to wear for a cloak. How lonely! How sad! Gone! A *sad* "good bye." Home on earth can never be complete again—never. What a wealth of love and sympathy went away with him. What deep tenderness we'll never have manifested and lavished on us again. "God be with us," till we meet again, and help us to grow stronger each day in Christian Graces for Jesus Sake. Amen.

February 2
Saturday A.M.

I feel if Papa were to come back to us this morning he would tell us not to grieve for him; that he was free from all suffering and sorrow. I feel that he would advise us to live close to God—not wander away but to live with a conscience void of offense in sight of God and man. To keep our conscience as the noon tide clear. He would I think advise our children that were so dear to him, to begin now in early youth to give their lives to God—to be Christians before bad habits are formed.

How strange it seems for us to be alone—our family and no Papa, no Grand Pa here. It seems to us that we are a very few, a small company without him. His presence, so much love, sympathy, good cheer etc. to make him a strong personality—Everything here in his home proclaims his absence.

When we went to supper last night all was so still in his room, and we felt like he ought to come in and feebly sit down and quietly eat his meal in his accustomed seat at table. I wonder if his [spirit] was not near us then. Askew seemed to be impressed at table. I felt as I've said and Ghu told me he felt like Papa ought to come in and sit down with us as he had so many years done. Ghu says the house is lonely, very, for him since Papa has gone. Rite here I wish to say Papa seemed to always have utter confidence in Ghu's integrity and entrusted to him many important money matters. All along thro' his sickness he would say Ghu will do thus and so—pertaining to buying, paying etc. etc. *Much* has gone from us. Life for me can never be the same. No one can fill Papa's place in my heart and in this home.

How, all this time (these years) since Papa has been afflicted and confined to the house has the old mill, the little homes on hill, the hills, the creak and bridge, all seemed to speak sadly to me of my old feeble Papa. How I've walked down to the mill "so silent and lone," where Papa has spent so much of his life and had a flood of sad memories to rush to my heart of my poor old Papa—nearing the grave—nearing a time to leave us. This old home is sweetest spot on earth to me and the saddest. I love every tree, every hill, the creak and branches.

But I am never to set my heart on earthly things deeply again. Papa has gone, Mama and loved ones. I must live with an eye toward a Home Beyond. At heart I don't feel I can ever be light and gay any more. Papa can not come to us, his home here in life was 85 years long—but the golden bowl is broken and our lives are saddened. But we can begin rite now to get ready to join him in Home above.

February 3
Sunday P.M.

I am home this Sunday P.M. without the beloved one whom I was
always with when Ghu and some of the children would go to Sunday
school. Papa and I and the youngest ones would always be here when
Ghu and older ones were away. And the company, the sweet company his presence was for me and the children. He always wanted
them to stay around him when lonelier than usual. He always wanted
them near by, but especially so if lonelier than usual.

Papa Ghu said he would not leave me if I rather he'd stay, but they
are to meet this P.M. to organize S[unday] S[chool] and our little
boys ought to be in S.S. and I told him I would read in some good
books here and write and not be lonely. I'm lonely without Papa
when Ghu and all children are here. Since Papa passed to Heaven
I feel that we, all of our family, are a very *small* company. I never
could have thought we would have felt in that respect just as I do —
I believe Ghu and Askew feel as I do about it. Papa's going away was
like a family leaving. We feel so small in No. — so lost without him as
we huddle together around fire side at night or gather at meal time
around table. When Papa was here I use always to feel we were a
good crowd — but his absence certainly does make me feel that we
are a small crowd now. He was father and mother and grand mother
and Grand father all in one. How we miss him! How the clock on the
mantle, chiming the hour speaks of him and Mama too — How many
cherished sacred memories the tick-tock of the old clock brings to
us. The old arm chair that his weary aching form has rested in for
a number of years looks so silent, so lone now. And the one that
Mama use often to sit in — they are both there in their quiet room
now speaking as it were in sadness of the forms passed from sight.
How strange for us to go in and not see Papa in his big arm chair or
on the bed or in veranda where he so often sat when up.

The memories are tender, sacred, painful. May we live so as to be
as ready as he was, when our time comes to go. May we keep our
conscience as he kept his the declining years of his life — unspotted.
He would not indulge in unfriendly or unkind remarks. He seemed
to always desire conversation to turn to another subject and seemed
to feel unpleasant or disturbed when people were indulging in unkind sayings of others — even tho' the saying were true. He wanted

to say no evil of none. He was very gentle to all animals. Often and daily fed our cat at his place at table and daily arose from table with food for our dog. He never wanted a dog killed or a cat drowned, no matter how unprofitable. He wanted them given away if any one would have them, or carried away near a home and dropped. He was Honesty itself allways. He was temperate in all things. A small eater of anything—victuals or fruits.

February 11
Monday Night

Two, yes three, men have been here today, trying to sell monuments for our dear Papa's grave. Mr. Middlebrooks of Locust Grove wrote, trying to sell one. Don't know who Ghu will buy from. I stay some of the time in Papa's room these days—just now and then; build a good fire and do some work in there. I love that room—'tis sacred—from memories of dear Mama and Papa. How much I miss Papa. How strange that he is not with us. Saturday night Ghu and little boys were gone from the house (down rite close by, in old shoe shop) where men had a rabbit supper and egg boiling. They were gone an hour—just after I had washed supper dishes. If Papa had not been gone I would hardly have missed them, but Papa's absence made the house seem so big and lonely. Mary seemed awed too because he was not with us; she was excited, and cried. We had a good fire in Papa's dear room, and 2 bright lamps burning. Mary, Maggie Wynn and I. We called "Rubie," Papa's dog, in; she helped our feeling considerably. Never did I love old Rubie so well as since her master died. I shall try take care of her in Papa's stead now. Never did I know a dog could comfort one so as I know since the night my two babies and I were alone in Papa's room. She was so much comfort—company too.

Today was Fred's and Travis' birthday—Fred 9 and Travis 7. I cooked them a birthday pudding and prepared a company supper (just little extra) in honor of their birthday. I could not cook the pudding till supper time because I had so much work to do and was so tired and overtaxed, could hardly keep going.

I copied, before time to cook dinner, a piece in sacred memory of my dear Papa, to send to Henry Co. Weekly for publication and baby Maggie was so cross that is was late before I had dinner and Mesrs O. B. Willis and Bill Childs took dinner. They came at late hour and I made them biscuit minus soda. I was very sorry I forgot the soda; but I was *so* overtaxed—so worried mentally and physically. I have a new book, "The Life and Sayings of Sam Jones." I am very anxious to read it—have not had time to read but little in it yet but enjoyed thoroughly what I did read. How Papa loved to read of, and from, Sam Jones! Were he with us and as well as before he took his bed, how thoroughly he would enjoy this new book. I can see him now as he used to sit and read.

I heard few days ago of Rev. Mr. Stilwell's death—he was our pastor last year. He baptized Mary and Maggie Wynn and I though performed the ceremony in a way that was earnest and spiritual. No doubt he was a good old man. He looked pitiful. Had trouble here, I expect plentiful.

I've been sick with cold, sore throat and hoarseness—my colds settle on my lungs. So does Askew's. I often feel uneasy about Askew's catarrhal affection. God be with us.

February 19

Yesterday was my birthday. I am 38 years old. 'Twas the first birthday I ever had without a father—am to be an orphan rest of my life. I was blest with a mother till 35 years old and with a father till nearly 38 years old. May the rest of my life be lived so as to be more worthy of such parents as I did have.

Little Maggie Wynn is one year and near one month old. She is very bright, very gentle, very loving. She is well now and a good baby. She picked up a piece of paper night before last, not much larger than my hand and mumbled and mumbled and ran her little finger over the print. She was reading—and so young to do such a smart thing. She leans her head very affectionately against us when we tell her to hug our neck. Oh, she is such a gentle affectionate little creature. She is fat and chubby. Eats a little nearly every day this week. She has never eaten enough to count till she was a year old.

Mary goes to Sunday School now and so does Charlie.* They never

*From here on, "Ralph" is called "Charlie."

began till lately. Have been twice. Neither Charlie or Mary had ever been anywhere much in their lives; so Ghu bought Charlie a suit—whole outfit and Mary a pretty cap and now they go to S.S.

I went over to New Hope Sunday eve—just before night—to the cemetary—my first visit to Papa's grave. How sad to see his grave and to be deprived of his companionship in our home. How sad to go to Papa's grave! Oh, how sad! Papa regretted deeply and talked of it on his death bed that there was no room for his grave rite close (side by side) of my dear Mother. I do deeply regret it too; the grave is not close—not far away, but not side by side. And he craved for it to be side by side but another grave was in the way and he knew it, and short while before dying spoke of his great desire to be by her side in the grave and spoke of the other grave being there.

February 26
Tuesday Night

Well, 'tis bed time and I'm anxious to write little. Received a note from Miss Ruth Jinks yesterday that I appreciated; she said that she had never taught a better set of children than ours. I am proud of that. I am glad they do not give her much trouble.

Bro. Marks and wife were here last Saturday. I enjoyed their visit—I felt benefitted by their coming. I love for Bro. Marks to come because he came and read with Papa and for another reason, because I think he is a good man. His wife's conversation and hearty laughs made me feel better physically. Bro. Marks had prayer with us—Ghu, myself and the children. I appreciated that; the last time he had prayer here previous to that was in Papa's room. May we live prayerful lives and be ready to join our loved ones in Glory when the summons come to "Papa Ghu," "Mama Mag," Askew, Fred, Travis, Charlie, Mary and Maggie Wynn is my prayer.

Oh, how we miss the loved ones gone ahead! How sacred sweet and tender are the memories of dear Papa . . . and Mama . . . that floods my soul. How strange I feel that they are not here with us in their home—sweet old home. How soon we all may leave this old home nest. This place will be sold this year—we may not be able to buy it; the highest bidder will get it. For memories tender and sacred

I would love to live on here—me and mine, till called to a home above to be reunited with dear parents and loved ones gone before.

February 27
Wednesday P.M.

This morning Mr. Sandford Rape, a friend of Papa's called me "Maggie" over phone. I appreciate it so much because Papa always called me [that] and Mr. Rape was first one to call me "Maggie" since my dear Papa called me to his dying bedside and said "Maggie—Goodbye!" Papa *always* called me "Maggie." I love the name because he called it that way and I consented for my baby to be called Maggie Wynn, because Papa always called me Maggie and the Wynn was for he and I too.

I sat down today in the old arm chair that Papa had been the occupant of so long—for the first time since he left us—and I'm the only one who has set down in it I believe since the day my precious sweet father was carried to the cemetary. I have felt a reverence or something akin to it, for the old arm chair that supported my precious aged feeble Papa's form. I have strongly felt enclined to pass behind, not walk in front, of the dear old chair. I wish the chair could be mine now as he no longer is here—to keep in memory of him.

March 3
Sunday P.M.

My dear precious Papa has been away (to Heaven) a month and how painful to be here without him! How *much* went away when Papa died! How much! How much! What a wealth of tender love, deep love and sympathy, great deep sympathy went from our home, our lives, when he died. How silent his room that before his going was where the family loved to be; especially how the children whom he always wanted near and around him, think it desolate. None of them like to pass thro' that room now after the evening grows on. None of them tarry in that room now at no time of day. How desolate this home—how the children loved and miss Grand Pa. How I loved and miss him! What a comfort he was to me! How lonely I am without him. Sunday P.M.'s we were left alone—he, myself and he baby, and usually, Charlie and Mary. Charlie and Mary go to Sunday School now and this Sabbath Eve no one is left but Maggie Wynn . . . and I. How unnatural it seems for dear Papa to be absent from us. How natural it would be were he here with us. How quiet his room! No sound save the tick-tock and strike of his clock. How I love that old clock because it was my dear Mama's and Papa's and kept time for them for a number of years and when it strikes now how many memories it brings of them. Baby cries so I can't write. God be with us here, sanctify memories of our precious parents to good of our souls and by and by unite us all in Heaven.

March 17

Wynn's Mill, Georgia

'Tis now a strange time of night to be writing. It is some after 3 o'clock. I had a nervous or wakeful spell and decided I'd rather get up and make a fire and write than to lie in bed 2 hours awake. I too, kept thinking of Susan Tarpley Col stealing a coat and pistol when she was here last. I decided to get rid of unpleasant thoughts I would write.

This is Sunday. If no one comes today I will go to Sunday School, unless otherwise prevented. I went last Sunday and enjoyed it. Last Friday P.M. spent an hour *very pleasantly* in Miss Ruth Jinks school room. I am very anxious to go back soon to her school room. That was a treat. What a pretty school room we have at New Hope. Rubber backboards, patent desks, veranda on front side, well close by etc. Ghu has taken great interest in getting these nice things here. He is wide awake on giving the school at New Hope his best, and in his children's education. Miss Ruth is a *very* fine teacher.

I visited the cemetary Friday P.M. too. How I do miss the companionship of my dear Papa in this home. Mary as small as she is—3 yrs old last Feb—missed him so much and she and Charlie speak of him yet. I know Askew's grief must be deep—he and Papa were so devoted to each other. How strange that Papa is not around fireside, in his room, on bed, in big arm chair, out on veranda etc. What a wealth went out of our home, our lives when he went away—a wealth of tender sympathy, gentleness and love.

I feel very much interested in our S.S. lessons now. The life of Abraham is so inspiring to better living; and the old testament characters are so helpfull, those we are studying now.

I've taken a step (forbid that I should seem to be boasting or self righteous) that is new: I try in my simple poor way to have prayer with my children at night—just begun one week ago—on Sunday night. I could not persuade Ghu to take the step. I told him as he was the head of the family that it was his place, but he wouldn't consent. "Not yet" he would say. Tho' he may be a better man than I am a woman, yet I felt a duty for *me* to discharge before and with my children, if he wouldn't. I believe every family should have a family altar. I believe we should honor God that way in our homes with and before our children. I never have been satisfied for us to live as animals and beasts—returning no thanks in our homes to our Creator for his goodness daily to us, tho' I've just turned 38 and mother of six (living) children (one dead) and our eldest eleven yrs and this is first time since we broke up housekeeping [that is, moved in with her parents] that we've read in God's word and had prayer with our family. I am thankful that I am not married to a man who would oppose me in this.

March 22
Friday P.M.

This is fine weather! Bright warm sunshine. Dry. Fine for one's health—outdoor exercise—but my duties keep me indoors most of the time. I long to get out more. I think I would be less tired, more refreshed were I to take more outdoor exercise or bask in this beautiful sunshine. For health's sake I walked up to see Misses Mat and Babe yesterday P.M. The sunshine was perfect. I rolled Maggie Wynn nearly all way there—Ghu rolled her piece of the way. Mary and Charlie went with me. I met with Della C. and Willie S. up there; also Mrs. Manerva McK., Mrs. Ida C., and Mrs. Lula M. Little Maggie Wynn loved quiet Mrs. Loula L. and stayed with her; crawled up to get in her lap twice.

Little Mary, by some means, pulled wash stand over on her one day this week. A very heavy home made wash stand. It seemed to be enough to crush the life our of her—the weight was so great—and she was (and is) the worst bruised child I ever saw in my life—both eyes, (left one awfully bruised) forehead and bridge of nose. I was uneasy until yesterday about her. She is just a playful as a child can be and I trust will get over th terrible crush soon as nature can heal.

Little Maggie Wynn can say new words—"Shoo! Shoo!" at chickens when they come in the house. She is now about (liking 2 or 3 days) 14 months old. She learned ½ month ago to walk few steps and contrary to the way all our other children did, she doesn't walk any better yet. The other children would walk—cease to crawl altogether, when they began to take as many steps as Maggie Wynn does.

I'm having help now to clean up the house every morning. She has helped me all this week. A negro girl, named Ada, 14 yrs old. How much I did need that much help at least, and how relieved I feel to have it. She is (by me being rite with her) a nice hand to clean up house (we make beds, wash dishes, and sweep floors together) and she is good hand, nice hand, to scour buckets.

Little Maggie, Mary and her devoted little brother Charlie, are all going barefooted. They all seem to enjoy it. Askew, Fred and Travis are too; they go fishing these fine evenings too. Papa Ghu went seining yesterday; we had fish for breakfast. Fish for breakfast brings memories of Mama and Papa; both liked fish and we have had no creak fish since Papa was in bed until today. He chewed up piece of fish when he'd had those. I remember, too, that the first fish we had on table after dear Mama's death, how Papa cried and he could hardly eat for thinking of her.

These warm days bring memories of Papa. Seems that he is here in his big arm chair out on front porch reading or talking to my little ones that he loved so tenderly. And when we see his chair, his room, his bed vacant, how we miss him; how strange it seems that Papa is not here, where he has been all the 37 years of my life (so far as I can remember). I was perhaps 2 yrs old or near that when we moved here. I was 38, 18th of Feb.

How strange for us to be in Papa's home and Papa nor Mama either one here. I believe they "are near us, tho' unseen," often. Yes, I love to think that they are. How strange it does seem that spring and summer are coming to us and no Papa here to mingle with us and converse with those who come in to see us. He seemed a part of me, especially since Mama died. I love and treasure their memory. I pray that the memory of my dear parents will restrain me when tempted to return evil for evil or to enter temptation to be or feel unkind toward any one, even those who may be so to me.

Maggie Wynn is just learning to climb up in chairs—stand up in them and hold to the back. She occasionally gets a *hard* fall out of doors, off of doorsteps. (Age 14 mo's liking 2 or 3 days).

Meetsie Crumbly played some sweet music for me one night this week. I heard it over 'phone.

March 25
Monday

Little Maggie Wynn is 14 months old today and can't walk any better than she did 2 weeks ago.

We have some beautiful white lillies in the garden now. How they fill me with admiration and sad thoughts too. They speak of my parents who admired them before they went to Home Beyond. I carried some of the white lillies to church Sunday and Ghu and I put them on Mama's and Papa's grave.

How this balmy weather makes me miss them. It seems that they ought to be here now. Seems that we ought to see Papa in his accustomed place—in arm chair—out on front porch—and that Mama ought to be passing thro' house and over yard. Seems like we ought to see Papa's warm smile, that always lit up his face when Askew and children came home from school and seems we ought to hear the warm greeting he always gave them. I imagine they miss it, especially Askew; Askew had roomed with him so long, all had part of the time—I think Askew misses him most at night.

Little Maggie it seems hasn't forgotton him. I carried her in Papa's room today and I said "Maggie, where is Grand Pa? Where is Grand Pa?" and she looked at once over on his bed. His room is the sweetest room in the house, a sacred chamber. I go in there and kneel at times by Papa's bed and pray for a better cleaner heart—by the bed where his life left his body. I ask my Maker there in that sacred spot to help me live a purer truer life—to be a true Christian.

Ghu assists in family worship now. Let me have it one week and then he took it up. We have it together now and I am so glad to have it thus—a family altar in our home.

Little Mary has "a new wrinkle in her horn." She wears p——t——ts. Has been wearing Napk——s till today. She has done very well with her devoted little Bro. Charlie to help guide or direct her new "outfit." Mary also donned one of Charlie's dresses today and she likes the dress and feels very much dressed up. She is a blessed sweet child. Happy and gay—merry as a sunbeam all the time. She went fishing today in a "jack hole" in front yard and caught two "jacks" and was just overjoyed and excited—just laughed and jabbered and ran around and squealed about catching 2 "jacks" with a jonquil top. These "jacks" are a flat headed worm shaped like a horseshoe nail; our children fish for them; put a small straw or jonquil top down in their hole until it moves and jerk it up quickly and often a "jack" is still holding on it biting it I suppose. The jacks make little holes in the ground in the yard.

So this week I must save some eggs to paint for the children; next Sunday is Easter. Miss Ruth will give an Easter egg hunt at her school.

April 3

Wednesday Afternoon

Askew stayed at home sick yesterday—not very sick, but did not seem well. He was help and company, too, for me. I enjoyed his presence all day. He made me a shelf to put my prettiest cups and dishes on. He carried Mary and Charlie to gin branch and gathered honey suckle and dog wood blooms. Today Fred is at home; he was too sick to go—not prudent for him. He has helped me too very well. He draws water, wipes dishes etc. etc.

Today has been a busy day—starched and Ada did not come to help me clean up house.

I saw on back of my Missionary Magazine a picture of a cousin of mine, Norwood Wynn, daughter of Oscar Wynn; I never saw her and have not heard of her before since she was a little girl that I remember of.

We had a letter from [brother] Charlie today; his health is still bad. I am afraid he will never be any better but I hope he will.

We've been having a cool spell since Easter. We keep fire all day and till bed time in Papa's room, or Mama's room, the sacred room. We may not have the pleasure of being thus in my dear parents room after this year. How helpful it is to me at nights this week around a good fire in the room that my parents stayed in so many years, to have a few verses from Bible read and a short prayer offered as we kneel in this sacred room to the God of my parents. What a sweet privilege it is to me. How helpful it is to me. How it does help for all our family of little ones and Ghu and I to be around fireside and to read a portion of God's word from the Testament used so much by my dear Mother and Father and in the room made sacred by memories of them, and to ask the care and blessings of their God to be with us and ours till life's end and afterward to reunite us with our dear ones in Heaven.

Ghu and I went to Miss Ruth's Easter Egg Hunt. Ghu rolled Maggie and both Mary and Maggie part of the way in baby carriage. I walked over there and back after working steady all A.M. and I think outdoor life would be a great blessing to me. Wish I could get out oftener and stay out more. Well, Ghu is not well; has boils on leg. They make him look and feel badly. Travis has roseola. Didn't hurt him. We (children and I) were alone Easter. Ghu went to Stark to Quarterly meeting and took dinner with Mr. Matt McMichael.

Askew has grated potatoes (ground them in meat chopper) twice this week for me. He and I are fond of potato puddings.

Maggie Wynn is doing a new thing this week. She is walking all over house and is so happy because she can do a new thing. Her little heart is filled with joy as she slowly walks (and sometimes fast) up and down the hall. Her dear eyes and face is lit up with joy as she walks. I thank our Maker that the darling baby can walk. My heart rejoices over it. All family are glad. Askew loves Maggie better than the others do I think. Charlie loves her but Askew loves her best and caresses her daily. Maggie loves Askew better than she does anyone except G. and I. Mary loves Charlie now best, of her brothers; she used to be devoted most to Askew; she loves Askew next to Charlie now I think. Maggie is always glad when the children come home from school especially glad to see Askew.

Askew was kind and good to Papa . . . and Papa loved Askew so *tenderly*, so deep—such a strong tie existed between the two. I feel sorry for Askew now. I feel that he missed his devoted Grand Pa sadly and daily. Papa loved each one of the children so tenderly—so devotedly. He was always so anxious about them when any of them were least bit sick. How he humored and sympathized with them! How his whole heart went out in sympathy to them at such times. We all lost love, sympathy, and a blessing when he left us. My dear mother was the same way about us all. Travis was the one who lay closest to her heart. How deep tender and true was her devotion to him and how true to all of them.

I am enjoying this cool snap (Apr. 3d) tho' beans, garden sass, corn, etc. are bitten and blasted. I love cool weather because I am not so worn out, so fagged. I thank our Creator for this delightful spell of weather. I certainly do enjoy it. Sunday was a lonely looking day as it was cloudy and the house was dark but I had a good time; weather was too bad for the children to go to S.S. and I read and talked to a friend or 2 on 'phone.

'Tis nearly time now for me to begin supper.

April 7
Sunday P.M.

Maggie Wynn makes sounds of words—after us—but doesn't say words. For instance, Mary says "Maggie wants more peaches" and Maggie will say "arut pe." Maggie (at 14 months old) will hug up a bottle, ball, rag, or anything, hug it close to her breast and rock her body too and fro and try sing—makes believe everything is a baby. She is so young to be such a motherly baby. I never, it seems to me, saw one at her age play as if things were dolls or babies so much.

Ghu is sick with boils on left leg—has severel. He has not been well in severel days or 2 weeks.

I am not feeling well.

Ghu couldn't go to S.S. on account of sickness today and he regretted not being able to be there. He loves the S.S. I love S.S. too. I wanted to go real badly too, but didn't seem that I could get off. How I wish I could go regularly. I love our S.S. magazine as well as any literature I get outside the Bible. It is a keen pleasure.

I've been sick for severel days this week+++ I pray that I may speedily be better and my strength spared to my family. I've been suffering the keenest anxiety in regard to my health. My fears are great that my health may fearfully fail, but I am praying yet that my strength may be spared to our family.

April 18
Thursday A.M.

Maggie Wynn is weaned. We began Sunday Night. She slept with Ghu Sun., Mon., Tues., night; last night she slept with me. She was wonderfully easy to wean; never cried a single *big hard* cry to nurse.

I am not well—lie down part of the time.

Little Maggie Wynn is learning to make sound of lot of new words, and learning to ask for water so that I understand.

Had a letter yesterday from Charlie and Willie [Wynn], a good letter. They are my warmest friends now since Papa left this world. (of course, I mean except husband and children).

1908

January 18
Home

A great many many changes have been made since I last wrote in this book—a great deal of suffering (physical) endured.

Today there is a fine baby girl one month old in our home. She came on Dec. 17th, 1907. She was one month old yesterday. I've suffered so with thresh in breasts etc., that I remain weak and can do almost nothing but take care of baby. Baby isn't named yet.

Laura Edge, husband and 2 children have been here a month—are here yet. Laura cooks for me as a good negro can't be found. Some things are not pleasant—two families of children for instance and so many of our own. 13 in number now in all in our home. We gave Laura 3.00 per month and boarded all her family besides. Ghu tried to get a negro girl for me today, so we could do without Laura and her family but failed to get the negro.

Travis had a nice letter from our former Pastor, Mr. E. C. Marks, this week. Travis enjoyed the letter and we all did. I had one from Mr. Marks also. I think a lot of Bro. Marks for more reasons than one. One thing he came and read and prayed with my Father . . . on his death bed.

January 24
Friday

I am sick—lump or caked breast—have been suffering since Baby came. Laura went home Tuesday night. We've been getting on up hill with housekeeping; lot going undone. I am very weak and can hardly sit up. Ghu does part of the cooking—most of it. My back is so weak and painful. My breast so painful! Baby wakeful!

Ghu is gone this week nearly every day. Charlie, Mary, Maggie and I eat lunches or cold snacks—Askew, Fred and Travis going to school. Miss Ruth, the teacher, boarded one and half months with us before Christmas—is to board with us again beginning in March. She is a very excellent young lady. While I have not health and strength enough to do for home and family as it should be done yet I feel to keep school going I will have to do best I can and board her. She is a noble woman and we feel it is good for us to have such a fine character in our home.

Ghu has gone to Locust G. today to Quarterly meeting. We are on Locust Grove circuit after being on Jenkinsburgh good while. I can't remember just now our new preacher's name.

Mr. Bill Ingram has married again. Told me to name our baby after his new wife: Minnie or Macy. Maud Holder suggested Nellie May; Leathy Upchurch, telephone operator at Locust G., told me to name baby Florence. Ghu suggested Lillie Frances (after two of my sisters) or Lillie Ruth. I thought of calling her Lillie James or Lillie Jim for my father and sister (both deceased) or Annie James, for both Mother and Father. Don't think Ghu wants the male name for a girl.

We had the coldest weather last night and today we've had this winter—the hardest freeze.

Names of those who came to see me while sick: Mrs. Ida Childs

> Misses Babe and Matt C——
> Miss Meetsie Crumbly
> Mrs. Athie Childs
> Mrs. Minnie Knott
> Mrs. Ed Peek or Jennieson
>   "   Nolina Thompson
>   "   Nannie M. Holder
> Miss Alice K.
> Mrs. Nora Ingram
>   "   Lizzie Mason
>   "   Lula Mobley
> Miss Della Childs

Della Childs suggested the names of Fannie Lee, and Le Verte, for our baby.

February 1

One year ago yesterday (Jan. 31st) since my dear father died.

During all this 6 wks illness how much he has been on my mind. Bro. Charlie is very low; I wish I could hear from him. Think it has been 2 weeks since I heard. He has consumption.

I paid one woman to wash some baby clothes for me until I could get well; after all her pay she was very unkind and would not do it. I had no one else to do it but I think the Lord was mindful of me in my helplessness and he sent a good old negro to me, old Aunt Harriett, who has recently moved to Charlie Childs. The old negro seems to be real Christian hearted — *kind* — no impudence.

I am suffering from my breast yet. Six wks I've suffered. Our baby was six weeks old yesterday. I would like to name her Annie James for my Mother and Father both and call her Jamie.

Ghu has been cooking, milking, churning, dish washing etc. since we have no one to help us. Four men ate dinner here one day this week. Laura cooked dinner then. All her family ate too. The men who ate here were fixing water works from well to house. I fear it will never do us much good. Cost $85.00.

Linda, a colored woman who assists now (Feb. 5th 1908) about the house suggests two names for our baby: Katie-Dell and Hattie Joe. . . . Laz E [Edge] suggested Daisy.

May 6

Our baby is going on 5 months old; we weighed her this morning for the 2nd time since she came to our heart, life and home: she weighed 16 lbs. At first hour of her life she weighed 10½ lbs.

We have named her Lillie Frances.* She was named in March I think (when about 3 months old). We call her Frances. "Papa Ghu" wished her to be named Frances and prefered her being called Frances.

(How much do I weigh? 172 lbs. How old am I? 39 last Feb — and Papa Ghu was 38 last Feb.)

*In the family Bible, Magnolia erased Lillie Frances and wrote Frances James over the erasure. "Miss Mag" was a determined woman.

We have begun at 4½ months old to tie Frances in little rocking chair—to let her sit out doors in baby carriage and watch children play. Little Frances is a blessed sweet baby. Has a bright face—laughs lot and is a good baby.

Little Maggie is cute and sweet. She is gentle as a lamb; mild and soft spoken.

Little Mary is a noble little Mother. She is a little Mother to Frances and Maggie. Mary is deeply *devoted* to Charlie and such playmates I never saw. She can't bear the thought of Charlie leaving her and going to school. Mary is a sweet child—unhealthy and nervous—but *so* sunny! She has weak lungs and coughs awfully and has spells of asthma. Had 3 spells this year. She is a tiny child to her age (4 yrs).

Charlie is a dear obedient little boy. Charlie tries to please us.

Ozella Shaw came back with Miss Ruth and spent night here. Col. Tom Brown and Prof. Duffy made a speech—both good. Words fail to express what I think of Col. Tom Brown. He is a man whom people think *so much* of.

Old Aunt Harriet kept Frances for me and gave me a chance to hear the speaches. A faithful old darkey.

May 12

Tuesday A.M.

This is last day of Miss Ruth Jinks' school term for 1908. I feel sadder than I've ever felt at the expiration of any term of school since any of my children have been in school. Miss Ruth is best teacher, *every way*, my children have known. I fear we may never have Miss Ruth to impart wisdom and uprighteous to them—right living and high thinking; for Miss Ruth is very bright and a true earnest strong Christian. We've enjoyed her Bible readings in our family devotion; we'ved enjoyed her as a S.S. teacher. As a literary teacher we've never known a finer.

"Papa Ghu" (the noble man, who is my husband; the big hearted sunny souled father of our dear children) has gone today to do some work on bottom land which he had rented from our colored friend, Fred Groggin. Ghu will be gone all day—left early. Askew's eyes failed so that he couldn't study and had to stop school. Askew has gone to help his Papa work. (Askew loves farm work and is indus-

trious on farm.) Also a negro man, Will Duffy—a wages hand—
has gone with them. They carried a basket dinner. And Miss Ruth,
Travis and Fred went to school—sad thoughts "last day of school."
So, Mary, Maggie, Charlie, Baby Frances and I are alone—I'm trying
to have a good day, doing some of the things I best like to do. We
have a cold lunch—don't expect to cook dinner. While I was getting
Frances to sleep, I read a child's book of "Longfellow's Life" and
enjoyed it as in early life I didn't have access to Longfellow. Miss
Ruth has *so* many *choice* books for young and older; I've enjoyed a
few of them. So many cares have prevented reading more of them. A
rare, rich, treat was her books to me. How I *love good* literature. How
I long for all of them to love to read—and to guide their reading in
right direction for to love to read and not love the purest and best
would mean great destruction of their morals. Good literature builds
character—sorry reading tears it down, lays no foundation to make
good men and women.

Well, I get blue sometimes after staying close at home and working with weak body—overtaxed strength. Often I wish I could go
more with Ghu and the children. Ghu has many warm friends and
who who ever had a truer friend than he is to his friends? I went with
Miss Ruth, Fred, and Travis, to Philippi to Sunday School Sunday
P.M. I had been away so long that I felt myself a stranger, where in
single life I felt so much at home. I saw some beautiful little girls
over there—and was treated so kindly by a sweet young matron,
Mrs. Vashti Kimble.

May 13

I read yesterday in Miss Ruth's books (the classicks she had for the
school children) the following books: "Eugene Field"; "Davy Crock-
ett"; "Louisa Alcott"; "Henry Longfellow"; "Evangeline"; "The
Pied Piper from Hamlin"; "Patrick Henry." 'Twas a day I spent as I
pleased, pretty much.

May 15
Friday A.M.

Miss Ruth left us today.

I felt like hiding to keep from saying good bye. "Good bye" to the best teacher and friend our children ever had. She was a diamond — a fine woman every way — intellectually and spiritually. What a wonderful privilege our children had to be in her school! Wonderful privilege!

Miss Ruth left me 2 cloth scrap books this A.M. to give Mary and Maggie and I knew Mary would be sad to know that Miss Ruth was gone, so to cheer her up, I gave her and Maggie the scrap books soon as they woke. She left each of the little boys a nice pencil and gave Askew severel copies of a splendid magazine, "American Boy." Ghu carried her to depot at Jenkinsburgh. She is a remarkable woman. One with so much life — such an animated woman at same time *deeply* spiritual.

Yesterday P.M. Miss Ruth, Maggie, Mary and I went to take a ramble to one of my *favorite* haunts. What a *sweet pleasure* it was for me, as I had not such a treat but once before in a long long, time. I am an enthusiastic admirer of nature; I love Nature with all depth of my nature; especially do I love these hills and woods that are made sacred because of memories of my childhood, because my parents owned them and lived here so long. How I love the oak trees around the house and in the grove on hill below house. What strong memories they bring me of my precious old father — my dear Papa — how the trees seem to speak of thee. How it seemed yesterday as we came back up hill that I could almost see Papa out on front veranda in his arm chair watching us. How often, in his life time, when coming up from these walks I used to fondly look at him, from first sight of the house and feel thankful to see him in his accustomed place. I felt grateful because I knew he was nearing life's end and that ere long the dear good man would leave me and my children whom he loved so devotedly.

Well, I enjoyed the ramble yesterday and was with a great noble woman; so in memory of it I picked up a peculiar rock to keep in remembrance of the walk taken with that noble woman, Miss Ruth Jinks.

I wonder if she will ever teach our children again? She told Ghu if she felt directed to teach here (by the Lord) she would come back. She said many fine things of our three children in her school and of our family. Even said surprisingly nice things of Ghu and I (I don't feel that I deserve them as much as Ghu does but I feel greatly helped by them and I feel inspired to live up to what she says I am).

Didn't I have a good time reading her books and papers! My, what a rich treat! Our boys enjoyed them too. I am glad to see them developing a taste for reading and trust the course will always be in right direction. So far it is good literature they've read.

Askew and Miss Ruth would sometimes have long conversations. I believe the whole family loved her much. One day before Miss Ruth went away she invited Mrs. Lizzie Mason over to spend the P.M. and also Mrs. L's three children. So after they came Miss Ruth took a number of beautiful Easter eggs (candy) out of her trunk and hid them out in the grove in front of the house. She pinned 2 up in trees. The eggs she had left over from her school hunt and she told the children 'twas a "Maybe" hunt this time. The tiny children went first: Mary Belle, Mary, Charlie, and Maggie—afterwards my boys and Olin joined in. Charlie found most.

Miss Ruth was a great hand to make friends with children and to make children happy. She knew of and did so many things to amuse them. She gave Mary, Maggie and Charlie some glue and bright paper links to join them. Also how to make tiny bright colored paper mats. Once while here she made sugar candy and treated to a large pan of parched ground peas.

Well she was a great help to Ghu and I—and to our children; they advanced rapidly. We felt honored to have her in our home, and grateful for the friendship of such a grand character. I am sure I'm not as narrow as I was when she came to board with us.

Misses Babe and Matt called on us yesterday P.M. I enjoyed their social chats and the memories of "auld lang syne" that they resurrected. They spoke long of my mother, my sisters and their family, and the good times they had with each other.

I had a letter from Cape few days ago. He is in Atlanta in Grocery Store of his own on McDaniel St. Askew wrote a letter to Mr. Leguin, his unknown Grand Pa. Askew saw his Grand Pa Leguin when he was wearing dresses; at that time Fred was 6 months old, or thereabouts.

Mr. Laster (an old fellow whom Papa was kind to and who seemed to care lot for my father) came and spent awhile with us also yesterday. I enjoyed his visit.

The summer is before us. I expect many will visit us ere its close. May the Giver of all good gifts, give me strength enough to cook, see after house and babies and to keep cheerful and to be in some way a help to all who may come.

May 26

Frances has on short dresses. Age 5 mo and about 7 days. She has on some clothes made for Mary and wears hose to keep her feet warm. Frances has a very bad stye on her eye; this makes 2nd one.

Mary is sick with very bad cough and asthma; she has had weak lungs all her life; she coughed badly when a baby in long clothes, and now at age of 4 yrs has asthma and coughs awfully and coughs most of the time, is easy to take cold and always coughs with a cold. Poor little Mary. No strength, not much strength at least, such bad health, such a tiny frail form—such a narrow chest, such a thin little body with shoulders stooped some. I am making her a cough syrup now of mullen and hoar hound. I trust little Mary will gain strength and outgrow her cough.

Maggie seems fairly healthy (age 2 and some over) and is fat.

Travis is suffering some with tooth ache. Charlie (at 5) had some pulled, because they ached.

Ghu, Mary, Maggie, Fred and I went to New Hope Sunday. Askew stayed at home and kept Frances; Travis and Charlie stayed with him. Frances slept and gave no one any trouble. Bro. Ward preached a good sermon. Banker Brown was with him from Locust Grove. Brown recited S.S. lesson with us and was very sociable when I met him after services. I've heard he is a good man. I liked him.

"Sarah Tollerson," Mr. T. and Mrs. T. took dinner with us Sunday. Sarah Tollerson (Crane is her real name) is a sweet girl. I like her very much. She comes with Mr. and Mrs. Tollerson each year and some times oftener to our house.

Charlie will be 6 yrs old next Sunday, 31st of May.

May 29
Friday

Frances is in short dresses the past 3 days—wore stockings 2 days and left them off yesterday. She began 2 days ago to say "mom, mom, mom," and "pop, pop" (said "pop" first). She is awful cute in short dresses. I did intend to wait till June but she kicked flannels partly from waiste and they seemed to annoy her greatly. Little Frances stays out in yard in latter part of the evenings and she likes it very much.

Poor little Mary is still wheezing with asthma; the longest spell the poor little thing has ever had; she plays all day thro' now and is feeling better than she did 2 or 3 days ago.

We have a new little calf that Mary, Maggie and Charlie enjoy now. Poor little Maggie fell off bed last night awful hard. She has been falling off the bed nearly all her life—am sorry we have no bed with railings. Maggie has always been falling somewhere. Has fallen more than all our family put together—a fact that is noticable and always has been.

Travis has been sick 2 days with tooth ache. We expected Dr. Cantrell here to pull his teeth—the decayed ones—yesterday P.M. but he didn't comply with his promise.

Askew and Fred are chopping cotton "like clever fellows" but Fred doesn't like to work in field; Fred says for Papa Ghu not to sell the mill—to let it be ours and he become miller as he doesn't like to farm. He says he doesn't intend to be a farmer.

Charlie is a lover of flowers—gathers *all* kinds he can find and talks a lot about them.

June 2
Tuesday

Poor little Frances fell out of baby carriage on ground Sunday P.M. I was dressing to go to S.S. Had dressed Frances and put her in baby carriage; she was nearly asleep and Fred was rolling her; he let loose carriage and the front hall is slanting; so the carriage rolled on out steep narrow steps and turned over on ground. Poor baby was knocked senseless and breathless for a while, but sustained no bruises. Fred crossed the hall and went in the room and before he could catch her she was gone—over the precipice. Seems as if it was enough to have killed sweet Frances. We were scared—I was pained and excited. But little Frances soon went to sleep and we all went to S.S.

After S.S. we went up to Ollie Mason's and stayed awhile. Mary and Maggie found a crowd of little folks up there to play with. They enjoyed some ripe May apples too and both want to go back.

(At 5 mo and some over, Frances was in baby carriage when it rolled out doors, throwing her out—Providence kept her limbs and body whole).

Charlie, Mary, and Maggie are busy now making animals of May pop, green, as they've seen me do for them. It is nice pass time for them.

Sarah Crane sent me about doz. flower plants and cuttings last Sunday eve. I am delighted to have them and have given Charles, Mary, Maggie, Askew, Fred, Travis all one. Hope each will live.

Fred, Askew, Travis, and Papa Ghu are chopping cotton today for Mr. Cornwell. Ghu needed the money and he and boys are working ½ day for Mr. C.

Charlie was six years old Sunday (May 31st) and I cooked him a layer cake and let 6 layers represent 6 yrs. Herman Ingram spent Sat. night and Sun. till P.M. with us. We had 2 freezers of ice cream out under the shady walnut tree in back yard. The family enjoyed that and no one better than Papa Ghu did.

I don't let small children make a practice of holding my babies. So, the larger boys are gone today and I let Charlie bring her a few steps to me. He felt he had suddenly grown good deal larger. He and Mary go down to pump now with a tiny bucket and pump up and bring a little water. They enjoy that. Mary has for first time (last week) begun thumping or pecking on organ and she tells people she can play an organ.

June 6
Saturday

Baby Frances can pick up, out of baby carriage, her play things when she drops them. Age 5 months and 3 weeks. She fell off bed yesterday very hard—2 falls and her first 2 in a week—fall from baby carriage and fall off bed. Terrible falls for a baby of 5 months.

Maggie isn't well; she has fallen off and looks bad. She is playing each day but rite fretful part of the time. Maggie was so fat and cute all the winter.

Yesterday I was ironing; the fire was large, of dry stuff, and the soot in chimney caught fire, and soon after 2 spots on top of house was seen smoking. Ghu and the little boys were at the house and Ghu climbed up on a ladder and carried water and put them out before the fire kindled to a blaze. 'Twas Providential that Ghu was at the house and that the smoke was discovered before a blaze had developed.

June 11
Thursday A.M.

Frances has a tooth—age 5 months and liking 8 days of being 6 months old—Askew carried Frances down to the pump—gave her some water and heard the little tooth "tink" "tink" against the tin dipper. So Askew discovered her first tooth first. Frances is stronger in back than most of our children were at her age—She can sit up a little while and often without toppling over so soon. Frances *crows* and crows, and laughs and laughs. She is a gleeful baby. She is a knowing baby—notices so many things that surprises us to see her noticing. Frances was sweet last Sunday at S.S. I went out to grave-yard and sat down on tomb of my dear father's grave and nursed Frances to sleep and then carried her back to church. Little Maggie Wynn is 2½ yrs. old. She hears my children play game that is called "Black Man" and the game begins this way: "What are you going to do when the black man comes?" They hollow out this interrogation. So Maggie can't talk plain, or join long sentences and she plays and this is the way she hollows it: "When Black Man comes, hanh? When Black Man comes? Hanh?"

June 19

This morning Charlie got up and went out on back veranda and looked out, down toward creak; he says, "It looks mighty lonesome down there. What is it?" There was a thick fog at creak and it had a depressing effect on Charlie and myself too. Frances is 6 months and 2 days old. She has 2 teeth.

Dora Wellmaker has written 2 post cards to me lately asking Askew to visit their home. So I guess in a few days Askew will board the train for Barnesville. Askew has never been to any one's home unless accompanied by Ghu, outside of this community, and not but a few times in this community; he and all my children have done very little visiting. James Lewis is living with Dora, hence came Askew with the pressing invitation. As he has never been away we all feel interested in it, and I feel sad to have him absent for a week, but I want him to go for the pleasure of the trip will be to him. I know we are going to miss him. I think each one of the family feel an interest in Askew's trip to Barnesville. Fred and Travis both want to go. Fred said if Askew backed out he would go in Askew's place. I hope that some time, while they are boys, that Travis and Fred may get to spend about 2 days with James. I abhor spunging, and don't want any of them to go anywhere and wear their welcome out; or go when I'm doubtful of a welcome for them.

Had a card from Miss R. J. [Jinks] today with Jackson Institute on it.

June 21

Monday

I am sick; was sick all night, with stomach and bowel disorder. Never had my stomach to pain me in such a way before and I was afraid we would have to telephone for Dr. Colvin.

Dr. Woods, in reply to my note, sent me last week, for Frances a package of teething powders. She cut teeth earlier if I mistake not than any of our children. At 6 months (and just before) she had 2 teeth.

I went with Askew and Travis to Philippi yesterday. Ghu was not well and stayed here with the children. Frances remained at home.

Yesterday was a very hot day. In P.M. I was not well and Frances and I stayed at home and all the rest of the family went to New Hope. A thunder cloud came up in P.M. They always excite me.

I feel that the months, weeks, and days will be trying on my strength from now til Sep. or Oct. Judging future by the past 14 yrs. Warm weather weakens me so that I feel all fagged out all time.

June 22
Wednesday A.M.

Askew left us early this morning on a visit to Barnesville. The first time he was ever away on a visit by himself. (He is 12 yrs old—will be 13 in Aug). Ghu carried him to McDonough to board the train. He will have to change cars in Griffin. He dreaded changing cars more than anything else I believe. How we *all* are going to miss him! How Papa Ghu and I wish for him, a *pleasant* visit! How near and dear the boy's going away made us realize he was to us. In our busy tired everyday lives, we don't stop as often as we should to realize how *dear* our home folks are to us and now and then some event makes the sacred relation stand boldly out—come boldly to the front of our minds. May out Heavenly Parent protect the dear little boy—guide him safely to B.V. [Barnesville] and bring him back to us—be with his "going out and coming in" and sanctify the visit to the good of Askew's life and our own as well. He expects to be gone about a week. How anxious we all will be for a post card from him.

June 26
Friday

We had one card from Askew saying "the first thing he did after arriving in Barnesv. was to knock a little negro down; the little negro asked him if he was a *white* boy." So Ghu and I laughed heartily at the first card. I guess the negro said it with impudence, or at least Askew thought so, 'tho Askew is tolerably dark and there are *white* negroes in cities. Askew can't bear "sass" from negroes—neither can I and my Father would not, and did not, bear it. He would do as Askew did first—"Knock a negro down." I answered Askew's card and told him his card reminded me of some lines I read when a child in "Lorenza Don." These were they:

> Where did you come from?
> Chucker-lucker town?
> Who do you belong to?
> Knock a negro down.

I quoted those lines on card to Askew. Well, 'tis near mail time now and we are anxiously looking for a card from Askew.

Travis and Fred went over to Nolia's after 2 cute little kittens yesterday. We've enjoyed the kittens (the children and I).

The mail has come. A card from Askew to Fred. Didn't say when he expected to return.

July 5
Sunday

We didn't go to S.S. this P.M. I wasn't hardly able and a thunder cloud came up but didn't rain but only sprinkled. I have been weak for a week. *Warm* weather has come and I guess I will not get much better much before Oct.

We had a fish fry yesterday—4th of July—Mrs. Lizzie Mason, her children and Nannie May Holder spent a part of the day with me. Mary was trying to ask Travis if he was putting turpentine on his leg—and she called it "rubber tine."

August 18

Askew is 13 yrs old today.

Frances was 8 months old yesterday. She crawls a little and has 6 teeth. Frances sat alone at 7—crawled at 8—2 teeth at 7—6 teeth at 8. She learned to sit alone with *very* few bumps. She loves Askew next to me—better than anyone.

We've had a busy hard summer. I've been sick with indigestion and dysentary. We've had "oodles" of company and protracted meeting and Bible School. Both good. Rev. Albert and Rev. Lundy Ward—

both among others with us some of the time during the meeting.
Misses Daisy and Nettie Gray during Bible School and a Miss Ger-
hart of Atlanta, Willie Wynn and 2 children from Augusta. Miss
Ruth Jinks to be here today. I'm sick and no help. Protracted meeting
at Philippi now. Ghu goes some. I wish to go but can't yet. A busy
summer—overtaxed strength, sick. Lot of company, lot of cooking,
lot of washing and ironing, but I am anxious to do it best I can—
patiently as I can and trust Lord to be in and with me thro' it all.

September 23

Frances is little over 9 months old—has learned to pull up by me,
the bed and chairs. Only 6 teeth are visible yet.

Sweet little meek, gentle lamb-like Maggie is sick; she has been
sick 2 days; she has been unable to play but very little—lies about on
bed—sleeps good deal—has some times good deal of fever and has
coated tongue. Ghu and I have been giving her pergatives.

Askew is not well today; he is in the house. Ghu and the boys are
picking cotton. Travis is a fine cotton picker and Askew too.

I heard Denis Burford was buried today; he leaves a wife and 2 little
fatherless children. Mule ran away with him and hurt him; he lived
just a few days afterward.

October 21
Wednesday A.M.

Oh, so many things are on my mind that I wish to write!

Charlie has started to school; he began Oct 19th (2 days ago) at
New Hope and Miss Trella Castellaw is his teacher. We've been with
Miss Trella only a short time, but I care much for her. She interests
me deeply. She is a violet—so modest and unassuming—so gentle
and refined—so easy for me to approach. How I love her pure sweet
character.

How busy my life is! Much of the time now overtaxed my physical
and mental strength, but withal how nice to be with Miss Trella. I
did not see how I could take a boarder—no one else was willing and

it seems it was Lord's will for me and I say that with a Divinely appointed task will be given strength to perform. How rich a treat to come in touch with such a girl or young lady as Miss Trella is.

How poor little Mary misses Charlie since he started to school as they've always been so closely associated. She can't talk much about Charlie being away without crying an she watches him so closely at night with his new primer and does not quite know why she can't have one and go with Charlie to school. Poor little Mary! Her first separation from her dearest playmate. She and Maggie play nicely and sweetly but she loved Charlie better and much prefers to play with him.

November 4
Wednesday P.M.

Charlie is learning fast—can read—hasn't been quite 3 weeks to school. Frances is nearly 9 months old—has 7 teeth. Is bright, very bright. Can call "Tarl; Tarl" (Charles) says or tries to say *many* single words—makes the sound so plain we all understand the word she is trying to say. She does not join any often. She fell out of baby carriage yesterday, for first time. She was asleep in it; we use it for a cradle and roll her away in front room to keep her from noise and she awakes and plays in it and she overbalanced herself yesterday but fell on all her cover and wasn't hurt but little.

Olin Lindsey is working with Ghu and at present is rooming with our boys.

Mary isn't well much; has been lying about on a pallet nearly all day. My back aches so that I can't turn off work fast and see after baby; so I get very little sewing done and yet I stay busy nearly all the time. Sometimes back aches so I can't do anything until I lie down and rest. A chronic weak back and lots to do. Wish I could have some good help each day. We wash and I iron too. I don't think I ever could keep doing with my weak back if it were not for the Divine help that I implore twice each day—morning and afternoon. I often give out and go aside about one o'clock and ask for help or strength to get necessary things done by time Miss Trella gets here or some after.

November 20

Last Friday (a week ago today) I began to wean Frances. She liked a few days of being 11 months old. I had thresh (or thrash) in breast and couldn't let her nurse longer—so very painful. She has thrash in her mouth worse than any baby I ever saw. I learned by her experience with it that babies *suffer* worse with it when they have teeth, than they do before they begin to cut teeth. Frances suffered and is still suffering tho' she is better. She was easier than most of the children to wean. She didn't cry to nurse at all first day but cried till 11 or 12 o'clock that night and more now and then for 2 or 3 days. Frances is 11 [months] now (on 17th) and has a good appetite; she has 8 or 9 teeth—(8 I know of).

I can't sew at all—just cook and clean up and attend to Frances. I have no nurse and where there are so many children a nurse in many ways would be a great nuisance. I don't want a nurse. I'm hiring most all my sewing in order to avoid a nurse.

December 8

Frances sleeps well now. Did not have to give her milk in the night long after she was weaned.

Christmas nearly here. May the Lord be with us this coming Christmastide and bless each member of our family.

1909

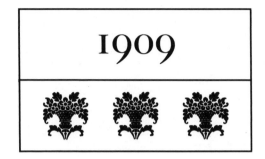

January 17

Another New Year has dawned; busy days, many little things to be constantly doing—and three meals and a boarder; 9 of us in family and a not very strong body; company dropping in etc. etc.—so I'm kept *pressingly* busy.

Well, we have organized S.S. at New Hope again; I've been one Sunday this year—one balmy Sunday and all family went. Mr. Hooten is Sr. Quarterly teacher and Oscar McKibben asst.

Mr. Tollerson (Sam) lives near us this year. Sarah Crane (who is one of their family) is very kind to me; she sends me things to read and also sent me a nice little pin cushion; I am not accustomed to that much or that kind of attention from my neighbors of late years. 'Tis a pleasure to have her friendship.

Frances is fat as a pig and drinks more sweet milk than any baby we ever raised—drinks cup full often. She is bright as new dollar.

Charlie has been to school 3 months, reads *well* and makes splendid figures. He is doing *finely* in school.

Frances can say lot of words—new ones each day—can't join any often—sometimes joins two words—for instance when she tries to say "thank-you mam" she says "mam-mam." She takes 2 steps some times, has only 8 teeth—and today she is 13 months old. Smart, sweet *good*.

January 23

We've had about (or near) 3 wks of foggy weather; foggy in forenoons and some days the sun shines in P.M.'s I never saw so much foggy weather, and we've had such a *mild* winter up to date—very little ice.

Mr. Jack Crumbly said this foggy weather was something unusual and strange. I traded a little with him today and he gave me a New Year's present—about 3½ yds of black worsted.

Little Frances fell over on andiron this week; a chair was close to the fire, and had a heavy quilt drying over it. She and the chair fell. I was out of the room busy—fire had burned down and was not a big fire, or else she would have burned worse. Mary called me excitedly and I ran fast to her.

Ghu has a crook in his neck—back of neck; 'tis bad and makes him look badly too.

January 25

Warm indeed for the season.

February 7

We had out phone taken our Thursday. We needed money, I guess, worse than we needed 'phone just now; may have it back ere long—don't know just what Ghu may do.

We had a blizzard about 8 or 10 days ago that lasted 2 or 3 days. Never was I so pinched by a cold wave—took ulcerated sore throat and have never gotten entirely over it. Cape was here—I had to cook more than if we had been alone and throat was worse than it has been in severel years but not near so bad as spells that I had prior to my marriage.

February 21
Sunday Night

Mary was 5 yrs old yesterday and weighs 33 lbs. (Maggie was 3 in Jan. and weighs 38 lbs now) And Fred and Travis were born on 11th of Feb. Fred was 11 and Travis 9. And Ghu's birthday and Mary's are on same day of the month—the 20th of Feb. Ghu was 39 yrs of age. And last, but not *least*, my birthday was on the 18th Inst. and I was how old? Ans. 40.

I have not been strong somehow this winter.

Frances is 14 mo's old—walks a few steps. Says words—rarely ever (but sometimes does) join two words.

Ghu went to Jackson today to get Dr. to relieve an inflamed and painful sore eye.

I've been sick all day—stomach and bowel disorder—loss of sleep and weak.

Three largest boys went to S.S. Ghu is Supt and as he was gone and only a few present they had no S.S.

March 3

Frances is walking well now; begun real walking about 4 days ago—is fourteen months and half old.

Mary (just five) wipes or dries the dishes sometimes and does it *real well* and helps little at times about, spreading cover on beds. When Frances began to walk (at 14½ months old) I am 40. When Mary arrived at 5 yrs old I reached 40 mile post. When Travis reached 9 and Fred 11, I reached 40. And Askew is 13—I 40—Charlie going on 7— I 40. And Ghu during all this reached his 39th birthday, Maggie her 3d on 25th of Jan.

I *love trees*. The trees that are anywhere near the house that my father and mother left here. I don't want one sapling cut; but Ghu has had a small piece of ground near the house cleared. He wanted the land I wanted the trees—the land is mine on this side of the creak—I am not "Boss."

Ghu has gone to McDonough today. Ghu is the miller. My little girls run down to the mill to be with their Papa—I ran to mill almost daily as far back as I can remember at the same place (not same house) to play in mill where my Papa was (he had a miller but he stayed at mill. The mill then was a two story mill and ground corn and wheat).

Last Sunday I went to New Hope (Ghu, Askew, and Travis went too) and Fred stayed at home and kept Frances, Mary, Maggie and Charles.

I've quit cooking so much on Sunday and have plainer dinner so that I can go to church and not be so miserably tired when I get there. But last Sunday Mr. Bill Hooten gave out and taught S.S. lesson for older people. By the way, I think much of Mr. Hooten. I regard him as one of my best old gentleman friends. In Sunday lesson Mr. Hooten related this incident: a good many years ago Uncle

Chris Davis preached at Mt. Bethel from this text (I think this or one of these verses was what Mr. H. said was text,) "Thou hast neither part no lot in this matter: for thy heart is not right in the sight of God." Acts 8–21.

"Repent therefore of this thy wickedness, and pray God, if perchance the thought of thine heart may be forgiven thee." Acts 8–22.

"For I perceive thou art in the gall of bitterness, and in the bond of iniquity." Acts 8–23.

And Uncle Chris Davis was talking about Peter and said that every man did not sell out or there were men who would not sell at no price. And when he said this that Dr. Wynn spoke out "Amen." Mr. Hooten added that Dr. Wynn (tho' dead now) was a man that no one could buy. I record these things of my dear father who was in lot of things, a great man. My mother was in many ways, a great woman.

June 21

Monday A.M.

How long a time has elapsed since I wrote in this book. I live a busy life—my time is necessarily taken up in work; lot of my time, most of it, in doing drudgery. But we can serve the Lord in doing drudgery—as well as going to a house of worship. We do our own washing and a large pile of clothes we do have but Ghu and children help and it is easier with their help than to hire impudent lazy negroes and have badly washed clothing and I thank the Lord for the strength and the help of home folks to wash with.

Askew is down with fever; this is 14th day. Dr. Horton says it is typhoid fever, of a mild form. This is Askew's first sickness to amount to enough to send for a Dr. Dr. Colvin came at first, twice, and carried a patient to Atlanta to hospital and while he was gone we needed a Dr. and so telephoned for Dr. Horton. I had the impression that Dr. H. was a christian, tho' we had never seen him. I also asked in prayer that the Divine direct and send us the Dr. that we ought to have. I think the Giver of life has wonderfully helped us and answered prayer in that Askew is no lower than what he is. In the beginning of Askew's illness I picked up Bible and opened to a verse in James about the prayer of faith saving the sick or restoring them: "And the prayer of faith shall save the sick, and the Lord shall raise him up; and if he have committed sins, they shall be forgiven him. Confess your faults one to another, and pray one for another, that ye may be healed. The effectual fervent prayer of a righteous man availeth much." These verses I turned to accidentally. They are found in 5th chap. of James and 15 and 16 verses. And they seemed as a promise given me and I've been hopeful for Askew's recovery all the time; at times more uneasy than others, but never without hope; the verses have calmed and assured me all along so far. Life is in God's hands—Dr's. can't give or save it. Dr. H. seems to be a fine fever Dr. tho'. His wife came with him yesterday. She was a perfect beauty. Dressed in height of fashion—like a beautiful doll. I never saw many such daintily dressed ladies. I must seem like an Indian to people of such high social standing, wealth, culture etc. etc. I am so plain in dress and manners. Nature cast me in that mold and environment kept me so I guess. All can't be lillies—some have to be sunflowers.

June 24
Thursday

Askew is very much better. In this illness (and the first time he ever had a Dr.) he had met three physicians: Dr. Colvin, first, Dr. Horton and today Dr. H. could not come and he sent Dr. Smith in his place. Dr. S. is next to Dr. W. Ghu's favorite physician; I never met him till today. I like him and am glad to have met him.

Frances is 18 mo. old. Had a spell of teething and fell off. At present she is well and fat again. She talks rite well and is having a good time these days out door with other children.

People who have come to see how Askew was (up to date): Mr. W. B. Kelly, Tom Holder, Tom Martin, Jim Holder, Mr. Bogue Childs, Mr. C. Childs, Bro. Jim, Mr. Prim Shaw, Misses Mat and B. Childs (2 visits each), Mrs. Ida Childs, Mrs. L. Mobley (2 visits), Mrs. Rhoda Shaw—2 of her children, Ollie Mason and 2 of his children, Mr. Bill Hooten, Mr. S. A. Tollerson, Sara Wynn, Sara Crain.

October 4

"The Oaks"

Cotton picking time with the farmers!

The grandest season of all the year to me!

I am not a cotton picker however. My back is always very weak and I can't pick cotton and I think a mother of a large family has *always* plenty to do in the home. I live closer at home than is best for me, physically and mentally, and if I could pick cotton I would pick some, in order to get fresh air and out door life; and I would hire sewing done with the proceeds of my cotton picking.

Well, I've been a visiting twice this summer. I had not taken a meal away from home in 5 years until this summer and I spent one day at Joe Wynn's and in one week from that day I spent one day at Will Wynn's. I had not been to Mt. Bethel before in 10 yrs.

Sarah Crain, my warm friend, has seen it best for her to make her home with her sister and is no longer my neighbor. I am glad she has gone where she has better advantages and more of her rightful liberties. Sarah came to see me and spent Saturday and Sunday with us. We attend Sunday School regularly. Ghu is Supt. I am Sec.

October 9

Saturday P.M.

This is a beautiful, beautiful day. Sun shines radiantly. What a glorious month October is! And September this year was enchanting, bewitching. How I love Nature! And how glad I am that I do love it; for my life is filled with drudgery—working in the home and for the large family we have. How weary I'd be living close at home and as constantly busy as my strength will permit. But I go to porch and enjoy, revel, bathe my soul in scenes of Nature that has been so lavishly scattered around our old home. The oak trees, how I love them! The hills! The creak. All *so* beautiful.

Dr. Jarrell and Dr. Charles McDonald own part of the beauties in nature that I so much love and daily admire (land my father owned in his life time) but it was fixed by the Giver of all good gifts for the home of my parents among this beautiful scenery to be ours. God's Hand was in it, or this home would not today be ours. There were others who wanted it very much. Tho' Dr. Chas. McD. and Dr. J. own some of these beautiful hills — yet they are mine to enjoy — mine, mine. I look at them and feel so glad they are mine to look at — to enjoy — to love and Dr. J. and Dr. McD. do not get the wealth from them that I do; they get money. I get something richer. "I am lord of all I survey" (All my eyes can see). How often I feel when gazing on them: alright Dr. J. and Dr. McD. They are yours to get money out of. They are mine to get sweet delightful pleasures from.

And the natural groves around our old home — are grand but Ghu has *spoiled* one view to my sorrow. He doesn't love nature as well as I and too, he had some, several reasons for obstructing the lovely view, by putting an out house (a cotton house) on lower front side of our sweet old home. It is with deep regret that I daily look at this building; yet I know that Ghu felt sure it was best. I hope some time the cotton house may be removed — set out toward horse lot. I would be proud of the large roomy cotton house if it was down in or near horse lot or the old buggy house. Ghu had severel good reasons for putting it there as it saves many steps for him; and he works *so very* hard and takes so many steps. I never saw a man with more energy. He works with too much vim I think. Goes in *too* much rush. He works all day and occasionally grinds corn till bed-time. Ghu is a true hearted man; a warm hearted man — "a friend to *every body*." He may not be as thoughtful at times in moderating his tone (and I have the same fault — and it may be to a greater extent than he) as might be best but his heart isn't hard or cold, if occasionally his voice is little harsh. He is the soul of *honesty* and has been better to me than I deserve and sometime more thoughtful of me than I of him; often times perhaps.

Did I record in these pages that I've taken two meals away from home this summer — first meals in 5 years — when Mary was a baby. And I think it a lot of help in severel ways to dine away — to go away from home occasionally — yet I see no chance to do it. My strength fails as I plod along and it would be so helpful to me to lay aside housekeeping and go out once a week. I would hold up better — be better off every way but the way isn't open. I've been housed up since first baby came and now are so many that I'm needed all time here only when I go to church but I do *long* and *crave* to go *out doors* and enjoy nature more. Heavenly Father grant that ere long a way will be made for me to be out doors more. I always welcome wash days because I can get out doors one half day each week. I ironed today and I'm nearly exhausted tonight.

Ghu has gone to Mr. Kelly's store. We have a boarder, Mr. Garner.

I almost despair sometimes of ever having a chance to leave home, to stay in open air and enjoy out door life, birds and sunshine, blue skies and moon and stars, trees and hills, water etc. etc.

Our boys (except Charles and he worked some) have been picking cotton away from home all fall; they are industrious boys and I think stayed in cotton fields too close. I think young children ought to have good deal of recreation. They worked and paid for them a suit of clothes, hat and shoes. So they didn't waste their money and I think that was noble in them. Travis is frail but worked hard. Fred can't pick as much as T. and Askew but sticks to it. They will soon start to school. No rest in a long time. I don't believe young children ought to work so steady. May the Divine guidance be about each of our boys. May they be workers early in the Master's vineyard and labor there earnestly.

November 2

The greatest trials I believe of my life is to be obliged to have on our home place impudent, disrespectful, saucy negroes. One by name of Millie High has been here all this year and has traded to be here another year. She lives with a peaceable negro man; the man we like. She has been very impudent towards me on severel occasions: the last insulting thing she did was to be enraged *with me* because I wouldn't let her talk "sas" and she went up to Mr. Dolph McK[ibben]'s and they say "preached funerels," talking against me. It is very trying to me. I trust in the Lord to relieve me or help me out of power to thus weaken, sicken and depress and unnerve me. I want to be right before Him in my dealings with her.

November 17
Tuesday P.M.

Maggie often says "I am the prettiest little girl in the '*cumfry*'"; Ghu often tells her she is the prettiest girl in this country. Sometimes he adds except two more—to keep Mary and Frances from being jealous. Mary and Maggie fell out with our yellow cat "Buster-Brown." Buster went in safe and carried his companion cats, reckon, and ate 8 nice cat fish. We had 7 left but there are 9 of us in family and cat fish is a treat to us. But they should not have been too severe on Buster; Frances opened the safe door to get her some sugar (and she waisted a whole lot, which told on her) and she left the door open and I suppose watched the kits and cats devout fish, and it never entered her baby head that it was wrong for cats to eat *cat* fish.

This morning old Buster Brown ran out doors from Maggie with a good size rabbit in her mouth; Maggie came running and crying to me and said Buster Brown had her kitten in his mouth and was eating it up. Maggie was in distress. She thought Buster would eat not only cat-fish, but her pretty pet kitten. She thought he was a cannibal. I went and saw what Buster had and relieved Maggie. Mary went first and affirmed Maggie's tale. I became excited and informed my own eyes of true facts.

Well, Mary and Maggie have a note like this to send to Mr. Kelly:

Mr. Kelly,
What are you giving for cats? Our Buster Brown ate up 8 cat fish—stole them—and we will swap him to you for chewing gum.
    You Little Friends,
    Mary and Maggie Le Guin.

Frances is awful cute, talks lot. Is devoted to my old dressing saques. Has a queer fancy and love for them. Has favorite sacks—and will cry for one when she gets sleepy and when it is given to her, day or night, she will hug it up in her arms and go to sleep delighted. She loves it like some children love a favorite doll. But such a queer plaything. Ghu says to her sometimes when she is crying for the "shawl" (she calls them all shawls), "You have not rite good sense no how, have you?" A queer love! A curious plaything. A funny baby! Ghu calls my dressing saques "Frances' step mammy." He says she loves me best and my old saques next best when she is sleepy. She sleeps with me but if we get a "step mammy" for her she will gleefully hug it tight and go rite on to bed and to sleep. She is a funny baby. She has a course voice. I predict that she will have a bright intellect. She is very mishievous and playful.

Mary is sunshiny and quick and can help me just a little now. She often goes to the mill and brings me a bucket of meal for dinner.

She says when she gets grown she wants to be a teacher just like Miss Trella Castellaw. She often talks of being a teacher like Miss T.

Maggie is pretty and very meek and gentle.

Charles is growing and likes school.

Fred and Travis are advancing nicely I think. Askew too. Prof. H [Harkins] said Askew was a bright boy. If my father were living how *glad* he would be to hear that. He loved Askew *so*, and he was so proud of Askew from infancy on till he died. Mama would love to know her little Travis is a bright, peaceful, industrious boy; he was my mother's joy and pride.

November 18
Thursday

One week today will be Thanksgiving-day. If bodily strength will permit, I'll fix for company on that day.

Travis is wearing shirts and suspenders! Every boy I have, except Charlie, are wearing shirts and don't a little boy feel proud of his first shirt and first pair of suspenders! None are old enough to wear long pants and I'll be sorry to see them going out of short pants—and to see them leaving boyhood, entering manhood.

Prof. Harkins says Askew is doing good work. I'm glad to hear that. Miss Trella says Fred is doing fine—advancing nicely. And glad of that. And I think Travis and Charles are doing well.

Mary begs to be allowed to go to school, but owing to a weak constitution and a lifetime cough we can't send her yet.

December 11
Sat.

(Written in Askew's hand:)
First time I ever shot a gun. Killed a joree. Age 14.
     Askew L.

December 19
Sunday

This is a cold rainy Sunday; last Sunday was an all day rain too. Christmas is nearly here. I have worked *so* hard trying to get all needed sewing done and to be up with Xmas work. I have worked nearly to prostration but am not ready for Xmas; hope to be by time it arrives. Am to go to Locust G. in few days.

Mary has been in bed this past week. She had croup — *severe* — attack. Dr. Colvin came at 2 o'clock in the night to see her and came by one day to see her. Although Mary is nearly 6 yrs old and never was healthy — always delicate, this was first time we ever had a physician with her. The Giver of all good gifts has spared her life to us, tho' she was seriously ill and we feared she was taking pneumonia after croup ceased; she had fever 2 days.

Dr. Colvin's remedies were fine and helpful and he was most kind to come so far at such an hr and in such *cold* weather. He has always been nice, kind, good to us. So was Dr. Woods, and Dr. Horton, especially Dr. W. He did a lot of practice for us. . . .

1910

February 18

I am 41 yrs. old today. And my health is not good. It seems to be failing on a line that I had hoped and prayed it would never give me trouble on again.

Frances is 2 yrs old—or was in Dec.

If it is the Lord's will I trust that the calamity may pass—that it may not fall on me. If it is the Lord's will for this ill health and great suffering to be my experience again I want to trust Him to help me to be resigned and to be able to say "Thy will be done."

A sad, sick and low-spirited woman on this my 41st birthday.

Lost sleep all thro' last night. Mary was sick and she sleeps with Frances and I. She is coughing badly.

Sara C[rane] sent me a pretty handerchief for a birthday present.

We are having a blizzard today. . . .

March 8

Mary started to school yesterday at New Hope, to Miss Trella Castellaw and Miss Ruth Rape. So now our first girl is in school: four boys and one girl in school. Mary is delighted, overjoyed. Charles and Mary are devoted to each [other]. They carry their dinner in same lunch-box. Maggie misses Mary but is cheerful and happy playing all day with Frances. Frances loves Maggie better than she does Mary—Maggie and Frances are good partners—both babies, age 2 and 4. Mary's face beams with joy over being a school-girl.

July 15

Mary fell out of the front room window and the fall was so hard. I was sitting out-doors by the window when such a *thud!* and Mary was lying on ground with breath out almost; she fell on breast and right arm and turned purple but was soon out of pain. 'Twas Providential that she wasn't seriously hurt. God's mercies are over us. We ask Him in beginning of the day to shield us each member that constitutes this home and to let His protecting arms be around and over our home and homefolks. "He shall give His angels charge over thee lest thou dash thy foot against a stone." The ever watchful loving Heavenly Father kept Mary's bones whole and from a serious injury. We should be grateful and encouraged to more trust in Him and to careful obedience to what we see as our duty to Him.

Askew is doing his first plowing this week. Bish Ponder's time was out and Ghu is not able to plow, but little at a time. Askew is working well and doesn't complain. He is a fine boy. Fred and Travis are working steady and no complaint tho' the weather is very hot.

Mary cut a tooth or two lately at age of 6½.

Frances is full of life and very mischievous. She is bright and interesting, but for past few days not rite well.

Maggie is same quiet spirited child — gentle and good.

Mary's health is much better this summer than any time during winter. Mary, Maggie and Charles have a good time now playing all day long. Charles is a good obedient little boy and most of the time kind to all.

Frances cleaves to me like my shadow almost. She loves me best — she does not love Ghu as devotedly as all the other children did at her age.

Am sewing all I can. Hot weather and a weak heart makes my progress [a] little slower.

September 7

Ghu and Askew have gone to Indian Springs; Fred and Travis are picking peas; Mary, Maggie and Frances are playing out under the beautiful trees in the fresh morning breeze. I think Charles is picking peas.

I am feeling cheerful and contented — am doing as I please, but must get up soon and go to work in earnest.

I had company yesterday and day before, i.e., in the P.M.'s. Mesdames Millie Morgan and Nannie Cowan came Monday P.M. and Misses Babe and Eunice Strickland came yesterday P.M. We had lot of company during meeting and I was overworked and worn out, tho' Ghu did lots toward dinner each A.M. and Jane Miller helped me one day too. Our preacher, Mr. Strickland, spent one night here. Joe Wynn, Dollie Ruth and Tommie Lou spent one night. We had no other comapany at night. Misses Ruth W. and Rosa L. took dinner with us one day. Owen Wynn and Ralph Morgan one day. Mr. Kelly and Olin Mason one day. Rev. Mr. Kleckly, Rev. Mr. "D.-Bar.-D." [De Bardeleven], Rev. Mr. Strickland, Mrs. D[e Bardeleven] and their three children one day. Mesrs Bill Cowan and Julian Cardell one day. And others—Sarah Wynn, Sarah Crain, and Miss Thurston. Will Wynn, wife and child. There was some *powerful* preaching done at New Hope during meeting—Four different preachers—Ed Cowan, Bro. D., Bro. S[trickland] and Bro. Kleckly one sermon. He is pastor of church in Jackson and what an intellect he had. And a *good* man too.

Miss Daisy Gray came once this summer and spent 2 nights here. We love her! We enjoy her visits.

A traction engine stopped in front of out house last night and furnished great amusement for the children and I had pasttime too watching it.

I've been going to see Mrs. Adams occasionally. She is 82 yrs. old, and very feeble. I was there one P.M. at preaching during meeting week. I've never heard Bro. D. preach but one time and that was at the evening meeting for Mrs. Adams. I regret being a "shut-in" this year, more than I ever can express: one *deep regret* was to be compelled to be away from church, from good preaching.

I don't know when I'll write in here again. In one month from now—oh, the dreadful unexpressible suffering that will be my lot to bear, but I trust in One who has kept my life thro' the same suffering 8 times and is still letting me live to be with my children. Surely after 9 times the suffering so deathly, will not be mine any more. May the Lord preserve my life again and spare me to my children is my prayer, in Jesus name. Amen.

October 6
Thursday

October! The sweetest month of all the year to me.

October 7

This is a joyous morning to me. It is 9 o'clock. A delightful breeze is singing in my much loved oaks around the house. I've been most of the time, since breakfast, on front porch resting and reading but when I cease writing I must go in and make beds, sweep floors, churn, wash dishes and cook dinner. Ghu and little boys are picking cotton for Mr. Tollerson; Askew is miller. Mary, Maggie and Frances are near by playing beautifully and I never loved my children so much as in these last few months.

I've never seen a sweeter baby than Frances; she is so cheerful, so joyous, so healthy and happy. And Maggie always so gentle and so kind. And Mary a good hearted, kind child. Travis works. He is very industrious. Fred can't pick near so much cotton as T. Charles does quite well picking cotton. Our crop is very short. Ghu and all boys except Askew are picking good deal away from home.

Some of the days lately I've been so downhearted because of the undescribable physical suffering before me—and that which is expected daily, hourly. But I read the Word and claim His promises and some of the hours are joyous ones. Sometimes I look at suffering and do not trust His promises as I ought and then I brood and cry a good deal. But I trust Him to help me in the awful suffering and I pray to be spared to my little children and to all family.

Life is sweeter to me it seems, than ever before. I seem to love my children better and life is richer, more sweet than ever before. I feel more content, love my home and surroundings so much.

Well, I pray the Lord to sustain me. I trust Him and His promises. I welcome the new life that I expect to be soon entrusted to my care. I pray for Ghu to have His help when I am on bed and his cares and responsibilities are heavier. I ask Thee our heavenly Parent to keep and bless all my loved ones when I am helpless and can not add to their comfort. Now I must go to work and Lord be with us all and bless us and cause thy face to shine upon us and help us to live so that our lives will be used or lived well pleasing to Thy sight—a blessing to others. We ask in Jesus name. Amen.

October 10
Tuesday Night

I have never had more peaceful, more enjoyable day it seems than
this one has been. How october weather does give me soul rest. I
never felt more contented. I never loved husband and children better
and I seem to be spiritually uplifted—have a strong desire to serve
my Maker earnestly.

I read a verse that helped me not worry over the awful suffering
that I expect any day or any night to be mine. It was this: "Cast thy
burden upon the Lord and He will *sustain* thee." And I am trusting
Him to sustain me tho' I can't say I've overcome *all* dread. Another
verse of a poem has helped me to be cheerful . . .

> "Build a little fence of trust around today,
> Fill the space with loving work and therein stay;
> Look not thro' the sheltering bars of tomorrow,
> God will help thee bear what comes of joy or sorrow."

Lucile McKibben has been giving me a *rich treat:* loaning me "The
Ladies Home Journal." She expects to loan me one whole year's subscription if I can find time to read them, and lately I am not allowing
myself to be greatly overtaxed; I am trying to take care of myself and
keep strength for the ordeal which I must soon pass thro' and so I
am taking time to read and words fail me when I try tell how I enjoy
those magazines. Bed time! Must read from the Holy Word and all
retire.

1911

February 2

A little over 3 months has passed since I wrote in this book. And oh, what suffering has come into my life since then! And a joy has come too. A sweet, a rare, unusually sweet baby girl came on the P.M. (About 3 o'clock) of October 26th [1910]. And that blessed baby has been sick 9 days — seriously sick! How much sleep I've lost, and how much I've prayed that our Heavenly Father would let the dear little life stay with me! And how much it seemed that she was going away to the other side — going to cross over and leave me empty arms and crushed with grief. But on 9th or 8th night a change came and for the better. Before day she lying in her little cradle began to "coo, coo" (calling me) and it seemed so sweet and so strange, as she had never done it before and I pulled her little cradle up to my bedside and she filled my heart with joy trying to *converse* ("Coo coo coo") with me and I talked to her and she would coo back to me.

I thank our Heavenly Father that her sweet little spirit has been left to me and I can look into her bright eyes and let her nestle near my heart yet longer. I pray that she may grow up in "nurture and admonition of the Lord" and be a shining light to others while she stays on this earth. A gleam of Heaven seems to be mine today because baby is better.

She is the only bottle fed baby I've ever raised and she is so tiny and so delicate and so sweet and so bright eyed.

April 25

Our little baby will be six (6) months old tomorrow; the frail little life has been spared thus far and I bear her up to our Heavenly Father in prayer daily. She is so delicate that I feel His help so much needed to work with her. She has a stubborn exzema; have been doctoring her for it long time, but it doesn't get well.

Have medicine from Dr. Woods, Dr. Smith and 75 cts worth of

patent medicine. Well! She was weighed yesterday for first time! Ghu bought her a little go-cart and I rolled her up to Miss Childs' and Miss Babe weighed her — 16 lbs — Miss B. said, but I could see only 15 lbs. for her — the little *bright eyed* kitten.

I have never been to church since our baby had been entrusted to my care, until Sunday.

Travis is a good boy and kind and attentive to baby and he knows how and when to feed her. I left baby in cradle in his care and she stayed there till I came back.

And she has a name at last! Florence Trella. Ghu named her Trella (for Miss Trella Castellaw) and I named her Florence. My youngest brother whom my baby *resembles so* had, in his last days, a warm young lady friend who at this time was Miss Florence Bramblett of Forsythe, Ga. but now she is a minister' wife (Mrs. Henry Mays) if I am correctly informed.

Baby has been suffering night and day with exzema and our doctoring seemed to make it worse till this week and I began to be very heavy hearted and feared she would be not better this summer and prayed earnestly for her: for what better can we do than pray when in trouble? And what would we do in deep trouble if we had no Lord to trust in — to commit our cares to? So we left off all ointments — used cuticura soap freely and talcum powders and bismuth freely night and day, and her face is better now, for which I feel thankful and though her body is broken out and raw in places, yet I trust she will soon be well. This week, she has, so far, diarrhoea and she looks so wan, so weak and *so* tiny. She has lost flesh and looks so hollow eyed and weak. I pray that the little life may be spared and that she may soon gain strength and flesh.

August 26

Baby is sick. She has been sick two nights and going on 2 days. She has the highest fever and it seems never to leave her entirely. This is 2 or 3 spells she's had this month and never was well long at a time. I was up with her much of last night and night before. She had just gained enough strength to get on all fours and crawl just about a yard. She had done it only a few times — perhaps not over three times. She loves a dog we have here and she can say Jack "J-a-c-k."

She brings the word Jack out so long and it sound so sweet to us. One day I was feeding her and I said good! and she said good (but only twice and no more) and she has said doll a time or two and she can say "cat" and "scat." Says scat when she sneezes and when strange children come near her. We thought it funny that she would say "scat!" to strange children and no one taught her to do so.

August 27
Sunday A.M.

My little Trella has been very sick 5 days. We had Dr. Smith with her yesterday eve. She was so bad off yesterday that her eyes lost their lustre and a dim unnatural look came in them—a listless, lifeless, deathly look. She has had 5 bad nights; she is quieter today than she was last night. I trust the Giver of her dear life will leave her with us longer. He knows best and we trust Him but how we are praying for our dear sweet sick baby. And Lord if it is Thy will leave her with us but Thou knowest best.

A great intellectual, gifted and spiritual man conducted Quarterly Meeting at New Hope yesterday. I was at home with a heavy heart working with our dear little Trella. I feel that I missed a *very rare* treat, but if Little Trella gets well I will try to be content at the loss, though I *do crave* such treats.

Trella is 10 months old today—has never weighed over 14 lbs. She is a rare gift—a rare flower—a brighter eyed baby I never saw.

August 29

What a sweet song of continual gladness or thanksgiving has been singing in my heart all day: our little Trella is out of danger and we feel today that she is on way to recovery. She seemed to be too weak to pull back to life and she was; but the Life Giver has strengthened her and left her with us, after she was so near gone. On last Saturday (today is Tuesday) her eyes seem to have the appearance of the seal of death and she was wholly unconscious and I couldn't arouse her, or get her to take any nourishment for awhile. Ghu and all the children except Fred were at Quarterly Meeting. I 'phoned for Dr. Smith and

sent for Ghu. She didn't notice, or regain consciousness until Ghu
and children came, and I gave her a little warm water in nursing
bottle, and took her on my lap and called the children around. She
opened her eyes and smiled a faint smile of recognition to Mary and
Frances and after a little was over the spell. She has never looked that
way before, but was brighter when Dr. Smith came.

I've been up with the baby much for 6 or 7 nights. We slept till 12
last night before she awoke. I found before day that she was better,
enough better to give me relief from 6 days of anxiety and prayers
for her recovery. And the Giver of her dear life heard and answered
our prayers; and if she lives, I trust her life will be a shining light
pointing and influencing others Heavenward.

Lot of company came to see Trella, but talking and company was
against her. She needed, and wanted, absolute quiet. Most sick people
need, and *prefer absolute* quiet. But our friends mean to show us their
kindness by visiting us when sickness enters the house. I appreciate
the kindness, yet *very few* know how long to stay in sick room, or
how quiet they should be in the room, or if not in the room, they do
not know how I long to be in room alone and quiet for good of the
sick—to minister to their needs; or how I am sorely needed when I
am entertaining them outside the sick room. They can't realize how
much there is for me to do in house and especially for the sick—
and to keep sick room quiet I am out with the company much when
needed by the sick. From the troubles and heavy cares sickness has
brought to us and ours I've learned how to do when I visit the sick;
whether or not to go in sick room at all; how *quick* to leave. To help
somewhere in house if I can; if not, never to hinder others by staying. Unless I am needed to stay and can work to be an advantage for
some one in the home—the patient or the tired ones of the home.

To our Bountiful Father above, we would offer tribute of praise,
for the glorious gift of His love and the blessings that hallow our days.

And Askew joined church last Sunday [August 27, 1911]. We were
surprised as he had never hinted that he intended doing so. We are
thankful that he did and we believe he will make a good and useful
man. We believe there are noble traits in him. As is characteristic of
him, in a quiet manner he walked up when an invitation was given,
and shook Bro. DeBardeleven's hand and quietly went back to his
seat. We believe noble things are budding in his soul and bye and
bye will blossom into usefullness.

And Fred joined church during protracted meeting and we are glad he did (and wish Travis would have come out with them, and taken a stand with the Lord's people). I trust they will remember their Creator in the days of their youth and that they will obey the Bible teaching every day they live. I pray they may *forward* go—not willfully committing any known sins and get ready and keep ready to meet the Lord in peace at any time; and to live a consecrated life, so as to do as much for God's glory in this world as they can. They who are most faithful in this life will have a larger capacity to enjoy Heavenly things. There are higher places in Heaven for those who live closest to the Lord, who obey him most implicitly. I trust they will never enter into any sin that will be a weight to their spirits.

I suffer remorse and will as long as I live for six years of a back-slidden life of my own. Six dark years—after I became a mother—six dark years in sin in my mother and father's life when I should have been a great blessing to them, and I suffer remorse because I was so led by Evil Agent as not to be a loving obedient, patient, sympathetic, dutiful daughter to them in all ways I should have been.

September 4

Askew went away this morning. He was never away from home but once before to stay. That time he went to his Aunt Dora Well-maker's in Barnesville on a few days visit. Now, for the first *real going* away! He has gone to Young Harris, in North Ga., to enter school; to be gone 9 months! This morning it seems but such a little while, that I can now see him in my imagination, a little boy in blouses and kilt skirt, pencil in hand, making or copying letters and words from a sign on an old storehouse door! And he was the "pet pride" of his Grand Pa Wynn—(until Papa died) and now this morning he is a rite good size, rite tall youth, age 16, and gone away from home. I believe his going away will be for his good both mentally and spiritually. We (Ghu and I) are glad to make sacrifices so that the best things in him may be developed. He has always had some fine traits. We expect him to develop into a good, noble, manly man.

It seems now as this new thing has come into Askew's life, that his Grand Pa ought to have been here the past few days and this morning. He was so proud of Askew. He loved Askew so and Askew loved him so; they each seemed to constitute a part of the other's life. So Papa kept coming strong in my mind in connection with Askew. How proud he would be of him now, could he be here and yet how inexpressibly sad my Papa would have been for Askew's separation from him and how anxious Papa would have been about him. Who knows but that Askew's Grand Pa was not (in spirit) near him when he left and previous to his going. I believe it was, because he loved Askew with an undying devotion, and love for our loved ones goes on in Eternity—it does not stop at what we call death. Good and strong minded authors say it is stronger after they leave us here and go to another world. "Absence or separation makes the love stronger—the tie stronger."

Ghu is a noble man; his education is limited but as Askew wanted to go to school away from home Ghu nobly and generously fitted him up with needed things, and gladly makes sacrifices for him to go. We did not feel able to urge him (financially) but we suggested that he ought to go on to school at Philippi. He wished to go away. We are *glad* he wanted to go and went of his own free will, choice, and accord. Young Harris was our choice. Mr. Oscar McKibben goes too; he is a religious young man. We think lot of him and hope he and A. will room together if it is best.

Askew felt a deep regret at leaving home and home folks for such a distance and such a stay. I'm glad to know that he did feel thus. No true soul could thoughtlessly leave the home that for 16 yrs had sheltered it, and the parents and brothers and sisters he had closely associated with. He was kind and thoughtful to me; sweet to his baby sister Trella—a bedfellow of Charles' etc. My and Ghu's dependence in some things, being the oldest child.

By the way, one of the sweetest, most cultured girls in this part of the country, an intelligent, violet-like character, a school mate and classmate at Philippi (where he went last year); and the girl he was most interested in of all the Philippi girls, and the *first* girl he ever felt *any* interest in (except kin); called him up on 'phone to tell him goodbye. He is so very timid that he never spoke of her to any one unless others called her name first and yet *I read him* and saw that he was glad she called. He appreciates her kindness highly and I am glad she was so thoughtful and nice in telling him goodbye. I appreciate it myself much. So does Ghu feel a keen interest in things likewise—things that are helpful to him and that are beneficial. So we feel towards all the other children in the home.

September 17

Trella has one tooth: cut it when 11½ months old. Her health seems so much improved with the advent of her first tooth and with this Sep. weather.

October 27

Little Florence Trella Leguin is 12 months (one year old) today. The crowning month of all the year I think. I *so much* love the delightful month of October.

And wee little Trella, the invalid baby, has lived to see her birthday! So much of the time her life hung by such a slender thread. No Drs. prolonged it. Althou' Dr. Smith was sent for twice when it seemed she couldn't survive. (He is a good Dr.) But 'twas the "Lord of Life," the "Giver of Life" the Great Physician who has spared and strengthened Trella up to this, her first birthday—first 12 months. She, who has been so weak, so helpless, who couldn't use her back much in so long, or her legs, can now stand awhile, often, by chairs and be in a sitting posture all day only when asleep. It is wonderful how she has improved the past month and half. It seems like a miracle to me and *I think it is*. I feared she had infantile paralysis, and lo! what strength came! Many anxious hours by day and night have I watched and prayed by her cradle. The Master heard, answered, restored and strengthened little Trella! Today she is round, plump (not large or robust) but round—eats some solid food; sleeps well, crawls, stands by chairs, is a very *mischievous* baby; cuts up many, many funny capers; laughs much—has a merry bright eye. A joy to the whole family; a sunbeam perpetually shining (almost).

John 20th Chap., and 31st verse: "But these things are written, that ye might believe that Jesus is the Christ, the Son of God; and that believing ye might have life through his name. . . ."

December 1

Yesterday was Thanksgiving day. What do these holidays mean to me: a weary overtaxed body and mind, because my strength is small, family large and much to do and no help; but after all, I enjoy and like to mark the days.

Olin Mason, our best little boy friend, spent last night here; Mary Dell, his sister, took dinner with our little girls and Mary spent her first night away from home! The first night of her life away from home. I have not spent a night away from home in 15 yrs—Askew was the baby; he could walk; I spent the night with my sister Lil at High Falls.

Well, this was the first Thanksgiving day of Askew's life that he was not at home and we miss him and I have him on my mind somehow, sadly. His absence makes me sad. His first Thanksgiving away from home. And won't we miss him sadly Christmas? Oh, I know we will.

When I have any extra work to do like holidays demand, I lose my patience more with the children, trying to clean them up—hair to plait, bathing them and my home and dinner to see after—my hands to do all except what little they may do, and I grow worried, easily scold, am more or less harsh with them, till the strain is over and then my conscience condemns.

I scolded Mary yesterday and did it in a wrong manner. I was condemned all day. I will talk it over with her and tell her how wrong it was in me and how sorry I am. I always so do when I grow irritable with them. But yesterday was Thanksgiving Day and I should have prayed and trusted the Lord for the needed patience and strength. And then I left a memory that I can't efface. Mary will remember the harsh word on the Thanksgiving day maybe *all* her life. Poor little Mary is frail and we all ought to exercise much patience with her. She's been so weak, delicate, all her 7 years of life. I prayed to God to forgive me the words of impatience and reproof and I will trust Him to help me more on this line. But I look strong and my body is weak; my health was wrecked—my strength sadly impaired when I first became a mother: when our little baby girl, our first born, came in this world my strength was wrecked for life; when last precious girl baby came into this world, the affliction became more aggravated. So I

am large, fleshy and people think I have strength. But what fatigue
it costs me, and more than fatigue — to try cook a good dinner —
prepare for holidays etc. etc. Each day's ordinary duties sometimes
exhaust all my strength and much of the time, many of the days, I
fail completely — have to rest, lie down much.

And so I never can do for my children near what I wish. I can not
do for my friends as I wish.

December 2

One thing I feel grateful for is that my hearing is appearantly
(or so far as I can perceive) perfect, tho' I can't read without my
glasses. Went to New Hope with a well prepared S.S. lesson; forgot
my glasses — could not read. But had the pleasure of hearing from
Bro. DeBardeleven a *good* sermon; it was perhaps the last I will ever
hear him preach; our new preacher is F. R. Smith. We haven't met
him yet.

I love nature — out doors! Fields, Hills Woods Rocks, Creaks,
Rills! And autumn leaves! What a rich treat to gather them! We
had some beautiful ones for Thanksgiving decoration; and Travis
brought me some Bamboo vines full of leaves and berries. How beautiful they were! And some of the sunsets that I pause in my busy life
to view, are wonderfully beautiful! Glorious to behold.

1912

March 4
Monday P.M.

Trella is an unusually sweet spirited, fun loving baby. She is so jolly! So full of pranks and funny "didoes" and capers. The light of our home. She's devoted to Travis, her Daddy and myself—She is next fond of Frances. Trella is 16 months old; she had infantile paralysis for a long time and that is why she can't walk any better now. She can take a few steps alone. One foot is not quite straight, caused from infantile paralysis; this foot she drags when we lead her; the shoe for this foot wears out first. Today I am taking bottle from her most of the feed times and learning her to drink from a cup. I will continue for an indefinite time to get her to sleep at night without one. She drinks from her cup without a protest—did the first time.

Mary has been seriously sick some this winter; she coughed so much—became so weak and was in bed a few days one while; she can't go to school the past 6 or 8 weeks. She is at present much better and not coughing. Mary and Ghu were both sick awhile and both sick in a way that made me feel deeply troubled and much in prayer. I feel thankful today that each are appearantly getting on very well. Ghu busy and appetite fair; Mary playing and eating as usual; she never had big appetite.

Even little Maggie and Franke [Frances] have both been sick and also Fred and Charles. Travis the only one who kept well.

Mrs. Manerva McKibben is to be buried this P.M. at New Hope. I talked with her a little while Christmas; didn't expect then to hear of her death so soon. Died without any one whom she spent her last years giving her, to their home, a warm welcome, but they gave her I am told the reverse.

Maggie is just so much help to me! She takes willingly and cheerfully so many steps for me! What will I do when Maggie starts to school? I've nicknamed her Susie Lou, after a fine character I read of. Mary and Maggie help me with the dishes now; taking times apart. This is some help that counts. I call on Maggie to assist me much more than I do Mary because she has better health.

Charles is good to mind me; he is so obedient and uncomplaining and a good little boy too. Travis helps me so willingly and uncomplainingly with Trella. I can trust him night or day for awhile. I can go see a neighbor at night or day and safely trust her with Travis. He is noble hearted and sees *well* and carefully after her when she's in his care.

March 28
Friday P.M.

Trella was 17 months old yesterday. I prayed for her life to be spared so many times when it seemed going out; and I asked our Maker to help me to be reminded by her life, if it should be prolonged, to discharge my duty more faithfully to God and man; to be so grateful for her spared life as to overcome useless worry; to strive to accept each day's cares and trials submissively. I pray the same prayer today. I feel grateful for her spared life and feel that the Lord of life is keeping her.

One day this week our home narrowly escaped catching fire. I have for severel years daily or as a rule asked God's protection over our home; his protecting care over the home. I look upon our escape from a fire as nothing short of His Providence, *over-ruling* Providence. There was a fire in fire-place Sunday (in best room) where we entertained Mesrs Lewis Garr and Will Cowan. On Monday A.M. I went in, swept up, and saw no fire, only a bed of (appearantly) white hickory ashes. I put on some chips, two sticks of wood — to be prepared for any unexpected or sudden visitor — to be ready for next company; I put a fire-screen made of cloth and paper over fire-place, came out and shut door; in one or two days after I opened door one morning and saw the black ashes of my burnt screan; some of the screan frame burned, but none of the wood that makes the mantle even scorched. I regard it wholly an over ruling Providence in answer to prayer daily or as a rule, for protection of the home.

Another time a few years ago, I was ironing. The weather was dry; I had on a big fire and the soot in chimney and pieces of soot that was caked like lime (only it was red as a fire coal) kept falling down the chimney so fast that I stood by with a broom to sweep them off floor to prevent floor from burning. We didn't have any water in any well close by and Ghu was a good distance from the house. At that time our house had *old* shingles (perhaps 35 or more yrs old) on it; the pieces of heavy burning soot fell on these old rotton, dry shingles and Ghu just happened (as we say) to come just as the old shingles were smoking in two different places and we had a ladder on one side of the house and Ghu grabbed a water bucket containing some water and went excitedly, almost breathless, and put out the *very* dangerous fire. Do I believe it *just* happened that Ghu came in then? No. I believe it was God's doing to save us from being without a house and all we had in the house.

Not so very long after that Ghu had the house recovered, which it so badly needed a long time before it was done. And God's Providence and care is over and around us and we should see it thus and acknowledge it. Why should we be recipient of such great catastrophes and not acknowledge His Hand?

June 12

Wednesday Afternoon

Trella (our 19 month old baby) has been brought back again from a spell of severe illness. Dr. Smith, the only physician we have ever had with her, paid her several visits. She was low and chances were against her, but the Author of Life, The Giver of all good gifts, prolonged her life, kept her thro' a 14 days fever (or 15 days) and that rite after she had been ailing 2 wks for effects of measles. We feel that the loving Heavenly Father alone brought her thro', cooled the fever, healed the stomach and lungs from which she suffered so much. In answer to prayer, she has been spared by The Almighty, and our lives are richer for her being left with us. I feel that her spared life should be a constant reminder to me to love more prayerful; be more submissive and obedient to the One who healed and spared her. The measles made her very sick and she was never well afterwards and in 2 wks was down with hot, burning fevers, swolen and hard hot burning stomach and a lung trouble which made her breathing hard, loud and difficult much of the time. Now she is so weak she can't walk but fever left her about a week or nearly so, ago. She has an appetite now better than at any time since she took measles. I trust that Trella's life will be a blessing to all she comes in touch with, with God as her friend and under his Divine guidance I trust that she will with her whole life do good. I hope her life will be a daily thanksgiving from me. Through these low spells God has raised her. To him I would be loyal at all times for His goodness to us in hearing and answering our prayers—in sparing dear little frail Trella to us, to our hearts, arms, and home.

Enable us, Lord, to live close to Thee and to be used by Thee all our days, and continue to bless and strengthen little frail Trella and to abide with us all now in this life and afterwards receive us, an unbroken family, in Heaven. We ask in Jesus name. Amen.

1913

February 8
Saturday P.M.

As evening shadows descent I pick up this book that I haven't written in (concerning our homefolks, our boys and girls and babies) since June [1912]. How many things have happened since then! How much sickness among the children—whooping cough.

Yes, in October Mary, Maggie, Charles, Frances and Trella took the dreaded whooping cough. Mary hasn't been able to go to school since, tho' two or three days she (at different times) tried but is still coughing and weak and not able to go to school. Mary had it the severest of any one we ever knew of and for a long time it didn't seems she would ever get over it. Well, she isn't over it yet, but for a good while it seemed she couldn't stand the cough any longer. We had grave fears but the Lord has spared her life and prolonged it where it didn't seems she could get as well as she is now. She has always had bad health and has never been able to go to school but little.

Maggie started to school and whooping cough stopped her. She didn't have whooping cough as bad as Frances. She and Charles had it light. Maggie has started back to school, went two days this week. Miss Rosebud Garr is Maggie's teacher. Miss Franklin is Fred's, Travis' and Charles. They are fine characters. We like them.

I sold (or rather consented for Ghu to do so), Trella's little cradle this P.M. He sold it to Lewis Ellis; I felt sad to part with it and regretted letting it go. I have sat by it and rocked it thro' so many anxious hours when the spark of life seemed to be going out of my precious baby's body. Oh, that tiny pale form that seemed to be loosing hold of life so fast! I can't forget it! And I have so many tender heart aching memories connected with that cradle that I wish I had kept it. But how much I have to be grateful for! The baby Trella, the occupant of the cradle is doing fairly well—not over effects of whooping cough entirely, but playful and usually hearty. To God be the praise.

A sad sad thing happened in our family last summer, or fall. Askew was out a short way from the house and Fred could see him by an oft repeated lightening flash, and Fred thought it was a white dog that had been annoying us and he asked Ghu twice if he should shoot that dog. Ghu was tired and had headache and lying on porch floor playing with Trella and he scarcely looked around but saw by lightening flash the white (Askew's shirt) and said in reply to Fred's question, "Yes, shoot the dog if you see him." Fred fired and it was Askew who received 40 shot in his body, and words can never tell of the agony we all endured for a short while. We heard Askew's groans inaudibly at first, but after a second more definite and at first Ghu thought a dogs groans but the next instant we all recognized Askew's voice and how thankful I am every time I think of it that the Lord shielded Askew and that it was not fatal. How thankful that he was spared from the grave that night. I conceive it to be one of God's wonders that prevented Askew being fatally wounded. How much sorrow filled Fred's heart! How deeply plunged into deep distress we all were for a short while, but to end of my life I shall be grateful to God for shielding Askew at that time. I regard it as plainly Providential.

Trella cried when the darky carried her cradle away. I felt so sorry for her that I wanted to send and have it brought back, tho' she never uses it (since last summer) but I am going to buy her a little chair with the money we received for the cradle. When it was brought out on porch to await the darky to carry it home, Trella just talked gleefully about her cradle and put her doll in it and rocked it and then had me to put pillows and cover in it and bring it in my room and put her and her doll in it and rock them awhile. So I guess my dear little unusually sunny disposed Trella has not only rocked her last time in her own little cradle, where she lay so many sick hours, but has rocked her last time in any cradle. She is 2 yrs and 3 months and 8 days old—no longer needs a cradle so I guess a little chair will be hers instead.

But she still keeps her bottles and milk, and eats some food, tolerably hearty most of the time this winter. Trella loves all the children but Travis is her best beloved brother. Askew and all the children pay her lot of attention and yet she is not spoiled. She is such a sunshiny, beautiful, sensible little fairy that we all are devoted to her and we all love her merry unceasing prattle and enjoy her quick words, witty sayings, and quick movements. She, ever since she could walk, reminds me of a bird; she gets about so quickly and so gracefully. She calls Fred "Fedley."

Travis is the quietest child in our family—Has a peaceable, gentle disposition and sympathetic nature.

Askew's health was not such to warrant his going off to school this term and so he is running the mill. He looks healthier now than he has in nearly 2 yrs. I feel glad that he is here at home. He needed rest and a change badly from school. It is a rich treat for us all to be together; I didn't know how to appreciate it till Askew spent nearly one year at Young Harris and I felt sad oftimes when he was away and our family temporarily broken. Askew loves home too but tho' a great lover of home he expects to go off again to school. He was a bright pupil so all his teachers say. Is is a blessed pleasure now that we are enjoying—all of us together at home.

Charles is a good obliging child, and so is Fred and the rest—all together a very good set of children. Of course, at times, some little things occur among some of the older ones that is not best. May God's love and protection be around them as a shield to the end of their days; bless them, comfort them, be with them in every sorrow, every affliction, and be near to overshield and bless to life's end and after that may we be a united family in heaven—not one lost, and this we ask in Jesus name. Amen.

February 8

Saturday Night

Trella says so many funny things: "No sire ree!" when she means no decidedly. She is a great curiosity and we all think that she is "wise beyond her years."

Mary weighs 45 lbs; Maggie 42, and Frances 40. Mary will be 9 yrs old in few days and Maggie is 7 and Frances 5 yrs of age. Charles is ten (10) and weighs 55 lbs. Trella is 2 yrs and 3 months old; 24 lbs.

February 10
Monday

Frances started to school today. Trella had a lonely time and could not content herself in forenoon — was unusually dissatisfied.

Frances is five years old — her birthday was 17th of Dec.

September 11

Askew went back to Young Harris last of Aug. We miss him much because of many things, one principal reason is that he is oldest child (living) and the oldest holds a place in home that when absent makes the vacancy keenly felt.

When he went to L. G. one term he was at home at end of each week and we did not feel sad about his being away.

Askew prefers home to any place, but he is deeply in earnest about getting a better education. I pray God's love and protection over and about him. May he grant him health to allow him to study. Askew is not a very strong boy in some respects. He was 18 on 18th of Aug.

HERE THE DIARY ENDS.

AFTERWORD

MAGNOLIA WYNN LE GUIN DIED IN ATLANTA, ON A VISIT TO her daughter Frances, on November 6, 1947, in her seventy-ninth year. As was proper, her body was returned to her home above the Tussahaw; her funeral was held in New Hope Church; and she was buried in the family plot in the adjacent cemetery, where she lies among those she loved.

The years between the conclusion of her diaries and her death continued to be eventful for Magnolia, increasingly filled with pleasures but not lacking in pain. World War I ended an age, a way of life, at Wynn's Mill as elsewhere. Her children began to leave home; the eldest son, Askew, had already gone away to college before the diaries conclude. After the United States entered the war, he was inducted into the army. Magnolia notes, on 6 October 1917, that "Askew has written us that he has been called to Camp Wheeler, in Macon. He will leave today or tomorrow. . . . 'God be with you till we meet again.'" In her second copybook, Magnolia expressed her distress at Askew's induction in a characteristic way, by copying a long, sentimental, patriotic poem, "Go, My Boy, Where Duty Calls," which concludes:

> To you Mother ever faithful,
> To your county ever true,
> Go, my boy, where duty calls
> And my heart shall follow you.

Askew escaped harm — as he put it, during the war he fought the battle of Camp Wheeler — but the influenza epidemic at the war's end took its toll: Charles Ralph died on 8 November 1918, at age sixteen.

Magnolia's remaining children reached maturity and established themselves in various occupations: farming, railroading, teaching, nursing, business; some married and provided Magnolia and Ghu with nine grandchildren. Only one other of her children, her beloved Travis, died (in 1941) before Magnolia. Ghu continued to mill until 1927 and to farm. Like most, his fortunes suffered during the Great Depression, but his position among his neighbors did not. Like Magnolia's father, her husband was a pillar of the community. In the larger world of Henry County, Ghu became a road commissioner, a justice of the peace, a tax assessor, a member of the board of education, and finally a judge of the Henry County court.

With the passage of time, the "historical" Magnolia of the diaries became the grandmother I knew in my youth. Having weathered the difficulties of her early life and some slings and arrows of fortune, she was able, in the last decades of her life, to enjoy serenity, peace, and happiness.

These are the bare facts of her life. What is significant about it, what it stood for, is clearly set forth in her diaries. Their pages reveal the woman my grandmother was and the times and locale that helped make her what she was. Much that was characteristic of the time and place revealed in the diaries may affront today's standards, but the evidence of these diaries as historical documents must stand, without judgment, to represent a life and a view of life in middle Georgia three quarters of a century ago.

Certain continuities, themes, appear in the diaries and reveal the sort of woman Magnolia Wynn Le Guin was. Prominent among them are the pain, anguish, and difficulties of childbirth and the ever-present problems of child rearing in modest circumstances, against which is balanced the love she had for her children and the joy she felt in them as they grew up. In a life too full of people, with too much hard work and too many household responsibilities, she had ample room for love of family—parents, husband, children—and affectionate and discerning relations with relatives, friends and neighbors, and pleasure in them all. Overriding the burden of the everyday and trivial was her deep pleasure in nature and her devotion to reading and writing, pleasures she could indulge all too infrequently. Above all, sustaining all, was her faith, secure, accepting; it was a refuge that got her through difficulties and provided her with strength and joy.

Magnolia Wynn Le Guin's death was deeply felt by all who knew her, as her obituary in the *Henry County Weekly Advertiser* (13 November 1947) proclaims with simple eloquence.

On Thursday, Nov. 6, 1947, in the usual quiet of Autumn dawn, a stillness we seldom know seemed to hover over New Hope Community. Our hearts were pierced with pain and yet, relief mingled together when word came that Mrs. G. G. Le Guin, familiarly known as "Miss Mag," had moved to the "Home not built with hands," a reward she so richly deserved, for such a beautiful life she lived!

She was a loving mother, devoted wife, friend to humanity, a good, kind neighbor, and indeed a true and faithful christian, if there ever was one. We know nothing too good to speak or write of her. To know her was to love her. These words were equally fitting for her while she lived as they are now. No one knows just how many lives were enriched nor how many blessings she rendered.

Mrs. Le Guin was before her marriage, Magnolia Wynn, and spent her life at old Wynn's Mill where she was born. She was in her 79th year. She loved people, loved to talk and loved old New Hope Methodist Church where she will be missed as the oldest member and where she has been a pillar. Many think of her as their "second mother."

APPENDIX I

RECIPES

MAGNOLIA WAS A GOOD SOUTHERN-CUISINE COOK. WHILE THERE WAS neither time nor means to prepare fancy gourmet dishes, she did enjoy "fixing up," especially for holidays, and especially baking treats for her children. Below are such of her recipes as she included in her copybooks; mostly they are "special," but there are some ordinary recipes, arranged alphabetically.

Boiled Irish Potatoes and Tomatoes

Boil Irish potatoes until almost done. Drain and slice thin. Butter a baking dish and put in a layer of potatoes with 2 teaspoonsful of grated onion and a layer of canned tomatoes with salt and pepper. Add layer of potatoes and onion and tomato with seasoning until pan is full. Cover with bread crumbs and tomatoes. Add 2 ozs. of butter in small pieces and bake.

Candy

Candy Made of Sugar

2 cupfuls of granulated sugar
½ cupful of water
A pinch of cream of tarter

Put the sugar and cream of tarter in kettle which cooks evenly all over bottom; pour in water, and when all the sugar is wet place over the fire and boil. Try some in cold water to test for pulling.

Candy

3 cupsfull of light brown sugar
A small lump of butter
15 cent can of condensed milk [1906 price]

Cook until candy forms a small ball when dropped in water. Add flavoring and nuts. Beat until creamy. The candy will be more creamy if allowed to cool somewhat before beating.

Chilli

Grind up any kind of cold meat (chicken, beef, ham, etc.)
2 or 3 big onions
red pepper
little water and butter

Cook well.
Add garlick if you prefer to onions
In winter this will slice when cold.

Chocolate Cake

1 cup butter
2 cups sugar
2 eggs
2 cups sweetmilk
5 tablespoons of cocoa
4 cups of flour
2 teaspoons baking powder

Seafoam Filling for Chocolate Cake

2 cups of sugar
1 cup of water

Boil until hardened when dropped in cold water; remove from stove and beat in 2 stiffly beaten egg whites. Add 1 teaspoon vanilla and beat until cool enough to spread.

Chocolate Sandwiches

3 lbs. white sugar
butter size of walnut
1 cupful of water
½ cup of cider vinegar
6 tablespoonsful of grated chocolate

Boil all together till crisp when dropped into water. Put in buttered tins and pull when cold.

Cocoanut Cream Bars

Melt 2 teaspoonfuls of butter in a granite pan; add one cupfull and a half of white sugar and half a cupfull of sweet milk. Heat slowly to the boiling point, let it boil for 12 minutes, then take from fire. Add a third of a cupfull of shredded cocoanut and a teaspoonful of vanilla. Beat until creamy and pour into buttered tins.

Coffee Substitute

1 cup full corn meal
2 cupsful of graham flour
Add 1 cup full of syrup

Mix to a paste and spread on a baking dish and brown carefully in the oven. If too sweet, add less syrup.

Crisp Ginger Cookies

1 cup of sugar
1 cup of shortening
1 cup of molasses

Let this come to a boil, add 2 level teaspoons of soda, let cool and add 2 eggs, 3 tablespoons of cold water, 1 teaspoon full of ginger, 1 teaspoon of cinnamon. Add enough flour to make stiff dough.

Fruit Cake

1 cup of New Orleans molasses
1 cup of grated cocoanut
raisins
nuts
figs
blackberry jam

If plain four (not self rising), use soda: add one cup of vinegar in which has been dissolved one teaspoon soda.
Use eggs and butter
Use some cinnamon and some nutmeg.

Fruit Rolls

2 cupsful of sugar
½ cup of water
1 cup finely chopped figs
1 cup finely chopped dates

Boil sugar and water till it forms a soft ball when dropped in cold water. Remove from fire and beat until it creams. But be careful that it doesn't get too stiff. Then add the chopped fruit and beat as long as possible. Roll in a wet cloth and leave in a cool place overnight. Slice in thin strips.

Horse-Radish Sauce

This sauce is especially good for roast beef.

Grate a tablespoon of horse-radish, mix with three teaspoonful of cream, a teaspoon of mustard, the same amount of vinegar and sugar, with salt according to taste.

Jam Custard

2 eggs
1 cup of jam
½ cup of sugar
2 heaping teaspoons flour

Butter large as an egg
1 cup sweet milk

Put whites of egg on top
Beat it thoroughly before placing on crust.

Light Bread

Sift two quarts flour into bowl or tray
Add a teaspoon of salt
two tablespoons of sugar
a tablespoon of lard

Dissolve half a compressed yeast cake in a cupfull of slightly warmed water and one cupful of warm sweet milk.
Stir and add more sweet milk or warm water until dough is formed
Set away and let raise for 2 or 3 hours
Then work (knead) again and this time grease a pan and put it away till it rises well and then bake.
Bake slowly until quite brown.
Grease the top of the dough when you put it to rise.

Mayonnaise Dressing

Recipe 1

The yolks of 2 eggs
½ cup of vinegar
1 tablespoon of sugar
Little salt
Mustard
1 big dip of butter

Put all the ingredients on stove in boiler and *stir constantly* 'till it thickens.

Recipe 2

Take four eggs and beat them slightly; add 1 cup full of sugar, ½ teaspoon full of mustard and one half teaspoon of salt and mix thoroughly. Put butter the size of walnut into half pint of vinegar; let it come to a boil and add the egg mixture. Stir til it thickens and let it cool.

Orange Marmalaide

3 thin skinned lemons
3 thin skinned oranges
Cut it all up—skins and all, in little pieces
3 qts of water (I think)
Let it stand 24 hrs.
After standing 24 hrs boil the juice hard ten minutes
Then let it stand 24 hours more.
Then measure 1 cup of sugar to 1 cup of juice
Cook until it jells

Soak or let this marmelaide stand only in crockery ware—water pitcher for example.

Peanut Goo

Roll shelled peanuts into a paste. Make a syrup by melting 2 cupfuls of sugar in the chafing dish. Pour over the peanut paste, let it cool, cut it and presto—peanut goo!

Tea Cake

1½ cup sugar
¾ cup of butter or lard
2 eggs
½ cup buttermilk
¼ teaspoon of soda
1 teaspoon of flavoring
And flour.

Wood Chuck

1 can of tomatoes
½ lb of cheese cut into small pieces
2 eggs beaten until light

Cook tomatoes until lumps have disappeared; then add cheese stirring constantly till it is melted; add the eggs and stir until all thickens somewhat.

APPENDIX 2

ILLNESSES AND
REMEDIES

DURING THE DOZEN YEARS OF HER DIARIES, MAGNOLIA RECORDS A
steady litany of illnesses and diseases. When her aged parents were not ill,
her children were. Nor were she and her husband spared. Some of the illnesses mentioned by Magnolia are the expectable infant disorders—roseola,
eczema; others are not so commonly known today (or are known by other
names)—cholera infantum, cholera morbus. Her last child suffered more
seriously from an "infantile paralysis" (1912), though whether this means
polio myelitis I do not know. All her infants but the first passed into childhood and went through the catechism of children's illnesses: earaches, croup
(in some cases severe), whooping cough (three bouts: in 1903, in 1906, in
1913), measles. Pneumonia was "feared" (1909) and there was a mild form of
typhoid fever (also in 1909).

The ailments of the adults, when not fatal, are less specifically labeled.
In addition to her problems with pregnancy and childbearing, Magnolia
records that she suffered from such things as ulcerated throat, "nervous prostration," and "neuralgia of the head." Ghu, whose health was remarkably
good by family standards, was troubled with boils and, once seriously, by a
"bilious fever."

The Wynn–Le Guin household did have professional medical attention,
for what it was worth. Magnolia's father was a doctor, though retired by the
time of her diaries; in addition, nine other medical doctors, one of them
female, are mentioned in the text as attending the household. The diaries
reveal a number of instances where patent medicines and folk remedies are
used, sometimes with the advice or consent of the medical doctors. Some
of these remedies recorded in the two copybooks are included here because
they add another dimension to Magnolia and her world. The remedies are
arranged in alphabetical order.

Bloating

1 carton of dried horseradish in one pint of apple vinegar or cider. Drink two table spoons full for three, four times a day. Will cure dropsy if taken in first stages. Don't take too much—it would be injurious.

Cancer*

"Remedy for removing cancer from the system"

Make a tea of well dried clover blooms and drink it regularly; has been known to eradicate cancer from system.

A Cure for Cancer

Sheep sorrell, gathered early in the spring when it is full of juice. Wash it perfectly clean, drain it as dry as possible, place it in a food chopper (that is entirely clean) and grind to a pulp. Put this in a sack and squeeze the juice into a bowl of crokery ware or earthen ware or china, or glass. Beware of putting it in any kind of metal. In summer time the vessel containing the juice can be placed in the sun to thicken like salve or vasaline. Watch closely as it quickly evaporates and do not let it remain long in sun. If all the juice is not needed at once, it can be bottled and kept.

If the cancer is not raw, it must be made so—that is, if there is a crust or scab on it this must be removed in order that the remedy may "take hold" better and burn in. And it will burn, I assure you. Take a piece of old linen (clean), put enough of the paste or sorrell salve to cover the wound, fastening the linen in place with narrow strips of adhesive-plaster. Put it on at night; in the morning soak the plastor off and clean and bathe the sore in water as hot as can be bourne, having first made a suds of castile soap adding a few drops of carbolic acid. Apply a clean linen with any good healing salve and fasten with strips of adhesive plaster again, as before, repeating until the cancer can literally be pulled out by the roots, which will have the appearance of white threads.

Of course clothes, poultices, bandages etc must be burned that come in touch with the cancer, immediately upon removal, and the hands not allowed to come in direct contact with it. Always use plenty of hot Castile soap suds, with carbolic acid to cleanse the sore.

*Magnolia's "cancer" is probably a canker sore or wart.

Corns

Apply pinch of baking soda, dampened with water; repeat it till the corn is well.

Cough

"For coughs with a cold"

Make a syrup of mullen and horehound.

Croup

Fry onions enough to make a poultice large enough to cover the chest. Mix with sufficient lard to make them greasy and apply to the little ones lungs and throat before going to bed.

Eczema

"For stubborn exzema"

Use cuticura soap freely with talcum powder and bismuth freely, night and day.

Fever Blisters

Rub kerosene oil as soon as you feel the swelling on the lip.

Sore Throat

Take an onion about the size of a walnut, cut it up, sprinkle plentifully with salt and pepper, put all in a cloth and pound until it is mashed well, and bind on the throat at bed time. In severe cases the treatment should be repeated two or three times. If taken in season, this remedy will cure diptheria.

Finally, there are two remedies that may have not been taken seriously:

Simple but sure method of making hair grow: Take 2 tablespoonsful of sulphur and 1 teaspoonful of quinine, place in a pint of rain water and apply to the hair twice a day.

Abracadabra—the most mystic word known (or supposed to be); it is for an old cabalistic word and is believed by some to have magic powers for healing, especially when written in this form:

ABRACADABRA
ABRACADABR
ABRACADAB
ABRACADA
ABRACAD
ABRACA
ABRAC
ABRA
ABR
AB
A

It is said that these words were written and then folded so writing wouldn't be seen and then sewed with white thread and worn for fever and plague.

Nonsense and superstition, I say. M.L.
I write for amusement.

INDEX